LIVING LETTERS OF THE WORD

Also in this series:

This Is the Day: Readings and meditations from the Iona Community
Neil Paynter
Gathered and Scattered: Readings and meditations from the Iona Community
Neil Paynter

LIVING LETTERS OF THE WORD

Readings & meditations from the Iona Community

Neil Paynter

wild goose publications

www.ionabooks.com

First published 2012 by
Wild Goose Publications, Fourth Floor, Savoy House,
140 Sauchiehall Street, Glasgow G2 3DH, UK,
the publishing division of the Iona Community.
Scottish Charity No. SC003794. Limited Company Reg. No. SC096243.

ISBN 978-1-84952-214-4

A catalogue record for this book is available from the British Library.

Overseas distribution
Australia: Willow Connection Pty Ltd, Unit 4A, 3–9 Kenneth Road, Manly Vale, NSW 2093
New Zealand: Pleroma, Higginson Street, Otane 4170, Central Hawkes Bay
Canada: Bayard Distribution, 10 Lower Spadina Ave., Suite 400, Toronto, Ontario M5V 2Z

Printed by Bell & Bain, Thornliebank, Glasgow

FSC www.fsc.org MIX Paper from responsible sources FSC® C007785

CONTENTS

Concerns for the days:

Social action

Church renewal

Worship

Called to be One

Mission

Work

Poverty

Basic Christian communities

Non-violence and peacekeeping

Interfaith

Commitment

The rediscovery of spirituality

The thirty-first day

A mouse can do little but a nest of mice can work great havoc.

George MacLeod, Founder of the Iona Community

Introduction

Each day of the month Iona Community members pray for one another, for the wider work of the Church, and for the Community's shared concerns. Like *This Is the Day* and *Gathered and Scattered*, this book explores some of those concerns.

These readings and meditations were gathered over the past few years, during which I've been working as an editor at Wild Goose Publications and as Editor of *Coracle: the magazine of the Iona Community*.

Some of these readings are taken from Wild Goose books; some are from *Coracle*; some are from the *Iona Community e-zine*; many are original to this publication. Also included are short prayers for each day, and a list of scripture readings which readers might like to work through as part of a daily discipline.

The Iona Community believes *'that social and political action leading to justice for all people, and encouraged by prayer and discussion, is a vital work of the Church at all levels'* (from the Rule of the Iona Community).

I hope that these readings and meditations will aid in prayer and reflection, and serve to encourage thoughtful, committed action in God's world.

The collection is again dedicated to all who believe in the power of the Word (and of words), and to all those who are working to make their communities more just and peaceful places.

Living Letters of the Word is the final book in this series of daily readings. Thank you to everyone who contributed to them; and to everyone at Wild Goose, especially Sandra Kramer.

Neil Paynter, Biggar, 2012

MONTH 1

New Ways to Touch the Hearts of All

Returning home

Alone in an inner wilderness
and burdened by regret,
a place where the heart can rest
seems a long way off –
a distant country, barely remembered.

For when the soul is lost and
all around are disconnections,
battered hopes,
mounting failures,
and the pain of abandonment
is our daily companion,
we know that we are far from home.

Yet even in this darkness
the heart longs to return,
to find release,
to be touched by resurrection.

For our spirit
ultimately rebels against
these imprisoning disconnections

and the lifelessness of false desire.
We glimpse a different path
even when far from it.

A path on which
our search for light,
our awareness of failings,
our yearning for another way
are in themselves
propulsions to new possibilities.

To the possibility
that our tears are being witnessed,
that our cries are being heard,
that our soul is being healed,
by the One who accepts, understands
and tenderly invites us Home.

Peter Millar

Economic Witness

On money

A few years ago, with a couple of promotions adding substantially to our income, I decided, with my family, that rather than getting used to ever-increasing amounts of wealth and the standards of living that went with them, we would draw a line somewhere around the national average wage (it varies depending on whom you consult, but tends to be around £26K) and that would be our income. The rest we would give away.

This was not a hasty decision but one taken in the light of many conversations about money with friends and in my community. The second aspect of our Rule of life as members of the Iona Community calls us to account to one another for our use of money and resources and this includes a calculation, together, of our baseline commitments and a discussion, in our local Family Groups, about the decisions we have made and about our giving to a common pot, to the Community and to wider good causes. A rule of thumb for us remains the injunction to tithe, to give 10%, but this is not hard and fast and through the process of accounting to one another adjustments are made. Some of our number have chosen to live lives of poverty; some have not, but do because their circumstances place them in poverty. Some of our number are wealthy, and middle-class professions number in the jobs done by members in various parts of the UK and abroad.

The application of this Rule to our lives was one of the structures supporting our decision. A second was a series of pleasant and provoking, somewhat disquieting evenings we had over a year with two other sets of friends exploring the spiritual power of money in our lives. We spent time reflecting on the relationship our parents and families had to money, how it was used to control or to free, to force or facilitate. We considered the experiences we had had of learning to use money, of having it and of not having it. We told stories of first wage packets, of poverty in all our family histories, of mothers going without food to feed children and of surprising acts of incredible generosity. A feature of these stories was often the way provision was made at a point when least expected and most needed, provision that was just that, provision of enough, often anonymous or from surprising, generous sources. We studied the scriptures and especially the Gospels and the sayings attributed to Jesus warning of the spiritual dangers of wealth, and we considered how we might go through the eye of the needle, or store up spiritual treasures, or give a widow's mite or live with the knowledge that the poor are always with us. Such sayings run deeply through us, with their own proverbial power to taunt and test.

Together, in these groups we came to the realisation that money is rather like prayer: it requires discipline and right relationship. It is easy to put off this right relationship for the 'right time' for adjustment or amendment. It's also easy to fall prey, as a giving person, to a certain pride in the giving, a sense of power at supporting good causes with surprisingly sized cheques. Talking about this, accounting to one another, as friends and through the more formal processes of our Iona Community Family Group, means, for me at least, that the power of temptations to pride, to poverty, to greed, to belief in our immunity to the spiritual dangers of wealth could be, at the very least, offset somewhat and held up for scrutiny before others.

Spring is the time of year when we account to one another in our Family Groups for the use of our money. It fits with the annual tax year end and means looking hard at what we have spent, and what these spending decisions tell us about our lives and our values. As well as giving, which represents our most significant spending, we see how our decisions about food, travel, clothing, hobbies and fitness, books and maintenance are nuanced, expanded through ethical decision-making, and where we have had no easy control. We also see where the surprises come – the sudden, unexpected gifts of generosity to the legal fees we have had as we have tried to keep our adoptive daughter safe from harm, covering, to within £5, the bill from our careful lawyer, *'because we were praying for you and thought you should not be doing this all on your own'.* It's not been easy and we may not be able to sustain the commitment easily every year into the future. Our concern and care for asylum seekers and refugees in our home and neighbourhood means that our resources cannot be easily under our control in the rather too solid way they may have been in the past. The poor are with us and are ours to care for, especially as the state withdraws even the pitiful amounts of support it may have previously given. It is from the much that we have been given that much is expected, hoped for or just needed. We'd like to try to continue in this way though we know that ours is not really in any way a radical commitment. It's just a decision to have the average rather than to unthinkingly take all we are being paid through decisions made by arbitrary others.

Material poverty is a scandal but, as Leonardo Boff has said, faith involves a constant conversion to the way of the poor. I believe our economy needs radical redistribution of wealth. I believe that there is enough for everyone's need but not for everyone's greed. I believe that the wages paid to me as a professor in higher education are unnecessarily high, and I'd happily trade some of them in to secure a future that contains people capable of careful, deliberative thinking, capable of speaking many different, even obscure languages, analysing a work of art, understanding the patterns of life in regions of the world remote in time or geographical distance, or spiritual expression. I'd happily trade them in for more days with my family and friends, or digging my garden and away from the treadmill of e-mail production. I believe the research showing that in countries where the gap between rich and poor is lowest the well-being of the country is greatest. I believe this is part of what my family have been discovering through our commitment to cap our wealth and give, without strings, to others, perhaps so that others may have benefits that would not otherwise be possible, but far more so that we might know what it is to give and receive from others in due measure. I believe that the poor may well always be with us but that is no excuse for staring wealth in the eye and not blinking. 'We are all in it together,' says David Cameron as he attempts to take money from the poor and slightly above average to give to the already very rich. Money is a political matter but it is also, perhaps primarily for me, a spiritual matter. And that includes *my* money. I believe that it doesn't matter what I believe about money if I don't find ways of trying to practise it.

Alison Swinfen

Month 1 Day 3

Youth Concern

Jesus was young (a sermon)

Do not let anyone look down on you because you are young, but be an example for the believers in your speech, your conduct, your love, faith and purity.

1 Timothy 4:12 (GNB)

Jesus was young. That fact always strikes me with some force whenever I remember it. At least, young by Western standards, though judged by Ethiopia or Bangladesh you might say he was getting on towards middle age. But in Britain, he would be too young to be the Prime Minister, or even the leader of a party, too young to be a general or a bank manager or the chairman of the board, and eyebrows would certainly be raised, and are, when someone of his age is appointed the president of a trade union or the headmaster of a school. Our society would consider him too young for real power.

And not only was he young, he didn't even show any of the marks of the rising young man, any of the signs that might have endeared him to his elders. He was unemployed, and, what was worse, he had voluntarily given up a perfectly good trade to go wandering round the countryside with no fixed address – a kind of early

New Age traveller. He had no home, having left his family with some rather ungrateful and not at all 'family values' comments about anyone who did God's will being his family. He was not married, had no children, and was a perfect target for accusations of irresponsibility and refusing to play his part in the upholding of society.

His friends were questionable, and in some cases downright disreputable, including as they did criminals, drunks and prostitutes. He spoke out strongly against the status quo, the establishment, and corruption in high places – in the government, in the military, in the church. He refused to take part in a military uprising, and would not defend himself when attacked. He spoke a great deal more about money than he did about sex. He did all the things that we warn our children against doing, and very much about him went completely against the standards of success and status we set for young people. And not only did he do these things himself, he also actively encouraged other people to do them too. He invited people to go and give away all their money to the poor and join him in his vagabond life. He told them to leave their jobs and their families and their security and opt for a life of uncertainty. If we met him today, we might be warned against him as a bad influence on young people, and there would probably be a police file on him.

He had qualities which we tend to ascribe to youth (often in order to dismiss them) – idealism, a quick temper, a tendency to do things on the spur of the moment (have you ever noticed how often Mark's Gospel describes Jesus as doing something 'immediately', and how often he changes his plans, when he had any, that is?). What an irritant, how infuriating he must have been to the power-holders and power-brokers, this young upstart from an unfashionable place.

The church, most of the time, has tried to pretend that Jesus wasn't young. Sometimes, it has just ignored the fact, and has acted as if Jesus was a grave, sober, impressive elderly man. Many Protestants like this notion of Jesus. Elderly men in black suits preside over what bears more relationship to a funeral than a celebration, and dignity is the most important thing. We are exhorted in suitably elderly, even archaic language, to adhere to ways of doing things that have happened for generations, without the question ever being asked if this way of doing things is actually speaking to the real needs of people.

Or sometimes, the church has acknowledged that Jesus was young, but has still managed not to let it make a difference, by saying, in effect, well, yes, true, he was young, but he was different, so it doesn't count. As if it were accidental, a little mistake on God's part. But isn't the Incarnation, the life of Jesus, about the fact that Jesus was born like us? So, if he was young, not an old man in disguise or some kind of freak young man, then he really was a young man, with all that that implies. Is it not the case that what was different about Jesus was not the nature of his humanity, but the choices he made about its expression? Young man as he was, all the humanity and youthful quality of his life was offered up to witness to a radically different understanding of the world from that in which he stood. By being who he was, not in spite of who he was, he did what he did. The unique quality of a young man's love offered other possibilities for justice, for transformation, for a new way of being human. Freely choosing not to act out of his own urges for self-fulfilment, not enslaved to the gratification of his own desires, but equally not bound to any political or social system, any religious orthodoxy, not imprisoned in any dogma or doctrine, he chose a way that led to pain, humiliation, dreariness and death. Not because any of these things were good or desirable, because none of them are, but because they were the consequence and cost of that way. I find demonstrated in that way, at one and the same time, both a sacrificial commitment to the value and worth of people, and indeed of all that is created, which we might choose to call unconditional love, and a profound assertion of his own calling, worth, freedom, self. At the moment of most complete self-surrender, he was most completely himself.

Did he struggle with these choices? Every step of the way. Did he find them easy, pleasant, inevitable? Not according to the Gospels. He fought with God and angels and demons, as well as with great social and political forces. He dissented, groaned, sweated, shouted and despaired. No wonder he needed times of deep solitude – and no wonder that he liked parties and feasts so much, when he could simply relax and let things just be. But through all the tension and conflict, he returned again and again to that freedom and that demand which would not let him go. And from the abandonment of all ambition for his own happiness, success and power came the new life of resurrection, in which all that is surrendered is given back in new, mysterious, but real ways.

The very fact of Jesus' age makes this self-surrender all the more an act of love. It is hard to let go of life at any age. But voluntarily to give up all the possibilities that youth offers, to choose not to drink the cup of living to the full – there is a choice few of us would make willingly. Too many have that decision forced on them. It is not twenty-year-olds who decide to make wars, but they are most often the ones sent to fight and die. There is nothing good or noble about the curtailment of life by war, hunger, injustice, cruelty. And for Jesus, aware of the power he had, and could have to a much greater extent, feeling perhaps that there was so much good he could still have done, the pain of surrender must have been acute. Renunciation, for anyone, and for the young man Jesus too, is never easy. Only love and the exercise of freedom gives it any meaning.

I stress Jesus' youth not to slight or offend older people. For the rest of my life, I will be older than Jesus. And his good news, and the invitation to be part of the community of faith, was to people of all ages. But it is important that we allow ourselves to be challenged by the person of Jesus, in a world where being young is often seen as being a barrier to real responsibility, and where we think we can lay down what our young people should be like from a desire to relive our own youth.

And so, when we read the Gospels, we need to look at our own communities and cities and ask, where is the young Jesus to be found? Is it in the seats of power and authority? Or could it be that we see him, as in the Gospels, questioning the status quo, offending the respectable, outraging and threatening the mighty with his revolutionary message of love and justice and forgiveness, with his continual call to change economic priorities away from favouring the rich towards justice for the poor? And where do we find Jesus' contemporaries in the church? Are they pushed to the margins, denied a voice, unheard in the name of one who was too young to be a bishop or a church dignitary? Are our churches places where both young and old can meet a young Jesus, and not simply his pale ghost? If we are honest, we know that most of Jesus' contemporaries never come near the church.

They are to be found elsewhere. Instead of lambasting them for whatever imagined failing this denotes, we might more usefully consider what this says about the church and about our attachment to the past at the expense of the present. Many, perhaps most, of Jesus' followers were young, as many of those who have been prophetic have been. Perhaps their very youth allowed them to live more by trust and passion, and less by a conviction of their own wisdom and strength. Remember the Lord speaking to Jeremiah: 'Do not say that you are too young.' There are no barriers to discipleship. The young Jesus called young people. The church must recognise both that calling and the fact that it will not necessarily show up in the ways we think it should. The young Jesus does not need to be protected by us, but perhaps he sometimes needs to be protected from us.

Kathy Galloway, Iona Abbey, September, 1987

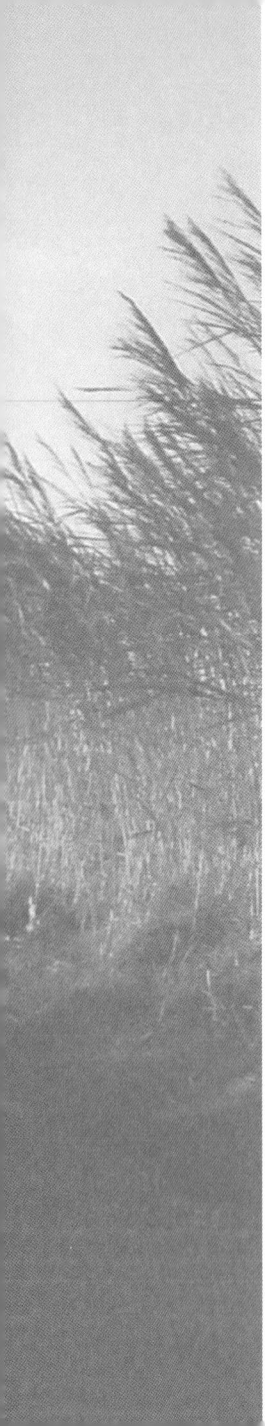

Month 1 Day 4

The Word

Steve the Satanist: unless a seed dies (a sermon)

John 12:20–33

He came into the church late one November afternoon.
It was pouring rain.
I'd just dashed in to get something from my office,
hoping to make a quick getaway.

'Can I use the phone?'

I looked at him more closely.
A young man, still in school, I thought,
not wearing a coat even in the pouring rain.
Thinking he'd had car trouble, I said,
'Go ahead, if it's a local call.'

As he dialled, he glanced around the church.
He chuckled and said,
'Imagine. A Satanist comes to a church to call for help.'

I swallowed.
A Satanist was using my office phone.
A Satanist stood between me and the door.
A six-foot-tall, strapping young Satanist
had me trapped in my office.
My Hollywood imagination conjured up a scene

as the young man spoke into the phone.
Would unsuspecting members of my congregation
find me sacrificed on the communion table
when they came to clean the church the next morning?
I began to edge toward the door.
This was not the kind of death
I would have chosen for myself.

Today is known as Passion Sunday in many churches.
It is a day to consider the death of Jesus
and its significance for us
as we move closer to the Cross.
Today's reading from the Gospel of John
provides an image of the kind of death Jesus would die,
an image to help us consider
the meaning of our own commitments in life and in death.

John pictures Jesus' death as a sign.
He believes that God is acting to reveal true glory
through Jesus' surrender of himself.
But this is not always the way people view Jesus' death.
Throughout history
and into our own generation,
Jesus' death has been seen as
weakness;
a tragic mistake;
a piece of gruesome history
covered up by rumours of resurrection.

Take my young Satanist, for example.
He was on the phone for quite awhile.
Then he asked if I would come and take the line.

'The youth worker wants to talk to you.'
My fear eased a bit.

I found myself speaking with a youth worker in the next city.
He explained he was part of a Christian team
advertised on radio stations that appealed to young people.
'We invite kids who are mixed up in Satanic ritual
to call us if they want to talk.
I'm going to come and talk to Steve.
I'll be there in an hour.
Will you keep him talking until I get there?'
I looked at the young man.
Steve the Satanist.
Somehow I'd imagined a name like Voltan or Draco.
Steve.
He was just 15.
And his mother's boyfriend had hit him in the face.
So he'd run out of the house in the pouring rain without a jacket
and come to the first place he thought he'd find help.
A church.
We sat in the sanctuary and talked as we waited.
Steve picked up a Bible
and flipped through it, glancing at the words.
He stopped when he read: Love your enemies.

'Do you believe that?' he challenged me.
'Yes,' I said.
'We believe that love is weak.
You should hate people who push you around.
Look here. It says turn the other cheek.
That's crazy.'

As Steve repeated to me some things he'd learned
from what he called the Satanic Bible,
I heard many of the teachings of Jesus turned upside down.
Hate your enemies.
Hit them first.
Whatever else it does,
this movement cannot accept the crazy teachings of Jesus
that insist we serve others and put ourselves last, not first.
Steve was convinced that strength is a master,
not a servant.

But let us listen to Jesus.
'"Unless a grain of wheat falls into the earth and dies,
it remains just a single grain;
but if it dies, it bears much fruit.
Whoever serves me must follow me."
He said this to indicate the kind of death he was to die.'

A seed must surrender its individual existence
in order to produce its fruit.
A seed gives life
by dying to its hard, smooth, perfectly packaged beginnings.
When the plant emerges from the soil,
the original seed has disappeared.
It has died to give birth to its crop of fruit,
its blossoms of beauty and the next generation of seed.

Jesus dares his followers to live by this pattern of paradox.
If we dream of life as a perfect package,
smooth, neat,
encased in a solitary shell of home and office

arranged for our own enjoyment,
we are like seeds that wither on the shelf.
Jesus challenges us
to plant ourselves in the common ground of God's world;
to give our energy-producing goodness
that feeds the goodness of the whole world,
not merely our own desires.

If we love life as a perfect package
and set our hearts on achieving it for ourselves,
Jesus says we will lose it.
We will know only the sterile loneliness
of a seed stuck in its own shell.
But when we die to the desires the world considers important,
when we give ourselves to others, for others,
our lives are enriched beyond measure.
It is a promise that only makes sense
once we have taken the risk and committed ourselves
to the messy soil of compassion –
loving our neighbours and our enemies.

Our fruitfulness,
our beauty and purpose
are only discovered in the midst of giving ourselves away.
Steve, my young Satanist,
could not understand this.
Instead,
he described sacrificing a bird
on the grounds of the church late one night.
'I had such a rush of power,' he said,
'as I watched it die.'
'Didn't you feel anything for the bird?' I asked.
He was silent.
He hadn't considered the bird until that moment.

I looked at him sitting beside me.
A bruise was forming on his cheek.
He was only 15.
He lived with people more concerned for their own interests than his.
He had little respect or support in his life.
The only power he could feel
was the rush of his own strength snuffing out a bird's life.

'Steve,' I said,
'I can only tell you what I believe.
I believe that love is the only force strong enough
to defeat evil in the world.
I believe that Jesus died for love's sake
and his love inspires us to care for others in every way we can.
Just remember that you came to a church for help on a rainy afternoon.
You can come back here if you ever need help again.
That's why we're here.
For Jesus' sake.'

I don't know what happened to Steve
because he didn't come back in my time at that church.
I pray for him
whenever I remember our encounter.
And I thank God for youth hotlines and youth workers
who are willing to invest time and energy and love for lives like his,
lives that know so little of hope and generosity;
lives that need some place to turn.

In his life and in his death,
Jesus reversed the values of the world.
Abundant life is not attained by the acquisition of things
or the triumph of force
or by achieving fame and popularity.
Abundant life is the gift God gives us
through the giving of others.
Jesus risked himself,
trusted himself
to the power of love that grows through patient self-giving.
A seed cannot see the results of its growth
when it surrenders itself to the ground.
We will not always see the results of our love

invested in lonely lives
and what seem like lost causes.

But if we would see Jesus,
then we are called to look into the midst of the neighbourhoods
where we are planted.
We are called to spend ourselves,
our time, our understanding, our money
growing relationships with vulnerable people:
with God's fragile world.
When we are rooted in the belief
that God's love produces abundance from tiny grains of generosity
and small seeds of compassion and commitment,
there is no other way to invest our lives.
We are called to be a place to turn.

Jesus died to promise us that God's love
can reverse the powers of death and destruction,
of greed and fear that have such a strong grip on the world.
Jesus committed himself to the fearless and hopeful generosity
held by every grain of wheat.
He died to feed the world with fearless, hopeful generosity
through which the true glory of God shines.
We taste it here in bread and wine.
We can share it wherever we go
if we trust the power of love to grow goodness
with fearless, hopeful generosity
even in the face of death.

Nancy Cocks

Hospitality and Welcome

Reflections on working with an asylum seeker: Michael's story

This is part of Michael's* story, told with his permission, but it is also part of my story. I work in the NHS in a therapeutic role. I also do unpaid counselling work for a counselling and training charity in a large inner city. Michael was referred here by his GP, who was very concerned about him. Michael was suicidal and self-harming. His moods swung between anger and rage and being almost totally withdrawn. A psychiatrist had seen him and said he was suffering from post-traumatic stress disorder and recommended therapeutic help. I was approached and asked if I would work with him. I had worked therapeutically before with asylum seekers. I was aware of the personal impact it can have: a kind of vicarious trauma.

Michael is 30 years old. He was born in an African country which has a long history of civil war. He speaks his native language and also English. His mother died from illness when he was 6 years old. He lived with his father and a brother and sister until he was 14. He remembered the soldiers coming and killing his father and brother. His sister was raped, then murdered. He was tied up and taken away and raped by a number of soldiers. He was released, as is the pattern in this form of oppression: some victims are left alive to tell others what has happened. It is a form of control and breeds fear. (As a result of this brutal sexual assault he developed a rectal prolapse which makes normal functions painful. At the time of counselling he was awaiting an operation. This caused him much anxiety, not least because he had no understanding of the concept of anaesthetics. Once I explained this to him he was much relieved.)

For the next few years of his life he lived with a farming family, who had taken him in, in a neighbouring country, where he lived happily, until the farmer's children, as they grew older, turned against him, seeing him as a threat to their inheritance. At this point he felt unsafe and left to seek asylum. How did he feel about that? (In what follows, Michael's words have been exactly quoted following his use of English, which is not always standard.)

He came to escape a dangerous situation. He arrives – and is put in another unsafe place:

'I seek asylum. I was put in detention, I was told – I call it prison – they said it was detention. I have never been in my life before.'

Michael's anger in these words can be felt. He felt he was being treated like a criminal. He had never been in trouble with the authorities in his own country, except for his experience with the soldiers. Having his movements restricted in this way reminded him of the restrictions they had placed on him: he was interrogated by the soldiers and intimidated. Feelings arising from the stress of the asylum process are similar to those arising from traumatic experiences – powerlessness, anger and humiliation. Psychological problems can be made worse by the asylum process.

'They ask me questions. I told them, and then they say "It's not correct." They don't believe it … They ask me more questions; they say it's going to be secret … I try to believe it. Then after a few months I went to sign. I was given a telephone to speak to my embassy … "You told me my words going to be secret, now leads to me talking to my embassy … you frighten me again."'

He was not only frightened by the officers, he was being retraumatised by being asked to recount experiences he wanted to forget.

'When I came here the immigration system was making me remember things I wanted to forget.'

His avoidance of these questions would be taken as suspicious by the officers.

It is not surprising that he became very withdrawn and would break down in tears for no immediate reason, for example, in a computer class which was full to capacity.

'So I just have to go to the art class. Then I said to the lady, "Just teach me how to paint." When it was time to leave there was a man that encourage me. I don't know his name but he will know that he was the one that came to me. He said to me, "How long have you been doing it?" I said, "This is my first time. That is why it's crap. That's why I left

it there." He said, "No take it," so he allow me back to the class to collect my painting. So that what inspires me, and I go from there and all this inspirations start on me.'

Painting was to be an important activity in his life. He would use it when he could not sleep. He would paint how he felt.

Michael, reflecting on his time in detention, said:

'Then after three months and three weeks I was released to somebody. I didn't even know the person they released me to. They said I cannot work, I cannot do nothing, I cannot receive house, I cannot receive anything to support myself.'

For Michael, as for other asylum seekers, there are these restrictions; therefore, they have little control over their lives. They cannot work, receive benefits or local authority housing. They rely on charitable support for food, clothing and pocket money. This presents an additional, secondary stress – they cannot provide for themselves. This conflicts with a culturally determined role of a man, who is the provider. It was made more difficult for Michael because the provider for him was a woman. He depended on her for everything. This was something that he was sharing with me because he did not want to upset her. He was very distressed when talking about this:

He is now moved to a big city he has never been in before, to a strange house and people. He is, on a daily basis, reminded that his future is uncertain. What is for most of us a simple act of receiving letters through the post became for Michael something to be feared. Every time a letter came through the door he was in touch with feeling that this could be the one to say he had to go home. This affected his mood:

'I am a little depressed when I think: Are they going to give me my papers to stay or are they going to take me home?'

The Home Office did send him letters about other aspects:

'The Home Office would send me letters to remind me at any time I could go; it's very panicking. It's very, very panicking.'

He was feeling trapped.

The Home Office is one factor in his life, but there is another. His partner is a local person whom he met through a charity, and their relationship developed. His mood lifted when he spoke of her. She was clearly concerned about him. She had arranged for him to see the psychiatrist. When therapeutic help was recommended he had no concept of counselling. It was explained to him. He recounts his own understanding after it had been explained to him:

'What are they doing there? They will just listen to you, then you will tell them your feelings, what is disturbing in your heart, then they can listen and give you advice. Not what I want.'

Michael's partner did not give up on trying to persuade him to go for counselling. She explained to Michael that she was experiencing him as angry, depressed, unhappy and suicidal. 'Counselling is good,' she had said. He finally agreed to be referred by his GP.

At our first meeting Michael seemed very low in mood. He described himself as feeling heavy in his heart and his head. He seemed burdened and lifeless.

He made attempts to be polite but it seemed a big effort for him. Suddenly he would let out a whimper and break down in tears.

It seemed important to say something about how I worked and what it might be like. I mentioned two things. One, that I was trying to create a quiet safe place in the counselling room in which he could talk. Two, that what he said to me was confidential and would not be repeated outside. I thought it important to emphasise that I had no contact with the Immigration Service or the Home Office. I did mention the exceptions to confidentiality regarding matters of personal safety and harm, etc. However, Michael immediately picked up on it being confidential. He nodded with approval.

As he recounted his story, his first and most immediate concern was the way he had been treated by the immigration authorities on arrival in the UK. As he spoke his speech became faster and there was growing strong emotion behind his words. It seemed that this experience was uppermost in his mind rather than what had happened to him back home.

I found myself becoming tense as Michael recounted his experience. I was in touch with anger, both his and my own. I managed to hold it in during the session. I did have a strong feeling of wanting to fix things for him. After many of these sessions I was totally exhausted. I found myself thinking that I was ashamed of my country for the way he was treated.

In other sessions his mood was very different. He described the best Christmas of his life with his partner's family. He felt accepted. Michael tells me with great delight that his partner is expecting their baby. He also speaks of wanting to do better for his child than his parents did for him. It is clear that this news has lightened his mood. He is thinking of a future with a family of his own and he speaks of his responsibilities.

Later on, after the child is born, he tells me of the joy of being a father. Yet he is also able to reflect on the further dilemma this places on him. He sees that if he is deported he will be making a problem for them both as well as for himself. It might have been better if he had remained single.

'Thinking ahead when I was just alone I was thinking if I am not going to stay, okay I can handle my life ... but now I have a son ... I want to protect ... to show human beings how to be one, to love one another, but to stop, to look for peace.'

He is expressing the pain of not being able to provide for his family and perhaps not see his son grow up.

'Do the Home Office really understand?'

He records how he feels in some words he brought to a counselling session:

I wish I never been born into this precious world, full of sorrows, too much confusion of being a human that knows not where his coming from neither where he is going. I feel sometimes many are left behind and many have been forgotten and fade away, as if they never exist in my life once before. I think about myself as one of those who are nobody, no reason to live as human, but trying to move life around to be normal person like others, but home wasn't home and outside home wasn't outside home. That's my feeling. What can I do when crying, no one can hear me, talking and they listen but not understand. Moving from one place to another yet no one see you exist as normal human.

He reflects on the mixture of feelings – anger, fear – and how it made him feel towards others:

'You see other human beings. You hate them, but you don't know why you are

hating them … is just because of what you see they want to do to you.'

'I could just kill somebody … I would pay dearly for it.'

Michael is very honest about his feelings but they are in control. Each time he had contact from the Home Office, these feelings came back; feelings he seems to have internalised, and which affect how he feels about himself:

'What is wrong with me, there is something that is panicking me. That is trying to catch me, which I don't want.'

As counselling progressed Michael learnt a breathing method for anxiety, and a body relaxation exercise for visualising a special place, which he called 'freedom'. These helped him not only cope with his strong feelings but also experience newer more pleasant feelings.

'A special place which I bring out of my mind, which I like to do, you know. A special place that is peaceful. No aggressive or fighting or hitting or bad things, you know. So, obviously I loose my mind to let it happen.'

Michael brought some of his paintings to our sessions. They became a kind of language we used to explore his inner life. One he showed me he had painted on Christmas Day whilst in detention. It was dark, brooding, the forms and shapes were difficult to see clearly and it was unclear what was happening in this painting. He said that was how he felt at that time. Another painting, he had completed after starting counselling. This was full of bright colours. There was what looked like an African scene. A man in a small boat on a river surrounded by lush green trees and shrubs. A strong yellow sun shone down and put the figure into silhouette. Michael used this to explain how his mood was changing. He could think with some good feelings about his homeland.

'It is from my heart.'

So Michael comes for counselling and describes his experience of being in counselling:

'They are very genuine. And the way they listen to you, it's like you stay so much close to your God or so much close to what you believe. They look at your eyes and give you some little guidelines which relaxes you to think nicely of your life.'

He then reflects on his own inner experience of being in this relationship:

'There was something inside me that makes me say that to him, because the moment I was speaking to him, I speak with all my heart, which I never speak to many people. I tell you what is really going on in my life and I was free to tell you. Sometimes I don't want to say to somebody, but I will say to you.'

Michael eventually shared two very difficult memories. I used a special method for dealing with trauma, Eye Movement Desensitisation and Reprocessing (EMDR), to target them. It is intended to stop people reliving past experiences.

He reflects on this process:

'He did the hands, and then he teach me to close my eyes and relax all my body. Actually I can see it depends on every individual, if I really want to do it. That is why I ... how can I put it? – a result and it is good.

'That was the most special aspect ... I forgive myself now because that what hurt me most.'

He asked, 'Is this magic?' Magic in his culture has a distinct meaning. I reassured him by reminding him of what we had done together. Later he reflects on it:

'I can feel it like "ahhhh" – it was relief. I was relieved. I can't any more remember the bad things.'

He realised that for counselling to work he needed to trust

me as his counsellor. What helped him to trust was his feeling understood.

'...You did something to cover me like, I can't explain it, it's just like you cover me with a wing and give me shelter inside ... a warm shelter. Then I am ... makes me to express all my feelings.'

Michael feels understood; this helps him in understanding both himself and other people. He feels able now to face and accept what is inside him.

'Counselling help me understand myself. It is you that will find the truth inside you and it is you will find the aggressive inside you, that will hurt you.

'I know there are things that you cannot change ... so not to be worrying about it. But if we can understand ourselves – best of all understand yourself before looking at other people then you will deal with them better ...'

Working with Michael was challenging not least because of the context of two cultures. I tried to be sensitive to his culture whilst respecting my own. It was important to learn to *be* with Michael rather than to act on the Western diagnosis of post-traumatic stress disorder, at least at the beginning.

I learnt that a specific task for me as Michael's counsellor was that of witnessing. Giving him time and space, listening to his felt experience as he recounted his story in his own way, without my judgement or need to interpret.

This is not an easy thing to do. But it is an important part of a healing experience as Michael finds his own voice again and a sense of himself, realising he has some choices, limited though they may be at times. It is recognition, too, that trauma is not just something that happens within an individual; it is something which happens between people. Relationships are traumatised. The formation of new relationships, with love, understanding, acceptance and trust, creates hope for himself and in humanity.

For me this work can be exhausting at times. After many a session, as I left to go home, I often had a sense that what I thought was important in my own life suddenly seemed less important or even trivial.

Michael does not now feel alone with his problems. He feels cared for. This helped him handle his self-harming behaviour and suicidal thoughts. These all eventually disappeared.

'I really wanted to kill myself. That's the point. It didn't happen because of you.'

He feels much more in control of himself and able to think about his future, which he realises is in his hands despite the restrictions on his life.

Perhaps the biggest indication of change is found in the painting which Michael gave to me. The upper background is dark, but with streaks of light. Central is a red heart. It has two white wings behind it as though they are holding it up. Below is a green field surrounded by a green hedge. Behind it all there is a beam of sunlight, yellow and orange in colour. It illuminates the background. Around the heart is a black chain covering it in three ways, with a black lock holding the three chains together. But in each of the three chains there is a break. The chain is clearly broken. On the back of the painting he has written:

'Peace of mind and passage! Without peace of mind, life is meaningless and world's worthless. But when there's peace of mind then you can see that life is precious and the world's beautiful.'

I am so grateful to Michael for sharing a part of his life with me and allowing his story to be told.

** A pseudonym*

John Prysor-Jones

Month 1 Day 6

This Is the Day

This day's grace

We bless you for the graces
of this day's journey:

For eyes touched
and vision re-coloured;

for ears unstopped
and hearing re-tuned;

for tongues loosened
and speech re-enchanted;

for minds freed
and the world re-imagined;

for hearts opened
and love re-kindled;

for dry bones breathed on
and lives resurrected –

we bless you for this day's grace.

Pat Bennett

The Iona Experience

A threshold experience

In a time of recession and so-called austerity the divisions within society become more apparent as they deepen. Education and health as well as wealth offer protection to some whilst those denied educational opportunity, those who cope with ill health, disability or discrimination, or who already suffer poverty, are made even more vulnerable. Rather than fostering social cohesion, 'we are all in this together', times of economic hardship see increased levels of inequality, mistrust, stigmatisation, resentment, protectionism and prejudice.

Since its formation, the Iona Community has worked and campaigned for greater social justice, engaging in projects through the years which have sought to combat poverty and address social division. In doing so it has advocated an incarnational spirituality which rejects any understanding of the Christian faith which seeks to keep faith, politics, prayer, action, body and spirit in separate compartments. The Iona Community believes that central to the Gospel of Jesus Christ is a rejection of that most pervasive and destructive dualism, Them and Us, from which all other divisions stem. A point emphasised by the Apostle Paul in his letter to the Galatians: 'There is neither Jew nor Greek, there is neither slave nor free, there is no male and female, for you are all one in Christ Jesus' (Gal 3:28).

Therefore, both as a movement and as an organisation, the Iona Community actively seeks to create and explore opportunities to overcome societal boundaries and divisions. Much of the Iona

Community's work is concerned with bringing together people from different backgrounds and with different perspectives in safe but creatively provocative encounters and situations.

In academic fields such as anthropology and psychology, such encounters and situations are described as 'liminal'. The Latin word *limen* means threshold. Threshold space is where all transformation happens. Richard Rohr, a Franciscan priest and writer who led a programme week in the Abbey, comments: *'Nothing good or creative emerges from business as usual. This is why much of the work of God is to get people into liminal space, and to keep them there long enough so they can learn something essential. It is the ultimate teachable space … maybe the only one. Most spiritual giants try to live lives of "chronic liminality" in some sense. They know it is the only position that insures ongoing wisdom, broader perspective and ever-deeper compassion …'*

Liminal time and space provide us with the opportunity to step back from our lives, from social and cultural norms, to look at them afresh, enabling transformation to take place. The Iona Community believes that Christians are called to threshold spaces and activities. Places where discomfort and disorientation, confusion and conflict may be experienced but which may ultimately become places of healing and hope, understanding and reconciliation.

Thus the Iona Community also affirms the fundamental need for safety during such liminal phases of life. This is where our liminal movement does not just meet our organisational structures but, more profoundly, is held by them. Ron Ferguson, a former Leader, once said that the most spiritual decisions are taken in the Finance Committee. Liminal phases will fail or, worse still, cause damage if order is absent. The work of administrative and support staff in Glasgow and of Islands Centres staff in bookings, finance, housekeeping, shop and kitchens sustains the common life and holds the space for the liminal to occur in safety.

The description of Iona by George MacLeod, Founder of the Iona Community, as 'a thin place' – only a tissue paper separating the material from the spiritual – is fleshed out by the concept of liminality. It also enhances the Community's theological understanding of its common task particularly of offering radical hospitality.

This is clearly seen in the work of the Islands Centres which welcome over one hundred guests each week during the season. Guests drawn from all over Britain, all over the world, from different Christian traditions and from none, each given the time, space and place for encounter and engagement, for worship, recreation and work, who often describe their stay as a life-changing experience.

Norman Shanks, another former Leader, explains in *Iona: God's Energy*: *'It is an experience involving grace and generosity, vulnerability and hospitality, in the course of which minds are challenged and hearts are touched … where risks may be taken and insights gained both into the nature and purpose of God and into what God is calling us to do and to be. It is an experience … that recognises the spiritual reality that individual fulfilment is to be discovered only in community, that self-development cannot be achieved apart from a concern for one another and for the world around us.'*

Peter Macdonald, extract from an Iona Community Annual Report

Month 1 Day 8

Life in Community

Among unchosen neighbours: a reflection from Iona

A reflection by Rowena Aberdeen, former Deputy Warden at the MacLeod Centre on Iona.

'To find my own life is a task I cannot undertake without the neighbour.' This comment by Rowan Williams from his book *Silence and Honey Cakes* in many ways sums up the reasons I chose to go and live and work with the Iona Community for three years. Of course, before I arrived I could not have articulated this thought so clearly. Still, in the years I spent as MacLeod Centre Warden I lived into the deeper meaning of this phrase – with all its attendant joys and challenges.

In our world today, most of us can choose our 'neighbours' – those we socialise with are usually people like us, who reflect the world as we see it. We struggle with office or church politics, and breathe a sigh of relief that we can leave at the end of the day or only have to see people once a week.

So what happens if you put yourself in a position where you can't walk away? Where your colleagues must also become your friends and family and support. Where, as we say on Iona, 'we choose to be open to unchosen relationships'. Well, then life gets interesting! The unchosen neighbour provides us with a different perspective. A mirror that does not reflect our own preconceptions but instead holds us accountable to recognising who we really are, rather than who we like to think we are. It is in this way that our neighbour gives us a new context: a different and perhaps more honest place in which we must put all our values and intentions into daily practice. We are all wonderful and loving people … until we have to engage with the messy reality of human relationships, where nothing is perfect and we must wrestle each moment with our ideals versus the interactions that make up our days. Am I really kind and generous? Or only when I'm not tired and stressed? Am I really good at communicating? Or only when the other person reacts appropriately? How do I react when I have to deal with the negative consequences of another person's actions? Especially when I think they were wrong in the first place. Am I really loving, or do judgement and righteous indignation creep in? …

We all know our ideals in these situations, what we believe about ourselves and how we think we would act, but it is in the testing of these that happens when we live among unchosen neighbours that we begin to see if these beliefs show through in our actions. In community living we can no longer pretend we are our intentions: we must recognise we are our actions, including our actions in tiredness, stress, hurt and conflict. In this, we come face to face with our own brokenness. Luckily, for me anyway, daily life also provided many opportunities for a stumbling and halting progress towards a truer love for those around me. A daily practice of love. Anywhere else and I would have run away from that practice. I know because even on Iona I tried. Everyone tries, because deep love is hard – uncomfortable and challenging. I had to give up valuing 'right' and 'fair' and instead seek the deep truth of another's story, no matter how foreign to mine. On Iona you can't run away. You need your fellow staff: they laugh and cry with you, support and socialise with you, give you what you need to survive a busy and challenging season. So eventually you turn up and try again (and again … and again!), and in that you find moments of grace, of a love you didn't think you had and moments where the Spirit moved when you'd thought it impossible.

Don't get me wrong – not all relationships are reconciled and not all people become close friends. But you can move a step or two closer to being able to love others for who and what they are in your life, whether that be a close companion who provides nourishment and support, or someone who mirrors to us our judgemental attitudes – because they trigger them all. Both are important for our journey; both help us to be open, to grow and to slowly move from brokenness to wholeness, as individuals and as community.

I love something one of my fellow Resident staff said: *'When I'm not living in community, I'm a lot more careless with relationships.'*

Angel in disguise

I hated him.
He undermined me,
threw daggered words and spiteful looks,
tore me down and tired me out.
He found every weakness,
entered every wound and insecurity.
And in doing so, forced me to look into my own shadows.

Am I truly a person of love and compassion?
Or does it fall away like an inconvenient cloak
when I'm backed into a corner?
I wrestled daily with him
and with my integrity:
like wrestling with Jacob's stranger –
an angel in disguise.

Rowena Aberdeen

Month 1 Day 9

WOMEN

Aliah bakes bread

She rose before dawn,
mixed the dough,
kneaded it in her neat home,
folded it like clean sheets
and set it aside,
to rise in its turn.
  Aliah woke her family
  and fed them,
  carried water, washed floors,
  left everything in order.
But now she is sitting
in her blue dress
in the bakehouse in the yard,

that ramshackle shelter
against rain and sun,
among the ashes of old fires,
while, in the iron stove, the new fire
for the new bread burns bright.
The dough is pliant, alive,
latent and, right now,
resting under a cloth
faded with much washing
and drying in the sun.
Roots and knots of olive wood,
hauled from the hillsides,
are piled ready to feed the fire.
She swings out the griddle –
which holds the heat of today's fire,
and years of sunshine
on the olive trees –
takes a disk of living bread
in her quick hand and
tosses it onto the hot metal.
At once it blows up –
a puffed pitta, a bread balloon!
Watchful, smiling, using a long spoon
as though supping with the devil,
Aliah turns the bread, lets it brown,
bake through, and then, deftly,
lifts it out to cool. Loaf by loaf
the pile grows, its warm aroma
wafting into the street; children
peep round the gate; neighbours
arrive to pass the time of day,

standing the heat of this kitchen,
approving the way she provides
for her household. They feast
on it with their eyes; some taste:
companionable work, baking.
The last disk of dough,
tossed onto the hot griddle
by hands swift and skilled,
is watched intently, turned,
not allowed to burn.
There is no waste.
The fire dies down, but warmth
lingers in the loaves, to be
passed on in nourishment.
Among the ashes see –
where there was no bread –
enough fresh loaves to feed a family:
enough to share, enough to give away.
And the fire still glows
in Aliah's face; right now
the making of bread
is her mystery; right now
she is skilled and fulfilled.
Right now
there is bread for today.

Jan Sutch Pickard

Prayer

Qualandia Terminal: First Friday of Ramadan

*A letter from the Holy Land from Warren Bardsley, who worked as an Ecumenical Accompanier (EA) with the Ecumenical Accompaniment Programme in Palestine and Israel (www.eappi.org)**

It is 7:15am on another hot Jerusalem day; in spite of a light, cooling breeze we know that by mid-morning we will be looking for shade. We arrive at the huge terminal by bus, just 15 minutes from Jerusalem. It is a soulless structure of steel and concrete that exists for one purpose only – to control and process human beings. The way through to the electronic search area is by means of narrow steel-barred lanes and a turnstile; the so-called 'humanitarian' entrance is for the elderly and disabled, though the whole system seems more suitable for cattle than for people.

Today the place is crawling with heavily-armed Israeli soldiers and police personnel. If you were unaware of the significance of this day you might assume that the military were preparing for a major political demonstration and expecting a riot. If so, you would be wrong. This is the first Friday of Ramadan, the most

important Muslim festival, and people are converging on this checkpoint from Ramallah and all parts of the northern West Bank in order to pray at the Al-Aqsa mosque in East Jerusalem. Let me repeat this, in case you may have missed the point: the thousands arriving by bus and taxi to this terminal are coming to PRAY, not to make trouble. Some will not be allowed through, either because they lack the appropriate permit or because they are the wrong age. This year the army has decreed that, apart from children 13 and under, only men over 50 and women over 45 will be allowed through. Men between 45 and 50, and women between 30 and 45, may pass, providing they have a special prayer permit to do so. Many are disappointed, and this year, to add to the confusion, a Palestinian source has indicated that all women over 30 will be allowed to pass.

The Palestinians wait and pass through the first checkpoint with dignity in a place designed to humiliate, women and men filing through separate gates. Young Israeli soldiers appear nervous. Occasionally they move forward to push back the pilgrims spilling off the transport vehicles. From time to time their commander barks orders through a megaphone. The army has created a clear area some 200 yards from the first checkpoint barrier as a way of controlling the flow of people waiting to go through.

The sun is relentless. Still people wait. Two very young children are in the line with an elderly woman; they cling to her, looking up at the soldiers with a mixture of curiosity and fear; an elderly couple, the husband walking with a stick, and supported by his wife, move slowly forward. Then a touch of humanity as a soldier takes the woman and her grandchildren from the queue and escorts them through the checkpoint. What stories are here! An Arabic teacher and his 12-year-old son sit disconsolately at the roadside; he is 49 but will not be allowed past the barriers. Stories are being collected by the large number of media personnel, which will be broadcast around the world later today. United Nations observers are present and members of Machsom Watch (an Israeli women's peace group), as well as the EAs, who, together, it is widely believed, act as some kind of restraint on the worst excesses of the military.

Restlessness and frustration grows among the waiting crowd as the time

approaches beyond which it will be impossible to reach Jerusalem in time for the prayers. Some are expressing anger when it appears that the army are not allowing any more people through. New orders maybe? Suddenly there is panic as the soldiers rush forward pushing the people back – there is the sharp sound of exploding sound grenades. Two teenagers are slightly injured. Some stones have been thrown by youths at the back of the crowd, who are separate from the pilgrims. Then (exactly as our training indicated) comes the tear gas and we begin to feel vulnerable. Our team leader rings and tells us it is time to leave. Meanwhile the people on the West Bank side of the checkpoint begin to disperse, to pray in Ramallah; there are three more Fridays left in Ramadan … we may get through next week or the week after, *inshallah:* who knows?

As we pass through the terminal cage and make our way back to the city I ponder two questions: What kind of legacy is being handed down to the next generation? And what evil has entered the soul of a nation that will go to such lengths to prevent people from exercising a fundamental human right – to PRAY in the place and after the manner of their own choosing?

Lord, where are you
in this unholy mess?
Muslim, Christian, Jew,
still reaping the
centuries-old harvest
of bitter enmity:
sowing new seeds of hate
for generations yet unborn.
Where are you?

When I begin to lose
much of my trust
in any kind of purpose,
remind me again
that it was here,
here on this ground
we call holy,
that you became
part of the mess.

Born, nurtured,
living, loving, dying,
in this place.
Not to sanitise it
but to redeem and transform.

Lord, in the mess we have made
of your world,
recruit us
in the holy work of
redeeming and transforming
our places.

Warren Bardsley

** The Ecumenical Accompaniment Programme in Palestine and Israel (EAPPI) brings internationals to the West Bank to experience life under occupation. Ecumenical Accompaniers provide protective presence to vulnerable communities, monitor and report human rights abuses and support Palestinians and Israelis working together for peace. When they return home, EAs campaign for a just and peaceful resolution to the Israeli/Palestinian conflict through an end to the occupation, respect for international law and implementation of UN resolutions. (From the Ecumenical Accompaniment Programme in Palestine and Israel website, www.eappi.org.)*

Month 1 Day 11

Justice and Peace

First on the list

He has told you, O mortal, what is good;
and what does the Lord require of you
but to do justice, and to love kindness,
and to walk humbly with your God?

Micah 6:8

I came into contact with the peace movement just over ten years ago. At that time I had been a practising Christian for thirteen years but despite that had never come across the 'justice perspective'. I had heard in many sermons about loving your neighbour, giving to those in need, etc, but never had this wisdom been put onto a political plane. Faith should have nothing to do with politics, some say. I'm sure that's right in certain circumstances, but because politics concerns the governance of our common life it is hard to keep the Christian viewpoint outside of it. It is about people's right to a decent life, our stewardship of animals and nature, the needs of the weak and much more.

It was the same when I worked in Paraguay: the congregation kept the moral teaching on a personal level. Together with the youth group, I visited orphanages and leper colonies. It was a faith that had social rather than political implications. It was only when I met Christians in the peace and solidarity movements that I understood it was a dimension that had been lacking. And what does this dimension involve? Well, I think it involves seeing the wider meaning;

daring to look at how our lives interconnect, South and North, men and women, poor and rich. Observing how we affect each other, and the delegation of power in our relationships.

Poverty, for example, is not a natural state. It is mainly created and upheld by political decisions on a local, national and global level. The interests of the different parties in the world are in conflict, and rich nations have institutions to protect their own interests. These often make decisions that do not benefit the poorest people of the planet.

A lot has happened during the last ten years, thank goodness, and popular movements have put global justice on the agenda. But for many Christians this perspective still seems problematical. I have heard young Christians sigh deeply when describing their attempts to bring up these issues in their own churches. Even simple suggestions such as using fair trade coffee at church can result in protests and anger. Perhaps it's time Bible classes studied the prophets?

Justice comes first on Micah's list. For the people of Israel, to act justly was fundamental to their belief; it was a crucial aspect of being a faithful Jew. The same word for justice as in the Micah quote is used by the prophet Jeremiah when he speaks God's word to the king. There it is obvious that the term refers to how we relate to the weak and those worst off in society. *'Do what is just and right. Rescue from the hands of his oppressor the one who has been robbed. Do no wrong or violence to the alien, the fatherless or the widow and do not shed innocent blood in this place.'* Where do we stand when it comes to violence and oppression? *'Do no violence,'* wrote Jeremiah, but also: *'Rescue from the hands of the oppressor the one who has been robbed.'*

It's not enough that we say no to violence ourselves, even though that can be a good place to start. As an individual I have to consider whether in my everyday life I contribute to violence or oppression, for example through the goods I buy or how I invest my money. But as communities – churches, associations – we must also ask ourselves how we can intervene when we know that others are suffering violence …

Annika Spalde

The Integrity of Creation

Heartbeat of creation

I love trees: they stand naked in winter, and burst with new life in spring. If you take a stethoscope on a spring walk and look for a young smooth-barked tree, you can hear what sounds like a heartbeat through the stethoscope: The sound of sap being 'pumped' against gravity, up the tree to the tips of the leaves. It sounds like our own heartbeat, and I often think of it as the heartbeat of creation.

We are connected to trees closer than you might think. I am no biologist, so it stunned me to discover, that if you take a single molecule of chlorophyll you have over a hundred atoms of carbon dioxide, nitrogen and hydrogen arranged in a complex and exact pattern around a single atom of magnesium. Now take a single molecule of haemoglobin and you have that exact same pattern of carbon dioxide, nitrogen and hydrogen around a single atom of iron. That is the only difference, that tiny atom of iron or magnesium. We can truly follow St Francis, calling trees, and all sap-filled plants, our brother or sister.

Chris Polhill

Columban Christianity & the Celtic Tradition

Reconnecting with the roots – a future for Celtic spirituality?

'Celtic spirituality' has been so popular for the last twenty-five years that it is widely accepted as a branch of Christian expression which developed in ancient times in these islands and lingered in remote places. It is often regarded both as factually true and as having a great deal to say to us about contemporary spiritual concerns, including the need to reintegrate faith with the rest of life, and to respond holistically to the environmental crisis.

'Celtic spirituality' was developed largely by evangelical Christians in England as a tool for mission in the 1980s but is also claimed by Catholics and by those who feel they are falling off the edge of church life. It has been effectual in helping people develop their spiritual life, and in some cases has led to the growth of dispersed communities, supporting members to undertake valued work. The current Celtic movement is not the first, and, like the previous movements, it seems to be a means by which people can address contemporary concerns in a prayerful and powerful way.

Yet, in spite of music and liturgy 'in the Celtic tradition' which are now part of the mainstream of church life, the movement is increasingly tired, less dependent on the rediscovery of ancient prayers that gave it its original sparkle, and more dependent on the derivative material, in translation and often at third-hand; or on poetry and prayers from all periods in Western culture that suit the selected themes and concerns of individual authors. Has it fulfilled its purpose as a movement, or are there aspects that could speak to us in new ways as the 'Celtic' spoke to people like George MacLeod in the 1930s and, a generation before him, to writers and artists of the Celtic Revival?

Modern Celtic Christianity has little in common with what is normally taught in a university department of Celtic Studies, but, at its best, while it may be historically wrong it can in some sense be theologically right, a path to deepening life with God, a response to modern concerns that finds its expression in ancient prayers and practices. While its attraction is limited, mainly to white, educated Christians, it has helped churches to recapture a sense of freshness, creativity and delight in Christian worship and personal prayer.

Since many of the books of the movement include prayers from all periods and cultures, it can be hard to define what Celtic Christianity is. However, in spite of its all-encompassing tendencies, there are certain key elements, and while these are found in many other spiritualities, when combined with the use of ancient poems or folk prayers from the Celtic-speaking countries, they provide a common core.

One element is a sense that God is present in all aspects of life. Celtic spirituality is seen as holistic, all-encompassing and capable of unifying apparently disparate aspects of daily life and work. There is an emphasis on the Trinity in the prayers used, whether folk prayers from the Hebrides or modern poetry that seeks to emulate them.

Another element is a belief in the spontaneity of the ancient Celts, who are viewed as having only the simplest church organisation. There is plentiful poetic evidence for another element: delight in the natural world and acute observation of it. Modern writers attribute to the Celtic peoples a sense of the divine as immanent as well as transcendent, and as living in harmony with the natural world, and, more controversially, with each other.

Storytelling is a vital part of the movement. Anecdotes about early saints are recounted, taken not only from writings from the Celtic countries, but from Bede's *Ecclesiastical History of the English People*. Many of the anecdotes selected are about women saints and reflect a desire to believe in the equality of women in the early 'Celtic' Church. The saints are presented as models for us today, and their stories means by which deep truths can be expressed, a form of narrative theology.

A sense of place is another element, and there is an emphasis on ancient holy places which are seen as spiritually and in our view geographically on the edge, which provide meeting ground for Christians who feel on the edge, spiritually and organisationally. Through pilgrimage to these places they can meet with like-minded people, ideally to form community.

There is much here that most Christians would value and would want to incorporate into their own prayer and public worship. But some of the assumptions contain interpretations that have diverged so far from fact that they are of little help in developing a robust spirituality. Sometimes, too, the term Celtic is used when another spirituality is in question, and most of the founder books on modern Celtic spirituality place England in the Celtic world, though very little use is made of English tradition. Because the 'Celtic' is known at several removes, it can become what J.R.R. Tolkien once described as a ragbag from which anything can be pulled. It also means that much that did belong to the Celtic-speaking countries hardly gets touched on at all, including most of ancient poetry; religious and secular writings; the artistry and theology of the great Gospel books and church metalwork; the physical remains of churches, wells and monastic settlements; and the folk tradition.

Celtic spirituality developed in Ireland rather later than in England and always used folk prayers. The most popular books were written by the poet and hermit John O'Donohue (1954–2008), who combined philosophical reflections with commentary on the native traditions and practices of the west of Ireland. At a time of rapid social and religious change his books gave a sense of connectiveness to Irish spiritual tradition. The extent to which his writings can be considered 'Celtic' may be disputed, but they touched people across the English-speaking world, while also appealing to those familiar with the vernacular religion with its visits to holy wells, the annual pilgrimage to Croagh Patrick, the

penitential journeys to Lough Derg, and other practices which use formal church rituals but are not dependent on them.

O'Donohue's approach may indicate one way in which what is good in Celtic spirituality can be drawn upon, by dropping the blander accretions, and seeking to root it in its origins. The same is true of the writings of Irish academics who have studied the ancient sources and tried to connect them to what concerns us today, in particular Thomas O'Loughlin and John Carey. There will be much that we cannot accept, but by exploring what is there and what has supported people down the centuries, we may discover something of how we can be stretched in our own spiritual journey with unlikely fellow pilgrims.

To do this, we need to give time to study the original sources and their languages, or at the least to learn more from those who do, using their knowledge as we use the knowledge of biblical scholars to more fully understand the scriptures. This may draw us closer to the writers who left us prayers of power and beauty, but who provided this spontaneity by living to strict monastic rules that gave time to prayer and study. Through study we can understand more fully what gave them their vision, in all its complexity, how it related to the ways in which they lived, and what we can take from it today, leaving markers concerning what we cannot digest, in case future cultures might find richness in the parts we discard.

We may also find much is not, and need not be called 'Celtic'. The Northumbrian missionaries of the 1980s modelled themselves on the missionaries of the sixth century, Irish or English. They took what was beautiful, publicised it and adapted it for the needs of mission as they saw it. This form of Celtic spirituality, largely book-based, might grow through rediscovering the great Anglo-Saxon religious tradition, the joyful freedom of medieval English spirituality, and the remaining vernacular religious practices.

As well as study of the past, we may need to ground the movement by looking more at what people actually do and express in the places in which we are called to work and worship, or have done until recently. We might find we can develop the 'sense of place' by asking people about their remaining traditions and practices, about what has bound them together down the generations, about the prayers they have learnt, and in doing so learn from their wisdom as well as that of the past.

Where else do we take this interest in the Celtic? If the derivative aspects outbalance use of the sources, its attractiveness will pall and limit its chances of enabling people to move towards the centre of Christian spirituality, the relationship with Christ which our ancestors saw as the purpose of their writing, copying, building and developing community.

Those who have worked with the Celtic have explored ways in which we might find resonances for contemporary lives. Among many other possibilities, we have chosen to explore in this part of the west of Ireland how we can combine using the prayers of the past in conjunction with the physical remains and the traditions of the inhabitants down the Christian centuries. We are seeking to relate more deeply to the place in which we find ourselves, and are developing a pattern of prayer-walks, following old routes over old boundaries, between high crosses, round towers and ruined churches where local people still bury their dead, and exploring also the beauty of the land which has been farmed for millennia. This involves our returning to sources and relearning from scholarship, and also seeking ways in which to break open the fruit of this study to serve our world. Walking involves meeting, and talking to, people who walk with us and those we meet on the way. It also provides for everyone to offer their skills and knowledge, and their music. As we grow in this practice, we tell the stories that inspired us in our faith, and we learn new stories, of how others have lived out their lives in faith, in their time. We pause at places made holy in ancient times, which have retained their holiness through the visits of praying people down the centuries, and we seek to respond to God with us today. We stop at places honoured by local people, to pause, and, if our tradition accepts, pray. We seek to connect through the stories and through the scriptures which were known to those who prayed in these places before us.

In a time of modern turbulence we try to connect also to the needs of our own time. We pray as the recession bites, revisiting some of the parables of Jesus that remind us that human relationships are the true focus when we handle money. We pray for the survivors of institutions where children were beaten and broken, for the priests and the lawyers who at best passed by, for the occasional Samaritan who protested to find that for these children of God there was no room at the inn. We pray for those who sit in the sun until the eleventh hour because there is no work, and that those in work may be generous in supporting those who do not. We pray that the roads that unite us will not be the source of death. We pray for farmers harvesting late after another wet summer, and, in a land whose national catastrophe was the Great Famine, for the places in the world where the harvest has failed. In a landscape full of the ruins not only of monasteries but of castles we pray for peace in a world racked by war. As we relish the plants, butterflies, birds and the poetry that delight in the world God gives us, we pray that we will learn again to tread the earth lightly and work against catastrophic climate change. We try to move away from congratulating ourselves for being on the margins, to focus on the people we have put on margins, the stranger, the economic migrant, the people who have remained poor through the time of wealth, and the people who centred their lives on work, homes and holidays, and have lost them.

Whether this approach is 'Celtic' or not, it is only one way to seek to honour the heritage in stone and writings, in farming and faith, in storytelling and silent prayer, in travelling to holy places, and to use what we have received for our common journey. There are many other ways, and each country and each culture will have its own variety. But it seems to me that the best heritage of the 'Celtic' is to reconnect us to the place and culture in which God has designed we find ourselves, to honour the past by discovering it again, perhaps at some cost to our expectations, and to honour the present by using it to break open the Christian story in ways to enrich our relationships to each other and to the wider world today. It is not particular to any culture or time, though the prayers we use may be, and in doing this we rediscover the core of faith in all its wonder and delight.

Rosemary Power

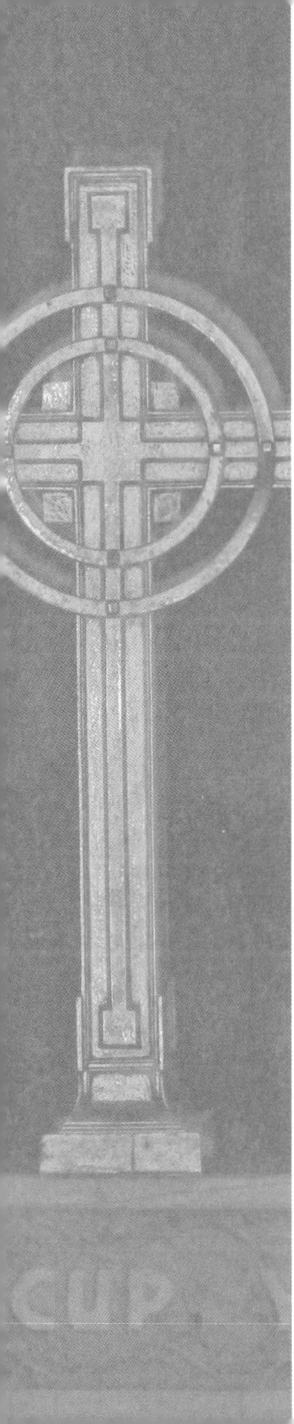

An phaidir gheal – the bright prayer

The blessing of God on you, Bright Prayer.
The blessing of God and Mary.
Where were you last night?
At the feet of Jesus.
Where are you tonight?
At the feet of the poor.
Where are you tomorrow?
At the feet of Saint Patrick …
Bridget with her cloak,
Michael with his shield,
the two shining hands of the Son of God
protect this house
and bring us safe to morning.[1]

Note:

1. *From an Aran islands' folk prayer printed in Béaloideas vii, 189 and Diarmuid Ó Laoghaire, Ár bPaidreacha Dúchais, Dublin, 1982, 220, translated by Rosemary Power*

Racial justice

Unite against fascism

On 28 March, 2009 the Hallam Diocese Justice and Peace Commission held a meeting of its parish contacts in Wickersley near Rotherham. During the meeting, Fr Shaun Smith, Chair of the Commission, spoke about the then forthcoming European Elections in which the British National Party (BNP) could have an elected Euro MP for Yorkshire and the Humber with as little as 9% of the vote. The Commission then asked Philip Jakob, Director of Music for the Cathedral and Diocese of Hallam, to provide a Christian response to this threat:

The British National Party has suggested that it espouses Christian values.

Archbishop Rowan Williams' exploration of the common ground between Christians and Muslims was ridiculed by the BNP as being instrumental in the 'Islamification of Britain'.

In the face of this and other views widely held by political extremists how does the Christian respond?

In 1992 the composer Bernadette Farrell set to music a wonderful text by Shirley Erena Murray. Written for Racial Justice Sunday it is entitled 'Community of Christ'.

The first verse is a powerful invitation to be Christ in the world:

> *Community of Christ, who make the cross your own,*
> *live out your creed and risk your life for God alone:*
> *the God who wears your face, to whom all worlds belong,*
> *whose children are of every race and every song.* [1]

The strong suggestion in the song that God wears my face and yours is mind-blowing. Look around you, as you go about your daily business, at the variety in the face that God chooses to wear!

Scripture reminds us that we are all 'made in the image of God'. The human race enfleshes God, and in the same way all things are created in God. 'Emmanuel' means what it says on the tin – God is with us! This is why we have respect for all created things, as well as for all humanity.

The BNP declaration of support only for indigenous British is to deny the indwelling of God in all regardless of skin colour, nationality, gender or status.

It was not for nationalistic reasons that a Scottish friend of mine once declared 'God's favourite colour is tartan!' God designs and embraces difference as the scene at Pentecost with all nations understanding each other confirms.

In Mark 7:24–30 we read that Jesus is pursued by a Syro-Phoenician woman seeking help for her child who suffers some mental disorder. Such is the depth of her faith that she harangues Jesus for a cure. However she is not Jewish and Jesus explains that he came only for the Jews. The woman will not take that lying down and lays into him with all manner of arguments. Under her persistence Jesus grows in his understanding that his mission, primarily to the Jews, must be all-embracing, that he has come for all peoples.

This is a critical moment of realisation for Christ as he moves from one perspective to a wider vision: Jesus, Son of God, changes his mind!

Human beings hold opinions which are formed by their experience. When these opinions are challenged we can choose either to cling to our initial position or to allow this to be modified by the challenge.

Unless we are very unfortunate or blinkered we will readily encounter difference in other people. Sometimes the difference causes a gut reaction which might amount to fear. This may be a natural consequence but the more we examine this reaction and the more we come to know the person of difference the more positively we will change in our attitude towards her.

Part of what makes Christ both fully human and divine in the story is that he transcends the ordinarily human and changes his mind. We can all move to a change of mind if our hearts are not hardened and if we refuse to allow fear to dominate.

So what do we pray for those who advocate and represent such views as those espoused by the BNP, those who have betrayed the image of God in which they are made? We cannot believe that they are intrinsically evil, for God, who saw all creation as good, does not create evil. However what comes out of them might be considered evil. We pray that their hearts too may be open to change, and that they might, in the words of St Augustine, 'give themselves back to God, the God who made them'.

All political extremists work on fear of 'the other'. Hitler did this with the Jews in times of economic depression in the 1930s and we are seeing similarly despicable attitudes in the present times of financial insecurity.

Fear stops you moving, stops you taking risks, narrows your outlook, directs you towards entrenchment and self-interest and thus makes you less human. We are communal beings and it is not good to be alone. No wonder that the most common saying of Christ and the angels of God is 'Do not be afraid.'

A dominant characteristic of the Christian is hospitality. 'See how these Christians love one another' is not a soppy sentimental observation but one drawn from witnessing those who show love for all, an all-encompassing, unconditional love.

Thirty-seven times in the Bible we are reminded to welcome the stranger. And all the miracles of Jesus reflect his intention to bring the outsider into the heart of the community. Jesus realises that it is sometimes necessary to transform the outsider, to give sight to the blind, to cure the leper, to give life to Lazarus, to set prisoners free and to relate to and energise the woman at the well, but the return of these persons to a community which had previously regarded them as different, challenges fixed opinions and transforms not only the healed individual but also the community itself.

There is a ludicrously comical scene in Monty Python's film *Life of Brian* in which Brian proclaims, 'We are all individuals' to which the crowd of thousands in one voice shouts, 'Yes. We are all individuals.' Then Brian adds, 'We are not the same.' And the crowd, again as one, replies, 'No, we are not the same.'

Despite the humour there is great truth in the statement. We are not the same, as another of Bernadette Farrell's songs indicates:

God made me as I am, part of creation's plan.
No one else can ever be the part of God's plan that's me.[2]

Paul, in his letter to the Galatians, writes that there is no such thing as Jew or Greek, no such thing as slave or free, no such thing as male and female, for we are all one in Christ.

Recently at an interfaith gathering in Sheffield, a friend put it differently. He said: 'There *are* people from different nations and cultures, there *are* people who are imprisoned whilst others are free, there *are* differences of gender, BUT all are one in Christ.'

I found that useful, more or less saying the same thing, but with different nuance.

And this Jesus Christ, in whom all are one, is Son of the God who created, and continues to create, glorious diversity through which, with which and in which the limitless breadth of God might be glimpsed.

Continuing with Paul's letter ... 'And if you belong to Christ, then you are the seed of Abraham,' *(you are Christ)* 'heirs to God's promise.'

And God's promise to be with us that we may all have abundant life, the common good, this is what prompts us to use our vote to bring about, not the pitting of community against community, but the reigning of God.

Amen. Alleluia!

Philip Jakob

Notes:

1. 'Community of Christ', words, Shirley Erena Murray; music, Bernadette Farrell, Hope Publishing Company

2. © 1995, 1999, Bernadette Farrell, OCP

Month 1 Day 15

Community

On the Victoria Line

She took a tumble on the Victoria Line,
my daughter damaged by a faulty gene.
She wasn't able to step firmly
from solid ground to moving stairs.
I, wrestling with too much baggage and worry,
was disabled too.

A stranger caught her –
Chinese … smiling … as I recall.
He waved at me as the escalator
carried me downwards, away,
helpless against the London commuters
surging, tumbling down towards the trains.
I waved back, thankful for his strong hand
holding my daughter safe in the crowd.
An act of kindness in the city –
two strangers met for a moment
and knew it.

Where does such goodness come from?
My daughter does not understand
her gift for bringing people together.

Bryan Owen

Pilgrimage

The M62 – a pilgrimage in everyday life

Not long ago I spent two unusually warm autumn months on a long-distance cross-country walk, following the acoustic footprint of the M62 Trans-Pennine motorway from Hull back home to Liverpool. I didn't regard it this way at the time, but in retrospect I can accept that it was a sort of pilgrimage. A pilgrimage in everyday life.

The idea came from my growing conviction that it was possible to see 'heaven in the ordinary', and that it is desirable, even essential, to look closely for it at all times, expecting to find traces of the divine in the details of daily life. I had become convinced of the psychic damage being done to us all by our society's obsession with the extraordinary, the spectacular, the successful, the huge (an obsession to which many Christians are by no means immune), and I was keenly aware of scripture's persistent suggestion that God is a God of small things, especially in the teachings of Jesus in his Sermon on the Mount and his numerous parables about mustard seeds, lost coins, food, clothes and ordinary creatures.

I was making these discoveries whilst taking walks around an ex-corporation housing estate on the edge of the big city where I lived, sometimes in company and in conversation with others, sometimes alone, looking at the details of life as lived on the ground, looking for God in the gaps. One consequence of these wanderings was that over many months I found myself composing meditations on the meaningfulness in life to be found in our interactions around such objects as wheelie bins, bus shelters, traffic lights and shopping trolleys. After all this, I was ready for a long walk, a slow meander across the post-industrial North of England, a search for heaven in the ordinary places alongside the M62, a pilgrimage in daily life. I was not disappointed.

It is liberating, to purge oneself of prejudices about certain types of places and people, to remove from oneself any preconceptions about spirituality as sanctioned by purveyors of pilgrimage, and about the limited range of activities which will bring oneself closer to the divine. It is a joy to discover that your spirit can grow not just in so-called thin places, but in places thick with carbon smoke: motorway service stations, for instance, which are the arenas for thousands of meaningful human encounters each day, refuelling stops for people on significant journeys, places of work for many, leisure destinations for those who live locally to them. Roger Green spent two years immersing himself in the life of South Mimms Services on the M25; his *Destination Nowhere* is a fascinating read, which inspired me to make the Travelodges and Days Inns of the M62 my home for days on end whilst on my journey. The generously-lit space of Cafe Primo became my living room: people-watching from the perfect comfort of a well-proportioned leather armchair, ready for unexpected occasional conversations, and enrichment.

In town centres the focus appears to be entirely on retail activity, but eating my chicken wrap lunch whilst sitting on a pivoting metal seat outside Marks and Spencer in Castleford I noticed that there is far more going on: that shopping isn't merely a series of dry economic transactions, it's what people do to meet other people in places like this. I came to understand newsagents shops as being hubs for the exchange of news and views; shop-fronts as bases for hoped-for encounters between occasional friends. In Goole I saw a husband, wife and newsagent share some gentle teasing, two ex-colleagues of different ages and genders having a warm 'catch-up' conversation outside Iceland, and a young woman enjoying showing her new baby to a friend who was equally delighted to hold the child – incongruously so, he being a generously tattooed punkish person. In the crisp September air outside the Co-op I warmed to shopping.

Even in the monstrously-proportioned Trafford Centre, entirely focussed on the business of merchandising, I sensed the human spirit present beneath the glittering lights. Delighting in the dissident extravagance of being there and not purchasing a thing, I spent a day at The Trafford Centre with my notebook, composing revised versions of the Lord's Prayer, as seen from the perspectives of the shoppers and the shop workers juggling their hopes and dreams through checkout counters and workplace interactions.

In taking on this sort of walk you find yourself adopting a visionary's eye. Trudging through the industrial estates of Warrington and Wakefield, I might have felt in the company of Blake and Bunyan, expecting to see heavenly visions in improbable places (shepherds working beneath motorway flyovers, people queuing up like eager communicants to receive free handouts at the Manchester city centre Food and Drink Festival). In Goole one night I awoke in a hot sweat in a grimy B&B above a Chinese restaurant where, in the sepia shadow cast on the wall by streetlights filtering through net curtains, I saw a cloaked figure with a crown on its head, looking somewhat like a nativity-play Magi. This figure felt like a quietly welcoming spirit. In my state of altered consciousness it didn't take me long to decide who this kindly visitor was. I gave this shape a name: the Goodly Spirit of Goole, and the next day (the ghost having disappeared in the daylight) I went in search for it around the town; successfully – I found it in many places where people gathered and went about their business, amicably, warmly.

The pilgrimage in everyday life is possible for anyone willing to open the eyes of their hearts to the latent divine in the midst of the normal. Besides the sanctioned mystics in our tradition, and the three who walked the road to Emmaus, I found myself inspired on the journey by the likes of Iain Sinclair, whose *London Orbital* describes his trudge around the M25, exploring the hinterland of London in the year 2000, and Nick Papadimitriou who spends his days investigating the 'deep topography' of places like Leytonstone: 'other lands woven into our land'.

A century ago a man called Charles Hurst walked south out of Manchester laden with a big box of acorns which he planted as he made his way through the English Midlands. A man on a mission,

Hurst felt that there weren't enough oak trees in England and he set about to put that right, recording his journey in a publication he called *The Book of the English Oak*. His philosophy is perfect for the pilgrim in everyday life. Having become proficient in 'the gentle art of strolling', Hurst wrote, 'I can now perform a feat which I believe few townbred men could accomplish with ease of grace: that is, *to walk a good English mile in an hour*.' 'The great secret,' he wrote, 'is sympathy both with humanity and nature, and this sympathy will open the eye and the ear to sights and sounds that the indifferent would miss. A rambler in the proper frame of mind can see a complex world in each clear pool of a brook: or he can regard the tumbling ocean as a mere moisture covering a portion of a whirling atom of dust.'

Walking with deliberate slowness, with attentiveness to people, places and things, and with a genuine openness to any possible encounters with the divine – this is the way of the pilgrim in everyday life.

John Davies

John Davies' Walking the M62 *is available from Lulu.com, and can be read in blog form at johndavies.typepad.com/walking_the_m62*

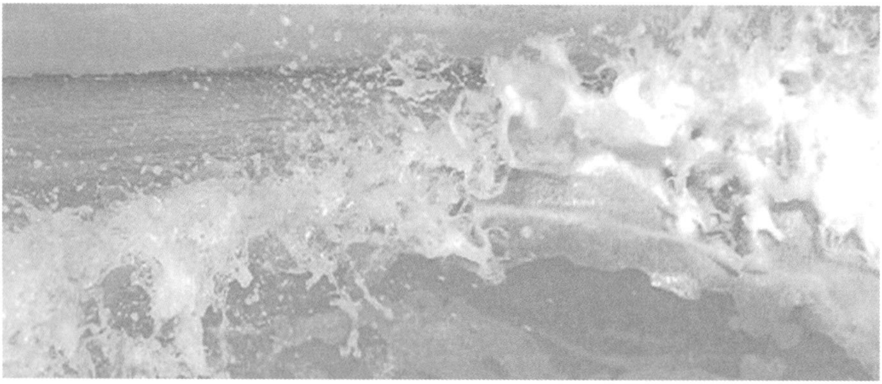

SEXUALITY

So many kinds of awesome love

1 Corinthians 13

There are so many kinds of awesome love,
I bless them all:

Love of kindred for their kin
Love of lover for their mate
Love of country for the native
Love of land for the explorer

Love of the labourer for his work
Love of the scholar for her truth
Love of the artist for the muse
Love of the preacher for the word
Love of the disciple for the way
Love of the mystic for their God

There are so many kinds of awesome love,
we need them all:

Love of brother, sister, father, mother
Love of parent, grandparent, uncle, aunt
Love of the beloved, love of the friend
Love of the stranger, love of the needy

Love of the woman for the man
Love of the man for the woman

Love of woman for her woman
Love of the man for his man

There are so many kinds of awesome love,
why must we set one above the other,
say some are worthy and others base?
Why must we choose one love
when we need all the kinds we can get?

There are so many kinds of awesome love:
The love that knocks you off your feet
  and sets you to desperate things
The love that is gentle and kind
  and swells the compassionate heart
The love that is joyous and life-giving
  and keeps you singing for days
The love that is steadfast and loyal
  and sits out long nights of pain

Young, jocular love
Old, wise love
Rich, extravagant love
Poor, pitiful love
Strong, encouraging love
Vulnerable, wounded love
Passionate, sensual love
Free, filial love
Fiery, prophetic love
Self-emptied, contemplative love

There are so many kinds of awesome love,
I bless them all.

Nicola Slee

Month 1 Day 18

HEALING

Starfish

In the morning early,
I saw the folk from the village
combing the sand for starfish
which the waves had washed up
and left vulnerable.

These, the villagers would collect, kill,
and sell for profit.
That was their way.

One morning I rose earlier,
and walked on the sand by the water's edge.

There, in the distance, I saw a solitary figure
who was also looking for starfish.

Whenever he found one alive or even just alive,
he would lift it, kiss it,
and lay it back in the blue water,
there to be revived and to swim again.
That was his way.

Now I get up every morning,
earlier than the villagers,
early as the man.

I, the strong, no longer stretch to survive:
I kneel down to restore the weak.

And I have found,
though some might mock me,
that even far from the seaside,
there are starfish on every street

John L. Bell, based on a story by Loren Eiseley

Month 1 Day 19

Social Action

Born into complicity

The reality of judgement is a note that resonates through the book of Micah. One of the things that gives the great prophetic voices of the Hebrew Bible (what Christians commonly call the Old Testament) such power is that they speak from and to all sections of society. But Micah, perhaps more than any of the others, speaks with the voice of the poor. This peasant farmer, with the suspicion of the countryman for a so-called progress which will leave the poor even poorer, calls the people of Israel to account for their crimes; and he is quite clear about what these are:

- the oppression of the weak by the strong
- the expropriation of peasants from their land
- the eviction of smallholders
- the enslavement of children.

Now we know very well that nearly three thousand years later, none of these crimes has disappeared from the face of the earth, and we rightly stand in judgement against them, and may be actively involved in campaigning against them. By the authority of scripture, with the authorisation of church and tradition, we read the prophetic texts against a world which practises such things, and the world is found wanting.

But it is also important to remember that the words of the prophets were addressed quite specifically to the community of faith, to the people of the covenant. The Hebrew prophets did not appear out of nowhere, their critique was not an external one; they stood within a prophetic tradition and it was because of their belonging within the community that they understood so well the nature of the faith of Israel. Their critique was historical, contextual, directed against specific concrete social and economic practices in a particular place at a particular time. In the words of George MacLeod, founder of the Iona Community, they were not prepared to tolerate 'the obscenity of the now'.

Although their interventions were political in nature, and had direct (and often for them unpleasant) political consequences, their motivation lay elsewhere. It was rooted in a passionate belief that the covenant relationship of God with Israel demanded that the relationships of the people with each other should reflect and replicate that covenant. It was precisely because they were people who had been liberated by the Exodus and had received both the Law and the promise that the community of faith was particularly under judgement. Of all people, they were the ones who should turn from oppressing and enslaving others. Through the voice of Micah, the religiously pious, those who were attached to their own pure identity as the chosen people, were being judged by the poor of the particular world of that little part of the Ancient Near East.

And as followers of Jesus, sharers in the new covenant, we too must take a relationship to the judgement of the world. By the authority of scripture, church and tradition, we stand in judgement on the world and find it wanting. But that judgement is a two-edged sword.

The first time I travelled outside the West, more than twenty years ago to an international peace conference organised by the Christian Conference of Asia, my well-meaning, white, Western liberal map of the world was shredded into tiny pieces. The experience shattered my illusions, my confidence and all but shattered my faith, as I knew myself for the first time, not just in theory but in reality, as part of an oppressive, dehumanising, environmentally disastrous world order. So many conflicts and injustices had British imperialism in there somewhere. Our considerable involvement in the global arms trade made it possible for many countries to make war. But war is not only waged with weapons. War is waged by economic policy, by market forces, by trade rules, by property rights of every kind, from land to intellectual. And it is waged by environmental choices and business interests, as uprooted, dispossessed and threatened people everywhere from Bangladesh to Brazil can tell us. We are always, somewhere in the world, complicit.

I became voiceless. I had nothing to say that could adequately express my shame. Silence seemed the only appropriate response. I had come face to face with the complicity with evil into which I had been born; what the church has classically called, in a somewhat misunderstood phrase, original sin.

This experience of judgement was for me the equivalent of hearing the voice of Micah. It was hearing all my texts, all my scripts, all my maps being read from another perspective. As a woman in the Christian church, I had some experience of what it is like to read from the margins; which has historically been to be overlooked, dismissed, talked down to and talked down, sometimes to be all but invisible. But it is a lifelong journey to hear the judgement that says: God is only colour-blind if you are white; it may be easier to be ecumenical in Scotland if you are Protestant; liberal democracy has a different ring to it if you're a sub-Saharan African country bleeding dry to meet your debt repayments to the IMF; hating the sin but loving the sinner may be a more loaded message if you're gay than if you're straight.

It took me many months to see that, though I had been born into complicity, I was not responsible for what I did not do. I had no choice about the complicity I had been born into – but I was responsible for the complicity I *did* have a choice about. I could say, 'This is the way things are – but I beg to differ.' I could be a non-conformist. I could choose in every way open to me to put an end to complicity.

Kathy Galloway

Month 1 Day 19

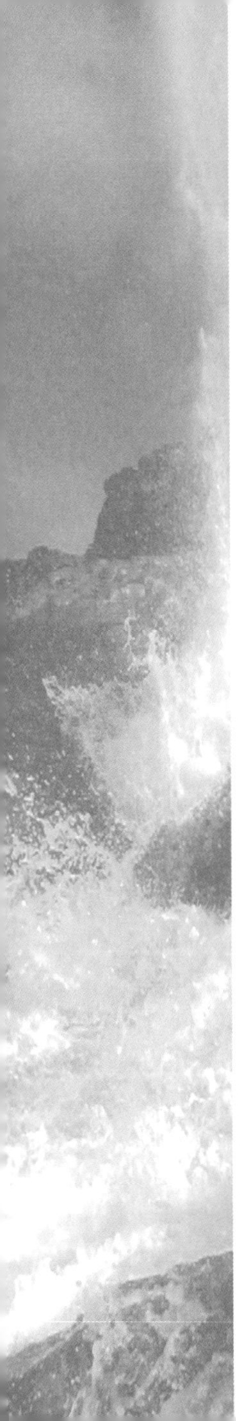

Month 1 Day 20

Church Renewal

Secularism

Pope Benedict XVI has targeted secularism as a demonic force in our time. In *The Guardian* of 31 May, 2010 John Hooper writes on the Pope's letter of March 2010 announcing a top-level investigation into clerical sex abuse in Ireland, and comments: *'In his letter, the Pope appeared to cast much of the blame for sex abuse on Ireland's secularisation.'* Pope Benedict is getting it wrong. But then popes do.

The meaning and emphasis of the word 'secular' have changed throughout history:

a) Originally the Latin word *saecular* is referred to an identifiable, lengthy period of time which needed to be understood in its integrity without importing ideas and questions which belong to a different era. Some people such as Richard Dawkins ignore this scholarly point, treating the early chapters of Genesis as a crude, false attempt to say how creation started. The interest of the writers and editors was much more practical: how to understand and live significantly the created life bestowed on us. They point to the need to begin with God: 'In the beginning, God …' They then take stock of creation, sorting out the different aspects in hymnic form: 'In the beginning, God created …', giving God praise. They go on with a parable of a garden with Representative Man and Representative Woman occupying it, indicating relationships to God, to the natural order and the creatures in it, to one another and to the mandate they are given. The Big Bang theory belongs to a different era.

b) In mediaeval times there was a shift of meaning accompanying a move to the autonomy of spheres of responsibility which had previously come under the church's direct patronage. When Constantine the Great gave legal recognition to Christianity, it meant relief from periods of persecution; but when the Roman Empire collapsed, the church was left to pick up the pieces, to provide a basis of order in spheres of education, health care, social provision, justice, parish relief, for instance. This issued in a paternalism which was ultimately resented, and which inhibited progress in these areas. Over time the civil sphere achieved independence from the ecclesiastical. These spheres came to represent separate areas of responsibility, whether they were thought of as working in partnership or whether the religious sphere was dismissed and given no credence.

To make the religious way of thinking separate from the rest of life was rejected by Jesus in his time. He said of a centurion who recognised his authority and trusted his word: 'Truly I tell you, in no one in Israel have I found such faith. I tell you, many will come from east and west and will eat with Abraham, Isaac and Jacob in the Kingdom of heaven, while the heirs of the Kingdom will be thrown into outer darkness.' He saw that the practice of religion could be both superficial and oppressive.

Speaking to religious leaders who resembled 'whited sepulchres' he said, 'You on the outside look righteous to others, but inside you are full of hypocrisy and lawlessness.' What Jesus looked for was faith which stemmed from a tried and tested bedrock of reality and found practical expression in compassionate, committed lifestyle.

Human experience echoes that of Jesus. Fidel Castro had a religious background. He discarded it: As he grew up he became more acutely aware of the church's collaboration with the oppressive and corrupt regime of the dictator Batista. He found in Marxism a reading of life and emphasis on justice which he could affirm. In the early 1970s I just missed him in Chile, when I stayed with members of the recently formed Christians for Socialism. Fidel had met and talked with them long into the night. His conclusion was 'With Christians such as you, Marxists such as I am can have not only tactical but strategic alliances.' True, he invested in the USSR connection, and led Cuba into membership in COMECON. But he was ill at ease with hardline elements in Cuban communism, and when the USSR collapsed in 1991 it was with some relief that Cuba disengaged and became a lay state. In his recent biography Fidel states his position as that of a Christian whose social analysis is Marxist-Leninist.

There remains a problem if the element of transcendence is missed out in defining 'the human'. That leaves powers-that-be to tidy their favoured understandings into line with their favoured ideologies. For Hitler, Aryans, for Stalin, the Party faithful, for Mao, aficionados of the Red Book were taken to provide examples of authentic humanity.

c) Secularism may be recognised as a practical resource which insists that the realities which have to be faced in life are addressed squarely without evasion or cover-up, honouring the terms available for getting purchase on situations. This approach found supreme expression in the Incarnation. Jesus Christ came without privilege or protection, exposed to all the vagaries of human nature, enduring its contrasts – 'valiant, ignoble, dark and full of light' as T.S. Eliot put it. He knew what was in human nature and accepted the consequences. His prayer for followers was not that they should be taken out of the world but that, there, they be kept from succumbing to evil. The Incarnation happened because God loved the world. Jesus came announcing not church but Kingdom – the whole fabric of created life transformed so that it is marked by justice, truth and peace. That we take the world seriously, exactly as it is, is accordingly an article of faith.

In the letter to the Colossians, Paul lays emphasis on the claim that Jesus Christ, the Head of the Church, is also the Lord of the world. He is presented as the source and sign that commanding forces, 'thrones, dominions, rulers, powers', need to change their ways. To validate their existence and to contribute to a world order which is just, they must take 'the form of a servant': 'The rulers of the Gentiles lord it over others and their great ones dominate. That is not to be your way. Whoever wants to be great among you must be your servant, and whoever wants to be first among you must be your slave: just as the Son of Man came not to be served but to serve and to give his life a ransom for many.' Not only persons but institutions,

corporations, nations will fulfil their purpose when they learn his servant way of working.

A corollary of this emphasis on the Kingdom, on a world to be transformed under Jesus Christ's Headship, is that religious language is not a requirement for authentic responses, personal or corporate. When it came to true ways of living, the church may instruct the world, but the world may also instruct the church. The church's role is provisional as is the world's. In fulfilled life, depicted as a City, there is no Temple.

I do not know what form of secularism Polly Toynbee of *The Guardian* embraces, but I believe that life is enriched by her determination to dig into and expose the underlying reality of situations, her good judgement in illuminating what should be supported and what combated, her acute concern that justice and truth should prevail.

Don't forget that, in the Parable of the Last Judgement, those whom Jesus affirms do not even recognise him and have no religious words in their response. They exercise straightforward secular responsibilities: feeding the hungry, giving drink to the thirsty, clothing the naked, giving hospitality to the stranger, caring for the sick, visiting prisoners. That is enough to merit his 'Well done!'

This is not a time to square up to secularism but to recognise and receive the gift that it contains. This is not a time when humanity is ignoring the call for a new world order ('the Kingdom'), but when the church is being told, 'You have your part to play, but don't try to hog the agenda. The call goes to all earth's people, and those who respond do so in their own way and language.'

Month 1 Day 20

The saints of God

The saints of God are down our street
and round God's throne of light.
There's some with formidable minds
and some just live aright:
together in God's family
their different gifts unite.

They serve at checkouts, empty bins;
they teach and make and mend;
they feed the hungry back from school,
the victimised defend;
to voiceless folk they lend an ear
and immigrants befriend.

Their efforts gain no accolades,
they simply earn that grace
which heals the world of many sores,
renews its battered face –
through such who live and love and care
in their own time and place.

When death comes knocking at their door
they'll look at Christ askance –
how could such ordinary lives
his Kingdom ends advance?
But Christ will say 'It's party time –
come, friends, and join my dance.'

Ian M. Fraser

Worship

Participative worship: Head and heart

It was the end of our three years in the Resident Group on Iona. I was sitting there in the Abbey, listening, watching, reflecting, as a group of musicians in the piano loft improvised with an interesting array of instruments, preparing for the evening service. 'Worship is so creative here!' I thought. 'Worshippers are so responsive! However will I cope with being an ordinary minister in an ordinary church again?'

By good fortune, though, we were going to Trinity, St Albans, where they had been doing imaginative things with their Sundays for a quarter of a century. Different teams taking turns at organising programmes for groups of mixed ages, with the worship drawing the threads together at the end. Coming from Iona, we were well used to teams preparing worship; but here they prepared *everything*, and spent weeks rather than hours doing so! They had the reputation of being a step ahead of the average church; one of those places where Christian education material was tried out before being made generally available.

Yet, after all those groundbreaking years, we found that it was beginning to look rather tired and conventional. Only a minority now seemed interested in the groups. Some folk were longing for worship that was not interrupted by discussion or other unwelcome surprises. We started to get complaints. Two longstanding members could stand it no longer, and left. It was time for a rethink.

But what to do? This church had travelled too far to suddenly retreat into being ordinary again. Whatever we needed to do, we had to keep moving forward. But why, we wondered, did people with such a rich history of group exploration and activity object to being asked to do a simple thing like talking with their neighbour for a few minutes in an all-age service?

I happened to mention a theory I had had ever since visiting the Taizé Community. There are three distinct elements to each day at Taizé: worship, formal teaching and group discussion. But each is kept separate from the other. Above all, discussion and teaching are never mixed with the worship. The Taizé Prayer, as it is called, is an uninterrupted flow – no announcements, no explanations, no sermon even. The result is powerful and deep.

My theory, I explained, was that worship is a heart thing whereas teaching and discussion are head things. People might be happy to talk together in small groups, yet they groan when asked to do so in the middle of a service – because in worship something entirely different is going on for them, I suggested.

'Well, if Taizé does it, why can't we?' someone asked. We began to think of what we could do to involve the whole congregation in Christian education again, but in a new way, without mixing elements that did not go together. And this is what we came up with:

We would try splitting the morning into three parts. First, Worship: readings and intercessions led by members, Holy Communion on the first Sunday of the month, on occasions a baptism, all in the first half hour. Next, Time to Share: news and notices, coffee and socialising; business strictly forbidden. Finally, Time to Explore: with the sermon or some other kind of input, led from within the semicircle of chairs rather than from the raised position of the lectern, followed by thoughts and questions from the congregation.

Flexibility was built into the morning. If they wished, people could come for the first part or for the last. All we asked was that they be there for the Time of Sharing, the news and notices. In fact, though, nearly everyone stayed for the duration.

For me it was the last part of the morning that was the most rewarding. The congregation would reassemble as our ad hoc singing group chimed up with an

Iona song. I would not be wearing my clerical robes now. The atmosphere would be more informal. Far from pulpit oratory, I would talk in a relaxed, open-ended way, leaving space for other contributions. The comments would often shed new light on the subject or Bible passage. Somebody's story would move us. And every time I would be delighted afresh by the sense that the Word of God was not dependent on me. It was coming from the people. From the interplay between us. From the Spirit!

And so it still is. We have been away from St Albans now longer than we were there. But this pattern, which began so tentatively, goes happily on. For some ministers and lay preachers the prospect of leading it must be a little daunting. Yet I suspect they actually find it liberating, as they experience the support and goodwill of the people and discover they do not have to pretend to have all the answers themselves.

We left them to it. We went off into retirement, into a new place, searching the churches and denominations for a congregation where we might be participants, rather than an audience.

Brian Woodcock

Month 1 Day 22

Called to be One

An ecumenical agenda

It is all gain that churches act now in comradeship in place of in rivalry or even hostility. But the gain must not be wasted. It should bring churches to the starting line to tackle major obstacles to unity – that deep unity with himself and the Father for which, through the Spirit, Jesus Christ prayed – that the world may believe in him.

Churches which continue with separate development mentalities need to use the trust which has grown between them to be critically engaged in sorting out what in their life adds colour and richness, and what presents obstacles impeding gospel mandates.

I believe that the following obstacles have to be dealt with if the unity we seek is akin to the unity for which Jesus Christ prayed:

Gender disinheritance

The argument that to open all church offices and responsibilities to either sex is to give in to social pressures is a distraction from the reality. That move is an imperative of the gospel.

In his earthly life, Jesus rejected the low standing of women. In the Resurrection he turned the tables on male assertiveness. His first personal appearance was not to Peter but to Mary Magdalene. Those whom he made primary witnesses were not the apostolic band but a bunch of women whose testimony was at once dismissed as 'idle tales'. He said we are to enlarge this work, do 'greater things' than himself by drawing on his resurrection power.

** What male preserves need to be opened up so that the unity on which churches may go forward together fulfils God's intention in Genesis 1, which affirms that women and men are together made in God's image, together blessed, together mandated to act as trustees and stewards of created life?*

Church disinheritance

Laity have been made a category. But the word *laos* describes the whole people of God. Those of us who are ordained are also laity. Cardinal Newman pointed out that the Pope and hierarchies had no mandate to establish true doctrine in their own right – that had to be done in vivid inter-relationship with the rest of the church membership.

Vatican II, conscious of the overemphasis on hierarchy of Vatican I, interpreted church as 'the people of God'. Theirs is the ministry which works in double harness with the High Priesthood of Jesus Christ. All leaders are called to 'equip the saints' (the punters) for their parts in that communal ministry to the world.

** What changes may be taken in hand so that the gifts of the people are drawn upon for worship, theology and dealing with major issues?*

World disinheritance

Jesus does not act only through the church. The letter to the Colossians points out that the Head of the church is also Lord of the world. The world is depicted as rejecting this lordship, but also as responding to it. The church, as well as enlightening the world, has to be prepared to be instructed by the world, learning from positive responses.

** Jesus came proclaiming not church but God's Kingdom. How are we to get over obsession with the fortune of the church, when it is 'the* world *God so loved that he gave his only Son'?*

Disinheritance of 'deviants'

In parables and encounters Jesus affirmed the humanity of Samaritans, rejecting their rejection. Whatever orientation people may have, 'there is no longer Jew or Greek, there is no longer slave and free, there is no longer male and female – all are one in Christ Jesus'!

When Jesus left us Holy Communion he provided an action uniting us to him and to one another more telling than words could convey. So why, in some churches, is a word understanding and tradition imposed, debarring 'deviant Christians' from partaking?

** Will the faithful be nourished and the world believe as long as such unity makes fish and flesh of Christians?*

Month 1 Day 22

Living as servants

Jesus warned disciples against a way of exercising power which mirrored the way of the rulers of the Gentiles, who wanted to impose their own will and still be called benefactors. 'That is not to be your way,' he said, and advocated a servant way such as he took himself.

** How may churches deal with internal top-down power tactics and with claims to primacy over others within their ranks? What effect would that have on the world – 'that the world might believe'?*

Ian M. Fraser

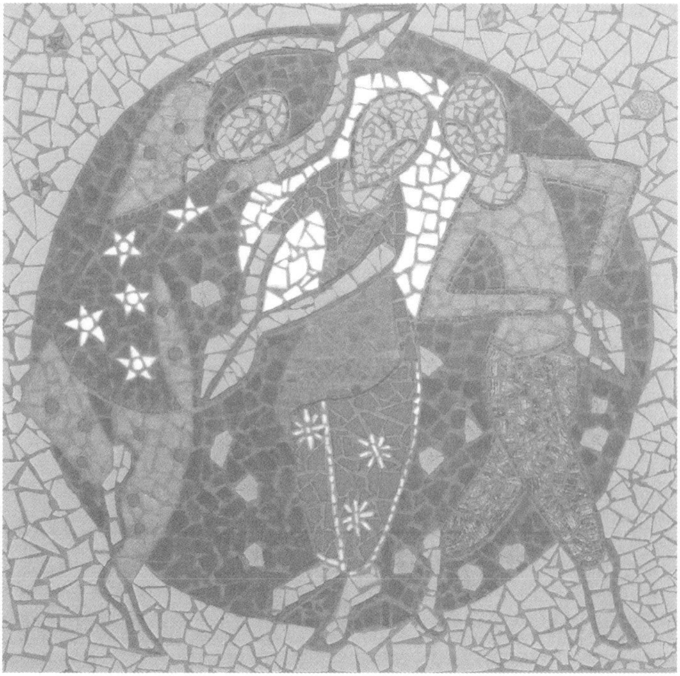

Mission

Lighting up the ordinary

If we met you, Jesus Christ,
we might not think that you were on a mission.
Your talk would be of common and curious things:
salt, dough,
lost lambs, lost coins,
paying taxes, hosting a meal,
wise virgins, and foolish house-builders.
We would not know you were on a mission,
we would think you were making sense of life,
lighting up the ordinary, identifying the truth.
When next you look with compassion on the world
and need mission done in your way,
Lord, send us.
AMEN

Wild Goose Resource Group

Work

Work is a curse – until you don't have any

At the age of 21 I was made redundant and joined the ranks of the unemployed. It was one of the most formative experiences of my life, if entirely unwelcome.

I found myself unprepared for a difficult journey: from being a young engineering apprentice learning skills which ought to have set me up for a long working life, to suddenly being an outcast, reduced to signing on each fortnight, and unjustly regarded by unsympathetic critics as being 'work-shy', a 'sponger', etc. As a young Christian I was disappointed by the response of the church to my personal plight, a situation which many of my peers were also experiencing (this was the early 1980s, a hard time for thousands of young and newly-unemployed people). It seemed that church people had little to say, in their sermons, magazines, youth ministry or in personal conversations, about the situation I was in. Little comfort, reassurance, or hope. It was during this period that I left the church.

Fortunately the faith which had nurtured me all my life did not desert me. I knew very little about God, but enough to suspect that he did have some feeling for me in my situation, and that the scriptures probably had quite a lot to say about the state I was in. So, with friends and companions outside the church, I embarked on the most significant course of theological learning of my life. Self-taught, over many months spent reflecting on our experiences, and drawing on influences from all over society (philosophers, poets, publicans, priests and pop singers amongst them), we discovered that God valued all people equally, regardless of status (the 'ranks' of the unemployed alongside society's generals); we noticed that in the story of Adam and Eve work is a curse – but that elsewhere in scripture God validates and celebrates work (as the Creator of the world – quite a job – and as the carpenter of Nazareth); we read Psalm 104 where work is as much a part of the

natural order as the rising and setting of the sun; and we realised to our astonishment that whereas our society belittles and marginalises them, God has a special place for the poor and struggling people of our world.

All of this is fresh and raw to me now in the light of the uncertainty which hangs over the working lives of so many in our area – in the recently announced factory redundancies and in the ongoing challenges faced by many, often hidden, who struggle to make a living in our rural area, where costs of fuel, transport, accommodation, etc are so high and resources so stretched. In my years of unemployment I learned something else about our faith – that God demands that his people demonstrate his justice in the world: a justice based on loving compassion, which means helping people in need (such as by contributing to a food bank) and joining them in their struggles (for more and better employment, fair wages, realistic and supportive benefits, and for dignity and equity).

'If one part [of the body] suffers, every part suffers with it; if one part is honoured, every part rejoices with it,' writes Paul (1 Corinthians 12:26). We might embrace these words of empathy as we work out how to respond to what is happening to the people of our area at this time.

John Davies

POVERTY

Metanoia

Why do you look for the living among the dead?' (Luke 24:5)

It was on a bright, sunny, stiflingly hot day one week after Easter 1994 that we drove out from the centre of Manila. I was glad of the air conditioning in the van and still reeling from a visit to Smoky Mountain the previous day. Father Ben Beltrane had introduced me there to some of the thousands of people who eked out a living making a few cents daily from scouring through the rubbish on the 200-foot-high smouldering heap from which the place took its name. Ben, a Catholic Priest and academic with a razor-sharp mind and charismatic gifts of leadership, was a man who could command big money from taking up one of the many offers he had received from US colleges over the years. Instead he chose life on the hill, living in community with the poorest of the poor, running a project with slum-dwellers repairing and painting the jeepniks, which are the main mode of transport around Manila.

Not content with survival, however, Ben's whole way of living spoke of transformation: of the physical conditions of the poor; of the lives of the ravaged and abandoned; of the spirits of the downcast and downtrodden. As a community organiser, Ben has few equals. He puts his intellectual and political skills to taking on the government – not alone, but in partnership with those most affected, the dwellers of Smoky Mountain. As he put it himself:

'You have to have a dream, and believe that it's not your destiny, that it's not God's will for you to be impoverished like that. We marched on the street and forced the government to rehabilitate the dump. That got us to where we are now.'

And where are 'we' now? The dump was officially shut down in 1995 and new blocks of social housing began to appear, funded by a coalition of partners, including the government. More than 20,000 former slum-dwellers live in these basic but adequately resourced homes, a far cry from the old shanties of the Mountain. The benefits are not only for those folks; the removal of a huge source of pollution and disease brings renewal and transformation for all around. It may only be a drop in the ocean of what is needed in terms of resurrection for the poor of Manila, but it is a start, a tangible sign of hope. Here at least, the living are no longer among the dead.

As we came towards the shoreline, the sun suddenly began to disappear in a haze. At first I thought it was a fog blowing in from the sea, but the acrid smell was all too familiar from the day before. The stench of burning rubbish in the slums of the world is something you can only comprehend if you have breathed it in. After a few minutes we drew to a halt outside a high, white-washed wall. It took a moment in the fog of smoke to realise that we had stopped outside a cemetery.

Stepping from the van, we entered a graveyard. The first impression was that it had been a grand setting some time past. This was a place where the rich had come to rest. A number of the tombs were small houses, with a little courtyard at the front, Grecian pillars opening into a room where a large sarcophagus (or two) looked rather like a kind of macabre table. I was immediately struck by the irony that, even in death, the rich had a far better place to occupy than the living of the shanty towns.

Then came another shocking realisation – something moved in the corner of one of the marbled rooms. Another, and another appeared, emerging like spectres in the blue-grey haze. Hundreds of people were living in this place of death. A whole new ring came to the angel's question: *'Why do you look for the living among the dead?'*

Within seconds, people appeared from every corner of the cemetery, gathering around Ramos, my guide, an aid worker involved in community organising in a number of the slums of Manila. They chattered excitedly together in Spanish and I caught no more than every tenth word. What was self-evidently clear was that they knew and trusted one another. We pressed on towards the back wall of the graveyard, which was broken down in places. I began to make out the sea in the distance, but in front of it was a 'beach' made up of tons of rubbish, not dissimilar to the mountain we had visited. It was covered with people sifting and gathering, hauling bags of plastic bottles or aluminium cans unearthed with bare hands from the mass of rotting garbage. The scene was a hellish kind of Costa del Sol: a crowded beach of a different magnitude. A filthy black sludge replaced lapping blue water – but children still paddled and swam in it.

Ramos explained the excitement: As squatters in this graveyard, the people were vulnerable not only to the disease that such squalor inevitably brings, but also to the violence of the authorities and the rich landowners. On several occasions, they had been raided at night by thugs with baseball bats and even guns, beating and terrorising them out of the tombs. Each time they were evicted, however, the people gradually drifted back, but always with the same fear of violence and death. On more than one occasion, people had died from injuries sustained in the eviction 'process'. But through a series of peaceful protests, followed ultimately by a round-table meeting, the people had found the courage, with the help of community organisers, to confront the authorities. The cemetery had been unused for many years and it clearly provided shelter for many people who had nowhere else to lay their head. There was no question of the land being used for development and there were no relatives of the long-deceased occupants who wanted to visit the tombs. Agreement had been reached, therefore, that no more evictions would take place – a huge relief to those for whom this was home. It might not yet be the social housing being built elsewhere, but at least this place of the dead could be put to better use as a place of the living!

Month 1 Day 25

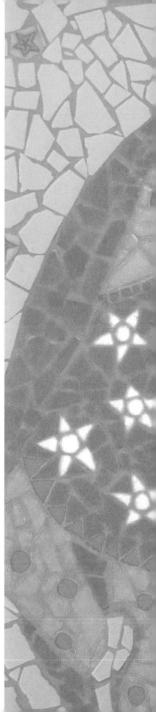

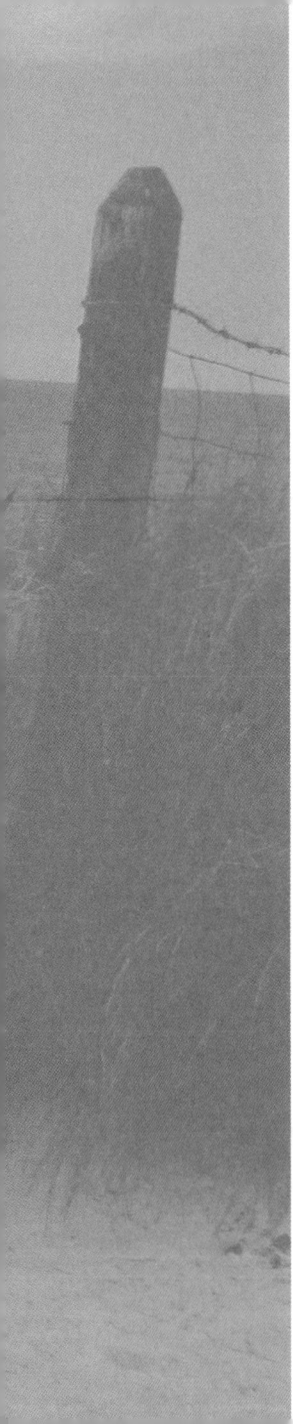

In time, small businesses would be seeded around the cemetery and along the seafront: home industries using the skills of the people to create crafts, often from recycled goods. The long-term aim would be to transform the place in the same way as Smoky Mountain, not simply through pouring in aid money, but much more through harnessing and enabling the skills of people whose human worth and dignity would at the same time be restored.

It may seem like a small step, but these small green shoots of life are the signs of true transformation. With the Easter story of resurrection from the depths of human violence and suffering still fresh in my ears, these encounters with the poor of Manila brought home the joy of what real transformation is all about. Where dignity is restored and hope engendered, the resurrection life is no longer merely 'a conjuring trick with bones', as theologian David Jenkins once so rightly put it. When the path to justice begins to be opened up for the poor and the discarded, the transforming love of the risen Christ takes on a tangible presence. As small signs of life poke their incredibly vulnerable heads above the injured soil, the healing of the earth and the wholeness of humanity become a dreamed-of possibility.

'Why do you look for the living among the dead?' – because that's where transformation is taking place. By definition, resurrection can only come when death and suffering are experienced. They leave their mark upon us, in the same way that the Risen Christ bears the marks of crucifixion. We must not imagine that resurrection masks fear or disguises death. Rather, it is in the very midst of death that the transformed life takes hold and hope springs eternal.

Martin Scott

Basic Christian Communities

Christ in the face of the stranger and prisoner: the Open Door Community, Atlanta, Georgia

The Open Door Community is a residential community in the Catholic Worker tradition (we're sometimes called a Protestant Catholic Worker House). We seek to dismantle racism, sexism and heterosexism, abolish the death penalty, and proclaim the Beloved Community through loving relationships with some of the most neglected and outcast of God's children: the homeless and our sisters and brothers who are in prison.

We serve breakfasts and soup-kitchen lunches, provide showers and changes of clothes, staff a free medical clinic, conduct worship services and meetings for the clarification of thought, and provide a prison ministry, including monthly trips for families to visit loved ones at the Hardwick Prisons in central Georgia. We also advocate on behalf of the oppressed, homeless and prisoners through non-violent protests, grassroots organising and the publication of our monthly newspaper, Hospitality. *(From the Open Door Community website: http://www.opendoorcommunity.org)*

To the left of the dining room at the Open Door hangs a Fritz Eichenberg print called *Christ of the Breadlines, 1950*. Underneath the print is the poem:

> *I saw a stranger yestreen.*
> *I put food in the eating place,*
> *drink in the drinking place,*
> *music in the listening place,*
> *and in the name of the blessed Triune,*
> *he blessed my house and myself,*
> *my cattle and my dear ones.*

As the lark said in her song:
Often, often, often,
the Christ comes in the stranger's guise,
often, often, often,
the Christ comes in the stranger's guise.

We have seen that at the heart of the community's practice of hospitality is the conviction that God's presence is encountered in the poor, the homeless person, and the prisoner. The Open Door draws from liberation theology, the Catholic Worker movement, and the Black struggle for liberation, all of which urge that God sides with the poor. God acts to liberate the downtrodden from oppression and enjoins hospitality for the stranger. Reflecting its association with Dorothy Day and the Catholic Worker movement, the community consistently turns to Matthew 25:31–46 as a key text for its life, along with Isaiah 58:6–14, Romans 12 and Hebrews 13:1–3. In the homeless and the imprisoned, especially those imprisoned on death row, the Open Door finds Christ.

This is a crucial faith commitment in the community that structures community life. In numerous articles in *Hospitality* and in conversations with members of the community, the theme is continually present: 'In the faces of the stranger and the prisoner we see the face of Jesus Christ.' Residential volunteer Elizabeth Dede writes:

The question 'Lord, when did we see you?' is a question central to our faith because seeing, recognising and understanding are acts of faith as we live in the post-Ascension world. Jesus has left this earth, and we can see him now only with the eyes of faith. Often at the Open Door we read Matthew 25 and ask the question, 'Lord, when did we see you?' In the answer to that question … we find a clear explanation of our calling and work: to be faithful to the risen Christ, we must feed the hungry, give a drink to the thirsty, receive strangers in our home, give clothes to the naked, take care of the sick, and visit the prisoner.

For the Open Door, the homeless and the imprisoned are sacramental. In those who are marginalised and rejected, God is present in a special way. Ed Loring, a founding partner of Open Door, explains what this means for the community:

The reality and the presence of God is mediated through the presence and suffering of the poor. So as we live our lives in solidarity with the poor, we are able to discover who God is; and God's reality, changing reality, confronting reality is mediated to our lives and calls us to new life which has two foci: life together in community and servanthood.

Seeing Christ in the homeless person and in the prisoner, the Open Door affirms their dignity and worth as God's children created in the image of God and sharing in the redemption of Jesus Christ. Founding partner Murphy Davis emphasises the centrality of the redemption in the community's understanding of its commitment to those on death row:

Death row is one more ragged edge of our torn world where we must take a stand for life. It is a matter of worship: worship of the God of Life, the God of Hope, the God of Peace, the God of Redemption. It is not a stand to be taken out of myopic sentimentalism. While people are at times wrongly accused and sentenced to die, death row is not a place where we frequently encounter 'innocent suffering'. It is a place that pushes us to the depths of our belief in God's redeeming power. We acknowledge with Paul that 'we have all sinned and fallen short', and we claim only the power of Christ's redeeming love for our salvation. We claim no less for our sisters and brothers on death row. In so doing we meet the Christ who suffered and died for all of us.

Here it is also evident that the community rejects any sentimentality about the poor, the homeless, or the imprisoned when it affirms that God is present with the poor. Such sentimentality is inadequate because it does not take seriously the evil of which human beings are capable, and does not take seriously the evil that has been inflicted upon the homeless and imprisoned.

Affirming God's presence with the poor empowers the community to confront the strength of evil without acknowledging it as the ultimate power in human life. Such faith does not have an easy optimism about progress and the perfectability of human life. This faith is lived out in the heartbreaking experiences of the Open Door. Murphy writes:

We are not indulged in the luxurious illusion of 'progress'. Our friends from the streets are more likely to get older, sicker, and even die than to 'get themselves together', get jobs, have their own homes, to – if you will – be 'rehabilitated'. Of our friends in prison, a few make it out of the cycle of despair and death. Many do not.

And this realism about sin roots the community itself in the graciousness of God, as it is God's love that saves, that makes persons whole, not the work of the community. Murphy states:

How difficult to hear the word that the Gospel calls us to be failures. After all, what are we to expect when we are invited to follow a homeless wanderer whose best friends were uneducated fisherfolk, prostitutes and other misfits. It is hard to learn that salvation comes not because our work builds steady progress toward the coming of God's kingdom, but because God is full of love and grace for us and the whole creation. Perhaps one reason that God calls us to love the poor is because the reality of the poor mocks our assumptions about progress and success.

Peter R. Gathje

The Open Door Community is one of the Iona Community's sister communities.

Non-Violence and Peacekeeping

A reflection by Jan Sutch Pickard, working as an Ecumenical Accompanier with the Ecumenical Accompaniment Programme in Palestine and Israel (EAPPI) (www.eappi.org).

Boundaries

The tiny village of Yanoun is only mentioned in the Bible once. In the book of Joshua there's a very long account of how territory was divided up among the tribes of Israel. Chapter 16:5,6 describes ' … the boundary of the Ephraimites family by family … going round by the east of Taanath-shiloh and passing by it on the east of Janoah.' Janoah/Yanoun then was just a marker in the making of boundaries. Yanoun today is a small farming community, where boundaries have positive and negative meanings.

I talked to Rashed, the mayor and one of the farmers who work the valley which runs between Upper Yanoun, at its head, and Lower Yanoun, where the land opens out. As well as a flock of sheep and goats, he has olive groves and fields under plough. We were looking out over the valley bottom, a patchwork of green – with hay, chickpeas, broad beans and wheat. 'You don't build walls or put up fences,' I said. 'Then how do you know where your land begins and ends?' He laughed, 'It is my land – I plough it and plant it. Kemal's land is right next door. If he want, he can put a stone at each corner. But if he don't put a stone, I know. Each year I plough the land. I know where the rocks are, underneath the soil.'

He knows the land well. This is where his father and grandfather farmed before him. But the landscape has changed. The tops of the limestone hills, which were once open grazing land stretching all the way down to the Jordan Valley, now bustle with watchtowers, telecommunication towers, watertowers, caravans, polytunnels and big chicken barns. These are the illegal outposts of the settlement of Itamar.

Rashed says that the traditional lands of Upper and Lower Yanoun amounted to 16,500 *dunums*. But now only at most 500 *dunums* are actually accessible to Upper Yanoun. 'Lower Yanoun is better. Here, we are in the middle of settlements.' He gestured round the hilltops, wearily.

There is limited access to another 400 *dunums*. The previous week he was able to get a one-day permit from the DCO to plough some of his own land, which is high on the hill near the settlement. But the next day, when he went back to graze his goats nearby, he was chased away by masked men. Soldiers or settlers? It wasn't clear. What was clear was that he had overstepped the mark.

Who sets the mark? 'Who decides where the boundaries will be?' I asked.

'The soldiers and settlers together decide. When the settlers want to change it, the soldiers agree.'

How are the boundaries marked? 'On this side' (to the west of the village) 'they make a fence.' It is visible on the skyline – not a huge structure like the Separation Barrier – just the way anyone might define their property. But whose property? These outposts are illegal in Israeli as well as international law. The young men who have come out from Itamar to stake a claim here are squatters on the land of Rashed and his neighbours. But now that this settlement expansion is becoming a 'fact on the ground', maybe it's good to have the ground marked out – don't 'good fences make good neighbours'? It's not as simple as that: 'There they made a fence – we can see the fence. But we can't go near it. If we even go so far,' he indicates several hundred metres, 'they will come out and give us trouble.'

I was struggling to understand what was going on, when I read this 'idiot's guide' from the organisation that brings together former Israeli soldiers and Palestinian fighters, Combatants for Peace:

So this is how it works: *The settlers arrive at a certain hill and construct an outpost, which is actually a caravan or a wooden shelter. This hill is usually privately owned Palestinian land. The army and the state give legitimacy to these actions by the fact that when these outposts are constructed the soldiers arrive straight away and guard it, of course, protecting the settlers. The owners of the land cannot harvest it any more.*

Month 1 Day 27

The party isn't over yet: around a settlement a special security zone is announced; the Palestinians aren't allowed to enter. Its size and area, no one really knows. The Palestinians find this out through trial and error: if they get caught and beaten they know they reached this zone. Of course there isn't any official decision, and when the units of soldiers change, so do their ground rules. And so the game starts over. (Combatants for Peace Newsletter, July 2009)

The invisible boundaries encroach on the village. And they are constantly being redefined. For instance, barns for battery chickens or other huge agricultural buildings, such as those above Yanoun, not only attract subsidy from the Israeli government, but also carry with their large footprint the need for a bigger 'security zone' – which effectively enlarges the settlement area. As we talk, Rashed and I watch several Palestinian shepherds grazing their flocks along the roadside or in the olive groves – while the hillsides lie inviting and empty, they are no-go areas for the farmers. Meanwhile the settlers sometimes choose to stroll through this landscape with impunity – almost as though they are 'beating the bounds' – defining their territory.

Here is Rashed's story of a recent incident – an attack not with weapons but with humiliating words: 'I go with my sheep … maybe 200 metres beyond the house. One settler came … he approached me with an M-16. I saw there were two more settlers on the hill. He asked me what I am doing here. I say "Feeding my sheep." He says, "No, this land is for me. Go to your home."

'I say, "You ask me to leave this place. Where shall I go? When I go to another place another person ask me to leave. So where shall I go?" He says, "You want to make problems here? You need problems here? No! Go to your home!" What to do? Perhaps they shoot my sheep … I leave with my sheep.'

All the time we are talking, a bulldozer is working on the

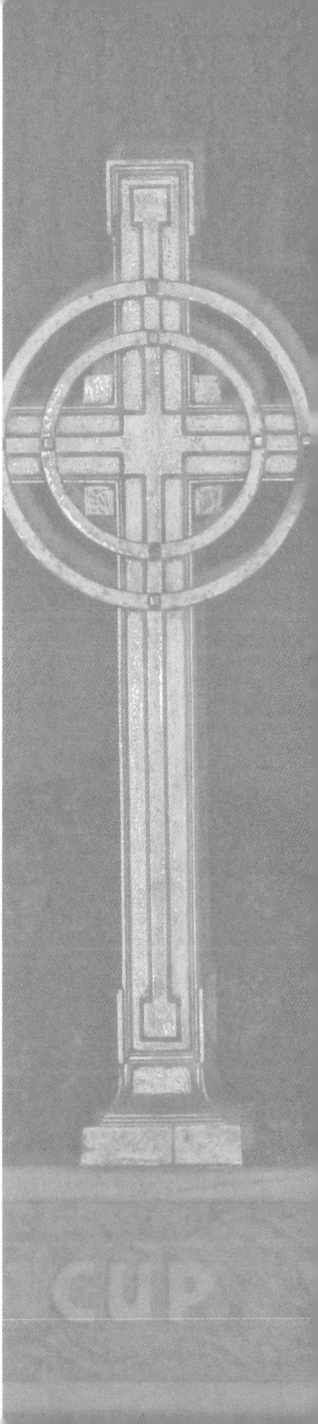

hilltop to the east, breaking new ground. Rashed points out that it's not a contractor, but an army bulldozer: 'Not settlers, army. That is bad.' Whatever military structure is planned there, this activity identifies the army of occupation more closely with the planting of settlements. The appropriate boundaries in their relationship were crossed and abandoned some time ago.

Rashed makes this connection, remembering a time before 1993, when Itamar was founded. He was 15 years old and was with his father and their flocks up on the hill where the chicken barns now stand. 'Soldiers come and start shooting over our heads. That was before the settlers. We go back to our house.' It was as though that was an early sign of the boundaries being redefined by force. Since then, when first the settlement and then the outposts came, Yanoun has suffered, but survived the crisis in 2002, when its people fled escalating violence. It's now the eighth year of international presence here – embodied most of the time by EAPPI – which seems to limit the aggression of the settlers and the military. But there's little we can do to hold back the invisible boundaries which are tightening like a noose on this valley.

'You know the settlers, the Israelis, want to take over the whole land – want to take Palestinian people outside the whole land. But if soldiers want to take me and my wife and children outside our home, if they want to shoot us, I not go. Where will I go?'

Jan Sutch Pickard

Interfaith

A heart broken open

An excerpt from the book A Heart Broken Open: Radical Faith in an Age of Fear *(Wild Goose Publications): a reflection by minister Ray Gaston on his grassroots engagement with Islam – from inner-city parish ministry in Leeds to the streets of Karbala at a time of rising Islamophobia and the 'War on Terror':*

… It was just before Christmas, 2003 that Hussein Mehdi, with whom we had developed a growing relationship following on from the Love & Resistance event in Leeds, invited me to join him on his pilgrimage to Karbala for the 10th of Muharram, Ashura and the memorial of the martyrdom of Imam Hussein, which he was planning for the following February. It also became a pilgrimage into the story of the sufferings of the Iraqi people under dictatorship, sanctions and war. It was a privilege to embark on this journey, a privilege to be asked, and it was beautiful in so many ways – beautiful and humbling – beautiful because of the depths I discovered in the Shi'a Muslim faith that touched me deeply. It was humbling in the wonderful hospitality I was shown right across the economic and social spectrum, including from Hussein's now sadly deceased aunt Umfareed – whose friendly, warm, open face I will always remember – who, along with her son Muwafaq, his wife, Abeer, and their lovely children, Jasimine and Tamara, made us so welcome in Umfareed's once-large home in Baghdad: the home had been divided into two – half having been sold in order to survive the austerity of the effects of Western sanctions in the 1990s. It was in her home that I broke bread and celebrated the Eucharist on Ash Wednesday with the help of her and her family, who went in search of grape juice and helped me burn the palm cross I had brought with me for the imposition of the ashes upon my forehead. And I remember the hospitality of Abdulilah, who was a

distant relative of Hussein's in Karbala, who took us into his sister's tiny home and moved us with his beautiful singing and poetry, while his sister fed us simple, delicious and carefully presented food. She had been forced to move to this house following the execution of her son, who refused to fight in the Iran-Iraq War. Abdulilah showed us the letter his sister had received that demanded payment for the bullet that was used to murder her child. Just one of the many stories I heard about the brutality of Saddam Hussein's regime.

When Hussein and I went to Iraq in 2004 there was much talk in the Western media about the liberation of Iraq, and so – as someone who had resisted the invasion, marched and indeed got arrested for non-violent direct action against the war – I went to find out how people felt about this so-called liberation.

It is true that one of the first things that struck me on entering Iraq was the immense sense of relief amongst those I spoke to (predominantly Shi'a) that the old regime had gone. But did this – as politicians at the time were claiming – amount to liberation? Salih, a teacher in Baghdad, told me off, in the way teachers do, for using the term 'invasion' about the US forces. He said to me: 'Mr Ray, do not call it invasion, it is liberation!' Contrastingly, Uraainib, whose brother was in an Iranian prisoner of war camp for 16 years, said to me: 'The Americans talk of liberation, anyone can talk of liberation. Saddam Hussein talked of liberation, liberation for the Palestinians, liberation for his people, but it was empty words. As far as I am concerned, Saddam and the US are two sides of the same coin!' Two very passionate responses to the language of liberation – one claiming it, the other rejecting it.

The truth is that politicians, tyrants and military chiefs all use the language of liberation very easily and for their own purposes. But liberation for a people is a deeper process that involves much more than the relief of the removal of tyranny. It is both material and spiritual.

It requires not just being rid of a tyrant but truth-telling; it requires not so much 'reconstruction' and 'democratisation' as healing. It requires the building of trust and the possibility of real hope, and it needs to arise from the people themselves …

When I look at Iraq today in 2007 and see the horrendous escalation of violence that continues day by day, I reflect on the misguided belief that violence, of any kind, whether 'terrorist', Iraqi resistance, militia army or occupier, can lead to liberation or healing, and I am reminded of the story I was given by a young woman at the University of Karbala after I had addressed a conference.

She passed me a letter written in Arabic. Through my companion, she asked that whenever I speak or write of Iraq I tell her story:

She wrote about her mother, who lost her own mother and sister and uncle, all of whom were murdered by the old regime. Her mother never recovered from this deep loss and was deeply depressed and disturbed for the rest of her life: the young woman felt that she had no mother. She wrote: 'It is easy to show when someone has been killed, there is a body that is dead. How do you show when someone has killed someone by destroying their soul?' She felt she experienced no love in her childhood, that her mother was absent – too traumatised, too destroyed, too broken; and she too had felt soulless, because she had not experienced love. Then, in her late teens, she was introduced to a man who was to become her husband. He showed her love and kindness and through this love brought her healing, confidence and hope. They were married and set up home together in Baghdad; then the 'Coalition' invaded and, during the bombing of Baghdad, her husband went across the street from their home to get some water from a neighbouring house, and a bomb dropped upon the building and he was killed. The man who had brought her healing and spiritual liberation from the effects of the brutality of Saddam Hussein's regime was now killed by a bomb dropped by those claiming to bring liberation from dictatorship.

It is too easy to forget that the bombs dropped from aeroplanes by states, under the so-called legitimacy of war and for the cause of so-called liberation, can easily be as indiscriminate as the bomb attached to a twisted soul who sees walking into a marketplace and killing himself and those around him as martyrdom or an act of liberation. Violence can never bring liberation or real hope, only destruction and death.

On our way back to England, we found ourselves – because of border difficulties – with some time to spare in Damascus. Hussein wanted to go shopping for a present for his wife in the markets of Damascus, and as we wandered through the streets talking and remembering the last few weeks, we also shared our frustration at not being able to return home to friends and family. 'Maybe,' I reflected to Hussein, as we looked at shops, 'God has something else for us to hear, to discover before we return to England.' Soon afterwards we entered a clothes shop and were met by a friendly young man who, in the process of showing Hussein some clothes, entered into the conversation, realising that we had just returned from Iraq. He then told us that his brother had been killed in Iraq. He was a martyr, he said; and he revealed to us that his brother had been the person who had driven the truck into the Red Cross building in Baghdad in 2003. Hussein and our new acquaintance had a long conversation in Arabic: this kind-faced man slowly revealed to Hussein that he was not very sure that his brother's actions were those of a martyr, and he told us that his family were not convinced either. He told us that his brother had a wife and two small children whom the family now cared for. 'Was he a martyr?' the young man asked Hussein. 'Or was he indoctrinated by people giving him a false belief in the righteousness of such an action?' Suddenly we were faced with the reality of the suicide bomber: an ordinary young man with a young family in Damascus, a brother who works in a shop, and a family who were left distraught and confused by his action.

How do we react to such stories? How can we respond as people of faith to the increasing insanity in our world and the continuing violence in places like Iraq? As a Christian I find comfort in Jesus' words that in the face of violence, wars and catastrophes we are not to be despondent or to speculate but to hold on to the truth of our faith *(Mark 13)* …

Mother Teresa of Calcutta said we should all pray: *'O God, break open my heart so that the whole world may fall in.'* In a world of violence we are called to cultivate compassion; in a world of self-righteous judgement and retaliation, we are called to practise mercy. 'Be merciful,' says Jesus, 'as your Father is merciful'; and as the Qur'an states at the beginning of each surah, 'In the name of God, the compassionate and the merciful.'

Compassion is a beautiful thing and it is only our turning again to embrace God's compassion and mercy that will save us in the end – we need to lament – we need to break open our hearts for the suffering in the world, for the victims of violence and torture and, yes, for the perpetrators of violence and torture, those twisted souls – be they powerful and ruthless tyrants or democratically elected presidents and prime ministers, or an indoctrinated young Syrian man with a family and a brother who works in a market shop …

Ray Gaston

Month 1 Day 29

COMMITMENT

Isn't it awfully nice to be a Christian?

Isn't it awfully nice to be a Christian?
Isn't it terribly good to have a faith?
The others are all wrong and we've known it all along.
We're the only ones who're sure about our resting place.

Isn't it simply lush to be a Christian?
The happiness and joy just never end.
All problems disappear and we never have to fear.
There's no more tears now Jesus is our only friend.

Well I'm a bloody useless crappy Christian.
I've fucked it up most every way I can.
My light is very dim and I'm dancing on the rim
of the toilet bowl of life and heading down the pan.

So give me all the bent and broken Christians.
The ones who know they're weak and full of strife.
Who walk in spite of rain and embrace the joy and pain
as they celebrate the wonder of this messy life.

David McNeish

Month 1 Day 30

The Rediscovery of Spirituality

The return of Godflesh: barking back

24.10.10. Sunday-morning thoughts following an extraordinary Saturday night: a first visit to the Supersonic Festival …

I've known Ben for over 10 years, grown to love him but not understand the supersonic world of music that has partially shaped him. Brought up on the Beatles and the Beach Boys I wonder what drew Ben into hard rock, into 'the world of extreme music, apocalyptic sounds and images, steeped in a Birmingham setting'. His music emerged, he says, as a sound of protest in the late 1980s, the end of the Thatcher years, a protest from working-class east Birmingham youth, 'a barking back', 'an act of cleansing and purifying' from so much that poisoned the air, dehumanised political and social systems, holding down the people.

I have grown to know something of the Ben who, after years of touring the world with the influential band Godflesh, chose to withdraw from everything associated with the almost deafening noise, into a whole year alone, hidden away in the silent folds of the Cambrian Mountains in Wales, a small and simple cottage his solitary home. This Ben, I begin to know. What I can't understand is how Ben, and other gentle, sensitive, thoughtful men, are drawn into supersonic hard rock music. All this exploding noise and within it these gentle human beings.

And last night?

Late last night we went to 'The Custard Factory' under the large railway arches near the bus station in the centre of Birmingham. Why? It was an opportunity to enter Ben's world and to attempt to understand more. I was really glad to share the middle of the night with Nicola and Joe (our daughter and grandson), Jenny and Ken (Ben's mother and stepfather), Sarah and Harris, and Jane and Adrian (friends).

It was freezing cold when we passed through the entrance gate for performers' guests, walking into the open-air corridors lit up by strong spotlights, watched by large, vigilant, yellow-vested security men, past halls already pulsating with music, and on into a building resembling a large empty aircraft hangar. No heating, no chairs, only a cold concrete floor.

Godflesh was headlining the Supersonic Festival. And men, lots and lots of them, between 35-45 years of age, wrapped up warm, some with woolly hats, flooded in just before the band took to the stage, filling the hall, waiting. And when

the crashing interlude music faded, Ben and Justin appeared amidst rising, swelling cheers, and then an explosion – swirling red, yellow, green and white lights, a rhythmic bludgeoning, primal pounding within an almost overwhelming sound and billowing white clouds enveloping the stage and hanging over us as a hovering evening mist. (Incense filling a temple?) And then the waves of chanting, the lifting up of hands and arms, the punching of the air, the gentle slow movement of heads, the swaying of bodies. Godflesh travelled the world until the late 1990s and had not returned to Birmingham, their home city, since 1991. The reuniting fans, including some who had travelled from other countries especially for this performance, sang – sang along with the songs as if they had never left their hearts. And the chanting? 'G.C. Green'– the rhythmic repeating of our Ben's name.

And the paradox?

Such an erupting explosion of noise, such tortured images, including a yellow cross, flashed across the blue screens, and the gentle swaying, relaxed, content, benign movement of young men and a few young women. It was much more than I had expected. I hesitate to articulate my wondering: is there, somewhere within all this, a public ritual, an exorcising of what some experience as their demons? 'An act of cleansing, a purifying'?

And then the lights went up, the volume of the noise went down and people hung around, well-pleased. A group of them, recognising my age and culture, asked if I had enjoyed it. My explanation for being there was that I had followed Ben to the Festival to try to understand the world he had once inhabited. 'Tell him: He's a mean bass. Tell him – congratulations.'

Sounds re-emerging from 20 years ago. What new throbbing rhythms, what protesting lyrics, what 'barking back', what stark restorative images, what form of social exorcism waits to emerge in Coalition Britain now?

Donald Eadie

The Thirty-First Day

(On the thirty-first day of each month, Iona Community members pray for fellow members who have died and for their families.)

Surprising gifts

The communication of the dead is tongued with fire beyond the language of the living – T.S. Eliot, 'Little Gidding'

I'll be seeing you, in all the old familiar places … – Popular song

Following retirement from full-time ministry in 2001 I took up (mainly for financial reasons), a part-time job with the library of University College, Worcester. In the dark days of January and February this gave me a reason to get out of bed in the morning, and my lovely, caring colleagues looked after me with real sensitivity, encouraging me to talk about Joan, but also respecting my need at times for space to withdraw and be on my own.

I don't normally dream much, but one night I experienced a deep physical need for Joan and eventually fell into a shallow and tearful sleep. This was followed by the most vivid dream, in which she was beside me, holding me and talking with me about ordinary family matters. When I woke up I was strongly aware of her presence. I wrote in my diary:

I have no recollection of ever dreaming like this before. It seemed to be totally real. Call it what you like, but I have little doubt that it was her coming to comfort and reassure me. This was followed by a peaceful night's sleep.

I read somewhere that the translation of the Hebrew in Psalm 127, verse 2, which reads in most versions, 'he gives to his beloved, sleep', actually means, 'he gives to his beloved *in* sleep'. Apparently we spend a third of our lives unconscious. Why, then, regard that area of our lives as being outside the touch of God's grace? Perhaps we need a theology of sleep!

Apart from this, I had no strong sense of her presence, but there were some definite indications that she was around. C.S. Lewis, in *A Gift Observed,* which he wrote following the death of his wife, Joy, spoke of, 'the impression of her mind, facing my own, an extreme and cheerful intimacy'. As with life's deepest and most personal experiences it is not easy to put into words, but for the recipient, the reality is undeniable.

Over the Christmas and New Year period during the time immediately before and after Joan's death, I worshipped regularly at Worcester Cathedral. I wanted to be anonymous, to come and go without having to talk to anyone. On Christmas Day, the Dean spoke of 'this vulnerable fragile baby, the very imprint of God's nature saying, I LOVE YOU, not in order to manipulate, but totally without condition and thereby liberating us'. A fortnight later, the baptismal liturgy contained the promise of God to his people in Isaiah: 'When you pass through the waters I will be with you. I have redeemed you … I call you by name, you are mine' (Isaiah 43:1–2). Once again the Dean preached, reminding us of our true identity, and that our names are graven on the very hands of God. The following Sunday being the beginning of the Week of Prayer for Christian Unity I decided to go to the Baptist church. To my surprise, the Dean was the invited preacher! His reflection on the set passage from John 14 spoke powerfully to me, as did the last verse of the closing hymn:

Green pastures are before me
Which yet I have not seen.
Bright skies will soon be over me
Where darkest clouds have been.
My hope I cannot measure …

So it was, that in those dark days, through this man who was until then only a name, God ministered to me. When I wrote to thank him, I said that it was as if God were putting his arms around me and saying: 'All is well.' I experienced a similar feeling when Luis, a former colleague from Peru, phoned from Lima late one night, having just heard the news of Joan's death, and simply said: 'I am weeping with you.'

There were other gifts too. A book on the stages of grieving co-authored by Evey, a friend from Dorset, with helpful quotes from many sources was a constant reference point. The discovery of a collection of songs by John Bell and the Wild Goose Worship Group, entitled *The Last Journey,* full of bracing comfort and deep understanding, helped me considerably, as did two powerful recorded sermons by an Irish-Canadian preacher called Maurice Boyd. I played these recordings again and again.

There *were* lighter moments. Joan and I had discovered Scrabble as missionaries serving in West Africa in the 1960s and played often down the years. One evening in February I had a game with our elder son and his family. I won, which was unusual because when Joan and I played together she invariably emerged the winner! Later that night, lying in bed and thinking of the evening, I found myself laughing aloud, when the thought was suggested: 'You don't think you did that on your own, do you?!'

I confided in a fellow-minister, who was also a widower: 'I really don't think I could face going back to the places which were special to us.' He was thoughtful for a moment, then replied, 'Then where will you go? If you are anything like us, you probably did most things together. For me, going back to those places is a kind of communion.' So I decided that over the following three months I *would* visit some of the places where we had lived and worked together.

I returned to Southport to attend the tenth anniversary celebrations of 'Facets', a highly successful church-community project, which in its origin and early development had owed much to Joan's vision and imagination. One of my journeys took me to Bakewell in Derbyshire where we had done much of our courting. I

walked over the town bridge and up the road, looking for the wooded area where we used to picnic. Inevitably it had changed, much of it having become part of a golf course. As I skirted the edge of the car park, a tall man, about my own age, greeted me and asked if he could be of any help. I suppose I must have looked a bit lost. When I explained why I was there he was quiet for a moment, then told me that he had just received results of his wife's medical tests, which had indicated a terminal illness. He paused, then said, 'Life gets rough, doesn't it?' We stood there, total strangers, united in that moment by our shared pain. Walking down the hill I paused to admire the view across the valley and spotted, in the field immediately below me, a hen pheasant followed closely by the brightly coloured male. 'See,' she seemed to be saying, 'they're still at it!'

I travelled to East Anglia, to Hingham in Norfolk, the scene of our first married home, where John, our elder son, was born. So many lovely and vivid memories of that scattered rural circuit came crowding back. I went to Norwich, and coming away from the cathedral, was deep in my own thoughts when I heard someone call my name. I looked up. He had recognised me from our college days, though we hadn't seen each other for over forty years. David and his wife, Kathy, were spending a post-Easter break in the Norwich area. We talked briefly and then exchanged telephone numbers. That seemingly chance meeting was to prove significant. Not only did they open the generous hospitality of their home to me, but David was to become a soul-friend. Vulnerable himself, he allowed me space to be myself and share some of my deepest feelings. He described himself as a 'wounded healer', and I believe that his coming into my life at that point was an important step in my *own* journey towards healing.

Mid-Wales was a place where we had enjoyed many great holidays. We returned most years to a cottage overlooking the Dovey Estuary kindly made available to us by a doctor friend from one of our former circuits. The family shared our love of 'Cae Top', and I wondered how I would feel, going back so soon after Joan's death. When I parked the car and walked up the drive, the house was empty. On a windless day in early June I sat for about half an hour on the front step, drinking in the quiet beauty of the special place and remembering the good times we had shared. It was, as my friend had said, a kind of communion.

Returning home from Bedford on a sunny Saturday morning, I turned aside, on an impulse, into the village of Sharnbrook, where John had spent a year at the upper school, during our days in the Bedford North circuit. I wandered through the village, and went into the parish church. One of the leaflets which I picked up contained this prayer:

'Lord, where tears fall through tragedy or heartbreak, enter the silence and hold me tight, lest in bitterness I blame you, or those close to me when I should be trusting you with those I love and *groping towards gratitude* for the time I have been privileged to share with them.' (my italics)

Groping towards gratitude. God's grace mediated through the most unlikely people and in the most unlikely places. Surprising gifts ... but then with the Bible in our hands perhaps we shouldn't be *that* surprised!

Warren Bardsley

Surrounded by a cloud of witnesses

Each occasion
we glimpse them:
that turn of a head,
that smile,
the way she walked,
his sense of humour,
each time
a knife turns
in our heart.
In time,
through the windows of our tears
we see them
and smile.
In time
we let go of sorrow.
In time
beauty and music,
remembered places,
bring solace not pain.
In your time,
God of all time,
may what we have sown in pain
be reaped in joy.

Kate McIlhagga

Month 2

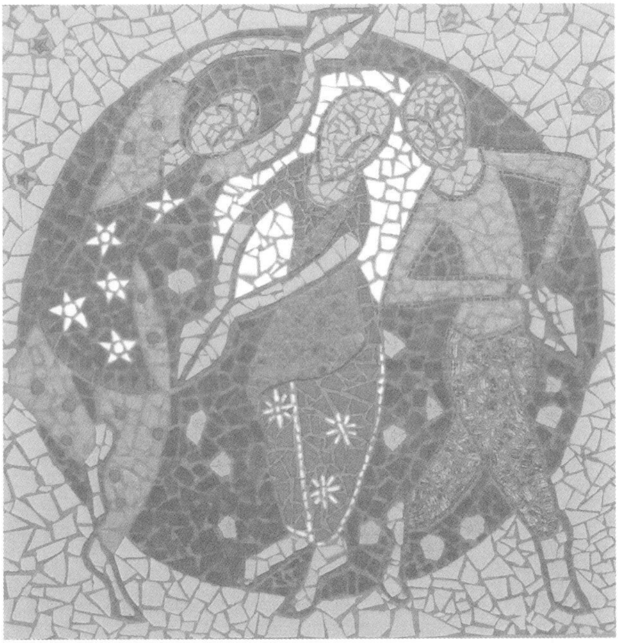

New Ways to Touch the Hearts of All

Khamal Aiteen: the eighteenth camel

There is a story of a man who left seventeen camels to his three sons. He left half the camels to his first son, a third to his second, and a ninth to the third. Despairing of their ability to negotiate a solution – because seventeen could not be divided by two or three or nine – the sons finally consulted a wise old man. After pondering the question, the old man announced, 'I don't know if I can help you, but at least take my camel.' That way, the sons had eighteen camels. The first son took his half – that made nine. The second took his third – six – and the third took his ninth – two. Nine and six and two made seventeen. They had one camel left over. They gave it back to the old man. Like the seventeen camels to be divided, the nuclear dilemma seems intractable. It sometimes provokes despair. But looking at the problem from a fresh angle, as the wise old man did, we may hope to see ways out.

– William L. Ury, from Beyond the Hot Line, *quoted in the booklet* Prayers for Peacemakers, *Pax Christi*

A soapstone camel graces our mantelpiece. A nicely worked piece about 14cms high, purchased long ago in Port Said, it stands sneering with a recalcitrant back foot ensuring a degree of isolation. Over the years it has gained in significance for us and for several of our visitors. Why?

William Ury's little story reached us at a time when, thwarted in their efforts to challenge the legality of nuclear weapons in their own national courts, peace campaigners, doctors and lawyers from many countries were coming together to create the World Court Project. This set out to lobby the United Nations General Assembly to request the International Court of Justice (ICJ) to give its opinion on the legality of the threat or use of nuclear weapons. This was an enormous task for ordinary citizens to attempt but hopes were high that the opinion of the highest court in the world would support the arguments of nuclear abolitionists, save activists from more fines, prison terms and burnout, and make the planet a little safer. The Project was formally launched in Geneva in May 1992 and took off worldwide.

My and Alan's part in it was tiny but it did produce some shocking and some golden moments as those to whom we spoke thrilled at the idea of supporting the formal approach to the World Court by completing individual personal Declarations of Public Conscience. How golden is the memory of seeing one activist literally dance round the room. These declarations harnessed the Martens clause from the 1907 Hague Convention which required the World Court to take account of the 'dictates of the public conscience' when deciding any legal question. By the start of the proceedings in The Hague in 1996 three million declarations were stacked neatly in boxes around the walls of the room in which the distinguished judges conducted their deliberations. And Alan was among the British group to deliver our boxes.

Opposition from the nuclear powers and their allies was colossal. It was a shock to hear that in the General Assembly countries supporting the ICJ Reference resolution complained that 'They are not just twisting our arms, they are breaking our legs!' When the proposition was debated in the World Health Assembly, one delegate asserted that 'nuclear weapons had nothing to do with world health'!

But hope was sustained by support from unexpected sources. When a friend from New Zealand visited us en route to attend the

World Conference of the Anglican Communion in South Africa, he departed clutching our information pack about the World Court Project, and left behind his official delegate papers, which, following frantic courier activity, were safely reunited with him next day at the departure gate at Heathrow. We were well rewarded when the Anglican Communion of Primates then became one of the first international religious organisations to sign up in support of the World Court Project.

After the UN General Assembly passed the ICJ reference resolution in December 1994 came the long wait for the court hearing. No wonder camels store fat and fluid in their humps to sustain them for long periods. At last, on 8th July 1996, came the historic result that any nuclear weapon threat or use is generally illegal and countries which possess them have *'an obligation to pursue in good faith and bring to a conclusion negotiations leading to nuclear disarmament in all its aspects under strict and effective international control'*.

The ICJ's opinion was strong enough in its condemnation of the threat or use of nuclear weapons to enable governments and campaigners to use it as a tool in support of the struggle for elimination. It confirmed that the Nuremberg Principles applied to nuclear weapons and implicitly undermined their status, placing them in the same category as biological and chemical weapons, only worse. In October 1999 the 'Trident Three' were acquitted by a jury at Greenock on a charge of damaging laboratory equipment used to support the Trident nuclear-armed submarine force. Their defence was that they had been compelled to act in order to prevent a crime of potential genocide. The Sheriff accepted their arguments based on the ICJ opinion that the deployment of Trident is illegal, and she instructed the jury to acquit them.

Afraid that this acquittal would set a precedent that would encourage other courts to acquit anti-nuclear protesters, in 2000 the Lord Advocate referred certain legal points to the High Court of Justiciary. The Lord Advocate's Reference Opinion (LAR) No.1 of 2000 on these points has been the subject of controversy ever since.

Unfortunately, the Scottish government has been advised that the LAR is the pre-eminent and binding law on nuclear weapons in Scotland. At an international conference held in Edinburgh in February 2009, distinguished experts demonstrated where the High Court went wrong in its interpretation of international law and the ICJ Opinion, but the Scottish government considers itself legally and constitutionally bound to abide by the law. So progress has ground to a halt, and once more we must start looking for an eighteenth camel to solve our problem. Which brings us back to our ornament.

After years of shuffling from house to house, occasionally lost or forgotten, our camel has become a symbol – a proud icon of action breakthrough. Now named Khamal Aiteen, once a year he leaps across the great chasm from our fireplace to our little Nativity scene. His recalcitrant foot rapidly removes sheep. His exasperated expression seems to summarise both our faith journey and the whole World Court Project experience. You might forget or disguise them for a time but the Incarnation and the World Court Opinion are both here to stay, to challenge and guide. Ornament or icon? Story or parable? Well, we know why we keep Khamal, but watch out for that back foot!

Maire-Colette and Alan Wilkie

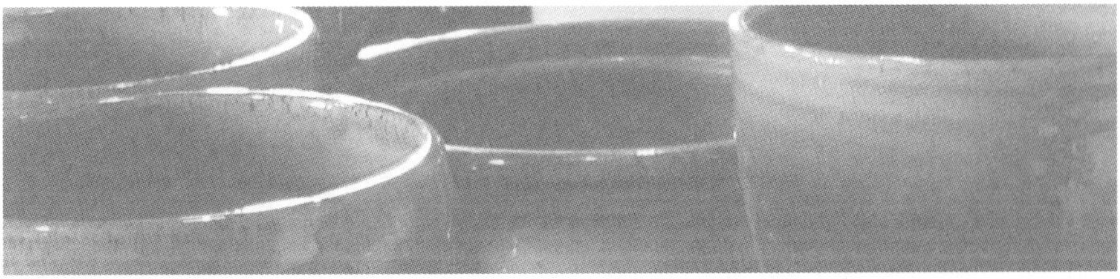

Economic Witness

Financial obesity

Some of my dearest friends have been drug addicts. Heroin and alcohol, mainly. Most of them are dead now.

I remember them with love – but not everybody loved them. The police didn't love them: they sometimes stole to feed their addiction. How else could they pay for their drugs? They lost their jobs and their homes and many ended up on the streets.

And of course they were looked down on with contempt by the rest of society – even though it was often the brutality of society that drove them into their addiction in the first place.

People who are addicted to food and become obese are similarly looked down upon. They are treated with scorn. Obesity is 'ugly'. Just as drug addiction and alcohol abuse are ugly. And, these days, we do not like ugly.

What we like is beautiful people – the ones who seem to be exactly the opposite of my 'ugly' friends. These are the celebrities, the mega-rich: the millionaires and billionaires. People who live in mansions and offshore tax havens.

All of them fabulously wealthy. All of them addicts.

They are addicted to something far more dangerous than heroin or booze or fattening food. They are addicted to money. And no doubt many of them have resorted to stealing to feed their money addiction, because tax avoidance and tax evasion are theft.

But, unlike my friends on the streets, these addicts are regarded as attractive and their addictive wealth is described as fabulous.

Maybe we need to think back to the words of Jesus, who proclaimed that he had been sent to bring good news to the poor, and who warned the rich that they had had their reward already.

Maybe we need to start being more objective about 'fabulous wealth' and name it for what it is. An obscene addiction, far more grotesque than drink or drugs.

My friends on the streets do little harm to anyone and relatively few people suffer when someone has an eating disorder. But the financial obesity of the rich causes untold damage to others. It makes attractive an unjust system of values and rewards that consigns millions to poverty and death.

We condemn alcohol and drug addiction but honour the rich. Maybe we should see the wealthy for what they often are – people who have grown obese on their addiction to money.

And perhaps see all addicts for what they are: people in need of help.

David Rhodes

Month 2 Day 3

Youth Concern

Suffer the little children: A reflection from Uganda

I have spent six years in Uganda as Country Director of the Elizabeth Glaser Pediatric AIDS Foundation. What we are about is the elimination of pediatric AIDS. It has already been achieved in America and Europe and our job is to work with each Ministry of Health to assist each country to achieve this goal. We have the science and the medicine but need to make it available to everyone who needs it. Without preventive medicine HIV-positive mothers will have a 25-30% likelihood of transmitting the HIV virus to their children. If the mother is already on highly active antiretroviral treatment before pregnancy, the transmission rate to her baby is a mere 0.7%. In between these extremes there are a variety of transmission rates

depending on which combination of preventive drugs the mother receives, but generally the transmission rate should be as low as 2-4%.

So far we have held five camps for children who are HIV-positive. Here is a little story from one of them:

The only sound I could hear under the forest shade was the creaking of branches in a copse of bamboo. The wind was gentle, blowing in from Lake Victoria, the famed source of the Nile River. Just ahead of me, 35 children from all over Uganda, all of whom were HIV-positive but taking antiretroviral medication, waited patiently in line at the beginning of the jungle gym course, which included swinging bridges and tightrope balancing.

The children were participating in the second annual Ariel Children's Camp, a week-long camp sponsored by the Elizabeth Glaser Pediatric AIDS Foundation. The camp is named for Elizabeth Glaser's daughter, Ariel, who died from AIDS-related illnesses in 1988. Would the campers manage to stay the course? Were they afraid?

The silence was broken as the first girl, Diana, started swaying on tyres hung from ropes and tried to cross from one platform to another. For the next two hours, there were screams of fear, encouragement and laughter. The finale came as each child – I think Agaba was first this time – climbed high into a huge tree-platform, and then, in a safety harness, launched along a zip line, down 100 feet to the ground at the far end of the course. The theme of the week was 'Journey of Life: Hope and Peace on the Way', and the zip line represented each of our worst fears as we launched off the tree platform.

The week also included a visit to the source of the Nile River as she begins her 90-day journey to the Mediterranean Sea, as well as many other games and exercises. There was a soccer game that never seemed to end. For me, the most significant event of this year's camp was the exercise 'Journey of Life'. Each child made a linear drawing of his or her life so far. Each drawing looked like a meandering river – along the way were key life events: 'I was born.' … 'My mother died.' … 'My older sister died.' … 'My aunt told me I was HIV-positive.' … 'No money, so I stopped going to school.' And so on …

One twist of the river on one boy's drawing said 'suicide' … I took the young boy aside and we talked. He told me things had been so bad in his life that he had swallowed his whole month's supply of antiretroviral tablets at once. He is still alive despite the dangerous overdose, and luckily feeling much better now.

Just behind the jungle gym at camp, there is a 10-foot anthill. It represented the mountain still to be climbed by each child on his or her journey of life. But Camp Ariel remains for each of us the base camp for reinforcement, renewal and refreshment. The children's prayers each night were for a cure for AIDS and for protection from evil.

With so many negatives in these children's lives, each positive event is momentous. Our camp is a series of positive events. New friends, encouragement, prayer, songs at night around the campfire, silly jokes. At the end of the camp, each camper was asked to name one thing they would take with them, and one thing they would leave behind. I said I would take the memory of the children's animated faces when they danced, and I would leave behind any discouragement.

And so my favourite week of the year at the Elizabeth Glaser Pediatric AIDS Foundation in Uganda came to an end.

The kids called me *taata wa baana* (father of the children). I am looking now at a card they gave me. 'Thanx' it says. Inside, each child has written their name: Mulindwa, Immaculate, Kenneth, Balaba Willy, Rose, Alex, Eric, Asasira …

The elimination of pediatric AIDS can be achieved. It needs commitment and, of course, cash. Each year as a world we are spending $10 billion to treat 4 million people, including children, who are HIV-positive. Today there are 14 million individuals, including children, who are in need of treatment. Still a long way to go.

Jesus once held a child and said: 'Whoever receives this child in my name receives me and whoever receives me receives him who sent me' (Luke 9:48). Children, especially the most vulnerable, take us a little closer to God and our understanding of what God wants for the world and for each of us.

Willie Salmond
www.pedaids.org

The Word

I don't like the dark

I was babysitting.
I sang quietly by his cot till his eyes closed,
then tiptoed from the room and carefully shut the door.

Minutes later came the sound of muffled crying.
I returned, ready to sing more songs.
But he simply said, 'I want the door a little bit open.
I don't like the dark.'

You can hardly blame him at two and a half.
Or at any age really.
He's certainly not alone.
Darkness is for owls and bats, not humans.
That's probably why we celebrate Christmas in late December.
Not because Jesus was born then.
But to let some light into the darkest time of the year.

You don't have to be a Christian to want that.
Everyone enjoys light at this time of the year.
Lots of lights, in fact. Whole strings of lights.
The more the merrier.
Merry, merry Christmas!

For those who do believe,
it's like opening the door of heaven

to let in the light that really matters.
And for believers and non-believers alike,
it matters because most of us, if we're honest,
don't like the dark very much.

But occasionally things happen
to believers and unbelievers alike
which make the darkness too thick for light to penetrate.
Then, come December,
the laughter is hollow, merry-making is a mockery
and it doesn't feel like Christmas at all.

It didn't feel like Christmas *then* either.
God forgive us for making the stable sound cosy!
Beneath the festive wrappings it's a hard story:

A scandalous pregnancy, a homeless couple.
A squalid birth and a refugee family.
Roman occupation.
A paranoid king.
A little town running with young blood.
A risky protest song, forecasting reversal of fortunes
between powerful and powerless, haves and have-nots.

If angels said 'Fear not!' it was because there was so much to fear.
If they announced good news for all it was because news was usually bad.

And if indeed the light had come,
it showed up, and meant so much, because of the night;
because the people were walking in darkness.
But what I want to know is this:
Did *he* say it, too, this child who had been born.
Did he, too, say, 'I don't like the dark!'?

Month 2 Day 4

Not *then* of course.
But when he learnt to speak.
Or when the sky turned black.
'My God, my God – why?'

Brother Roger, founder of the Taizé Community,
said, 'Even in the darkest night a light shines.'
I need to know the truth of that.
I need to know that it was still true
when a disturbed woman stabbed him to death
in the crowded sanctuary there.
For I don't like the dark either.

But I seem to recall him being asked, long ago,
when a terrible earthquake had shaken Mexico,
whether it had shaken his faith as well.
His reply was that sometimes
God doesn't seem to be there at all;
but that when you can't find him
that's when he may be closest.

I have another recollection.
A Hindu temple in South India,
where the focal point was a dark place.
Out of the dark place a flaming platter was carried.
It was taken round the worshippers,
who each in turn
cupped their hands through the flames
and over their heads
in single movements, as if bathing in divine light.
But though the flames had been brought from
the inner sanctum,

and were taken back as they died down,
the inner sanctum remained dark.

'God dwells in darkness,' they explained to me.
'God created light. God gives light.
But God was there *before* light.
God's home is the *darkness*.'

It is with such recollections as these
that I face the dark side of Christmas.
And the darkness in the world,
and myself.
I find glad tidings of great joy not by escaping reality
but by embracing it.
Festive hopefulness comes from the depths,
or it is nothing.

You don't have to like the dark.
But if you can accept it,
and know you are not alone in it,
even when it seems as if you are,
that may just be enough.
Enough, maybe,
to stay with it till you find your way through.
Enough, even if you don't feel Christmassy,
to know what Christmas is.

Brian Woodcock

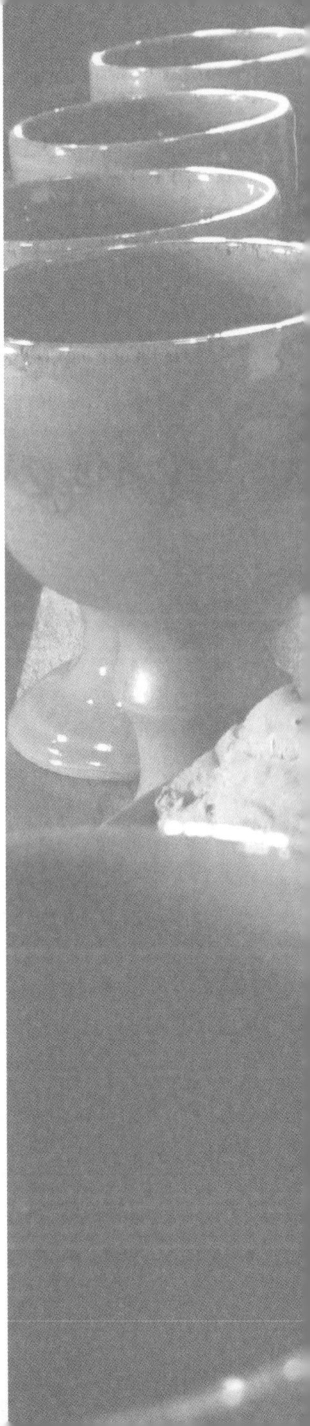

Hospitality and Welcome

Lessons in love and anger: Rima and two weeks in May

Early March 2009

I'm in California when Robert rings and says that Positive Action have called to ask if we will take in a destitute 16-year-old Eritrean girl. Ahead are days of public speaking and a long transatlantic flight. 'Yes. It's what we do.'

I've been back home barely two hours when the phone rings again. 'Can she come tonight? We really don't know for how long.' Twenty-five minutes later she is in the house. Rima.

There follow several months of legal complexity and endless frustration with the Home Office, and not just on our part. The judge at her destitution tribunal in London was clearly angry with the 'respondent' (Home Secretary) for her failure to supply any evidence or any representation in court.

We learn much about the utter desperation of refugees from Eritrea – a country with more refugees than any country other than Iraq at present, a tiny fraction of whom have made their way to the UK. Our house guest shows us YouTube postings of her arrival by shipwreck into Europe. Gradually we learn more of her story, gently, fragment by fragment. Families in the neighbourhood and at church take an interest, invite her to spend time with them and befriend her. She misses her family back home so much. She misses her dad, who was taken away by soldiers, who came back for her before she escaped. We learn how little she actually understands in English, and how few of the crucial aspects of her life are understood through the complexity of the bureaucratic systems which frustrate more than they serve …

Friday, May 8th 2009

11am: The colleague opposite me is talking about performance indicators for postgraduate study in the arts and humanities and how we would ensure appropriate audit. Another day in the University of Glasgow and the birth of another form, with another tick box to ensure accountability. I'm a little on edge and distracted. Rima has to report to the UK border agency in Brand Street, Govan for the first time and Robert has gone with her. There is a slight pause at 11am between items on the agenda for colleagues to refill their coffee. I check my phone for messages:

Received: 10.46. 08-05-2009. Message from Robert. click. 'Rima in Dungavel. Italy in a week unless solicitor can stop it.'

All the clichés are true. Time and space slow down. There is a sudden shaking in my hands. The sound of colleagues talking about submission rates fades and I feel surrounded by silence. My fingers are heavy. I can't get the phone to close. My fingers are trembling. I drop the phone. Pause. Breathe in. I turn to the colleague on my right – a gentle man – and make some stumbling apology about needing to phone home. In my feet, the blood from my face. Robert picks up. 'It went about as badly as is possible.'

'I'm coming home.'

Who will share this heavy load? Who will bear our sorrow?

At home there are what the press teaches us to call 'emotional scenes'. I'm trying to get practical, trying to hear the story, trying to understand, trying to concentrate, moving into rapid action. Moving into tears. 'We have to take her things up to Dungavel.' Robert's face drawn. There is more to come later, more to be told of the questioning at Brand Street. The moment when the key turned in the lock behind her and he felt he'd betrayed her, handed her over to the authorities. The only box on the forms for what we do as hospitality, it seems, is trafficking.

Italy may not immediately sound so bad. But Italy is where she lost a finger, was entirely reliant on charity. Italy is where she lived in a massive, mixed, derelict squat under curfew. Italy is where she had to walk two hours a day to a feeding station for her breakfast, and then for her lunch, and then for her supper. Italy is where, with infection taking its toll, she was given money by the community to leave and make her way to the UK where she would, they believed, have better care. When she hears that she will be returned to Italy she sobs uncontrollably. Italy, at present, according to Amnesty International, is unable to keep to the terms of the Dublin II Regulation. Italy is where Berlusconi has stated his aim of 'cleansing Italy of is multi-ethnic population' and is now turning boats from Africa back and refusing to allow them to land. Italy is where government coalition partners are demanding Italian-only buses.

Robert is in shock at the questions he has been asked and from his experience at the Home Office. I proceed to pack her belongings into her tiny suitcase. She doesn't have much and quite a bit of what she has she has been given in the last couple of months. Pictures drawn for her by young children at church, Easter eggs and cards. We begin initial phone calls and e-mails, starting with Family Group and our own near friends, neighbours, family. I'm shaking as I pack. I've visited Dungavel for years as a befriender and had recently ceased visiting to attend more fully to the hospitality we were offering at home. Dungavel is a prison. It is no place for a 16-year-old girl.

We speak to her lawyer. I go back and teach my Friday afternoon classes and by the time I get home she is in Dungavel. We borrow a car and drive the hour south of Glasgow to Dungavel with her belongings. Much of what we have taken up – the Easter eggs, the nail varnish and hair oil, her belt and scarves, we cannot leave for her. They are bagged up in HM prison bags for us to collect on our way home. At last we are able to enter the visits room and she meets us, sobbing. We all are. Apparently she'd been told in the UK Border Agency cell, in Brand Street, that she didn't need to worry because 'Dungavel is like a big cinema.'

Month 2 Day 5

Saturday – after a sleepless night – we begin to piece together the possibilities of a campaign.

Sunday we ask for prayer.

We get used to the Dungavel road. As luck would have it I am on annual leave for the week so on *Monday* morning I begin contacting our MSPs, MP and her solicitor, and all those we know in the asylum campaign networks. Out goes the first request for action and prayer. The response is incredible. Letters and e-mails begin to pour in to the politicians, responses come, creative ideas – the resourcefulness of good people is alive and escaping and full of hope. We watch in wonder as our worlds connect and we learn more of love and more of anger day by day. Driving up the Dungavel road every evening that week in the car I listen again and again to the words of singer-songwriter Tim Spark's (of Camas) album, *Nikko Fir*, and his track based on the words of Isaiah 58:

Give shelter to the homeless;
feed the hungry
and you shall rise like the dawn.

What does it mean, I wonder, I still wonder, to rise like the dawn?

By *Thursday* we have an application in for a Judicial Review with release. By *Friday* we have an advocate. In between times we learn via the networks into the Home Office that she is to be moved on the 19th and deported on the 21st.

Friday night: Text from Rima in Dungavel: 22.53. 'Hi alisn this crazey peple talk to me to get ready on 20 min to move and I refes them. good night love u by.'

And that was the last message we received from her before her SIM card was taken too and she no longer had any means of contacting us. *Saturday* was a crazed day of searching Scotland for a lawyer to prevent the movement south and out of the reach of

the Scottish Judicial Review. We were thwarted. On *Sunday* she was moved to Yarl's Wood, near Bedford, and then served her removal papers.

Sunday evening: I'm on hold, for ages. In the background the music playing on the Yarl's Wood switchboard is a song on repeat with the words 'Don't be afraid that I'm leaving. Be strong on the surface.' The song is interrupted: 'I'm sorry. She is probably having her hair done, or her nails,' says the voice. A new track 'Summer is over. The Innocent have never laughed. Drenched in my pain … here comes the rain.' Over and over and over again. Another interruption: 'We are having trouble locating her. She has a lot of freedom of movement so has probably made new friends. No, we can't take messages. Do you want to hold?' Another song 'Baby, keep my head above the water. Help me swim for my life.' The line disconnects and I don't know what to do with my frustration or anger, other than cry. That night Robert and I sit together quietly, hardly speaking. There is nothing to say. 'I'm afraid,' he says. 'I'm really afraid.'

Monday: Another night, another day on the phones and with the campaign. This time the press are involved, a photographer comes to the house, a new lawyer is instructed in London, money transferred, everything is now speeding up in a race against time to beat the deportation deadline set for Thursday. All our communications are now by text – with the press, with the lawyers, round the campaign, and for those who are praying. More letters are written, more urgently, with love, with anger.

The door bell rings; it is one of my students with a casserole. 'It was the only thing I could think of left to do,' she says.

Karen Reeves, a fellow Community member living near Bedford, volunteers to visit Rima in Yarl's Wood. The right person in the right place. She has to register her visit 24 hours in advance.

Who will share this heavy load, who will bear our sorrow?
The Lord has promised us peace and freedom.
Who will help this promise to come true?

Tuesday: We have strong contacts to Italy and the various church and community organisations that look after asylum seekers. We are beginning to see the tracings of an immense network of love and advocacy, of compassion and action that is always there, but only now present to us, in our very particular need. Friends, family, colleagues, neighbours, members of the Community and of our church – all are creatively, intelligently, remarkably doing amazing things to keep hope alive. Rima has sent us her deportation papers. We know the flight number and the time of her deportation on Thursday. I organise a small, quiet vigil for Wednesday night. I eventually get through to Rima on the phone. Tears.

Wednesday: The story is in the press. Replies are now pouring in from MPs and MSPs, government ministers and all the others who have been contacted by the campaigners (now in the hundreds). There is no news from England or the lawyer. 4pm Robert phones. 'I think we have done all we can. We just need to wait now.' So we wait. We hold our breath.

Text from Robert: 17.34. 'Flight Stopped. JR with release.'

Alison Swinfen

An open letter to the UK Border Police

Dear Sirs,

I'm not sure when you will come. Others I know who you have come for say I should expect you between 4 and 5 o'clock in the morning. That's very early. You will be weary, I expect. It may have been a long night and you probably don't relish the visit you have been ordered to make to our house.

We may be asleep when you come. You will wake us. First with the doorbell. Then with the banging. Just give me a moment to find my dressing gown and slippers and run down the stairs to let you in. We know you are coming. We expect you now. Every time the doorbell rings we think it might be you.

It is possible there will be other guests in the house. We often have folk staying with us; they come like the ebb and flow of the tide. Always welcome.

You too will be welcome, though it will be harder for us: it is what we do and what our home is for. I've been baking, so there will be fresh bread and homemade jam or marmalade. It's hungry work, this work you do, taking children away from their parents, putting them in prisons. 'Removal' is what you call it. It's the law. 'A future fair for all.' 'Every child matters.'

I'll make sure there is milk in the fridge. You will probably need a cup of tea or coffee.

Our child, the precious one given into our care for a while, has already been separated from her parents once. The police have already taken away her father; she has already seen inside Dungavel and Yarl's Wood. Apparently last time you told her that she doesn't need to worry about Dungavel: that it is just like a big cinema or a big disco. That wasn't how she described it when she was released to us, so she will take some persuading this time, I expect. And she may not understand; you say strange things about laws and rights and you do it in English, and even I will struggle to recognise it as a mother tongue.

I'd like to ask you not to be rough. I've seen the bruises on others. You may say it is necessary to use force. I was on the Ethiopian Airlines plane that recently landed at Heathrow Airport and I saw how you took the young girl off the plane there. I know you are 'only doing your job', but please, don't do that to our lovely daughter.

Yours in expectation,

Alison

Alison Swinfen

This is the Day

In the midst of the 'ordinary' (from an Iona Prayer Circle letter)

… This letter seems to be very practical and it would be easy for me to begin to worry that it wasn't 'spiritual' enough. As I was thinking that, I had a memory pop into my mind. I had been doing MacLeod Centre cover and had been unable to go to the communion service in the Abbey on Sunday morning, as I was the person who had to be available in the MacLeod Centre.

I received the message that the bread and wine had been brought down for me. I went into the kitchen where the hustle and bustle of preparing lunch for 50 was going on. Just visible on a shelf in the cupboard was the bread and wine. It was a picture I will never forget, so clearly symbolic of how Jesus' presence is in the midst of the ordinary and how He can be easily missed if we only think in terms of the spectacular. Rather, He appears in the very humdrum and is often hardly visible at first glance. In that case, an ordinary loaf of bread and some wine in a earthenware jug in a pantry. Perhaps in our present predicament He is to be found in computer files and piles of paperwork. I have certainly encountered His presence in the many letters, cards and e-mails from you all. May you meet Him in whatever your 'ordinary' happens to be at the moment.

Much love to you all,

Prayer Circle Coordinator

Polly Burns

The Iona Experience

'I would have almost certainly guaranteed come out of jail in a box'

Many different folk come to volunteer with the Iona Community on Iona. Chris Chamberlain, a volunteer with Jacob Scotland, a project which supports ex-young-offenders, speaks here (at a press conference promoting the Jacob Project) about his journey from prison to Iona …

'Right, I'll start from the very beginning.

'Five years ago now … I was in Reading Young Offenders … and didn't have a lot to go out to. At the time, I would class my mental health as being quite poor: I made several suicide attempts while I was in, just due to the fact that I didn't have anything whatsoever to go out to when I got released. There was nothing.

'And I would be lying on my bed, in my cell, moaning about the world to my cell-mate. And I got a knock at the door. And it was the Resettlement Officer. And I remember him going: "You haven't got anywhere to go when you get out, have you?!" And I said: "No." He said: "All right. OK," and went away. And that was it. And I was like: *All right. Thank you very much …*

'But then it was a couple weeks later, that this woman from a project called Time for God, a woman called Leslie, came to visit me in the jail. And she sat down with me in the chapel, and she said: "If there is *one* thing you want to do, what would you want to do?" … I said, "Well, I've always wanted to do youth work. But, obviously, you know, that's not gonna happen now, is it? I'm in prison." And she said, "No, no, bear with me, bear with me." Then she saw someone else. And went away.

'About three weeks later, she came back and said: "Chris! Have you ever been to Scotland?"

'I'm like: "Ahhh ... no."

'"How does a small island off the west coast sound?"

'I went: "Is there a pub?"

'She said: "Yes."

'"Then I'll go." I said …

'And then a few weeks after that, Helen from the Jacob Project, and Andrew, one of the staff on Iona, they came to meet me. I always remember when I was on my way down the wing to visit them, the Resettlement Officer said: "Right – no bullshit, all right? They can tell – they can smell it a mile off." So I'm there going: *Oh no, I wonder what's gonna happen now.* So I walked in, and I had quite a long chat, with Helen, with Andrew, about the island and such. Anyway, I got released (Jacob was working on my release). And once my tag came off, 'cause I got released on tag, I flew up to Glasgow … And if you haven't been to Iona – it's bloomin' miles away! And I got the ferry, got the bus. I always remember saying to Leslie: we were on the small ferry going across to the island; I looked out and I said: "Look, if I see Christopher Lee or a wicker man – I'm outta here!"

'And then, when I got off the ferry, the only people I saw were people with long hair and beards and sandals. So I'm like: *Oh, what have I got myself into*? So then, I got taken to the Abbey. And anyone who's been there knows that at your first meal you have to stand up and introduce yourself. And I'm like: *What do I say?: "Hi, I'm Chris, the ex-con"*, or whatever? But the welcome that I got. The warm feeling. Afterwards, everyone just came up to me and hugged me and said: "It's really good you're here. I'm really pleased to meet you."

'And I spent six months there, working as a housekeeper. Folding bed sheets and stuff like that. And it enabled me – well, obviously it was so far away from my hometown, I had no connection to any of my old friends, or any of my old things – there was no Internet, no mobile phones, it was complete cut-off from everything – so I was able just to take a step back and just completely to rewire my brain and just start concentrating on what I actually wanted to happen.

'And then, I left the island. I came here, to the Iona Community's Glasgow office, where I was working with Helen and the rest of the Youth Team, as a trainee Youth

Worker. Part of that role was, I started going into schools and doing a talk on my time in prison, under the title of "Choices" … And I always remember best, I went to this school. And then I think it was three years later, or something like that, I was working part-time on the door at a pub, and I remember a kid walked past me as I stood there and went: "Ah! You're that dude that was in jail! You came to our school and talked." And I was like: "Ah, right. How you doing?" And there's this kid, he was about fourteen then, and he said: "You know, I was very similar, on the same path as you were going. But after you came, I went home and talked to my mum and I said: Mum, I need some help. Because I don't know what's going on. I'm hanging around with these people, doing these kinda things."

'You know, it was kind of heartwarming to see that my mistakes somehow managed to help someone else …

'I'm not being melodramatic, but without the Jacob Project I would have almost certainly guaranteed come out of jail in a box … No one gives a monkey's about you when you come outta jail. No one does. My last job working in prisons, you could see it time and time and time again. It's like a revolving door, these guys are in and out, in and out. And you say "Why?" … "No one gives a crap about me: why should I give a crap about anything else?" Whereas the Jacob Project actually says: "We do. We want you to fulfil your potential."'

Chris Chamberlain

Life in Community

Time and timelessness

'Where's Iona?' asks my family.

'On the western edge of Scotland,' I tell them.

My son, always the sceptic, looks it up on Google maps and is truly impressed. 'That's a long way. How do you get there?'

'I fly from Sydney to Glasgow via Heathrow. Then I take the train to Oban, a ferry to Mull, a bus across Mull, and finally a smaller ferry to Iona. I'm guessing the trip will take around 36-48 hours.'

'So you're going on a 2-month holiday!'

'No, I'm going on a pilgrimage, and to work as a volunteer.'

Was such a long journey worth it? I was setting off to live for eight weeks in a community, to do a physically demanding job (housekeeping in Iona Abbey) and live in dormitory accommodation with a group of people I did not know. Fear was part of my initial reaction – fear that I would find travelling so far too demanding, fear of not coping with a new, perhaps uncomfortable, environment, fear of meeting strange and difficult people and not being able to handle the situation – and the busyness of community life. And let me say: it was busy.

Of all its diversity and differing aspects, the overriding experience has to be one of community. Many of us are looking for community, feeling that our modern materialistic, individualistic society values are failing to offer us the nurturing, the caring, the meaningfulness, the loving support that we assume is what community means. Do we find that on Iona? I make two points.

First, we have the experience of having a task or activity enhanced by doing it together (hanging the washing in the drying room was a great occasion for a chat) and having to rely on others. We each have tasks to do – cleaning bathrooms,

changing sheets, washing up, pouring tea; singing and laughing together as we do them – and the quick completion by each person of their allocated task benefits everyone.

This experience of community seems to mean that people come to trust one another more quickly and to share more openly, to somehow be more real and authentic than ever seems possible in 'ordinary' life. And I'm sure that what helps brings this about in working together is the physical proximity of bodies – there's not much space when eight or so people are washing and wiping up in the scullery of the Abbey or the MacLeod Centre. And then, passing from the Refectory with wet sticky hands to the Abbey for worship – to be reminded that we are profoundly, deeply loved by God – we respond by trying to love others.

This sounds very idealistic. It sounds like I might have closed my eyes and ears to the reality of this place. So, yes, there is a second side to this experience. That it is also a place where what you are is what you bring with you. If you come in order to escape something, particularly yourself, then you will be disappointed. Collective living isn't the escape one might hope it to be. Collective living brings into sharp focus all your faults, your failings, your weaknesses. Here we come up against the obdurate realities of others, and, worse, come up against ourselves in the mirror of those others. There are some who do not cope, some even sliding back into the neurotic or psychotic state which is their demon; some, finding that a small isolated island, surrounded by sea, is a terrifying prospect – no city distractions, no big supermarket, no coffee shop, no cinema to enable one to escape oneself.

Was it the spiritual experience I anticipated? I tried to go without expectations, so that the experience was 'itself', not something I fantasised about and then was disappointed in because the reality didn't match the expectation. Although I was aware that I was in a very special place when I worshipped in the Abbey, my God experiences came when I walked the land, climbed Dun I, gathered stones on the north beach, woke to the sun sparkling on the sea and sand and hills of Mull, or watched the golden sunset over the western seas. The sheer beauty of nature in this place drew from me a wordless 'thanks' to its Creator.

I sought a way to understand my Iona experience. It seemed to be beyond my understanding, an experience of the sublime, and I was searching for words and images that might express this experience. I wrote home:

Time seems extraordinarily different here, both to stand still and to race by; one becomes aware of the ebb and flow, of constant change, and yet of absolute permanency. No wonder the early people felt very close to God here, a place closer to 'heaven' than we find in our normal places of living. The immediate is the community life; the context is Nature herself – here, the two flow together: time and timelessness.

It is always a great experience to travel, to fulfil a dream, but it is also nice to return home. I had made the journey to Iona, I'd lived there for eight weeks, I'd worked and worshipped with the Iona Community. Travel heightens one's awareness of 'there' and 'here' and throws into relief one's understanding of life. And so, I find myself remembering T.S. Eliot's words from 'Little Gidding' (*Four Quartets*): '*We shall not cease from exploration, and the end of all our exploring will be to arrive where we started and know the place for the first time.*' Home is 'here', but now tinged with the beauty and wonder of Iona and heightened by a deeper experience of God's amazing love for all creation. I was not merely a traveller, I was a pilgrim.

Bonita Frank

Bonita was a volunteer on Iona in 2007. She is currently Editor of Wellspring's newsletter Pipeline. *Wellspring is one of the Iona Community's sister communities.*
www.wellspringcommunity.org.au

WOMEN

Not counting

(Exodus 12:37; 15:20)

They were tired:
tired of cajoling the children,
tired of packing and unpacking and packing,
tired of carrying the food and the baking pans,
tired of walking.

I didn't think that they had any energy left,
but they did.

They were anxious:
anxious about their enemies,
anxious about their older ones and their little ones,
anxious about the future,
anxious about the unknown.

I didn't think that they could let go of their anxieties,
even for a moment,
but they could.

It was a risk.
I thought I might be on my own,

that no one would join me,
that I'd look a fool.

I wondered if, after my brother's long song,
my sisters would have had enough of singing,
but they hadn't.

And so I sang for them,
and I sang with them
and I danced,
and I played my tambourine.

And the dry ground was beaten firm
by the feet of six hundred thousand women dancing,
not counting men
and sheep and goats and cattle,
and children.

Ruth Burgess

Prayer

Passionate about the city: a sermon

Luke 13:31–35

Jesus was passionate about Jerusalem. It drew him and yet it frightened him too; he was angry with it with all the heartfelt anguish of a lover, and yet it evoked his tenderest maternal feelings. In the end, he wept for it.

Jerusalem was not the place of his birth or upbringing, and yet in a sense it was for him, as a Jew, and still remains today for observant Jews, a place of enormous spiritual and psychological power. To a people for whom the land was all, who believed that God had promised them the land, and brought them out of captivity in Egypt into it, Jerusalem was the paramount symbol of that promise. It was a concrete representation of their identity. And more, it was the place where God was to be found and worshipped in the temple. God lived above all in the temple. So it is not surprising that it evoked such strong feelings in him. It was his history, his community, his religion.

I think it is not fanciful to say that this moment, on the road to Jerusalem, was a liminal one for Jesus, for here he stands on the edge of transformation, of something new coming into being. With deep prophetic insight, he sees at one and the same time what is, and what is to come, and is weeping for a moment that contains within it both birth and death. History, community, religion are taking a new turn. God will no longer be found and accessible only in Jerusalem. This is a moment between the no-longer and the not-yet.

Jerusalem is still a city of huge symbolic significance, not only for Jews but for Christians and Muslims also, a city still wept over, a city in which the way that leads to peace is all too often ignored and blocked. Pray for the peace of Jerusalem today. And yet for most of us, it is not the city which claims our love. For us, the most important question is, what does it mean to love *our* city? What does it mean to pray for it, as Jesus did?

I am passionate about my city, though it is not the place of my birth or upbringing. I live in the West End of Glasgow, in a friendly environment. A few years ago, I heard an ecologist make a very good case for it as a paradigm of green urban living – tenement houses, solidly built and energy-efficient; good public transport; excellent small local shops; schools; services, parks entertainments; sports facilities; hospitals – a neighbourhood where places of work, living, service and recreation are integrated in a multicultural and extremely socially mixed environment. And indeed, it is a good place to live. In such a place, community responsibility and ecological concern are very high. People are always cleaning up the River Kelvin, campaigning about the use of the parks and the maintenance of the public spaces; every street has its residents' association. People value their environment, so they take care of it. And find it takes care of them. They experience it as friendly. It meets their needs. We take care of what we value. Why do we value what we value?

To a great extent, we value what in turn values us – what meets our needs, what affirms us in our life and aspirations, what gives us enjoyment and delight. This is a kind of symbiotic process – we know it with our friends, with our children; if we are fortunate, we know it with our work. It's not usually easy to tell, and probably it doesn't matter too much anyway, which came first, the valuing or the being valued. They reinforce one another. I think one can make a very good case for people in the West End of Glasgow living in a symbiotic relationship with their environment. The environment is friendly to them, so they are

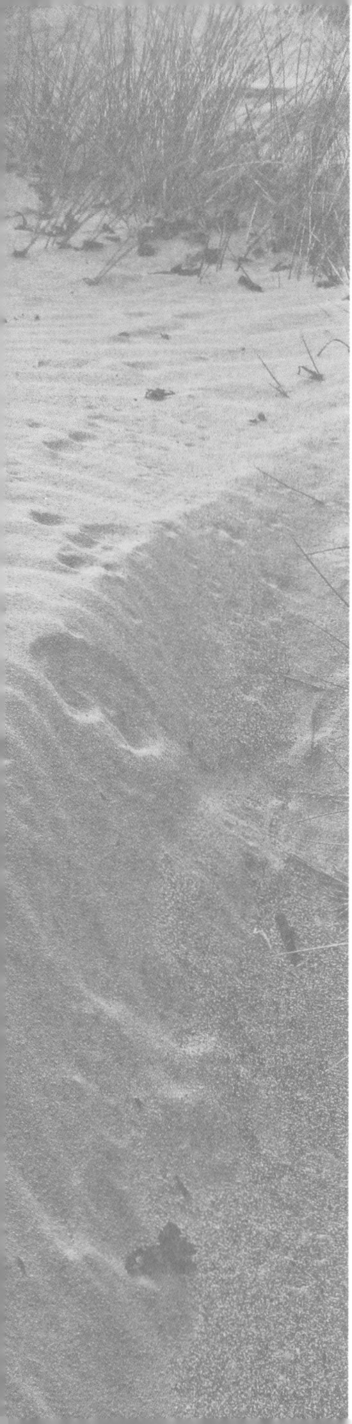

friendly back. They take care of it. They invest time and energy and talents, and often money, in it – all of which makes the environment even more friendly.

But even in a community such as the West End, which is essentially one which still works, you don't have to look far to find pain and anger underneath the surface: the pain of the young people leaving care who live in the house next door to me, or of those living in the many homeless hostels and DSS hotels in the area, or of the survivors of domestic abuse in the refuges; the anger of students struggling to survive in an area where three of them have been burned to death in three separate incidents, whose flats were unsafe because unscrupulous landlords did not maintain them properly; the anger of asylum seekers treated with contempt by those who do not understand anything of their experience; the anger of disaffected, unemployed young men in a city with a sectarian history. For them, the environment is not friendly; and I have lived in other parts of the city where the environment is even more hostile.

People's lives are lived in the context of their environment, and to probe the roots of their pain and anger is a process that inevitably leads to the need for change – change that will involve both healing and justice if it is to be any kind of good news for those who live in our cities.

The pain of a city is complex. The suffering that cripples our inner cities is often the pain of lifetimes and generations. The pain of individuals is bound up with the pain of the whole community. An abused child is sometimes the child of parents who were, in their turn, abused by their parents. When a child is killed on a busy road that runs through a housing estate, or an old person dies of hypothermia because they cannot afford to heat an all-electric flat, the whole community suffers. The community suffers because all their children and all their pensioners are at risk, and will continue to be at risk until there is change.

And how do I pray for healing for this community? When I begin to pray for the individuals I meet, I find myself praying and acting for the whole community. I cannot pray for an old person with bronchitis if I do not also put pressure on a council or a landlord who is responsible for the damp and substandard housing that is the root cause of the illness.

How can I pray for those who are lonely, old and disabled if I do not take time to visit them, and, at the same time, ask why there is so little funding to provide sheltered accommodation and to staff day centres? I cannot pray for families living in tower-blocks, whose relationships are at breaking-point, and whose children are distressed, if I do not raise questions about the way that government and local authorities allocate housing stock and fund play space and nursery provision.

I cannot pray for a young person in prison if I do not look for ways to relieve the boredom of unemployment, the pressure of advertising, the board and lodgings legislation that keeps him on the move, and the lure of drugs, which have combined to destroy his liberty. I cannot pray for poor people in my community, for refugees and asylum seekers or for that matter for hungry, oppressed and poor people anywhere else in the world, if I do not challenge the way that my country's government spends its resources and the way its popular media engages in relentless poor-bashing and racism.

I say I cannot pray. What I mean is that I cannot pray for the healing of others with integrity without also acting on my prayers. If I am blind to the sources of injustice around me, and divorce the needs of an individual from the pain of a whole community, my prayers for healing are nonsense and bear no resemblance to the good news of the gospel.

Has prayer any validity in the context of the cities' pain? Is it not rather naive to spend time in prayer when what is needed is action? What good can prayer do? Most of the people I pray for have no idea that I am praying for them, so what is the point?

I find it much easier to ask these questions than to answer them. When I prayed in the midst of the city, I discovered that my prayer changed me. When I prayed, I let God's love into my life, and the healing and forgiveness that that love brought made it far more possible for me to live out the gospel than if I had not prayed. Prayer made me open to change. It was not a substitute for action; rather the source of action's motivation. Prayer made me aware of God's love for me and for the people around me, and that brought a sense of healing amidst the anger and pain. But the pain within me and the pain around me did not go away, and the injustice continued and at times overwhelmed me and the community, filling us with rage and frustration and fear.

Jesus, you wept for the city you loved – in your words and actions the oppressed found justice and the angry found release …

Weeping for cities and working for justice is rarely dramatic or sensational. It is not an activity that brings instantaneous results. The suffering of a dispossessed community, in Britain or anywhere else in the world, has no easy solutions. For healing and justice to occur there needs to be change – change in values and attitudes; change in political policies and social conditions. And change for those in need means change for everyone, and none of us change easily.

Perhaps it is easier to pray for the peace of Jerusalem than for the peace of our own cities. When we pray for the peace of those around us, are we willing to live out the implications of our prayers?

Jesus, teach us to pray.

Kathy Galloway and Ruth Burgess

Justice and Peace

On war and peace

Everything that happens in this world happens at the time God chooses. He sets the time for killing and the time for healing: the time for war and the time for peace.

– Ecclesiastes 3:1

The king of Syria was at war with Israel …

– 2 Kings 6:8

'You are going to hear the noise of battles close by and news of battles far away. Countries will fight each other, kingdoms will attack one another.'

– Matthew 24:6

'We cannot go back to operating as we might have done even 10 years ago when it was still tanks, fast jets and fleet escorts that dominated the doctrine of our three services. The lexicon of today is non-kinetic effects teams, counter-IED [improvised explosive devices], information dominance, counter-piracy and cyber attack and defence … Attacks are likely to be delivered semi-anonymously through cyberspace or the use of guerrillas and Hezbollah-style proxies.'

– General Sir David Richards of the Ministry of Defence in the UK, speaking in July 2010

On the 2nd of July – thanks to the kind invitation of my elder son Eldon – I was in Buckingham Palace in central London. On that day, Eldon was being honoured by his country for his outstanding and courageous leadership in the war in Afghanistan. I was proud of Eldon as any dad would be on such an occasion.

As he went forward to receive his honour, I was thinking not only of Eldon but of his many colleagues who have been killed or seriously wounded in Afghanistan. I am sure he was also thinking of them because his pastoral care and concern for the women and men under his command has been a central component of his leadership, not only in Afghanistan, but also in Iraq, Bosnia and Kosovo.

But on that summer morning in London, surrounded by the pomp of the British monarchy, I was also thinking of the many local women, children and men in countless towns and villages in Afghanistan who have been victims of improvised explosive devices. Their names and narratives are largely unknown to us, and we shall never know the terrible sufferings they too have endured because of war. War in their own land.

And millions of us around the world continue to ask what is the purpose of this war in Afghanistan which is taking many lives and birthing so much sorrow. When will it end? How will it end? How many more will die? Are people on both sides dying in vain? What is the future for Afghanistan? And what of its cost? Endless questions.

And these questions, along with countless others, are being asked in many countries and across the board. Not only by folk in the streets, but also by our politicians and by our military commanders. I hope that they are also being asked by the churches, for this is a vast theological, moral and spiritual issue for those who seek to be guided by Christ's light and hope.

It is not easy to work and campaign for peace and for justice in the modern world. We all know that. The global military machine is far beyond the understanding of individuals, and words such as those from General Sir David Richards, himself a good and honourable man, send a chill down our spines. Yet without our military in place, would the world resort to total anarchy? And what of the role of the military as peacekeepers within a world of multiple conflicts, both large and small?

Centuries ago, those who wrote the Bible seemed to accept, as they reflected on God's purposes and the human condition, that war and conflict were inevitable. They accepted that there were times of war and times of peace. Times of breaking down, and times for building up. In the New Testament, Jesus and his disciples announced the possibility that one day our world may become conflict-free. I will not see such a day in my lifetime. Yet the invitation to look at our human condition through the eyes of non-violence, of creative love, is always present, as Gandhi in the 20th century so powerfully reminded us.

It is my conviction, as it is of many others, that we must continue to speak of the possibility of peace in our world. Ordinary women, children and men in every country on earth long to live their days in some degree of peace, even if that word 'peace' means many different things. But there are also those who do not seek peace, and sometimes we find that a hard truth. The addiction to power often leads to conflict, and that striving for individual power is also at the heart of human experience.

Through my elder son's work as a respected military commander and strategist, I have come to a range of new understandings about our world. Over these last several years that has not always been an easy journey for me, and I value the support of friends and colleagues in it, and for their untiring support for Eldon, especially when he is working in areas of high danger.

But surely the truth is that we are all on a journey of understanding when it comes to the complex issues of war and of peace. Yet it gives us all hope that the Bible writers were themselves on a similar path. They accepted the reality of conflict while at the same time illumining for us a pathway to a more tender acceptance of each other. I tried to express this biblical wisdom in a prayer I wrote last year:

God, illumine our minds as never before. Let us forgive this century and every other. Stop the war in ourselves and in the world. Remove from our hearts the illusion that we are separate. May every nation and every culture recognise the pain of our common fears and discover that one amazing heartbeat we all share.

Peter Millar

The Integrity of Creation

Looking at the environment through the lens of prophecy

Taken from a talk given to an Iona Community regional plenary, 2010 on 'being a prophetic church in the 21st century'…

A great deal of the church's thinking about the environment has been based on different understandings of creation. Creation theology has in some places been seen as a synonym for environmental theology: the fact of being created, being creatures alongside all other creatures, creation being good, humanity having dominion over the earth, the Sabbath as the crown of creation, etc.

I want to argue that it is a mistake to start from creation in order to understand a Christian approach to the environment. It is a mistake both theologically and politically. The appropriate place to start is prophecy.

Walter Brueggemann has argued that two distinct trajectories can be identified in the Bible. One encompasses creation, the Book of the Covenant, the wisdom tradition. This is the tradition of the kings, of the priests, the hierarchy. It was written and edited over a long period of time by those with influence, wanting to preserve their position.

It emphasises stability, hierarchy, reflection, changelessness.

This is all very well, but the Israelites, the worshippers of Yahweh, were founded and held together not by hierarchy or stability but by liberation: 'I am the Lord your God who brought you out of Egypt', that's why 'you shall have no other God but me.' The liberation from slavery is the founding narrative; the Exodus gave the Israelites their faith. As Dorothee Soelle says: They had to know they were liberated before they could know they were created.

So there is this other tradition, the prophetic tradition, with origins in the liberation from slavery and the Exodus, and includes the prophets who develop a narrative of returning to the liberator God. This tradition emphasises radical change – it is unsettling, divisive, exposing oppression, rousing the poor, condemning the rich. Brueggemann argues that this is the tradition in which Jesus locates himself.

So I'm arguing that we should look at the environment not through the theology of creation but through the theology of prophecy – and only then, secondarily, should we look at creation. Our approach to creation should be based not on the originator myths of Genesis, but on the prophetic utopia of 3rd Isaiah, of the new heaven and new earth.

So if we are thinking about the environment through prophetic eyes, we should ask: Who is suffering in the current state of the environment? Who are the oppressed? Who is the oppressor? Who are the environmentally poor?

Bound together through 'relations of actual harm'

The first thing to say about this is that we live in a globalised world. It is impossible to separate ourselves from the poor and oppressed because we are oppressors. The way the global economy is set up means that we cannot help but oppress others through our everyday activities. We may buy fair trade products, environmentally friendly products, we may make ethical decisions in every aspect of our lifestyle, but by being in the world as citizens of a European nation, we oppress. Andrew Dobson, who writes on environmental citizenship, calls this the 'relations of actual harm': the social relationships in which we exist cause actual harm to someone somewhere in the world. We cannot extricate ourselves from this (and even if we did manage to find a way to separate ourselves from all societies and live self-sufficiently in perfect isolation from everyone else, then notwithstanding the legacy of oppression we would take with us, we would also do nothing to challenge this oppression). This is the tragic dilemma of the parable of the talents – using the talents which have been allocated to us enables us to benefit from the exploitation of others, but burying the talents does no good either.

Month 2 Day 12

The second thing to say is that we live in a particular form of globalised world – a neo-liberal one. Neo-liberalism puts the interests of capital above all other interests. It is a breach from the policies of the welfare state, in which most countries accepted a compromise between the interests of economic growth and the welfare of citizens. Neo-liberalism tears this up. The state no longer has the responsibility for the welfare of its citizens. The responsibility of the state is to make things easy for capital accumulation or economic growth. All things must become commodity, to be bought and sold in a marketplace, so that businesses can make profits out of them – or if they don't, they go to the wall. There is a constant striving to turn more things into commodities. Carbon trading is a way of commodifying the atmosphere: companies can buy and sell portions of the global atmospheric carbon cycle.

Neo-liberalism was first experimented with in Latin America by US client dictators and juntas, then was introduced to the UK by Margaret Thatcher, to the US by Ronald Reagan, to Europe, Australia, Japan, the Pacific fringe, and then more recently to India and China, where it is currently leading to massive dispossession and, in India, civil war. The geographer David Harvey points out that, it is not quite true to say that neo-liberalism maximises economic growth. In many places throughout the world, when neo-liberalism was introduced, economic growth was lower than in Keynesian social democracy. The point is, neo-liberalism maximises particular kinds of economic growth: that which benefits the elite class, the owners of the big companies and their allies. So the point of neo-liberalism, to Harvey, is a shift of class power away from working people – who had achieved some influence through the welfare state – to the transnational capitalist class.

So the point is, we live in a time of globalisation but it is the particular form of globalisation which is the problem, the neo-liberal globalisation which puts the interests of the seriously wealthy, who need to find new ways to invest and make money, above the interests of everybody and everything else. But it doesn't have to be like this. Globalisation could mean many things which are in the interests of the poor, the dispossessed, the exploited. That is why the vast majority of movements – the environmental activists, trade unionists, tribal movements, land rights campaigners, peasant groups – who gather to protest at international meetings of the World Trade Organisation or the G8, or who gather themselves at the World Social Forum, call themselves the 'Alter-globalisation Movement' – not anti-globalisation but alternative globalisation, under the banner of 'Another World Is Possible' (which sounds very like a 21st-century secularised translation of 'the Kingdom of God is among you').

Dumping onto the poorest

And thirdly, I want to describe the global economy as based on a logic of dumping. The economy, whether local or global, is essentially a mechanism for extracting materials, turning them into things which we need or want or can use, or into the energy which we need or want or can use, distributing these to us and then disposing of the materials again. At each of the stages in this process, economic decisions are made. We are used to making our decisions as consumers, for example in the selection of commodities which we buy: do we pay that extra premium for the organic vegetables or the fairly traded products? Do we take the environmentally-preferred train to London for £150, or the plane for £50? We make these decisions – I guess we usually choose to pay extra for the ethical choice, if we can afford it. If we can't afford the organic potatoes sometimes we buy the chemically-produced ones and what we are doing is shifting the difference in cost onto the soil whose life is shortened, the contaminated rivers, the workers exposed to the chemicals. We shift costs, not because we are bad but because we can't afford not to.

Well, everybody along this supply chain is making similar choices – and not usually on the basis of ethics. They are making decisions on the basis of a cost-benefit analysis in a competitive environment, constantly looking for ways in which they can make savings in order to stay afloat. So when push comes to shove they try to shift costs off their budget sheet so that the cost-benefit equation comes out better. Shifting costs is part and parcel of the decision-making of economic agents. And costs need to be shifted in as cheap a way as possible – which usually means dumping them onto the poorest: those with least leverage to resist; those who can't buy themselves out of being dumped on; those whose own cost-benefit analysis means that they are so desperate for a job that they will tolerate being dumped on; countries whose foreign investment is predicated on providing a space which is 'safe' for dumping – such as the Special Economic Zones in India, where environmental and labour laws are relaxed in order to attract foreign firms.

So the three things to say about the wider world and the environment are that we are all bound together through 'relations of actual harm', that we live in a neo-liberal form of globalisation in which everything is commodifiable, and that the logic of the economy is one of dumping onto the poorest. In this context, who are the poor? Who are those whose interests are the core of a prophetic vision to which the Iona Community can respond in matters of belief and action in the world?

I want to talk about one group of people who are the environmentally poor in the present day, who some of you will have heard me speak about in the past – the survivors of the Bhopal gas disaster.

Twenty-five years ago, on the night of 2nd-3rd December 1984, toxic methyl isocyanate gas leaked from the Union Carbide insecticide factory in the city of Bhopal. It leaked because of the logic of dumping. The factory was set up by the US company Union Carbide, in the poor sector of the city of Bhopal, to provide insecticides for the new high-yielding crops introduced in the Green Revolution. As sales plateaued, profits were squeezed and savings had to be made. Maintenance was reduced, staff levels were cut, training was diminished, worn parts were replaced with cheaper alternatives, broken monitoring gauges were not replaced at all, refrigerator units were switched off, chemicals stockpiled, expensive safety equipment was removed. And so when water leaked into a tank of gas and started a chemical reaction, there was nothing to stop thousands of people being killed – an estimated 8,000 people in the following few days, some 25,000 to date.

I have had the privilege of working with the survivors who have been campaigning for justice for over 25 years, demanding commensurate compensation, economic rehabilitation and pensions, adequate healthcare, environmental remediation of the factory site and the contaminated water, corporate accountability from the company. But during this time, India got the neo-liberal bug and started doing whatever it could to attract multinational capital to invest in its high-tech corridors, its mineral deposits and its Special Economic Zones. Multinational capital from corporations like Dow Chemicals, which bought Union Carbide. The last thing which the Indian government wants to do is send out a message that such companies could be liable for expensive reparations if an accident happens during its ordinary cost-shifting, dumping activities. After all, one of India's unique selling points is that its population is cheap.

And the chances are, we have all benefited from the production of cheaper food as a result of Dow's pesticides, or nicer-coloured paint on our walls, or car engines which work, or printer's ink or computers or mobile phones – all the accoutrements of modern life in which we are, without much choice, implicated in the 'relations of actual harm'. And all around us, companies are still shifting costs as cheaply as possible – cutting corners, moving operations to India, increasing productivity; putting profit before humanity is an ordinary, everyday activity. As one of the Bhopal campaign slogans puts it 'We all live in Bhopal'.

Starting with prophecy

So, returning to the theological task of looking at the environment through the lens of prophecy, rather than of creation: what implications does this have for our action? Starting with prophecy means that we ask different kinds of questions about the world. What does it mean to look at the environment from the prophetic perspective of the environmentally poor?

When we start with creation, we have a tendency to ask: How can society sustain itself? Sustainable development is the mantra. We need to sustain things more or less as they are. How can we go on like this? How can we keep the lights on?

But when we start with prophecy, we ask a different question: How can society be transformed? How can things be different? How can we make another world possible, an alternative globalisation which isn't based on the logic of dumping? As rich and reluctant oppressors, our lifestyles would not be sustained in such a transformed world.

When we start with creation we ask: What lifestyle choices should I make? How can I make decisions ethically? How best to use the power of choice which I'm blessed with?

But when we start with prophecy, we ask: Where are those who are dumped on resisting? Don't start with those of us who have the power of choice: look at those who have least choice but are still challenging the logic of dumping which they are experiencing most acutely. How do we join them in their struggle?

The creation-focussed starting point asks: How do we become better stewards of our possessions; make sure what we have is environmentally friendly? What should we be doing with what we own the better to make positive impacts on the world?

But the prophetic starting point is: How do we lose our possessions? How can we engage with the world in ways that risk losing what we own? Ending injustice means ending the privileges that we get from being rich in a corrupt, unjust world, privileges like being able to be stewards of our possessions.

Making ethical choices, being good stewards, sustainable development: it is almost inevitable that we will want to support these. But these will never transform the world and the corrupt logic which dumps onto the poor. And the more we focus on our ethical choices, the more we will want to hold on to the privileges which give us the power to make them.

I want to finish with the prophetic insight of 15-year-old Amir, in Bhopal, whose parents were exposed to the gas and whose friends include those born with severe abnormalities: 'What has happened has happened and we can't change that but we will keep on fighting. We want to stop another Bhopal happening elsewhere. Even when we get justice we will keep fighting so that no company feels it can do what Union Carbide did, and nobody else will have to experience what Bhopal has.'

Eurig Scandrett

Eurig Scandrett teaches sociology at Queen Margaret University, Edinburgh. He is coordinator of the Bhopal Survivors' Movement Study and edited Bhopal Survivors Speak: Emergent Voices from a People's Movement: *www.word-power.co.uk*

Month 2 Day 13

COLUMBAN CHRISTIANITY & THE CELTIC TRADITION

Iona: Icon of marginality and engagement

In 2002 I committed a serious act of downward mobility. I resigned a university chair and full professorship in New Testament to live quietly and marginally on a hillside in my home state of West Virginia. I wrote a Rule of life modelled on St Benedict's and accounts of Celtic solitaries. But in spite of careful planning, I wasn't prepared for the jolt of being 'status-less'. When asked the commonest social question 'What do you do?' I had no response but 'Uh, nothing.' I tried saying 'I grow tomatoes', to which people responded, 'Oh, you're a farmer.' How strong is our need to have and give a label!

I could have answered 'anchorite', an unfamiliar word, or 'hermit', which carries heavy baggage. Whatever it's called, 'opting out' elicits strong responses. The most clueless is 'Well, wouldn't that be nice', as if it were self-centred, spiritually sybaritic. The 'look' I get recalls a story of Roman Catholic mothers returning from Mass on the Feast of the Holy Family. 'Didn't Father give a good sermon on family?' asked one. 'Yes, and I wish I knew as little about it as he does,' quipped the other.

People who imagine a life of chosen marginality and solitude is idyllic or escapist haven't tried it. It is what Sr. Jeremy Hall, O.S.B., a hermit for 20 years, calls a life 'of self-emptying openness to God'. 'All too often,' she writes, 'we take refuge in noise or words, sometimes almost unconsciously, to escape from inner abysses and outer tensions that we lack the courage, or … the fundamental honesty, to face.'[1] A solitary or marginal life is demanding, without ordinary 'psychic cushioning'. When you live alone, you live with yourself all the time, unprotected from your darker impulses.

The larger question this choice raises is the one American feminist theologian Rosemary Radford Ruether put to Trappist monk and hermit Thomas Merton in the 1960s.[2] What good is such a life in the face of the world's mammoth problems? Isn't withdrawal basically both useless and self-indulgent? Although the question presumes theological positions I don't hold, it is fair and of interest to the Iona Community which is devoted to balancing work and prayer, social justice and contemplation.

In Benedictine fashion, I make my living by the 'work of my hands'. I write, occasionally speak, give a retreat or spiritual direction – a modern equivalent of the desert mothers' basket-weaving. But how do I address the charge that I have forsaken a useful for a useless life? I hope I am 'fruitfully marginal', although society tends to equate 'marginal' with 'useless', 'unproductive', certainly 'unprofitable'. Society isn't keen on the marginal, not just hermits, but the physically or psychologically chronically ill, the poor or unemployed, refugees, prisoners, the elderly, children, the unborn. But chosen marginality, marginality for freedom and 'connected marginality' can be powerful, if quiet and subtle, Christian 'action'.

Chosen marginality

Consciously chosen marginality bears witness that the way things are is not the way they have to be, certainly not what God intended. It presents the challenge of deliberate irrelevance, of an authentically lived 'counter-cultural lifestyle'. In an informal talk in Calcutta in October, 1968 Merton said: 'The marginal person … calls into question the meaning of life … the office of the monk or the marginal person, the meditative person or the poet, is to go beyond death … to be, therefore, a witness to life.'[3]

This witness is often experienced by observers as a challenge, if not an affront. It raises painful questions. What if we aren't our 'label', professor or farmer, for example? Who am I without the 'identity' conferred by social groups or political party or parish or denomination or all the things I do? Could people who have opted out of mainstream society see something I don't? Marginality frightens people. It suggests something might be seriously wrong with the society, groups and life in which they are heavily invested. The witness of marginality is the challenge to change. And for individuals and societies change is not easy.

Marginality for freedom

One of St Paul's most important assertions occurs in Galatians 5:1: 'For freedom Christ has set us free. Stand firm, therefore, and do not submit again to a yoke of slavery' (NRSV). The marginal Christian understands much of what society passes off as routine and normal is slavery. Merton noted the 4th-century desert Christians (Christianity's paradigmatic marginal people) 'did not believe in letting themselves be passively guided and ruled by a decadent state, and who believed that there was a way of getting along without slavish dependence on accepted, conventional values.'[4] They incurred disapproval because 'the opinions of others had ceased … to be matters of importance. They had no set doctrine about freedom, but they had in fact become free by paying the price of freedom.'[5]

Chosen marginality offers costly, delicious freedom, the fresh perspective that comes from being 'outside the camp'. It is exemplified by the boy who, when everyone else ignored the truth, publically declared 'the king is naked'. When for the sake of Christ's freedom one leaves the camp, it is important not 'to carry the world with you as an implicit standard of comparison' which would only be taking along 'the negative standard of the world one had abandoned'.[6] In order to build God's Kingdom, Jesus needs some people content to be on the world's sidelines, able to see what the players in the game miss. Like Abbot Bessarion's monk, they must be 'all eye' and see with the clarity of one not deeply engaged in the clatter and the clamour of the daily game.

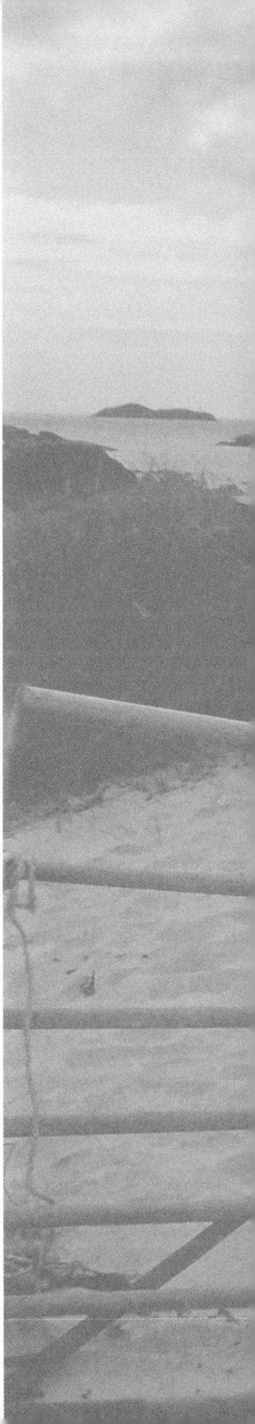

Paradoxically this kind of marginality is 'connected' to what it does not choose, perhaps most tenaciously by the clear-sightedness of its separateness. The desert Christians of the 4th century left the world not 'as though escaping from a wreck', but left 'a world that divided them from themselves' in order to help save it. 'They knew they were helpless to do any good for others as long as they floundered about in the wreckage. But once they got a foothold … they had not only the power but even the obligation to pull the whole world to safety after them.'[7] Isn't this what St Columba did by his self-imposed 'exile' on Iona?

The great paradox of chosen marginality is that one doesn't leave 'the world' and normal social life because one hates it, but because one loves it so much. To love the world without being of the world is a prodigious challenge, but central to the Christian witness of marginality. Sr. Jeremy reminds us that in Jesus 'we see the perfection of … self-emptying openness to God … infinite capacity to serve in love.'[8] Sometimes, as Milton's sonnet 'On His Blindness' so eloquently says, the service is passive, 'to wait'. Indeed, the Psalms and prophets continually admonish us to 'wait on the Lord', but that voice is silenced by the world's noise-makers, its lack of stillness. Bede Griffiths, O.S.B., wrote 'Stillness within one individual can affect society beyond measure.'[9] Earlier, St Seraphim of Sarov had said: 'Keep your heart in peace and a multitude around you will be saved.'

Christian marginality is far from self-indulgent. It is a call to growth in Christ's self-emptying openness. That opening happens in prayer, which is central to the whole enterprise. Our renunciations open inner space. The more open we become, the more space there is for God, and the more deeply we move into the heart of God. We begin to experience what Rabbi Abraham J. Heschel called God's pathos, perhaps even God's broken-heartedness. The marginal Christian's diminishing self-reference and growing freedom and open-heartedness creates a space that God and God's world perfectly fit.

Christian marginality is useless only if prayer is useless. Devoid of any power but that of the crucified God, the open-hearted person is also the broken-hearted person, because, although we don't take the world's standards to the margins with us, we do take the world in its woundedness. Our 'utility' is to love and pray it toward health.

Finally, the solitude, 'oddness' and patience of the marginal Christian images the 'inner plentitude' requisite for all authentic ministry. We know ourselves broken and being healed, sinners and forgiven. We choose environments where we can live in the light of healing Love and constantly reach out toward it in worship, prayer, devotion, stillness, study, trusting that it reaches toward us. Though we remain needy and sinful, we grow in inner freedom and expansiveness, serenity and security – for service, even if it is primarily Miltonian, 'to sit and wait'. The ability to wait characterises marginal people as lines by the homeless shelter and the unemployment office or monastic vigils attest. But 'doing good' from anything less risks using service to fulfil our own needs and devalues the process of love we see enacted in Christ's self-giving passion.

Marginality and Iona

People who choose marginality recognise how easy it is to be dominated by a false self, a world-conditioned ego. They choose not to be shaped and ruled by false values of 'a decadent state'. They recognise they don't have to live under Caesar, knowing that one can 'opt out', and doing so, exercises a radical freedom that ultimately overcomes alienation. It is also to be a 'scary example' of that possibility.

For Love's sake one takes to the margins the world one relinquishes. It is what St Columba did. As a result of his withdrawal to a small rock in the sea, from his marginality, a whole swath of northern Europe became Christian. Quite apart from its beauty, its mysterious natural, vibratory power, Iona is an icon of marginality and engagement. The point of an icon is to invite a step through it into the Reality it reflects. Iona hangs at the edge of the world inviting us to be in but not of it. When we take Iona's history and spirituality seriously, sometimes in reality, mostly metaphorically, we stand on its margins and, like the Macedonian to St Paul, invite others to 'come over and help us'.

Bonnie Thurston

Notes:

1. Sr. Jeremy Hall, O.S.B., Silence, Solitude, Simplicity, Liturgical Press, 2007, p.28

2. Mary Tardiff, OP (ed.), At Home in the World: The Letters of Thomas Merton and Rosemary Radford Ruether, Orbis Press, 1995

3. N.B. Stone, P. Hart & J. Laughlin (eds.), The Asian Journal of Thomas Merton, New Directions, 1968/75, p.306

4. Thomas Merton, Wisdom of the Desert, New Directions, 1960, p.5

5. Merton, Wisdom of the Desert, p.10-11

6. Merton, Wisdom of the Desert, p.22

7. Merton, Wisdom of the Desert, p.23

8. Hall, ibid, p.28

9. Quoted in H.Ward and J. Wild (eds.), The Monastic Way, Eerdmans, 2006, p.135.

Racial justice

Overcoming in Mississippi

'Y'all want grits?' Mr Peters asked me every morning as he put the bacon in the pan, at his house in South Edison, Greenville, Mississippi. It took some courage for Albert Peters to host a young student from Scotland who was helping out with voter registration and the Freedom Schools set up by the Civil Rights 1964 Campaign. White Mississippians were not exactly overjoyed at these 'agitators' who came from the north or elsewhere to support black citizens in establishing their long-denied rights. A local SNCC (Student Non-Violent Coordinating Committee) leader warned me: 'Your Scottish passport won't save you if it gets tough.' But I had nothing more than a few insults hurled at me and a cold feeling in my stomach as we were surrounded by members of the Mississippi State Patrol with menacing guns and huge shades when we went to 'desegregate' a cinema.

It was risky for volunteers and there was already that summer the chilling knowledge that three civil rights workers had 'disappeared'. But we could go home after a few days or weeks. On the other hand, many local African Americans who broke the southern taboos by hosting volunteers that summer had their houses fired on or were victimised by police or vigilantes long after the guests had gone back north.

I don't think that Mr Peters was ever going to be put off by that prospect. At 94 he had seen it all. He was born less than a decade after slavery was abolished and he told me some of his father's

tales. Mr Peters had lived through the reconstruction years and seen the terrible backlash from the Ku Klux Klan when the occupying Northern army withdrew. He had known what it was to get hopes of a better and more just South dashed on the corrosive altars of extreme poverty and racism. He had known some of those who were murdered in the lynching years of the early 20th century. He had learned how to survive the evil system of segregation and he had retained his dignity and never lost his humanity. He had endured all this and more.

Mr Peters was rooted in a very practical and basic (but far from simple) faith which had been honed by over nine decades of struggle. He was a wee bit disappointed that I wasn't a Methodist and quite incredulous that I had never heard of grits! And as he was coming to the end of his life he was determined to do his bit to assist a movement for justice whose fruits he almost certainly wouldn't see. I remember asking him if he was afraid for himself. 'Lawd no, what can they do to me now?' and he laughed, while his mouth revealed a diminished number of teeth.

I thought of my friend Albert Peters when I watched the joy that erupted at Barack Obama's inauguration, listened to the powerful prayer by a veteran of the Montgomery Bus Boycott and heard the President pay tribute to the legacy that was made possible by so many like Mr Peters who refused to accept the place falsely ordained for them by a sick society.

A few days later I reread the last letter I received from him, in September 1965. 'I often think of the pleasant hours we spent together,' he wrote, 'and if we don't ever meet any more in this world, I hope to meet in the great beyond where there is no parting.' I hope so too, and I also hoped on 20 January 2009, that wherever Albert Peters was in 'the great beyond' there was enough technology to enable him to tune in to Washington and to know, like millions of others, that he was part of that journey. 'Those who die on the march will renew their strength. They shall rise up on wings as eagles.' Mr Peters would give a hoarse chuckle at the idea of having wings or being an eagle. But to have been welcomed into the house of one who in his own quiet way said 'yes we can' was and is for me an awesome privilege.

Prayer

We give thanks for all those unrecognised yet heroic people whose steps taken in courage and suffering have paved the way for a better world.

We give thanks for hopes fulfilled after long struggle and for transformation only dreamed about but now made possible.

We give thanks for the privilege of being part of that community of saints whose lives have touched us and left us better for knowing them.

Iain Whyte

Month 2 Day 15

Community

I will leap into love

Over one hundred years ago, two young women encountered one another in Kirkcaldy, an industrial town in Fife. Jean worked in a bottling factory, and attended a Bible class for 'working girls'; Helen was the wife of a local Presbyterian minister, and the Bible class leader. They both believed in God and longed to be faithful Christians, but they disagreed about the right ways to express that faith. Jean loved to dance: in the midst of her difficult and toilsome existence, dancing was a source, and expression, of friendship, excitement and pleasure. Helen believed that dancing was dangerous – even wicked. She told Jean that she must choose, for she could not have both Christ and the dance. Jean replied that she could not give up the dancing. 'Then,' said Helen, 'you must lose your soul.' Very soon after, Jean contracted smallpox and died.

I read that poignant wee story when I was living in Kirkcaldy, and researching the lives of nineteenth-century Scottish Presbyterian women. It is recounted in a book extolling the good works and evangelical fervour of Helen Lockhart Gibson, but it was the image of Jean which haunted me: a woman of spirit, like so many of her Scottish sisters down the ages, who was told that, if she wanted to live a spiritual life, she would have to stop dancing.

I cried for all the Jeans and Helens who have been taught that spirituality cannot be embodied, expressed or celebrated in the glorious energy and rhythm of human dance, because in my own life, dancing has been, not just a powerful image or analogy for encounter with God, but real, sweaty, breathless, embodied, laughing experiences of profound connection – with my own self, with other people and with God.

Many religious traditions have, of course, used physical, expressive movement in the context of worship. I am glad that the Christian church is beginning to value liturgical and circle dancing as good ways to use and give thanks for all our senses. But that's not what I mean. In fact, I have to make a confession that sometimes, while participating in earnest and meaningful liturgical movement, a wee voice pipes up from either my feet or my gut, subversively asking, 'Yes, but when will the real dancing start?'

The real dancing, for me, happens at village hall ceilidhs and Hogmanay parties; in nightclubs and school discos. It's Gene Kelly and *West Side Story*; it's tango and salsa. It's the spectacle and beauty of ballet; it's the purpose and exuberance of South African township crowds. Real dancing is rooted – earthed in and nourished by diverse human cultures and traditions; but it is also dynamic – living and growing and reaching for the skies of human possibility. It can be sexual and intimate (and that is part of its thrill and universality) but dancing can also be a wonderful affirmation of inclusion, overcoming difference or awkwardness with humour and warmth. Real dancing can require intense discipline (even pain); attention to our own bodies and how they move, and concentrated cooperation with partners; it can also be playful, anarchic and unruly. Real dancing is movement, achievement, friendship, surprise, transformation, celebration. I have danced with young people and old people; with men and women; with folk of all ages, nationalities, circumstances and backgrounds; with graceful experts, and with those who have at least two left feet. Recently a lot of my dancing has been done (on Iona) with my young sons: we have discovered entirely new ways to Strip the Willow!

A community which dances is a community of spirit, which knows the need to affirm connections between self and larger reality; which knows the need to create spaces of energy, passion and delight, in the midst of hardship, pain or tedium; which knows that struggles for survival and justice will be afflicted by rigor mortis, if not enlivened by the breath of celebration. I am with Emma Goldman and Rosa Luxembourg – it's not my revolution if I can't dance to it. I have never been comfortable with the word 'spirituality', which somehow suggests an abstract package of acceptable religious behaviour. But I believe that I am a human being of spirit, animated and emboldened by a loving, creative God. I choose life, and Christ, for my partners in the dance. I believe and pray that my soul is not lost, but is embraced and challenged by that choice. For the potent language of dance has offered a vision and foretaste of God's promised community: the mystic connections of material and sacred; immanence and transcendence, which Mechtild of Magdeburg expressed beautifully in this medieval hymn of praise:

I cannot dance, O Lord
unless you lead me.
If you wish me to leap joyfully
let me see you dance and sing.

Then I will leap into Love
and from Love into Knowledge
and from Knowledge into the Harvest,
that sweetest Fruit beyond human sense.
There I will stay with you, whirling …

Lesley Orr

Pilgrimage

Through all these things

Whan that Aprill with his showres soote
The droghte of March hath perced to the roote …
Thanne longen folk to goon on pilgrimages

From the 'General Prologue', *Canterbury Tales*

But, having taken that plunge, how exactly *does* one pass the time on a pilgrimage? When I did my first Iona pilgrimage, back in 1996, I had no way of knowing whether it would be my only one, and so I was keen to adopt some sort of 'spiritual discipline' as I walked, in order to 'maximise the experience', as it were. I attempted to do this at a mental, rather than a physical level – something I hoped might perhaps be equivalent in effect to, but slightly less uncomfortable than, walking barefoot up Croagh Patrick! Thirteen years and many pilgrimages later, experience has taught me that while engaging in some sort of pilgrimage discipline can indeed be fruitful, there are many different ways in which it can be done. So … here are three different disciplines which I've tried to adopt, on occasion, to enable me to approach the pilgrimage mindfully, and which I've found to be helpful and rewarding. Of course it's not the case that doing one excludes other possibilities – often, in the end, a mixture of elements becomes involved.

Whilst on assorted pilgrimages through Japan in the 17th century, the Zen monk Matsuo Basho distilled the essence of what he saw, smelled and touched, the conversations and encounters of his journeys, and the deeper mysteries he sensed through all of these, into various poetic forms. Whilst writing haiku (a three-line poem of 5, 7 and 5 syllables respectively) is not necessarily everyone's forte, I've found that the process of trying to identify and articulate a key element from each of the stops en route around the island can be a really helpful way of focussing my thoughts, and of translating the pilgrimage experience from being merely(!) a very enjoyable and informative amble round the island, into a richly rewarding and sometimes life-changing journey. At each stopping place, I try to pick up one thing – maybe a phrase or a particular image – from the talk/meditation/prayer that is offered, and then, for at least part of the walk to the next station, turn it over in my mind and search for the heart of it. There seems to be something about the rhythm of walking itself which is very conducive to this sort of rumination. I'll try (or at least begin) to compose and scribble down a short prayer or meditation, a single sentence or maybe even a haiku, to capture and contain this insight so that I can remember it and return to it later for further thought. Of course there are different ways of doing this recording, by no means all limited to the textual – I happen to choose words because I'm hopeless at art! Often I've found that, when doing this, distinct themes and connections become apparent and the pilgrimage develops its own very specific and coherent narrative. I've also found that I remember these distilled insights, and carry on working at and benefiting from them long after the physical pilgrimage itself has ended.

But while this sort of mentally-disciplined approach can be a helpful one to adopt, I also sometimes choose to go with a much more 'unfocussed eye'. The Welsh priest-poet Euros Bowen, in his poem 'Litter Stick', compares the poet to a man picking up discarded bits of paper with a pointed stick, noting how, through what his eye rests on, the poet's mind is *'picking up an image here/and lifting an image there/and … putting them out of sight/in the sack on his back'*. I think that this too can be a good way to approach the pilgrimage: Simply letting its various sensations – sights, sounds and smells; words, patterns and textures – settle into the subconscious can be a good way to enjoy its gifts and realise their potential more fully. In this instance, I think it's more a case of consciously and deliberately giving oneself up to the physical and emotional experiences of the day – whether that be a soaking from the rain, the feel of pebbles under bare feet in Columba's Bay, the pleasures or difficulties of conversation, the thrill of seeing an unknown wildflower or a new vista, the sensations of achievement or exhaustion, etc – and embracing and accepting them without any great attempt at dissection or analysis, before letting them sink down into the subconscious. It may be that later you recall them and consciously evaluate or make sense of them; it may be that they remain hidden for a while, but are at work shaping your thinking and living, or enabling you to make different connections between things. I've also found that sometimes they resurface unbidden as an epiphanic moment, when you suddenly see the world differently. And who knows, they might even reappear as a poem!

Of course Chaucer's pilgrims famously told one another tales and this is also often a feature of the Iona pilgrimage – although those one hears tend to be more autobiographical. So my third approach is to go expecting and ready to share in any conversations that the day brings, and to not be afraid to share stories of my own. Sometimes I think this exchange flows directly from the *comunitas* which has already begun to develop as guests share work and worship at the Community centres. Sometimes, it seems that something about the rhythm of walking along side by side, or the act of helping someone negotiate a bog or scramble over stones, breaks down the barriers we put up to hide behind, and one finds oneself in deep and personal conversation with relative or even total strangers. Such encounters may be brief, soon curtailed by the inevitable shifts in groupings which occur as one walks; sometimes conversational threads are taken up, on and off throughout the day, becoming richer (and sometimes more heated) as they draw on what's been seen, said and shared during the course of the walk. For me, some of these conversations, begun with almost total strangers, have become the basis of enduring and supportive friendships. Others have been the locus of new insights, or have provided the starting point for the development of new understandings. Still others have taught me things about myself ... and about my own shortcomings! In some ways, I've found this sharing of stories to be one of the most richly rewarding ways of passing the time on the pilgrimage. It is also, I believe, through the demands it makes on our ability to both give and receive hospitality, as much of a proper spiritual discipline for pilgrimage as any amount of inward rumination.

At the end of the day though, the pilgrimage round Iona can be engaged with and enjoyed on many different levels. For me it's been a place where I've learned much about Iona's history, geography and geology; where I've enjoyed the natural world – wildflowers I'd never before seen, hearing the rasping song of the corncrake, taking in glorious scenery and enjoying invigorating weather of every shape and form. It's also been a journey on which I discovered more about God, about my fellow-travellers and about myself, although the lessons have sometimes been hard ones.

And through all of these things, my life has been expanded and enriched.

Pat Bennett

Month 2 Day 17

Sexuality

God's wide embrace: what is 'natural' and what is 'in Christ'

WALKING WITH THE SPIRIT

Jesus lambasted the scribes and Pharisees for being meticulous about paying tithes while neglecting *'the weightier matters of the Law: justice and mercy and faith'.* The church must always take care not to fall into some similar error, through fastening on one controversial subject and neglecting 'weightier matters' – even risking dividing the church on a matter which is not central to Christian faith.

The Mosaic Law condemned homosexuality. What are we to make of that?

Who said not to adopt ideas and practices just because they appear in the Bible (in that day, the Old Testament)? On the Emmaus road, Jesus walked some miles with two disciples who were thoroughly versed in the scriptures. They were told not to take the contents at face value but to sort out what in them belonged to his way – that alone had weight. The Holy Spirit would convey, to those who sought light, what belonged to his way and what did not. That left plenty of the Old Testament which was shown to be not of his way!

Jesus emphasised the newness of the Gospel, which required a fresh approach: *'You have heard what the old-timers say … but this is what I say to you …'* (Matthew 5:21–48). His was a position of authority which could affirm or disown elements of Old Testament teaching. We are called to sift out from the old writings what we should follow and what reject, guided by the Spirit who will work with us to reveal the mind of Christ.

Those who say that they believe in the Bible as it is, from cover to cover, delude themselves. It is impossible to hold that the way to deal with enemies is to get their infants and bash them against a rock (Psalm 137:8–9) and at the same time hold that we should love them and do good to them (Luke 6:27). A choice has to be made between Jesus' way and that of others.

In the Mosaic Law, homosexuality is explicitly forbidden: *'You shall not lie with a male as with a woman; it is an abomination.'* Yet when barriers to the Aaronic priesthood are listed, homosexuality is not included – and there are plenty other barriers! *'The Lord spoke to Moses, saying: Speak to Aaron and say: No one who has a blemish shall draw near, one who is blind or lame or one who has a mutilated face or a limb too long; or one who has a broken foot or broken hand; or a hunchback or a dwarf or a man with a blemish in his eyes or an itching disease or scabs or damaged testicles. No descendant of Aaron the priest who has a blemish shall come to offer the Lord's offering ...'* (Leviticus 21:16–21).

We have no right to pick out what we want from the Mosaic dispensation. In for a penny, in for a pound. We would have to adopt all the cleansing rituals – including that of women after childbirth (as if that made her unclean!), refusing to acquire shirts or blouses made of different fibres (such as cotton and 'man-made'), to name but two prohibitions. What we are called to do is to select what belongs to Jesus Christ's way and what does not – we must walk with the Spirit along our own Emmaus road.

DEALING WITH 'NATURAL' REACTIONS

In the New Testament, Paul will shift gear at times. He will argue from what is considered to be 'natural' in place of what is theologically valid. Lesbianism and homosexuality are a case in point. In the letter to the Romans he gives vent to his own aversion and disgust: *'Their women changed natural intercourse for unnatural; and in the same way also the men, giving up natural intercourse with women, became consumed with passion for one another. Men committed shameless acts with men, and received in their own persons the due penalty of their error'* (Romans 1:26–27).

What is deemed 'natural' or 'unnatural' refers to common social understanding of appropriate and inappropriate attitudes and conduct. These change from time to time and vary from culture to culture. Paul here deals with conformity to social and traditional norms as they were at that time. He also deals in the same categories when he addresses the question of women's hair – treated as having significance according to its length. The low status of women socially was marked at public worship by their wearing a veil or a hood – or at least having long hair as a covering. The tradition Paul faced is described thus: *'Any man who prays or prophesies with something on his head disgraces his head, but any woman who prays or prophesies with her head unveiled disgraces her head – it is one and the same thing as having her head shaved'* (the mark of an adulteress) (1 Corinthians 11:4–5).

Paul gets his knickers in a twist trying to deal with the situation on the basis of what is and is not natural. He seems to be impatient at being diverted from 'weightier matters'; and shows an awareness, at the end, of the weakness of the argument he develops.

It starts with the assumption that the husband is the head of the wife whom, in that society, he was assumed to own. Taking it at that level he asks what may naturally be looked for: *'Does not nature itself teach you if a man wears long hair, it is degrading to him, but if a woman has long hair, it is her glory?'* (1 Corinthians 11:14-15). He finishes lamely, as if unconvinced by his own thinking based on what is natural and unnatural: *'But if someone is disposed to contest this – we have no such custom, nor do the churches of God'* (1 Corinthians 11:16).

When Paul uses categories of 'natural' and 'unnatural' he is ill at ease compared with times when he develops a theological basis. No wonder! What professional male footballers or musicians or painters would consider long hair to be a disgrace? My mother thought that it was natural for men to smoke but unnatural for women; natural for men to wear trousers, unnatural for women. Times change. What is considered natural today will sound strange tomorrow.

ON BEING 'IN CHRIST'

Paul changes back to the gear which urges his life forward, asking what it means to be 'in Christ'.

Aversions may lead to understandable antipathy but must not provide the final standing ground of Christians.

Paul drives his theological thinking forward to deal with different forms of natural repugnance, relating these to the claim on Christians to guide their conduct by what it means to be 'in Christ':

'As many of you as were baptised into Christ have clothed yourselves with Christ. There is no longer Jew or Greek, no longer slave or free, no longer male and female – all of you are one in Christ Jesus' (Galatians 3:27–28).

Examples of overturning particular repulsions may be examined more closely:

Jew and Greek (or Gentile)

Peter's meeting with Cornelius (in Acts 10) was decisively influenced by a trance in which he saw a large sheet coming down, filled with every manner of beast and bird. The command came to kill and eat. Peter responded that he had never eaten anything which was profane or unclean. The voice of the Lord came: *'What God made clean you must not call profane.'* This happened three times and prepared Peter for a meeting with emissaries from Cornelius, that *'devout man who feared God with all his household'*. It led to Peter championing the cause of the reception of Gentiles into the church, with minor restrictions, at the first Council of the Church in Jerusalem (though Peter later went back on his own commitment and had to be put right by Paul).

The snag was that a party had been putting pressure on the church to make the sign of circumcision applicable to Gentiles when they became members of the church. Their case seemed logical but would have made Christianity a sect of Judaism in place of a world faith. The argument went: since Christian faith has its roots in God's work recorded in the Old Testament, the sign of that belonging, circumcision, should be adopted to confirm the reality. Paul contended that the sign was nothing in itself – it merely stood for allegiance to God. Gentiles who gave their allegiance to God did not need what would have been a constricting sign. True circumcision has to do with what we believe and how we live that out: *'real circumcision is a matter of the heart'* (Romans 2:29). *'In Christ Jesus neither circumcision nor uncircumcision counts for anything. The only thing that counts is faith working through love'* (Galatians 5:6).

Slave and free

Paul at no point directly challenges the practice of slavery. But there are hints in his dealing with Onesimus, a runaway slave of his master Philemon, a Christian. Paul commends to Philemon's love this man who has become a brother in Christ, in a letter on his return to his master's household. He does not tell Philemon how to establish a new relationship – which might result in the slave being freed. He simply says: *'Perhaps this is the reason he was separated from you for a while, so that you might have him back for ever, no longer as a slave but as more than a slave, a beloved brother'* (Philemon 15,16).

Male and female

Jesus had given full human status to women. In his meeting with them they were given dignity and place. This also governs his dealing with the antipathy of Jews towards Samaritans. The Woman at the Well whom he met in passing through Samaria became a missionary as a result of that encounter. The parable of the good Samaritan emphasised the need to appreciate and value underlying compassionate human characteristics instead of giving a stereotyped judgement.

Jesus' resurrection featured a turn-up for the male books. Would he appear first to Peter personally? He appeared to Mary Magdalene. Would he entrust the primary witness to his resurrection to the band of apostles? He did so to a small group of women bent on anointing his body, whose word would not have stood up in court!

The church had to deal with the phenomenon that women might be leaders in the small house churches which sprouted vigorously after Pentecost, and that they did not keep silence in public worship, as was supposed to be appropriate for their low station, but prayed and prophesied with the men.

We can trace a male backlash.

Three points are worth noting:

1. In 1 Corinthians 14:33–36 it is asserted that women should keep silent in church. For one thing, this text looks like an insertion which does not belong. The flow of argument moves straight from verse 32 to verse 37, and it can be bracketed to show this, e.g. in the New Revised Standard Version. For another it contradicts what Paul says earlier in 1 Corinthians 11:5: that it was accepted practice for women to pray and prophesy.

2. When Paul quotes the tradition conveyed to him, the full story as it is set out

in the Synoptic Gospels has been tampered with to reassert male dominance. It is said that Christ appeared to Peter and then to the Twelve, etc. The women had been airbrushed out (1 Corinthians 15:3–9).

3. Two old chestnuts appear in 1 Timothy: that man was first created and only thereafter woman. Accordingly, the male is superior to the female. The writer (not Paul but one of the school of Paul) also resorts to the old trick of reducing the parable of Adam (in Hebrew a collective word for mankind) and Eve ('Life-force', womankind) and a talking serpent to focus on the eating and sharing of forbidden fruit.

Take the whole narrative in Genesis and Eve comes out as much the stronger character. Adam is depicted as being constituted from earth brought alive by God's inbreathing – Eve was formed out of entirely *human* material. There was a reversal of the widely common understanding that the woman should go to where the man is to consummate union. The narrative says: *'Therefore the man leaves his father and mother and attaches himself to his wife and they become one.'* When the temptation is depicted, Eve at least corrects the serpent – there was only one tree which was forbidden. Adam turned out to be just an unprotesting fall guy. The witness of Genesis is that God chose us to be trustees of his purpose and stewards of his creation, women and men in their togetherness. The New Testament way of saying this is 'all one in Christ Jesus'.

HOMOSEXUALITY IN THIS CONTEXT

Jew and Greek, slave and free, male and female are representative of different types of persons whose beings and actions might produce revulsion in others. But what matters is

not what is 'natural' but what is 'in Christ'. That should determine their treatment.

The letter to the Romans, in which Paul shares the reaction of abhorrence he has with regard to homosexuality, was written around 57 AD. We see Paul clarifying his mind in the next five years or so, so that in the letter to the Colossians in the early 60s he broadens out his understanding of how people regarded as unacceptable are to be treated once they are seen to be 'in Christ': '*... you have stripped off the old self with the practices and have clothed yourselves with the new self, which is being renewed in knowledge according to the image of its creator. In this renewal there is no longer Greek and Jew, circumcised and uncircumcised, barbarian, Scythian, slave or free; but Christ is all and in all*' (Colossians 3:9–11).

Jesus said: *'The things I do you are to do also; and greater things than these shall you do because I go to the Father.'*

We are meant to build on and extend the understanding of what being 'in Christ' means for different types of people in different stages of history – the Colossians statement begins that process. Homosexuality is not means for fingering noses at society. It belongs to the makeup of a considerable number of the human race, created by God in the image of God. Traces of different orientations can be discerned in the womb. They are native to the selfhood of some human beings, not adopted by them. Samaritans, tax-gatherers such as Zaccheus, sinners, physical and social lepers are in Christ given new status and we are called to treat them accordingly.

But to leave it at that would be too ungenerous. We need to go further to see gays and lesbians who are Christians as a special treasure to enhance the life of the church. They provide witness to the fact that the church is to be an inclusive community, embracing especially those on whom sections of society frowns, where all excluded are given a welcome and a significant place at all levels of service in the church.

Month 2 Day 17

God's wide embrace

All sorts and shapes and sizes
in Christ the Lord belong:
lives spent in joyful praising,
the mute without a song,
the wayward and conformist,
the meek and mild, the strong.

Samaritans and heathen
Christ called into his fold;
he saw in little children
the Kingdom way unfold,
in those despised, disparaged
discerning Kingdom-gold.

The bachelor and spinster,
the partner and the spouse,
the straight and gay, whose natures
God's providence allows,
are all made in God's likeness:
to one God pay their vows.

We're one in Christ our Master,
a holy, hallowed race
in whom all rainbow people
are due a welcome-space,
all sorts and shapes and sizes
caught in God's wide embrace.

Ian M. Fraser

HEALING

Cracking up

A good laugh? A life-changing transition? A destabilisation of the ego? Just a joke among friends, or maybe a cataclysmic cosmic shake-up. What does 'cracking up' mean to you?

I woke up one August morning, some few weeks ago, to find myself transplanted. I felt I had been plucked out of a world where I shared my time between a lively English market town and a series of international airports, and dropped down in the wilds of Ayrshire, where all I can see is cows.

What happened? Not exactly an earth-shattering event, just a house move that I expected to be reasonably routine, given that I spend much of my life 'on the road' in any case. Where I hang my hat shouldn't matter too much, and in any case I have Scottish genes, so why do I feel so dislocated, and why would the feeling of 'cracking up' come to mind?

What a wonderfully ambiguous phrase that is! Visions of crumbling buildings and shaken certainties come to mind, but so do images of omelettes, which of course depend for their very existence on cracked-upness. Could that be true for us as well? Having just come through several years of painful transitions in various contexts, I am beginning to think that I, and perhaps the whole human family, will only move deeper into God's dream of all we can become, if we surrender to a bit of cracking up. That, of course, seems to run counter to the conventional religious language, which says a lot about being 'saved'. I wonder why that is? The song 'The Rose' reminds us that 'it's the heart afraid of breaking that never learns to dance'. Is it true that the 'breaking times' in our lives are in fact the points of growth? If so, why do we make such efforts to avoid them? The whole matter of being 'saved' has led me to ask myself: 'Do I want to save my life, or spend it?' Church language keeps on about the saving. Jesus seems to do nothing but spend himself. Why can't I quite connect the two?

In a wonderful Good Friday TV programme some years ago, John Bell interviewed a South African woman who was running an orphanage for the children of HIV/AIDS victims. Asked what legacy she hoped her life would leave for the world, she answered: *'I hope that when I die I shall have completely spent every gift God has given me, and I shall leave nothing behind me but a footprint.'* Life is a gift, and gifts are for spending. Jesus even warns us that anyone who tries to save their life will lose it, but those who are willing to spend themselves will find themselves. To spend ourselves we are going to have to get cracked open. And that usually won't be very comfortable.

Cracking up happens during transitions that pitch us into new situations, sometimes chosen, sometimes not, but always challenging. Times like these shake us up like a kaleidoscope, and bring the pieces down in a different order – a new pattern that we hardly recognise as ours. They destabilise our ego. None of us expects that. None of us wants it. But I guess all of us need it. I know I do, and if I doubted that, some of the issues that have demanded my attention during these years of transition have made it very clear that my ego is still fighting fit and not easily knocked out.

The nursery rhyme reminds us that Humpty Dumpty is a very accident-prone kind of egg. He was there when the first-generation stars met their spectacular supernova ends, and cracked open in explosions that released all the elements that would eventually make us. He has been particularly vulnerable to the forces of gravity recently, not just in my personal journey, but in our collective human journey. He has tumbled off the wall of ecclesiastical complacency in the face of abuse and other scandals. He has tumbled off the wall of predictable weather patterns. He has even fallen off Wall Street itself. But suppose, just suppose, that the resulting mess isn't the end of something, but an invitation to make a new beginning. Suppose these eggs haven't just broken – but have hatched! What kind of chicks might be emerging? Fresh ways of being church? Enlightened financial systems based on a more just and fair distribution of the world's wealth? Creative and non-violent solutions to world conflicts?

An invitation to use our collective intelligence to stop exploiting our planet and to work co-creatively with her instead? These chicks are still very fragile, but they are there because the eggs have cracked up and given them a chance at life.

How can we nourish them, so that their potential becomes a reality in our world?

But cracking up doesn't always have to be so heavy. We crack up in laughter too, and laughter is a wonderful midwife of new thoughts and new possibilities. Laughter can crack open our sorrows and give us a new perspective. Two friends of mine lost a dear friend suddenly and prematurely, and were broken in sorrow for her passing. They planted daffodil bulbs at her grave, and grieved for her all winter. In spring they went back to her grave, to discover an abundant crop of – onions! They cracked up. They laughed until the tears came and they swear that they heard their friend laughing along with them.

God has to have a sense of humour, and, more immediately, Jesus too! Why do we sit so solemnly through all those stories about trying to take a splinter out of someone's eye when you have a plank in your own, or about camels crawling through the eyes of needles. So many ridiculously exaggerated and caricatured situations that no one could forget – and we sit po-faced through it all. That must make God cringe! Look again – can't you see the tongue in Jesus' cheek? Or even the cheek in Jesus' tongue?

Something ridiculous that cracks us up can clear out some holy cobwebs and take us to fresh understandings of the immanent power of this man who leads us to God. In the midst of my own post-move disorientation I cracked up over a card I found in a Glasgow store. It had a picture of Jesus standing on the hillside, while a young boy solemnly offered him a basket of loaves and fishes. The picture could have been straight out of a Children's Illustrated Bible. And the caption? 'No. Mine was the herb-crusted cod with rocket and parmesan salad.'!

Let's not be so afraid of cracking up. It may be the best thing that ever happens to us, as we follow the one who cracked open the veil of the temple to lead us all through it and beyond it.

Margaret Silf

Month 2 Day 19

Social Action

Planting potatoes

April 4th 1984, the anniversary of the death of Martin Luther King. Faslane Peace camp, already over a year old, had planned an action to reclaim the land fenced in at Faslane, now used as a base for the UK's nuclear death machines. The idea was for as many groups as possible to converge secretly around the perimeter and, at the appointed time, to cut the fence and reclaim the land for peace.

Our group, the Gareloch Hortis, was very new. We had all done a non-violence training together in Glasgow and were keen and ready for action – even if our mouths were dry and our knees knocking with nervousness. For us it was a big, big thing to cross the boundary from law-abiding citizenship to responsible civil disobedience.

We had brought with us a big sack of potatoes which we wanted to plant inside the base as a symbol of growing food for the world rather than nuclear destruction. We wanted to reclaim the land from death to life.

At the appointed time, a quick, desperate snipping of bolt-cutters allowed seven of us to squeeze through the gap made in a chain-link fence. Hurry, hurry to get the task done. Out with the shovels and spades and forks, and then plant random rows of potatoes in the turned-up soil. Still no police!

And so we had time; time to look around, stop, reflect and rejoice in what we'd done. Joy, defiance, pride all grew in us as we stood by our reclaimed land waiting for our first-ever arrest.

Our voices rose in song:

'You say this land is out of bounds,
our lives and our futures are out of our hands.
This earth is not yours to put boundaries around.
We'll grow, we'll get stronger, our voices resound.'

Helen Steven

Month 2 Day 20

Church Renewal

Seek and ye shall find ... confessions of a church searcher

In 2006 I moved to Glasgow for work for eighteen months. I was in a new city and wanted to settle into a church. But how, in such a big city, could I find a church that suited me? Did I need to push my boundaries and go beyond my Church of Scotland roots? Was this a chance to step beyond my spiritual comfort zone? Could I find a church that could provide a sense of community and fellowship for a new guy in town?

I didn't know Glasgow well, and so armed with just a couple of recommendations and the wonder that is Google, I searched around for some churches and began visiting them for Sunday worship.

Glasgow, as you might imagine for such a big place, has a wealth of churches, from those that meet in some of the city's most historic and famous buildings, to more modest, low-key, even hidden communities. I cast my net wide and visited Church of Scotlands, Baptist churches, Anglican churches, Pentecostal churches and even a Roman Catholic church in my search for a community.

I went with an open mind and a prayerful heart, keen not to prejudge and keen to soak up whatever teaching, friendship or guidance might be provided. And boy – were the results varied!

I experienced sensationally dull sermons that lasted an ice age and were delivered by preachers with minimal public speaking ability, I met all sorts of wonderful people, faced rugby scrums of welcome teams in some of the more exuberant churches, but more often entered, experienced and left churches without a soul speaking to me.

The diversity of church experiences was a highlight – from the most traditional churches to some of the recent waves of post-modern church groups – and I found myself reassessing my own view of what a church needed; and what role I as an individual might play within it.

I reflected on these thoughts on my blog as my search continued, and as my reflections weren't always positive, so neither were the comments I received from disgruntled church members. But I was glad I could at least be accountable for my words and perhaps help churches understand how they were seen by an outsider visiting for the first time.

On my first visit to an Episcopal church in the city's West End, I found a lively, young, vibrant community, with very engaging worship and powerful preaching. I wanted to like the place.

But astonishingly, nobody spoke to me. I was clearly new, and the church was full, so I was near plenty of folk who could have and should have spoken to me. But none did, even when I stood like a lemon holding a cup of post-service tea wondering whether I was invisible.

How could a church that seemed so full of life be so blatantly unwelcoming?

And so I wrote that on my blog, only to be e-mailed within a few days by a very apologetic Rector saying that he'd read my blog and spoken about my comments with the church's welcome team. I later discovered my honest review had led to quite a debate within the congregation about how they treated visitors.

That in mind, I visited a second time some weeks later, and intriguingly, at the very last minute, a young woman shot into the church and sat next to me, in one of the very few spare seats. Looking around rather terrified at the opulent interior, she muttered to me, 'Is this a Roman Catholic church?'

We began talking, and it turned out she'd never been to anything other than a traditional Church of Scotland. I could empathise and began telling her a little about what I knew of the church in which we both sat. The unwelcomed had become the welcomer; and I pointed out the irony of this to the Rector when I introduced myself after the service. I told him I'd be there again in the evening.

And so it was a few hours later that I found myself back in the church before the evening service began, sitting quite far way from anyone else, just thinking and praying.

I surmised that the search – now several weeks old – ought to come to an end at some point, that I needed to become a part of a community and settle down into a church, wherever it would be. I prayed that God would provide me with some direction, with a sign of where he wanted me to be. I lifted my head to look at the screen on the stage, and there beneath the week's intimations scrolled the words:

Welcome, Simon Varwell

An instantly answered prayer if ever there was one. It turned out that, after the morning service, the Rector had spoken to the guy doing the visuals, little knowing that it would appear to me as a divine indication of where I was supposed to be.

Clearly my church search was over and this was where I belonged. I settled well, made many great friends and grew more deeply in my faith.

Some months later, I was asked to join the welcome team – I could hardly say no.

Simon Varwell

Month 2 Day 21

Worship

The candle we light ...

is more than itself.

It's a flame of many memories:
a lifetime of relationship:
lover, partner, husband, wife,
brother, sister, parent, child.

It's the fragile flicker of chance
that makes encounters
into friendships.

It's the touch of a lover,
the smile of a neighbour,

a child who puts a hand in mine
silently telling me
there is tomorrow
and all will be well.

It's a drench of fresh rain,
a garden of sunflowers,
impish daisies
that come from nowhere,
a good meal,
a cat to stroke,
a cup of clear water,
the last rays of the setting sun.

Where cure is impossible;
it's healing and peace.
It's closeness in loneliness,
comfort in mourning,
love to share.

It's a farewell
to the one who has died
and a yes of breath to the living.

It's the ripeness and wholeness
of all beginnings and endings.

We light the candle
to let go shattered dreams
and all that might have been
into the dark space,
into the greater hope.

This moment of shining
in a tiny bit of the darkness
is hope, prayer, blessing.

It will burn itself out
but never die.

I do not know what resurrection is
but I believe it comes quietly
in moments of light
where love is strong
to bear regrets
and banish fears.
And for now
that is enough.

Joy Mead

Called to be One

The crossing

For twenty years that nameless death
– the details grinding the soul –
Hung in silent memory.

All night he hung
Nicked with knives
In the empty mill
Wrung back to consciousness
When mercy intervened.

Towards dawn
A woman waking on the other side
Heard the shriek –
Eloi. Kill me.

They found the body
The throat cut
Beside the dustbins
Wet with rain.
Someone counted the wounds –
Over two hundred.
It was part of the job.

For twenty years that nameless night
Crossed with our fear.

One day the new neighbour told
Of the mild bachelor
Who mended the widow's latch
And wandered homewards
Taking a pint in a safe bar.
His last Eucharist.

'They killed my two uncles.
Tim they shot. Frank, that was worse.'

Christ, hanging in a tilting world,
Was your pain briefer?
Or was the mill your olive-press that night?

Rosemary Power

In memory of a victim of sectarian abduction, taken to a deserted mill on the Belfast 'peaceline' before being murdered. Northern Ireland currently has a process to explore the past.

Mission

Kissing the leprosy sufferer clean

'Will you kiss the leper clean,
And do such as this unseen,
And admit to what I mean
In you and you in me? . . .'

These familiar lines come from that splendid hymn by John Bell and Graham Maule, which begins 'Will you come and follow me?'. But no amount of kissing will ever cure a leprosy sufferer. If we're going to sing these words and mean them, they need to be understood in a different, non-literal way.

The rabbis said that the healing of leprosy was 'as difficult as raising the dead'. Throughout most of human existence, leprosy was incurable. So when St Mark reports that Jesus healed a man with leprosy (Mark 1:40–42), he was declaring a miracle, the power of God at work in Jesus' person. In Jesus' day, and right into the 20th century, the only thing society could do was protect itself from people with the disease. St Luke tells of an encounter Jesus had with ten men suffering from leprosy – ten because the only human contact they were allowed was with fellow sufferers (Luke 17:11–19). In later centuries, 'colonies' were established in which, by law, leprosy sufferers were obliged to stay. Well-known examples are the islands of Spinalonga, off the coast of Crete, and Molokai, in the Hawaiian archipelago, associated with the devoted ministry of Father Damian among the leprosy sufferers of these islands. Such colonies still exist today – in India (where there are about 1,000), China, Romania, Egypt, Vietnam and Japan.

Inspired by the example of Jesus, there have always been people who have cared for leprosy sufferers with great compassion and courage. The Leprosy Mission, whose symbol is a stylised version of the man in the St Mark story kneeling at Jesus' feet, was founded in 1874. Doctors and nurses served faithfully, metaphorically seeking to 'kiss the leper clean'. But there was no cure. However, at almost the same time, things were beginning to change.

In 1873, a Norwegian chemist, H.H.A. Hansen, working in Bergen, first identified the cause of leprosy – the mycobacterium leprae, making it the first bacterium to be identified as causing disease in humans. And that discovery has been of the utmost importance. Leprosy is a disease – not a punishment from God. In leprosy circles now, the word 'leper' is not often used; for a leprosy sufferer, the word 'leper' defines his or her whole being in terms of a disease, and that attitude is exactly what has to be changed.

This disease is not hereditary. It is not contagious. You can kiss the leprosy sufferer, or shake his hand, or bathe her sores, without any risk of contracting leprosy. It is infectious, spread by airborne droplets from the nose. But is not very infectious, being in fact the least infectious of all communicable diseases. Around 95% of the world's population are naturally immune. There are no 'leprosy epidemics'.

The discovery of the bacterium eventually led, in the 1940s, to the development of a drug called dapsone, which was very effective in curing the disease. However, so much was used that by the 1960s, the bacterium had become resistant to it and incidences of leprosy began to increase. Then in the 1980s, Indian scientists developed a cocktail of drugs – dapsone, clofazimine and rifampicin – which is now in standard use. This multi-drug therapy (MDT) cures people with leprosy. After a short treatment with MDT, a leprosy sufferer is no longer infectious, and if caught early enough, there are no signs that the person ever had the disease. But it's a big 'if'.

The leprosy bacterium, once inside the body, inhabits the body's cool areas, just below the skin, principally the feet and legs, hands and arms, and the face. The bacterium attacks and destroys the nerves in these areas, effectively anaesthetising them. As a result, people injure themselves without feeling pain. Hands become 'clawed'; burns and cuts become infected; eyelids can't work properly, people can't blink, and eye problems are rife. With these kinds of physical deformities, you would think that everyone who suspected they had leprosy would immediately report it and present themselves for treatment. Not so – because they are often afraid.

Leprosy is feared because of the stigma, ostracism and total rejection associated with it. Leprosy breaks up families. Children of leprosy sufferers are refused entry to school. People lose their jobs. In some parts of the world, people affected by leprosy are legally banned from holding a driving licence, travelling by train, or even contesting a divorce, since leprosy is itself grounds for divorce. So people often don't report the disease early enough. As a result, and even though after MDT treatment they are no longer infectious and they no longer have leprosy, the physical and psychological ravages are still there.

In some modern translations of the Bible, the word 'leprosy' isn't used, since it's not clear that in every case leprosy proper is actually meant. So a phrase like 'dreaded skin disease' is used. Leprosy isn't a disease of the skin, but it is dreaded – both by those who don't have it, and by those who do. The work of all those involved in treating leprosy includes not only curing the disease, and treating the physical disabilities, but also working to change attitudes.

Leprosy is still a global problem. India reports some 50% of the world's cases; other countries with a significant number of leprosy sufferers are Burma, Nepal, Bangladesh, Madagascar, Mozambique, Tanzania, DR Congo and Brazil. Leprosy occurs in some 91 countries, according the WHO in 2000. The numbers are coming down all the time, but the problem still remains.

In St Mark's account of the healing of the man with leprosy, there's a word in the Greek text which can be translated differently. It could be translated as Jesus was 'filled with pity', or as he was 'filled with anger'. Either way – or both – the example of Jesus still stands as a challenge in the 21st century. We can help to 'kiss the leprosy sufferer clean' – and not just by singing about it.

Stewart Smith

www.leprosymission.org.uk

Month 2 Day 24

Work

How to strip an olive tree

First, call friends, neighbours;
next, approach the tree,
with its cascading leaves like tears
and its clustering ripe fruit, green or black;
next, spread your cloths under the tree;
next, beat the tree (the way you might beat a donkey);
next, comb the branch-tips with your fingers,
till the olives fall pattering all around you;
next, use ladders to reach higher,
work together;
next, send small boys up the tree;
next, watch as they beat the higher branches
so that olives fall like hail;
next, the children edge out along the branches,
and their small weight tips the balance
so that laden branches
bend into the hands of the pickers;
next, check that the tree is stripped;
next, sit down in its shade
and drink hot sweet tea out of a kettle,
share bread and oil and herbs –
and olives of course;
next, put kindling aside;
next, with many hands, take up corners of cloth,

gathering the fallen olives together;
next, scoop the fruit and leaves into a bucket,
lift it above your head, pour it out, winnowing,
repeat;
next, scoop your olives (leaving the leaves) into a sack;
next, fold the cloths away;
next, glean the fallen fruit;
next, look up into the branches,
stripped bare of fruit, and say,
'That's a fine tree, old, but year by year, good fruit';
now move on; next …

Jan Sutch Pickard

Poverty

The Poverty Truth Commission

'A demanding common task alone builds community' – now where have we heard that before?

And here it is again.

Nearly three years ago, we were asked if regular meetings could be held in our house in preparation for the Poverty Truth Commission, to take place in March 2009.

This was an amazing event, which happened in Glasgow's City Chambers over one afternoon. 400 people came together, to hear the experts: people who were actually living in poverty shared their experiences – the Testifiers – and called for change. Also there, listening, was an invited group of civic leaders – church leaders, politicians, MSPs, MPs, representatives of the police and the media – the Commissioners who were there to hear the testimony of the former group, and respond.

The purpose of the meetings in our house was to bring together the group of people who would speak out at the event as the Testifiers, about their experience of poverty and exclusion – speak out either in spoken words, in song, in drama, in dance or in film.

And so began an amazing journey

- as this group met together to share their stories and to work out how best to present them;
- as we all came gradually to trust each other and to form a strong bond;
- as the task became more focussed and more urgent; and also more demanding, with expert facilitation from Elaine Downie, guidance from Paul Chapman (the initiator of the whole project) and overall leadership and

inspiration from Martin Johnstone (from Faith in Community Scotland);

- as we adopted the great slogan, first coined by the anti-apartheid struggle in South Africa: 'Nothing About Us Without Us Is For Us'.

For us, there were many echoes of the work of Glasgow Braendam Link with families living in poverty, where both Molly and Elaine had worked during the 1990s. The same values, of respect for individuals' dignity and integrity, were basic to the work of the group; the same desire, too, to enable people living in poverty and social exclusion to be equipped to speak out and to be heard in their own terms. We saw all this developing over the months of hard work, and counted it a tremendous privilege to be involved, even in a small way.

Many great individual stories were told, with much struggle, tears and laughter, as the group worked towards the event of March 2009. One of the most moving ones came from Ruchazie, a peripheral housing scheme on the north of Glasgow. Through the local church there, a small group of young people from the scheme travelled to Malawi, and spent time living with local families, and working with local young people of their own age. Four of the young people from Ruchazie were involved in the Poverty Truth Commission – and we were all deeply moved as we heard them speak of how they had come back to Glasgow, their minds blown open by the courage, enthusiasm and resilience of the young people they had met there, who, as one of the Ruchazie boys put it, 'just had nothing but were so happy'.

This story has a tragic part to it as well, which illustrates the huge difficulties that young people living in poverty in some parts of Glasgow have to cope with. It's well known here that in some of our peripheral housing schemes, there are territorial boundaries which it's often not safe to cross. One of the Ruchazie boys, with a group of friends, had to cross one of these boundaries one evening to attend a birthday party. They borrowed a car from one of their parents, as it wouldn't have been safe for them to cross the boundary on foot. Tragically, the car crashed – and the lad who had been to Malawi, and had his whole life changed, was killed.

In March 2009 the event in the City Chambers in Glasgow took place. The presentations on that day were remarkable: straight storytelling, rap, dance, film, song – the talent on show was tremendous. The Commissioners responded in the best way possible – came back after a brief meeting together, and instead of falling into the usual trap of either offering bland comments or instant solutions, simply said, 'We want to meet with you and see what, *together*, we can achieve.'

And so began the next stage of the Poverty Truth Commission, when some of the original Commissioners met with some of the original Testifiers – all now called Commissioners – and formed three small sub-groups, to start working on specific areas which they jointly identified as needing to be urgently addressed, if poverty was to be tackled seriously and effectively in this city. Tricia McConalogue, who had also worked with Glasgow Braendam Link, became co-chair of the Commission, first with Jim Wallace, and then with Maureen McGinn.

A group formed to see what could be done about *violence*. This group included John Carnochan, head of the Strathclyde Police Violence Reduction Unit which was already pioneering a radically new method of tackling violence. He said: 'The Poverty Truth Commission has helped shift my perspective and influenced our work.'

A second group set about tackling the issue of *misrepresentation of poverty by the media*, to see if the usual biased and sensational coverage that it so often gives could be changed.

A third group centred on the work of the *kinship carers*, mainly grandmothers caring for their grandchildren because their own parents were unable to look after them due to problems with addiction. This group was seeking to promote a level playing field of financial support for these women, who give so much care for their own family members, but who often, due to the uneven distribution of government help and benefits, struggle financially in a very serious way.

By now, two part-time administrators, Kat Watts and Miriam Rose, had been employed by Faith in Community Scotland, and their input was invaluable in terms of expertise, and of planning and following up meetings between these three groups and decision-making bodies.

Apart from addressing specific issues, two other significant outcomes of this phase of the Poverty Truth Commission were that several of the original Commissioners spoke of how the whole experience had changed aspects of their work practice. Also, at a personal level, labels came off, and firm friendships were formed across the old Commissioner/Testifier divide, as people worked at the demanding common task.

All of the above was working towards the final event on Saturday, March 16th 2011. Again, this was held in Glasgow's City Chambers, before a packed audience, mainly of representatives from organisations committed to taking forward the cause. For two hours, the Commissioners shared the story of their two revolutionary years – through film, dialogue, rap, stand-up comedy, and hard-hitting accounts of the three main issues they had tackled: overcoming violence, media misrepresentation and kinship care.

Martin Johnstone summed up the day, and the two years' work, by speaking of the legacy of the Poverty Truth Commission. He highlighted the two main outcomes. There was the confidence that the people in poverty had gained, as they had discovered their voice, and realised that it could be, and was, heard by the people in power. And there was the knowledge that the people in power had gained, that with all their wisdom and even a lifetime of public service, statistics and soundbites were never enough to deal with poverty – what was needed was a complete culture change.

So what is this culture change? In Martin's words, 'If it had been white people leading the black civil rights movement in America, nothing would have changed!' If people in poverty don't lead the fight against poverty, then nothing will change. The experience of the Commission has been that as people in power have come out from behind their desks – as people in poverty have stopped being treated as, and feeling like, victims, and have found their voice – so a whole new energy, and a whole new dynamic, for change has been set loose. 'Ultimately,' said Martin, 'this is about human relationships – getting rid of the labels and the badges – and putting real meaning in the bland phrase "We're all in this together".'

The work will go on. Over twenty-five organisations, in Scotland and across the UK, have already committed themselves to taking up the challenge, and the process, of the Poverty Truth Commission. The three working groups will keep at it. The lives of the individual Commissioners, by their own admission, have been changed for good. The event in the City Chambers ended with everyone in the hall being asked to turn to their neighbour and share the great slogan: 'Nothing about us without us is for us.' We left the building, very conscious that it was also up to all of us.

John and Molly Harvey

A simple prayer

God,
I have a simple prayer for the Church.
I pray that one day soon
I will be part of a church that when we pray for the poor,
we will pray for 'us' and not 'them'.
I pray for a Church that will not only have the courage
to work for the poor,
to struggle with the poor
but will also be of the poor.
And I pray that one day
there will be no poor people in the Church
because there will be no poverty.
And I pray to you,
the God of miracles,
the God of the rich,
the God of the poor.
Amen

Martin Johnstone, Church of Scotland's Priority Areas Secretary;
Chief Executive, Faith in Community Scotland

www.povertytruthcommission.org

Basic Christian Communities

The weak things of this world can overthrow the mighty

Affirmation

I believe in you,
my companion,
the human Christ, the worker Christ,
the conqueror of death.
By your measureless sacrifice
you have begotten the new human being
who is destined for liberation.
You are living
in every arm raised
to defend the people
against exploitative domination,
because you are alive on the ranch,
in the factory, in the school.
I believe in your truceless struggle.
I believe in your resurrection.
Christ, Christ Jesus, be one with us.
Lord, Lord my God, be one with us.
Christ, Christ Jesus, take sides
not with the oppressor class
that squeezes dry and devours the community,
but with the oppressed,

with my people
thirsting for peace.

From the creed of the Mass of Nicaraguan Farmers

Prayer

Holy Spirit of God,
who, by spontaneous combustion,
raises up small communities and house churches all over the world,
enlighten our eyes to see in them the fullness of church,
'self-convened' as they are 'before the living-Word-in-Christ,
without human masters'.

We give thanks for their unpretentious lives,
so that all kinds of seekers for the Way of Life enter into community,
accepted just as they are.

We give thanks for the gifts distributed among them,
brought into play with others to build up the life of the Body of Christ
for witness in the world.
And we remember it is 'not by might, not by power,
but by my Spirit, says the Lord of Hosts'
that new life comes, and the meek shall inherit the earth.

Glory to you, Holy Spirit, with the Father and the Son,
for whom the weak things of this world can overthrow the mighty,
who call us to be like children
if we would enter the Kingdom of heaven
in the manner of Jesus Christ,
the Servant King.
Amen

Ian M. Fraser

Non-Violence and Peacekeeping

The net is empty: reflections on John 21

A version of this text was used at the International Ecumenical Peace Convocation in Kingston, Jamaica in 2011. It reflects the hard, often seemingly futile work for just peace: the hours spent doing what seems to be right, in times of tiredness, despair and raw grief, and the sense of hopelessness as focus and energy is on the preservation of power and privilege and not on serving the poor. At the IEPC were many people who have worked all their lives in contexts of violence and oppression for justice and peace. There are times in this work when a resurrection moment is recognisable, tangible and we glow with delight and joy in the promises of new life. But much of the struggle for justice is far less glamorous. Being honest about the hard toil and difficulty is part of the witness to peace: the careful naming of the disappointments, the missed opportunities, the utter exhausted frustration of going out to do the work, being up all night, and coming back, it seems, with nothing.

'Peace be with you' he said.
'Happy are those who have not seen but believe.'

It is easier said than done.
Because I am not happy. I've been working so hard.
The net is still empty.

> The net is empty.
> The net is empty.
> The net is empty.

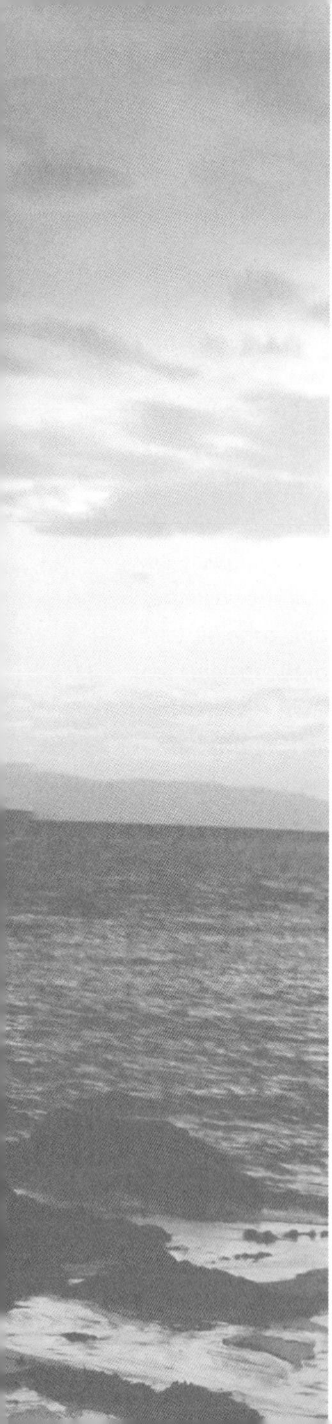

And the best I have to show for all this work is a set of doctrinal disputes in a church which equivocates, and mumbles about its budgets, and seems to put more effort into its precious feasts and its comfortable relationships to power, than its work for justice and peace.

I've been working so hard and the net is empty.

And I'm too exhausted now to know if I'm looking in the wrong place and what might be a good way to work. I don't know which way to turn or who to trust. Around me men and women cry for blood and celebrate murder, drowning out my critical voice, ridiculing my naiveté. Friends desert me as it becomes too hard, too costly, too much to bear. And I feel so alone.

Money, weapons, technology, security systems, comfortable lifestyles all endlessly frustrate my exhausted attempts at faithfulness, goodnesss, at gentleness and mercy, through their hideous and overwhelming power.

> I cannot win.
>
> The net is empty.
>
> It is all pointless.
>
> It is just like chasing the wind.
>
> 'Do you still not understand?' he said.
>
> 'How often must I tell you?'
>
> I am not happy.
>
> The net is empty.

God of the emptiness
God of the futility
God of the humble nothing

Forgive us our impatience

God of the wind
God of the waters
God of the shoal beyond our reach

Forgive us our limitations

God of the waiting
God of the watching
God of the early-morning light

Grant us your impatient peace.

Alison Swinfen

INTERFAITH

'The Charter for Compassion' (an historic day at St Andrew's Church, Lisbon)

During Easter 2011, I had the privilege of sharing in the services at St Andrew's, the Church of Scotland located in central Lisbon. (It was in 1866 that the Scots here first gathered into a Presbyterian church.) The present minister, Graham McGeoch, and his wife, Telma, are constantly welcoming visitors from around the world, and alongside that ministry of hospitality are bringing new vision and insight to this Lisbon congregation. Since they came to Lisbon, Graham has been sharing with me in e-mails something of this vision, and in our dialogue I had sent him details of 'The Charter for Compassion' which was launched worldwide by people of different faiths in 2009.

The Charter for Compassion (www.charterforcompassion.org), which expresses powerfully those things which the great religious traditions of the world have in common, has been taken up by St Andrew's here in Portugal. It was the first church in Portugal to affirm the Charter. Fellow signatories include the Central Mosque in Lisbon, the Buddhist Union in Portugal, and the High Commission for Immigration and Intercultural Dialogue – a department of the Portuguese government.

Among other things, the Charter says: *'We call upon all men and women to restore compassion to the centre of morality and religion; to return to the ancient principle that any interpretation of scripture that breeds violence, hatred or disdain is illegitimate; to ensure that young people are given accurate and respectful information about other traditions, religions and cultures; to encourage a positive appreciation of cultural and religious diversity; to cultivate an informed empathy with the suffering of all human beings – even those regarded as enemies.'*

A beautifully executed copy of the full Charter hangs in St Andrew's Church, and since Lent 2010, the congregation have been reflecting on its meaning and implications for daily life. In Lent 2011, as a demonstration of their commitment to the Charter, the church led a visit to the Central Mosque for people in the English- speaking community. The warm hospitality of the Imam encouraged the congregation to extend an invitation to him to visit St Andrew's.

In Easter week, Graham and the congregation released a Press statement about the Imam's visit. The Press statement reads:

Imam to preach compassion at church service:

On Sunday 8th, May 2011 the Imam of the Central Mosque in Lisbon will preach at St Andrew's Church. Both mosque and church are signatories of the Charter for Compassion, the global movement that affirms: 'The principle of compassion lies at the heart of all religious, ethical and spiritual traditions, calling us always to treat all others as we wish to be treated ourselves.'

The invitation to preach was extended to Sheikh David Munir, the Imam, by the church, following a visit to the Central Mosque by members of the English-speaking community in Lisbon during Lent 2011. This visit was part of the church's commitment to inter-religious dialogue and cooperation.

The minister of St Andrew's Church, Rev. Graham McGeoch said, 'It is a unique opportunity to explore our interdependence, transcend our fears and to discover the common cause of compassion that lies at the heart of our traditions.'

The service to be held in St Andrew's Church, Lisbon will begin at 11am on Sunday 8th May. St Andrew's Church is a charge of the Church of Scotland in the Presbytery of Europe. It has been offering English-language worship in the Reformed tradition in Portugal since 1866. It is fully committed to ecumenical and interfaith relations.

As the church prepared this Press statement, Graham shared with me something of his own understanding of the Imam's visit:

'1492 represents for the Iberian peninsula not only the discoveries, but the forced conversion or the expulsion of religious minorities (Protestants, Muslims and Jews). The Charter has enabled us as religious minorities to discover our common history across religious traditions. This had opened the congregation to a deeper understanding of their own faith as well as cultivating an awareness of the faith of others. As far as we are aware, the visit of the Imam to St Andrew's will be the first time that a Muslim cleric addresses a church in the context of actual Sunday worship in Portugal.'

My own view is that this is a very significant development in interfaith relationships. A small gesture such as inviting an Imam to preach on compassion in a local congregation has meaning far beyond local boundaries, and does much to lessen our ignorance of the Islamic world.

O Lord, grant us to love Thee:
grant that we may love those that love Thee:
grant that we may do the deeds that win Thy love.

The Prophet (Peace be upon Him)[1]

Peter Millar

Note:

1. Prayer from The Oxford Book of Prayer, edited by George Appleton, Oxford University Press

Commitment

A small part of the picture

'Still Human, Still Here' was the title of a conference in Glasgow one winter Saturday. It focussed on the increasing reality of destitution for asylum seekers whose status was still to be determined and who had not yet had their support and housing approved.

The conference appealed for hosts – those who had a spare room and could give this to a man or woman who needed it for a temporary period before housing was made available. A number of us signed up, and had telephone calls asking for help.

Overseas visitors have been a regular feature of our home-lives over many decades. Over the years, we have had several short-term refugee guests, mainly from Africa but also from Asia. Some have come from countries where there is a very obvious reason for them to be refugees. Others are from places that seem, on the surface, to be 'safe' and 'stable'. They might be from a minority that is unpopular with the government. Or they might, as in one situation, have traded with a rebel movement. A story from one of our guests was that she had a boyfriend who was in the liberation movement and she was threatened by both sides, neither of which believed that she was to be trusted. Stories are often told in pain and in part. They emerge at the table or late at night over a drink or a cup of tea. Some of them are contradictory, or like a jigsaw, they don't appear to fit together. In the confusion, which is partly caused by culture of language, there is the frustration of not having anything like the full picture.

It is a necessary lesson to learn that the hosts cannot begin to fully understand the problems, still less to solve them. We are so used, from our secure position, to want to be at least part of the solution and we can't cope very easily with a lesser role. Those who have had pastoral ministries are particularly susceptible to this. But we have to learn that we can't save the world and that sometimes what is asked of us is a relatively modest role of being one of a number of helpers in a particular situation. The task is to provide shelter and a welcome, food and the possibility, no more, of whatever level of friendship is appropriate for a short time.

Several of our guests have spent a lot of their time watching television in their own room. It is their space for a few days and we try not to intrude, whilst making it clear that they are welcome in other parts of the house. We fixed up one guest with some voluntary work where payment in kind was the norm and made contacts with a football team which needed players in which he expressed an interest. Conscious of the very limited resources which government makes for the support of asylum seekers, we agreed informally for him to do some work for us that needed attention and for which reasonable remuneration could be given. None of these ideas worked out. We were in contact for a while. He came to our house for lunch or tea from time to time. Then his telephone line went dead and the e-mails bounced back. He vanished from our lives.

When we stay with friends in Africa or Asia or they with us in Scotland, we or they may come with all too much physical luggage, but we come to renew friendships and deepen our relationships. Refugees in need of short-term shelter come with very different baggage to complete strangers. Their reception by us may of course have deep consequences in their future lives. But we have no rights of expectation of the relationship and no right to know any more of their story than that which they choose to reveal. The offer of shelter may be frustratingly limited, but it is enough.

Prayer

God give us the maturity to accept that
we cannot work miracles or save the world.

God give us the patience to offer support to those on the margins
without setting or altering
their own margins.

God give us the assurance that our limited assistance
is part of wider opportunities for growth that we will never see.
And make us content to be a small part of the picture.
Amen

Iain Whyte

The Rediscovery of Spirituality

Meeting the Black Panther of the Blue Mountains: A letter from Australia

Being with indigenous Australians in their own community puts your own life into perspective. Of course it is true that these – often remote – communities face enormous problems and that these will be present for many generations to come. At times the problems appear insurmountable. But what of our own values as affluent people? What of our own social and spiritual impoverishments? What of the cloying blandness which now characterises so many of our own choices? We are often told by our indigenous friends to 'keep listening' – not to arrive at quick fixes – but to listen, and to listen more. To listen to the Spirit, to the earth, to one another. To be present. To be. To be in harmony with a reality which transcends our ego. When I was in Indulkana, I saw for myself the many problems facing indigenous Australians, but I was also aware of the bleakness in my own soul as a person who has had so many possibilities and choices.

And this for me is one of the central dilemmas of our time. Many of us have so much but we seem to have squandered this rich inheritance. Technology companions an acute blandness of spirit. Travel does not often make us wiser. Our relationships at a personal and social level are often fraught and angst-ridden. As one writer put it: 'We have not only stopped believing in God but also stopped believing in ourselves.'

In my book *Waymarks: Signposts to Discovering God's Presence in the World*, I wrote about the plural nature of the modern world, and about the importance of accepting difference and 'the other', who is often seen as a stranger. This can never be a bland task. It demands that we reach into our depths in order to seek more awareness. To live not only with a strong moral imagination (which is a different thing from a narrow view of morality) but also with the knowledge that our own existence on this wounded planet is provisional and enfolded in mystery. Perhaps another way of putting this is to say that we are called from the edges to seek the heartlands. These are depths of spirit understood by our indigenous friends not only in Australia but in many continents. It is something to do with a communal replenishing of our spirits, which is a markedly different reality from being only concerned with our personal salvation.

Meeting the Black Panther of the Blue Mountains

When I woke up in sunny, but cold, Sydney on the morning of July 2nd, 2007, I never for a moment thought that the day would contain a once-in-a-lifetime experience! For the 2nd of July was the day when for the first (and presumably last) time I met face to face with the legendary 'Black Panther of the Blue Mountains' in New South Wales.

This is a true story! I was not drunk, or on drugs, or hallucinating, although, as you may know, all of those (or at least some of them) might have been possibilities. I was my calm self – aware and open to life! And in that openness to life and to new experiences I became the 281st human being to have had the privilege of sighting the big cat, which was first recorded in the Blue Mountains in 1835 (see the Big Cats of Australia website).

A little of the background: On the morning of July 2nd I travelled up from the centre of Sydney to the Blue Mountains to work on a book with a close friend and colleague, Anne McPherson, a former Leader of the Wellspring Community.

While with Anne in her small home near the beautiful village of Kurrajong Hills, I went out for a short walk to buy some apples in the neighbouring village of Bilpin, which lies at the heart of some amazingly rich and large apple orchards. The orchards themselves are surrounded by the ancient bush of the Blue Mountains – a largely uninhabited area (apart from on its edges) which stretches for hundreds of square miles and which, through the centuries, has been home to many indigenous communities.

On my way back from Bilpin, I walked about a mile into the bush. It was cold and it was getting dark. I walked down a steep path to a gorge and then on my return, a strange animal crossed my path, halted some yards above me on the slope, looked around and then, after a couple of minutes, disappeared into the darkening bush. I looked at my watch and it was 3:40pm. I had kept looking at this large black creature with its strong face and bushy tail but had no clue what it was. On the way back, I thought how little I knew about the animals of the bush – despite having walked so often in bushland. Who was my companion on the lonely trail?

Later that evening when I recounted this meeting in the bush to Anne she seemed very surprised, and asked me to once again describe the animal in detail. When I had completed my tale, Anne immediately came to the conclusion that I had seen, at very close quarters, the legendary big cat, known as the Black Panther of the Blue Mountains. (The panther has also been sighted in the state of Victoria many hundreds of miles south of the Blue Mountains.)

The rest, as they say, is history. My sighting has been recorded by various groups in Australia who are tracking the Black Panther (no one is clear how many panthers there actually are). In all my travels in Australia I have never met a person who has seen the big cat, and many friends told me that they thought it was only a legendary creature like the Loch Ness Monster in Scotland. (Several expeditions mounted over the years to track and film this big cat have never had clear sightings of it!) So there we are – the wee Scots guy, out to buy a bag of apples, and the elusive Black Panther meet face to face on a cold winter afternoon. A moment not to be forgotten.

But I can't leave it at that! As I thought about this encounter with the Black Panther, several things came to mind. When I saw this animal I had absolutely no idea what it was. At that moment it was just a strange animal. I had never heard that a black panther roamed the bush, and I knew nothing of earlier sightings. The historical and social narrative concerning this creature only came later. Now I am not able to go back to that 'raw experience' without knowingly being aware of all the other facts. When I met the panther, he or she had no hinterland of meaning; but now, having received so much information about the big cat of the mountains, the animal has a huge hinterland of history, etc. One example: I did not see it as a 'dangerous animal', but when I was later asked if I would have gone down that path on my own on a dark afternoon, knowing that a panther might be there, I replied that I might have thought twice before setting off! My initial experience remains the same, but my understanding of what I saw that afternoon has totally changed.

Which brings me to the person of Jesus Christ. None of us have had what I would call a 'raw encounter' with Jesus. Yes, we may have had a personal experience of Christ in our lives, as millions, through the ages, have claimed. I feel that in my own life I have encountered and been changed by the one we know as Christ. I can say that I have some certainty about that, as can many others. But in what sense was the Jesus who met me on life's road an 'unknown Jesus'? He could not be. The Christian narrative has been held in my family for centuries. It has been held in my culture for centuries. It has been held in the world's narrative for centuries. And it has been 'interpreted' by the Christian Church for centuries. We may be able to 'imagine' something of Christ's life 2000 years ago (a task which personally I find very difficult), but the meaning of his life does not, and cannot, come to us raw. We meet a Christ who is embedded in his story (a story of the centuries), and that fact interests me a lot. For the early disciples it must have been very different. Or am I wrong? Was their encounter raw, or also filtered through a wider story?

Who was that panther? Who is that panther? Who was this person Jesus? And what are the links to that Jesus of history and the 'filtered' Jesus we hear about today? Does it matter that we have never encountered a 'raw Jesus'? My encounter with an unknown Australian animal has raised theological issues! Who is this Jesus we meet in our lives? One thing is certain though: even if you've never seen our friend in the bush – I can assure you he's there!

Peter Millar

The Thirty-First Day

Step by step

Step by step,
in your footprints:
Brendan, Brigid,
Columba, Adamnan.

Step by step,
in your footprints:
Margaret, Cormac,
Anna, Michael.

Step by step,
in your footprints:
Sue, Kate,
Ian, Alice.

Step by step,
in your footprints:
all you saints,
all you angels,
step by step
I'm coming home.

Ruth Burgess

Month 3

Month 3 Day 1

New Ways to Touch the Hearts of All

The wilderness rejoices: a visit to Camas

Originally quarry-workers' cottages, then a salmon-fishing station, the Iona Community's Camas Centre on the Isle of Mull is run by a staff group with specialist skills, helped by several volunteers. Young people from the city and elsewhere, and other groups too, come to Camas for an adventure holiday with outdoor opportunities for canoeing, walking, swimming and camping, a visit to Iona, and the experience of exploring issues, building relationships, and facing new challenges through living and working in community.

'Mike, will you look in each direction and say what is the same, and what has changed?' asked Becky, the Camas gardener. I was with four of the Camas staff for the Morning Reflection. It was during the balmy days of April 2011, and we were in sunshine, gazing at a calm blue sea, standing a stone's throw from the Camas buildings, on the little island – the one that gets cut off as you daydream and the tide comes in. I was returning to Camas after a break of about 10 years, having first been there through the summer of 1990.

To the north, the outlines of Gometra, Ulva and Little Colonsay were familiar friends. Favourite rocks on the island in the bay still invited me to sit. It was people who had been agents of change. A few yards to the east there was a lovely simple stone labyrinth, and to the south strong new huts. To the west were the buildings, which I recalled as impractical, damp and cramped. Restoration has made the walls, windows and roofs weather-tight. An attic added to the lower building includes a drying room – another major difficulty solved. Solar panels heat water; a wind turbine charges a huge battery, mainly for a fridge and a washing machine – joy of joys: we used to boil the tea towels, and take the other washing to Iona.

Installing mains water has solved many problems. Showers – and flushing loos – have ended night-time stumbles on uneven stone paths. The rough paths have also been made smooth, both beside the buildings, and on the track to Camas, with slip-proofed wooden walkways over the mud.

I had heard nothing but praise for the renovations at Camas, and I shared that enthusiasm.

Camas remains a challenging place to live and work in though, and remains a place where only torches, candles, fireplaces and lanterns shine – and stars can still be seen. I had no doubt that the current staff would provide the energy and skills to use the place with the visiting groups – as has been done consistently for as long as I have known Camas. The people living and working there had of course changed, but the spirit, energy and humour with which they were preparing for the new season were familiar.

The previous afternoon we had been talking about how visiting groups could be encouraged to use all their senses at Camas, to build relationship with their surroundings: from that comes the impulse to care and conserve, and to share enthusiasm – expressed so well in the John Muir Trust Award scheme now an integral part of the Camas programme. So, on the island that morning we paused and listened … and I heard something that was different. There was new birdsong carried on the air of Camas. To the south, woodland planted not even ten years ago was already mature enough to give shelter to the birds, and protection from wind to a garden now vastly bigger and more verdant than the one that was struggling in the early 1990s. Helping Becky (or perhaps hindering) for an hour or two the previous afternoon had made me realise the huge effort over the decades in turning that rough ground into garden.

Looking from our island that morning, the wind turbine seemed a suitable symbol of Camas, responding to the possibilities and challenges of this age.

At our feet were other symbols of Camas. The very rock of the bay, pink granite, is a coming together of three minerals. Upon the rock the algae, then mosses and grasses grow, and an ecology, a natural community, develops. That same coming together of diversity, to build something beautiful and new, continues each week as new visitors are welcomed into community.

In 1990 there were concerns about localised issues of acid rain, pollution, the hole in the ozone. These were known to be reversible with rational policies. Yet these were the signs that unfettered commerce, industry and acquisition were unsustainable and damaged the planet. Today we know that we are generating global change – to the climate, in loss of biodiversity, in ocean acidification. Reversing these is not so straightforward. In many circles in 1990, talk was edging forward from being about domination of the earth towards the need for stewardship. We now know that the connection to the planet that needs to be recognised and recreated is not merely one of stewardship – but of us as an intimately linked part of the planet. At Camas I imagined air, water, land, life interweaving like the lines of a Celtic cross, an interweaving that included humankind.

It is a radical hospitality that the Camas staff offer – an offer of community with them, certainly, but also with the place, the land, the history of Camas, and with the earth and stars, without the masks and distractions of city life.

Camas embodies the attitudes and relationships needed to heal the planet. If a prophet hadn't started Camas in the 1940s then the Iona Community would have to start it now.

Mike Mineter

Economic Witness

A time of great taking: a global *saquao*

We hear of comparisons between the recent riots in UK cities and riots elsewhere. Window-smashing in Athens. Car bonfires in Paris. There are parallels: a spark set by police violence, a generation that feels forgotten and marginalised. There have been other mass lootings in recent years – and on a vastly greater scale than those in the UK. In the aftermath of the US invasion, Baghdad witnessed a frenzy of arson and looting that almost emptied the libraries and great museums. In Iraq, ordinary people, having for years watched Saddam Hussein and his family take whatever and whomever they wanted, felt they had earned the right to take a few things for themselves.

In 2001, when Argentina's economy was in free-fall, thousands of people living in poor neighbourhoods stormed foreign-owned superstores. They came out pushing shopping carts overflowing with the goods they could no longer afford – clothes, electronic goods, meat. The government called a 'state of siege' to restore order; the people didn't like that, and overthrew the government.

Canadian journalist Naomi Klein points out that this mass looting in Argentina was called 'El Saqueo' – the sacking. That was politically significant because it was the very same word used to describe what Argentina's elites had done by selling off the country's national assets in flagrantly corrupt privatisation deals, hiding money offshore, then passing on the bill to the people with a brutal austerity package.

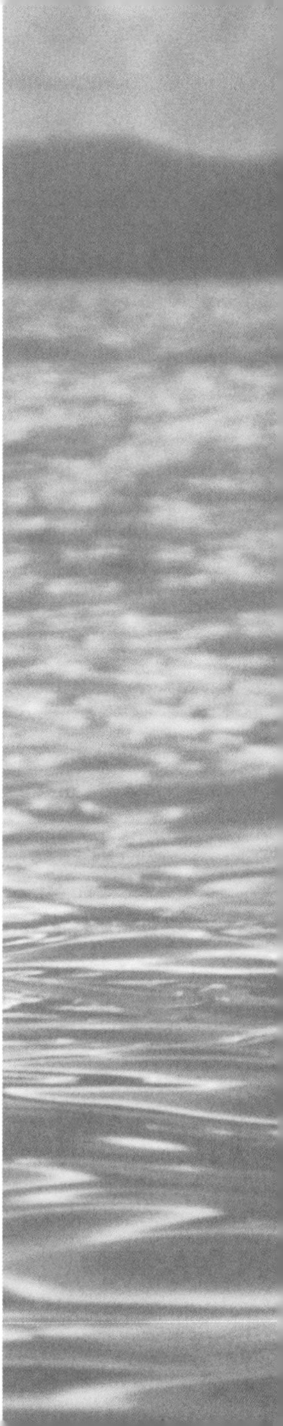

People in Argentina understood that the *saqueo* of the shopping centres would not have happened without the bigger *saqueo* of the country, and that the real criminals were the ones in charge.

We are being constantly told by politicians that the recent riots in the UK were not 'political'. This is said in all seriousness, as if the massive bank bailouts never happened, followed by what have so rightly been described as 'the defiant record bonuses'. And as in other countries, the UK government continues, in response to all of this, to force sacrifices on the most vulnerable, while the elites continue to pursue their insane lifestyles.

At present here in the UK we are witnessing daily: the firing of public servants, the scapegoating of teachers, the closing of libraries, the rolling back of union contracts, the botched up rush to privatise public assets … The list is never-ending, and once again we are being lectured at by the very people who sacked the economy in the first place.

In spiritual terms this is a time of 'great taking' – a 'global sacking' – fuelled by a pathological sense of entitlement. It is, as one commentator said, 'a looting with all the lights on as if there was nothing to hide'.

Of course I am not defending those who destroyed, through their arson and looting, a lifetime's work of a small shopkeeper. Of many small shopkeepers. But we are also failing to examine and to reflect upon these wider lootings which are endemic in our time. The evil (and it is a corporate evil) in these absurd bonuses is just one marker of this pathological belief that we are entitled to as much as we can grab. And the companion to this greed beyond description is the prevailing ideology that in an age of austerity to discipline the vulnerable is fundamental. We must keep the poor in place while the rich – by foul means or fair – flourish at all costs. Such is modern Britain!

In such an atmosphere of global looting, it is important that people

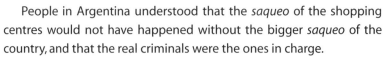

of faith remind society of an alternative narrative. A narrative with which we must reconnect if society is to remain sane. And that narrative – expressed in all the great religious traditions of the world – reminds us of certain basic elements needed to retain our humanity. It tells us that human beings who live only with a sense of 'entitlement' – grabbing all for themselves in their short life on earth – are in fact spiritually impoverished. Or to put it another way: they are not 'fully human', despite the seeming richness of their lives.

For several years, Dorothy and I, along with our three children, lived alongside many poor families in South India. That was a privilege. These Indian families taught us so much about what it means to be a rich human being. In terms of money and possessions they had little or often nothing at all, but in terms of the human spirit their wealth was limitless. Even the poorest family would make sure we had food before we left them. Sharing what they had was not something to be analysed. It was a fact of daily living.

The present belief in grabbing all that we can for ourselves raises many questions. Is it possible in our modern technological societies to reconnect with a culture of giving, of sharing? To move away from this blind belief in entitlement? To ask seriously of society and of one another: what actually are our rights, responsibilities and privileges? Or as the old slogan put it succinctly: 'To live more simply that others may simply live'.

These are political questions, but they are also questions for people of faith. Even within our secular societies many still believe in God and with the understanding that the earth is a sacred place. Many also believe that we are in a fundamental way accountable to each other, and that we are stewards of the earth in all of its diversity, beauty and wonder.

It is also true that our daily living can reflect an alternative narrative. Through our elected representatives and other channels thousands are campaigning against this culture of greed. That is a great hope in such times. We can all do something to express 'another way of living'. We have choices, and – despite its many flaws – most of us who read this are living in a democracy. Our voices can be raised in the public square without fear of persecution.

Month 3 Day 2

Gandhi's words are not new, but they are relevant in the struggle to witness for truth and for a renewed understanding of how human beings should interact with one another (and not just in his native India where recently millions have taken to the streets to fight against the rampant corruption at every level of Indian society):

'To recognise evil and not to oppose it is to surrender your humanity; to recognise evil and to oppose it with the weapons of the evil-doer is to enter into your humanity; to recognise evil and to oppose it with the weapons of God is to enter into your divinity.'

Peter Millar, 2011

Month 3 Day 3

Youth Concern

Rekindling community: on the 2011 UK uprisings

What's left to say? What can be said when a whole generation is accused of being looting, greedy, violent, reactionary good-for-nothings? When eloquent families, with such great upset, watch as their children are locked up for years. I'm guessing you've had many conversations about why the uprisings (or 'recession riots') broke loose and the political complexity of causes.

In such intense times, as a young person I think it's important that we articulate, to turn the tide of bile set against us, and look for solutions.

I spent the first 18 years of my life in the most affected areas, around Tottenham and Enfield. Since the insurgency, I have been asked to be on support committees for the families of youth being locked up – many people I grew up with at primary school. In my lifetime I have never witnessed such trauma and abandonment by the government. What can youth say when education is now priced out of comprehension; when up to 75 per cent of youth services have been slashed in local boroughs in the first half of 2011 and job prospects are so bleak that one in two young people in Tottenham are now unemployed; when we live with the fastest-growing rich-poor divide since WW2? Today we know that if you're twenty years old and white you will be three times more likely to go to university than if you're twenty and black, and that if you're black you will be twice more likely to be out of work. When the politicians are busily fiddling their expenses, the media is ridden with hacking scandals and the judicial system is swamped with unaccounted for deaths at the hands of the police (Jean Charles de Menezes, Ian Tomlinson, Mark Duggan …), seriously, who do we turn to? In times like this, we can only look to our communities to build systems of support amongst this mess.

The grounds for rekindling community must begin.

Of course the damage on the ground was horrific. But to understand the uprisings, the plasters must be ditched to look at the root cause of the wounds …

Dan Glass, 2011

27-year-old community activist Dan Glass is part of 'So We Stand'. He has also been an activist with Plane Stupid and Climate Camp. So We Stand: http://sowestand.com

THE WORD

He was a storyteller

He was a storyteller,
he drew pictures with words:
a tiny seed growing into a huge tree
a lamp under a bed
a lost sheep crying.
Buckets of fish
hungry birds gobbling up corn
a house built on a rock
workmen grumbling …

He was a storyteller,
and he told great stories:

Once there was a traveller … and the bandits attacked him …
One day a king threw a great banquet … and no one turned up …
In a certain town there was a judge … and there was also a widow …
There was this man … and he had two sons … and they were very different …

He was a storyteller,
and he asked his listeners questions:

Who was neighbour to this man?
Why do you call me good?
What do you think the owner of the vineyard would do?

Are you jealous because God is generous?

He was a storyteller,
and he knew how to deliver punchlines that stuck in your memory:

No servant can be the slave of two masters.
Whatever is hidden will be brought out into the open.
Whatever you do for the least of my brothers and sisters,
you do for me.
Your heart will always be where your riches are.

He was a storyteller,
with words he could draw pictures;
and people listened
and people remembered
and some of them followed him.

They called him
the Word of God.

Ruth Burgess

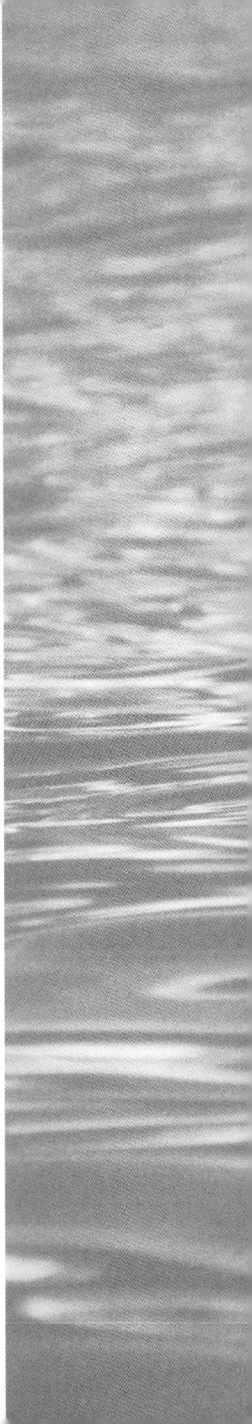

Hospitality and Welcome

No room for the mystic

I gave my friend a hymnbook when he left the university. Not an unusual gift from a chaplain. Except that my friend Abbas was a Muslim from Sudan. The hymnbook was his own request. He had attended services in the chapel and discussions in the Chaplaincy Centre. He sat quietly in the corner, observing, but with a concentration and an intensity of spirit. Only rarely could he be persuaded to make a quiet comment. The chaplaincy, he said, had been one place where he felt at home and he wanted to take something away from an experience which he had appreciated. Abbas had also attended the Gospel Hall. The folk there thought that he was a potential 'catch', and made strenuous attempts to convert him to Christianity. Abbas didn't seem to mind and he neither rejected this angrily, nor mocked it. But he and I knew that there was no more chance of his abandoning Islam than for Partick Thistle to beat Real Madrid. Abbas was a poet and a philosopher, who loved and cherished all expressions of faith that sought understanding. Sadly that was precisely to be his downfall.

When Abbas returned to Sudan he wrote several books. One was *The Freedom of Mind, Thought, Will and Creed in Islam*. His next book was *Islam Is a Religion, Not a Religion and a State*. Perhaps not the most popular of titles in that North African country. Although he came from a well-connected Sudanese family that advantage was not enough to save him. He was arrested, imprisoned and exiled. When we next saw him it was in Cairo, where he was writing poetry and trying to make a life for himself in what was a relatively tolerant society in the 1980s. He brought us gifts of crafts and flowers, which he could ill afford. He had met Robin Ross, former member of the Iona Community and Middle East staff member for the

Church of Scotland, a link that Abbas cherished.

Then disaster struck again. There were bomb attacks on tourists in Egypt and these were blamed on Sudanese extremists. Ironically, because Abbas was a loner and the Sudanese liberation movement in Egypt had never heard of him, and certainly couldn't vouch for him, he was arrested and expelled to Libya, being dumped, with few possessions, literally just over the border. Libya didn't want him, and so, after weeks of travelling in North Africa, he arrived in Morocco, where he has been ever since. His story is of one who forcibly wanders the world but is not at peace with it because the world cannot find a place for him.

Abbas would very much like to find an academic post in Britain. He has crossed to France several times and been turned back at Marseilles, fairly roughly by all accounts. He gave £200 to a stranger to fetch his belongings from Egypt and was genuinely surprised when he did not see the man (or his possessions) again. We might smile at the naivety of an other-worldly man, but that would be only half the story. The other half is, I believe, more accurate. Abbas is a man for whom honesty, toleration and scholarship are so deeply rooted that he cannot imagine that there are those who do not share his values. He would no more dream of taking money under false pretences than of planting bombs.

Is there a place in the polarised world today for people like Abbas? He points to a greater vision of humanity. He does not 'fit in' to any established structure. He is irritating to those of us who just want to get on with our lives. In a non-threatening but profoundly disturbing way he challenges our security and our selfishness. Doesn't he remind us of someone else who did all that?

Prayer

God of the wanderers and of those who fit no easy categories, help us to hear the voices of the visionary and to make room for those who carry the vision of peace to a polarised world. We ask this in the name of the prophetic nomad from Nazareth.

Iain Whyte

Month 3 Day 6

This is the Day

Meeting Hassan

I met a man today, relaxing on the beach
after we had marched against the arms trade,
and waved our flags for truth and peace.

I met a man today; we chatted about the sea,
how calm it was, how lovely
to feel so warm and free.

I met a man today; he asked where I was from,
I asked the same of him in return,
and he told me his home was gone.

I met a man today who had fled his land in fear,
his family had been bombed away,
he had lost all that he held dear.

I met a man today, who had run from Iraq
via homelessness and beatings,
he knew he could never go back.

I met a man today; I wanted him to know I cared.
So told him I was sorry and
of our protests and our prayers.

I met a man today, my words just sounded hollow in my head.
So instead I held his hand and
silently offered him my cheese and bread.

I met a man today:
we met through
the sharing of food,
the sound of the waves,
the telling of stories and
the sacredness of silence.

I met a man today, and for hope,
together we broke bread.

Rachel Mica McCann

The Iona Experience

Transfiguration – a moment in Iona Abbey

Candles flicker.
Silence grows.
We wait
for God to move.
The oboe
sets its haunting melody free,
wandering,
seeking,
aching
in our souls.
Its beauty
caresses,
embraces,
holds me
in that holy,
healing moment.

Let us build them booths,
these musicians,
magicians,
muses of the Holy Spirit.
I insist!
Let us keep them
here

with us
and hold this moment,
this beauty,
to replay it
again,
again,
again.

Forever
and ever!

Then I know.
I smile
at my presumption.
The presumption of disciples
caught up in mountaintop wonder,
shrouded in beauty.
Let us build them booths, Jesus,
so that they will never leave us.

Transfiguration.
We have what has been given –
wandering,
seeking,
aching
beauty
that holds us;
heals us;
embraces us with hope.

We cannot coax
such holy wonder
to remain.
We can only live,
changed by its gift,
changed by its moment.
We can live
trusting that a gift has been given.
The gift will come again.

Nancy Cocks, Isle of Iona, August 2003

Life in Community

Life in all its fullness: from the Camas Diary

Campfires on the beach, dancing dolphins, selkie stories, apple and fresh currant pie, Texas honey, basking sharks – Camas is life in all its fullness. The Camas Diary is a blog written by staff and volunteers of Camas, the residential centre of the Iona Community on the isle of Mull. Camas offers small groups of young people and adults a chance to learn more about themselves, the environment and spirituality, through a variety of outdoor, creative and environmental activities and a simple, sustainable way of living. Following are some extracts from the wonderful Camas Diary …

This week we welcomed a group of kids from a youth club in Edinburgh. One highlight for me was the wild camping trip. We packed our heavy bags full of tents, clothes, sleeping bags and food, walked up the track, then drove to Knockvologan Farm, stopping at Fionnphort's Ferry Shop on the way so they could stock up on some essentials (crisps). Some found the walk from Knockvologan along the coast difficult and it was slow going, but eventually we made it to the lovely beach campsite. We spent a pleasant evening watching the sun set, playing hacky sack and bocce, and sitting around the driftwood fire toasting marshmallows. The next morning we managed to pack up and get going despite the rain, and headed back to Camas, stopping for an involved session of the German Foot Game.

The week included a lot of time spent throwing things: the frisbee, the hula hoop over the fishing pole, rocks at the bell, plus the odd tantrum. At other points we had table tennis tournaments, built a raft and a shelter, learnt guitar chords and imitated each other's accents and slang.

At the moment the ground around Mull is covered with all sorts of wildflowers, including about 50 different kinds of small yellow flowers that are just about impossible to distinguish from one another …

A week has passed since our Sheffield group left us at the top of the track. We had an amazing week!: Fearless adventurers walking down a vertical cliff-face, valiant explorers investigating the area from kayaks, and heroic voyagers marching through the hills to hidden beaches in the middle of the Scottish wilderness.

A week full of laughter, adventure, good company, singing songs.

Peat-cutting was a success. Clean women and men walking up the track, and two-legged, sticky, brown mud-monsters coming down an hour later.

To end the week we had a campfire on the beach with some truly amazing entertainment. Never before has Camas had such a fine jug player present, and never before have the Simpsons been to visit …

The wind gradually began to subside and we settled into our preparation for a visit from children from Iona and all across Mull to take part in an array of activities, including storytelling, rock-pooling (exploring the wilds of the sea), games, art and poetry, and a trip to our very own organic garden just at the entrance of Camas.

The children arrived on Thursday morning as a cavalcade of stomping feet and excited voices all around Camas, and we had some biscuits ready for them all. We split them all into groups: the Crabs, the Starfish, the Seagulls, the Sharks, the Jellyfish, and the Whales. The sounds of stomping feet everywhere never stopped except for lunch and everything buzzed with curiosity and excitement. It was a thrill to be able to share the experience of Camas with so many children and leave them with memories of here …

This week was led by Kathy Galloway, and called Exploring Creation. We had a group of lovely people from all over the world. We went blackberry picking in the pouring rain, while others enjoyed tea in the polytunnel, as well as digging spuds for the tea. This was also a week of trees and their fruit – the plum tree gave us some beautiful plums which were made into an amazing dessert. The blackthorn produced sloes which we will also find good use for.

We went on a few day trips: to Ardalanish, where Aeneas told us the story of how they became organic weavers. We also went to the tidal island of Erraid and, after lunch and selkie stories at the lighthouse observatory, walked to the seal colony to see if there were any sealskins on the shore.

Our last night was filled with good food, songs, comedy and wonderful poems! …

This week Camas was visited by one of our longest-running groups: Abercorn School from Glasgow. It was a week of high-fives, arm wrestling, cook-offs and 'made you looks'.

Everybody had a great time, except Rob who lost out on the Camas Cook-Off and was forced to wear a Beard of Shame. Two of the group performed at the Iona ceilidh and almost everybody had a dance.

It was a hoot of a week, full of work and play and sunny days and starry nights. To top it all off, on the final evening we paddled out on the calm, clear and ever so magical water. We were not the only creatures out to play in Camas Bay that night. Four dolphins came to dance and dance around our kayaks! Breathtaking really. Here's to Camas Bay and all that dwell here …

This week we have had an older group of young people, ages 15-20, visiting us all the way from Harstad in north Norway.

Camas-typical activities went very well, thanks to the beautiful weather: kayaking, abseiling, walking to Trig Point, taking a boat trip to Staffa, camping on the Mac lawn, joining the evening service for peace, ceilidh, pilgrimage on Iona, doing a treasure hunt (with edible treasure, of course), going to Market Bay, a lot of games – shark attack, shipwreck, Norwegian rope game.

Finally, according to tradition, we let these guys take over Camas for their last evening here. Some decorated our dining room with flowers and flowery napkins on each table, some occupied our kitchen for the evening meal – they served a Norwegian version of Mexican food. Thank you all!

Another precious week has passed by like that. We all believe that the community and friendship we built this week will last long in our memories and will fill us with bright smiles and warmth throughout our lives forever! …

A new discovery! Becky, our gardener, has been harvesting the black and red currants from our garden like nobody's business. Where I live there aren't many currants to speak of, so I have not eaten them hardly at all before. But then – heaven opened – and a glorious thing happened.

Becky made pie! Not just any pie – she made apple and fresh currant pie – and holy smokes it was sooo good! I need to apologise to my mother as this pie was better than any I have ever tasted. At the first bite, my tastebuds sung with the pure bliss of all that sweet berry goodness. It was a party in my mouth that I never wanted to end. I have never wanted to eat, and re-eat, dessert so much; you can guess that I was definitely hoarding the leftovers of that pie for the next few days – and it never failed to wow me!

Now Becky is off on holiday, and there is no more apple, black and red currant pie, but it's memory will live on because I have tasted the best darn pie that the world has ever had! And even though that pie is no more, Becky has also seen fit to make black currant jam. I sneak into the kitchen in the morning to eat some because I dream of it at night …

We had a youth group from Texas here last week, and we had loads of fun! Let's see: we took these guys to the ceilidh dance on Iona, we went abseiling, we went to Market Bay, hiked up to Trig Point, and we kayaked, but my favourite bit was on the Thursday evening during our Camas Challenge (for those of you who don't know, this is when we let our guests take over Camas for the evening, and this means they are in charge of decorations, dinner, entertainment, and our evening reflection).

So, for Camas Challenge these Texans made us some brilliant stir fry, and decorated the common room nice and proper. They also put on a lovely reflection, and even awarded us with a special labyrinth plate from Texas. Then (this is the best bit) they taught us to two-step to some country music, how to do some other group dances, and even wowed us all with some brilliant performances. One very cool chap did a stand-up comedy act that was hilarious; we had a pair of lovely twin girls who sang a beautiful country duet.

These guys were such a fun group. They even left us Texas honey which we are still nibbling on. We bade them a very fond farewell with lots of 'yehaas' and 'y'all come back now, you here!' . . .

This week we had a group from Penicuik High School. These guys arrived after having just finished up their exams and so were really looking forward to getting away from it all for a week at Camas. On Sunday morning we all walked over to Market Bay for some games and art on the beach. In the afternoon we did some gardening and started to make some cob for our outdoor oven. Cob's made by mixing sand and clay together, and we found the best way was to use our bare feet and dance, twist, shake and boogie on top of it. We also found that coating our faces in clay protects us from the midges (sort of at least). The only way to wash it off, of course, was to take a swim in the sea.

Then on Monday it was off to Iona. The teachers generously bought us all an ice cream and we sat down on the grass in the old nunnery. In the afternoon we headed down to Sandeels Bay and relaxed in the sun for a while (ah, life is good!). These places are so beautiful and we wanted to do our bit to keep them clean and so picked up flotsam and jetsam as we walked back towards the Abbey. That night we ceilidhed in the village hall. There was also a group of young Swedes there who showed us the flipping freaky frog dance!

We came back to Camas on Tuesday after our night's camping. Then there was raft-building and racing and falling apart and getting wet! We also went abseiling down the quarry wall, which caused a few nervous moments and some shaky legs but everyone gave it a go and did their best.

One thing the group were keen to try out this week was to experience some solo time. As John Muir said: 'Only by going alone in silence, without baggage, can one truly get into the heart of the wilderness.' So this was some time to be by ourselves and let go of all the usual everyday busyness.

Thursday night was Camas Challenge night and our group served up some delicious spicy Mexican food – mucho gracias! We also had a lovely reflection where everyone shared what they enjoyed most about the trip and their high points. It was really great to hear that everyone enjoyed themselves so much and that they felt like they had got to know each other better and formed friendships. During evening entertainment we did comedic aerobics and an amazing game of sharks versus lifeguards under the kite. We were sad to see everyone go! …

Our group of guests were a crew of folk – some from as far away as Australia, some from as 'far away' as Bunessan, and all with an interest in sustainable living and discussing how we can reduce our carbon footprint. The group had come armed with data on how much energy they had used over the previous months, and looked into transport, home, food, to see which area had the biggest carbon impact. We then discussed ways of reducing this to one tonne per year in each area.

We gained inspiration and advice when going to visit the local eco-croft and Ardalanish Farm. The beautiful beach at Ardalanish was perfect for sauntering with our ice creams, and spotting all the wildlife, flowers and native woodland.

So many people have put in a lot of work to set up their own wind turbines and more sustainable ways of heating, insulating and looking after their homes. It was great to share ideas in the village hall, and have guests over for dinner on our last night …

This week we had an incredible group of young men from Glasgow come and stay with us. The week was full of tons of activities – and basking sharks! We went out sea-fishing with some of the boys and on the way we had basking sharks come right up to the boat, with their huge fins and humungous mouths; we all watched in awe as we could literally almost reach out and touch these whale-sized sharks! We even had sharks in our bay – the lads from Glasgow and the rest of us loved it! Oh, and did I mention that we all caught loads of fish, and some of us even learned how to gut and clean them!

So, we went abseiling, kayaking, hill-walking to Trig Point and Market Bay; there was lots of football, swimming (and those boys were amazing at swimming as they swam in the freezing bay at night without wet suits – they are definitely Scottish, and no mistake!). We went camping twice. First, we took the boys over to Iona and camped on the Mac lawn, and then we went to the ceilidh dance in the village hall – those boys definitely know how to dance! Then, they went wild camping near Terraragain at a beautiful beach, and the weather was definitely perfect for it!

Then, these young lads decided to do the Camas Challenge. We played loads of games, like football and ultimate frisbee, with their group going against Camas, and it was a close shot, sort of, but in the end those young men won the trophy (we put up a good fight though). They also cooked us dinner that night, using the local fish we caught – and it was delicious!

Finally, one of their leaders let me paint a treasure map on his head. It's kind of a dream of mine, I mean I have always wanted to see a bald man with a treasure map on his head, and well, I guess Camas is just the kind of place where dreams come true! …

http://thecamasdiary.blogspot.com/

Camas Centre, Ardfenaig, Bunessan, Isle of Mull, PA67 6DX, Scotland, UK

Month 3 Day 8

Women

Millenium Development Goals: Gender equality and empowerment of women

The adoption of the Millennium Declaration in 2000 by the UN General Assembly was a defining moment for global cooperation. The Declaration sets out the key challenges facing humanity at the threshold of the new millennium, outlines a response to these challenges, and establishes concrete measures for judging performance through a set of interrelated commitments, goals and targets on development, governance, peace, security and human rights. At this gathering of world leaders there was a palpable sense of urgency to *'free our fellow men, women and children from the abject and dehumanising conditions of extreme poverty, to which more than a billion of them are currently subjected'*.

The Declaration noted that national leaders have a collective responsibility to uphold the principles of human dignity, equality and equity at the global level and proclaimed that this was an opportunity to *'rededicate ourselves to respect for human rights and fundamental freedoms, respect for the equal rights of all without distinction as to race, sex, language or religion, and international cooperation in solving international problems of an economic, social, cultural or humanitarian character'.* The Declaration also affirmed that there were fundamental values essential to international relations in the 21st century, including freedom, equality and solidarity. A commitment was made to eight Millennium Development Goals (MDGs), intended to be people-centred, time-bound and measurable; based on global partnership; politically supported at all levels, and achievable.

If by any chance they got wind of these glad tidings, women around the world – and especially women who constitute 70% of those human beings living in extreme poverty – might have had cause to ponder, as they trudged through African scrub for hours in the search for usable water, or scrabbled through the garbage heaps of Sao Paulo, or endured endless unwanted sex in one of the squalid brothels of Calcutta, or screamed in the agony of giving birth through mutilated genitals, or struggled simply to get to a school and stay there. They might have dared to hope that their time for justice and dignity was dawning, that the way things are is not the way things have to be. That their right to a life of choice, integrity and freedom from harm and constraint would be secured by a radical redistribution of resources and power in every domain of human interaction. For the third MDG was a solemn commitment to PROMOTE GENDER EQUALITY AND EMPOWER WOMEN. In truth, if this goal is not fulfilled, there is little hope that we can achieve any of the others. Marginalisation and exclusion of women, and systematic discrimination against them, is a fundamental and tenacious cause of poverty, as well as being symptomatic of it. There is abundant evidence from around the world that gender inequality and systematic subordination of women has adverse impacts on efforts to tackle poverty. A recent OECD study demonstrates that countries which waste their resources by severe discrimination against women score badly on several MDGs. Where women have no access to ownership of land or credit, there is poor progress on the eradication of extreme hunger and poverty – up to 85% more than the average rate of malnourished children. Where over 50% of girls aged 15-19 are married, less than 50% of children receive primary education. In societies which tolerate and legitimise violence against women, maternal health is poor, and mortality rates for mothers and infants are high. There is a strong correlation between economic development and the extent to which women are educated and enabled to take up waged employment.[1] And women are widely recognised as key to sustainable development. So there are excellent pragmatic arguments for commitment to addressing inequality based on gender as a strategy for tackling endemic extreme poverty. But this goal is of intrinsic importance, and explicitly valued as a recognition of women's entitlement to the fundamental conditions of human well-being and dignity. It is in keeping with previous UN commitments, including

CEDAW and the Beijing Platform for Action 1995.

Although I am not a development expert, I do know what it's like to participate in struggles for gender justice, both here in Scotland and the UK, and also in transnational networks of women claiming their rights. Belonging to this global movement for change has been one of the great joys and privileges of my life. I have been inspired and moved by the courage, the wisdom, the humour, the persistence, the creativity – and not least by the righteous anger – of women in Palestine and Sri Lanka, in Romania and Zimbabwe, in Ruchill and West Pilton. We have heard the rhetoric, we have won some concessions, and yes, there has been truly significant social and cultural change in the status and opportunities available to at least some women in some places. But we've got a long way to go in this country, never mind in some of the poorest places on the planet. Gender equality and empowerment of women – that strikes me as the rallying cry for a radical transformation of the current global order. It calls for a major redistribution of resources, not just from the materially wealthy to the poor, but away from structures, traditions, symbols and systems which embed male power and privilege, limiting women's space and capacity for action.

From before birth until death, there is an enormous global transfer of resources from girls to boys, and from women to men. Women perform 60% of the world's work, earn 10% of the income and own 1% of the land. They contend with son preference and unequal nutrition; lack of access and encouragement to education; job segregation and discrimination at work; low wages; expectations of sexual services, unpaid domestic labour. Women work, cook, clean, give birth, give way, accept or endure control and limitations, and suffer degradations in order to benefit men. Even where individual men and groups reject the codes and practices of dominance (as many do) they benefit from what has been called the 'patriarchal dividend'. R.W. Connell writes:

'Men's dominant position in the gender order has a material pay-off, and

the discussions of masculinity have constantly underestimated how big it is. In the rich capitalist countries, men's average incomes are approximately double the average incomes of women. Men have ten times the political access of women worldwide (measured by representation in parliaments). Men have even greater control of corporate wealth (looking at top management in major corporations). Men control the means of violence, in the form of weapons and armed forces.

'I call these advantages the "patriarchal dividend" for men, and this dividend is not withering away. Yet not all men are corporate executives or mass killers. Though men in general gain the patriarchal dividend, specific groups of men gain very little of it. For instance, working-class youth, economically dispossessed by structural unemployment, may gain no economic advantage at all over the women in their communities. Other groups of men pay part of the price, alongside women, for the maintenance of an unequal gender order.'[2]

What hope for a millennium goal which implies a direct challenge to the privileges and entitlements of the patriarchal dividend? Let's take a look at the target and progress indicators for MDG 3.

Target 3.A: Eliminate gender disparity in primary and secondary education, preferably by 2005, and in all levels of education no later than 2015.

This is a very narrow interpretation of the Goal, but the progress indicators are more wide ranging:

> *3.1 Ratios of girls to boys in primary, secondary and tertiary education*
>
> *3.2 Share of women in wage employment in the non-agricultural sector*
>
> *3.3 Proportion of seats held by women in national parliament*

Each of these things – education, paid employment, political participation and representation – are essential to the achievement of gender equality and women's empowerment. But to set quantifiable targets for achieving them is really just to beg the big questions. Why is it that girls do not enjoy parity of access to all levels of education? Why is there a global gender pay gap and segregation, and exclusion of too many women from paid work, far less career opportunities? Why are men so extraordinarily overrepresented in national parliaments and other key political institutions – especially at leadership and executive levels? This is not primarily about technical machinery and adjustments to achieve numerical parity. It's about power. The 2010 Christian Aid Report *We're All in This Together* challenges the flawed understanding of poverty which lies behind the MDGs, arguing that it is not just a lack of material resources, but a lack of opportunity, of power over one's life and prospects, a lack of dignity. People living in poverty must be supported to take power to challenge and overcome the constraints they face. And crucially, those who hold and exercise power over others must be held accountable. Christian Aid criticises the MDGs for shifting the focus of the Declaration from empowering those in poverty, to telling poor countries what their priorities should be. Their mechanisms largely exempt the rich from examination and accountability. Poverty is maintained by systematised inequalities of power in personal, economic, social and political domains. Poverty is always relational. It is rooted in unjust human behaviour which creates inequality by giving some groups privileged access to make choices about their lives, while constraining or denying the right or opportunity of other groups to do likewise. Gender inequality is the social construct that results in women not having the same rights, opportunities and privileges as men. It intersects with and compounds other inequalities in profound and complex ways, so of course there are women who benefit from the privileges and entitlements related to class, race, wealth and so on. Sylvia Walby argues that gender inequality is structured by domestic labour, wage labour, sexuality, culture, violence and the role of the State.[3]

Empowerment is about people who have been denied choices acquiring the capacity for agency and control in their lives. It's about *change*. Poverty and disempowerment are two sides of a coin: an inability to meet basic needs and practical subordination to or dependence on powerful others rules out the possibility of meaningful choice. The normalised operations of power and entitlement make inequality seem natural or inevitable, as in societies where individual men and patriarchal institutions (in which many women are implicated) assume the right to make decisions about who and when to marry, where to live, children and their custody, freedom or restrictions of mobility and association – all of which severely constrain the possibilities available to women and girls. Women may simply accept their lot in life, or know that the costs and dangers of challenge would be too much to bear. Power has at its disposal a range of tools, including social norms; appropriation of religious institutions, beliefs and texts; legal instruments; kinship practices; control of money, property, education; inherited or assumed rather than delegated authority; ideologies of supremacy; stigmatisation of those who refuse to conform. And by no means least, the use of physical, sexual, emotional and psychological violence, exploitation or coercion.

Gender-based violence (GBV) against women and girls is a global outrage. It is the major cause of death and incapacity among women aged 16-45. Women living in poverty and adolescent girls are particularly vulnerable to the harm, fear and exploitation of GBV, and its destructive, disempowering consequences. Rape at home and in conflict situations, sexual assault, domestic abuse, intimate intrusions, commercial sexual exploitation, workplace harassment and exclusion, constraints on freedom of movement, female genital mutilation, forced marriage … the terrible list goes on and on. Violation functions as coercive control to keep women in their place. That's why it is outrageous that eradicating GBV has not been included as an MDG priority, because it is a precondition of genuine gender equality and empowerment of women.

Nevertheless, the three indicators of progress do offer potential for transformation of unequal gender relations, including GBV.

Education

The gender gap has narrowed, especially for primary school attendance. In 2007 the global average was 86 girls for every 100 boys. But research shows that education at secondary and tertiary levels has the highest payoff for empowerment, and here the gap remains significant, especially in sub-Saharan Africa and the Middle East. Disparity remains a problem, both in attendance and in the gender stereotyping content of education. Even where provision is formally available, other factors impede: girls are expected to stay at home and help with chores; they leave to get married; or they are sexually harassed by students and teachers. Far too many schools lack basic provision of sanitation and privacy. Pressure on girls to drop out of education peaks at puberty.

Access to paid work

The importance of economic independence has been one of the central planks of the women's movement. Even paid work done in the home has the potential to shift the household balance of power. The benefits of microcredit are well attested, including increased self-esteem, decision-making capacity and sometimes a reduction in domestic abuse. Collective participation has wider impacts in terms of greater political confidence, protest campaigns, knowledge and access to officials. Non-agricultural wage labour is associated with migration from rural areas, and often away from the traditional patriarchal controls of kinship and community. Women have used their newfound earning power to demand changes in violent or exploitative domestic circumstances, with the real option of leaving. In South Asia, it has enabled many to avoid early marriage, challenge dowry traditions, develop new social networks and a greater sense of independence. Even if factory work in itself is not satisfying, it can lead to positive changes.

But studies also highlight the extremely long hours, layoffs, lack of health or employment protection, low pay, ubiquitous sexual harassment and other exploitative conditions of export-oriented work under globalised neo-liberalisation. Women often face victimisation and intimidation from major multinational corporations if they complain of conditions or try to unionise.

What are the MDG indicators to measure conditions under which millions of women sweat and labour for a pittance? What mechanisms have been put in place to hold to account the rich world whose casual sense of entitlement to cheap jeans, Nike shoes or the sexual exploitation of women's bodies is so clearly premised on unequal power relations? Fashion to die for?

Around the world the vast majority of poor women working for pay are in informal, casualised, low-value and stigmatised work, selling sexual, domestic or construction labour. These economic activities are more likely to entrench than to improve women's subordinate status, and are more accurately characterised as basic survival strategies than means of empowerment. The double burden of poorly paid, low status work plus unchanged domestic demands remains one of the most tenacious and widespread gendered inequalities.

Political representation

The global average percentage of women in legislatures is 18% – that's about 7% better than in 1995. There are 58 countries where the percentage is 10% or less. At leadership and executive level, progress has been even slower, with 16% of ministerial posts and only twenty Heads of State (up from 14 in 2010). This level of underrepresentation should shock us, if it wasn't so normal. In countries where active efforts and measures have been applied, the benefits have been notable, for example in Kyrgistan, or Rwanda, which for a few years topped the international table with over 50%. Electoral systems are also a factor – multiple representative constituencies, proportional representation and party list mechanisms are all more likely to return women candidates. Single candidate simple majority systems, as in Westminster, are the worst performers, and generally are ill-equipped to accommodate diversity.

Month 3 Day 9

The story of the Scottish Parliament is instructive. I was one of many who took part in the 50/50 campaign to achieve equal representation in Holyrood, mobilising a broad alliance of women's organisations and other supporters. In 1999 Scotland's parliament was almost 40% women, and the Labour Party achieved 50% representation by a zipping system for constituencies. It made a difference to the political agenda and style of politics. Female MSPs, many with a background of active involvement in local communities, Women's Aid, etc, ensured that GBV became a priority for discussion, policymaking, funding and action. As a result Scotland has been a global pioneer for its strategic and serious approach to GBV. Other concerns such as childcare, poverty and early years education have been addressed. But even here in enlightened post-devolution Scotland (!) the political culture often remains stubbornly macho and difficult for women. Launching a recent report, Professor Alice Brown commented: *'While there were disappointments, we have to acknowledge what progress has been made. And we must remember what it was like before. Now there is a much better chance of policy reflecting the whole community. And there are concrete policies we can point at to show that a difference has been made.'*[4]

That is the hope and aspiration for women seeking justice around the world. But women who do achieve political office are not usually from the poorest communities. Their concerns often reflect the priorities of political and social elites from whose ranks they are drawn. And the extent to which national parliaments are able to make policy in the interests of the poor is hugely compromised by all the punitive dynamics and mechanisms of globalised neo-liberalism. Political power has enormous potential for transformational change, but only by the mobilisation of women and men most affected by poverty and inequality, in protest, resistance and challenge. Women's capacity to engage effectively in public arenas – to be heard and listened to, not ignored, ridiculed or patronised – depends on what power they have in other arenas of family, market and civil society.

Gender inequalities and disempowerment of women are multi-stranded and immensely complex. These realities make it difficult for the poorest women in our world to exercise meaningful agency and choice in their lives. The issues that affect them, and us, cannot be reduced to a list of targets to be implemented by the very people and institutions which benefit from inequality. The 2010 MDG3 Task Group report concludes:

'Some countries have shown that significant progress can be made. The key problem is not a lack of practical ways to address gender inequality, but lack of significant and deep change to bring about transformation of entrenched conceptions of men's and women's roles, responsibilities and control over resources.' [5]

In the words of Michelle Bachelet, Executive Director of UN Women: *'That gender equality and women's empowerment are goals in their own right and central to all other goals must be more than a mantra. It must become a lived reality for women and men and boys and girls in all countries.'* [6]

Lesley Orr

Notes:

1. OECD report: See the OECD Gender, Institutions and Development database, available on: www.oecd.org

2. R.W. Connell, 'Gender: A Short Introduction', 2nd edition, Polity Press, 2009

3. Sylvia Walby, Theorising Patriarchy, Wiley-Blackwell, 1990

4. Alice Brown, quoted in The Herald, March 18, 2010. See report 'Women in Power: the Impact of Women Ministers of Post-devolution Scotland', Active Learning Centre, 2010

5. MDG 3 Task Force Interim Report, 'From Promises to Action: Recommendations for Gender Equality and the Empowerment of Women', 2004

6. Michelle Bachelet, Executive Director, UN Women, speech to the UN General Assembly, October 11, 2010

Prayer

How am I supposed to pray?

How am I supposed to pray
with that racket going on?
Don't you realise I have to talk to my Maker
about important things
you know nothing of?

How am I supposed to pray
with you jumping all over me?
Demanding attention,
affirmation as I pull the duvet from under you
to screams of delight.

How am I supposed to pray?
How would you know?
You have no religion, just the expectation of
being heard at any moment.

I love that about you.
And I hear you, my little teacher.
I hear you.

David McNeish

Month 3 Day 11

Justice and Peace

We all bleed red

We all bleed red ...

Solyman Rashed, one of the detainees to whom the London Detainee Support Group's excellent report on indefinite detention is dedicated,* was my friend.

He was killed by a car bomb in Kirkuk, after accepting 'voluntary return'. The London Detainee Support Group/Scottish Detainee Visitors press release which was sent to me as one of the Scottish Detainee Visitors reads as follows:

'Refused asylum seeker Solyman Rashed, 28, was killed by a car bomb in Kirkuk on Monday, 6th September, 2007, after being returned to Iraq two weeks earlier. This tragic death highlights once again the dangers of forcing asylum seekers to return to Iraq.

'Solyman took "voluntary return": a misnomer as he did not go of his own free will. He had been in an immigration detention centre for 15 months, having been arrested when he was homeless and destitute. He was refused bail around ten times. After his last bail application was refused in July, he despaired of ever being released from detention and agreed to return voluntarily.

'Solyman travelled to Baghdad on the 15th August, 2007, and travelled on to Kirkuk, his hometown. He lived for only 2 weeks in freedom, before his life was ended by a roadside bomb.'

We all bleed red ...

I have a picture of Solyman on my desktop at work, so that as I work away at the screen, doing what I do as an academic, I do not forget. The picture is amazing – a great beaming smile, a flag of Scotland, and the Saltire painted across his face. It was taken in Dungavel IRC, where Solyman spent most of his time, and where Catrin, Thom and myself especially became his friends. Together, as his friends, we organised an impromptu vigil in George Square, soggy members of Scottish Detainee Visitors and Unity standing round the anti-poverty plaque in the pouring rain in gentle, awkward, tense quiet with candles and his picture and wrapped in PVC protest banners. The police came but seemed to accept that we were grieving; a vigil; people close to prayer, and they kept a distance, but watched on.

Solyman Rashed was a peaceful man, we said together.

We all bleed red.

Alison Swinfen

* *http://www.detainedlives.org/wp-content/uploads/detainedlives.pdf*

Month 3 Day 12

The Integrity of Creation

Walking the track

In May 2009 at Camas a group of adult guests on the 'Reading the Big Book' week were considering the theme of 'landscape'. At the morning reflection session we told of our journeys to reach Camas – then we visualised the walk we had all taken down the track …

You begin where the track leaves the main road among cars, mailbox, dustbin, firewood pile and wheelbarrows. Far away you can see a wind turbine, and the people who meet you tell you 'beyond that turbine is where you are going'.

A farm gate, usually with a large puddle just inside it, leads to a stony, farm track, with fenced fields on each side. After a short, steep slope it is straight and level for a while, though sometimes with deep muddy puddles. You can walk beside your companions and get to know them. When the track gets rougher a walkway of wooden planks appears on the left-hand side. Using this makes it easier to push the heavy wheelbarrow, if you are the one bringing supplies, especially when the track dips sharply down again.

Another gate leads to a wide, flat wooden bridge over a burn, and then to a smooth, wide, grassy track, open to the moor on either side. But the track turns sharply to go up and round a rocky knoll, and we've completely lost sight of our destination. After the sharp bends the slope is gentler, but the ground is so boggy that more planks have been laid. Walking on these should keep your feet dry, but sometimes an unwary step produces a fountain of black, muddy water.

Another gentle rise leads to a wider view. The track stretches away, apparently smooth and level, and there is a clear view of the small hills with the wind turbine on top. It looks a long way still, but all very simple.

It's only as you travel along that you discover the pitfalls – steep drops, muddy holes, places where you really need the planks, which are sometimes smooth and new, sometimes rough and worn, with flat stones filling gaps. Halfway along is another bridge over a deep burn. Now the track begins to rise again.

Reaching the far side of the level moor, the track bends again, becoming a stony stream-bed, and finds its way up between small rocky hills. A pair of gateposts on the right-hand side leads nowhere. Now there is a high stone wall on the right-hand side, and steep hills on the left. You climb steeply and can no longer see where you are going – while the turbine still whirs steadily on top of the hill.

As the track levels again, becomes smooth and grassy and bends to the left, a new view appears – a valley below you, leading to the sea. Soon you have your first sight of the rooftops of Camas – but now, suddenly, the track becomes a steep, stony downward slope. You need to walk slowly, trying not to stumble, but the heavy wheelbarrow, bouncing and clattering, is trying to run away with you. You are focussed so much on this that you hardly notice the back of the buildings getting closer and closer.

But you pass the blue name-post and suddenly you land on a wide, smooth lawn – the sea is right in front of you, doors open and friendly faces and voices welcome you to Camas.

Joan Jones

Month 3 Day 13

Columban Christianity & the Celtic Tradition

The 'new outline' of Christ's body for today

I am writing this on the isle of Iona, where for me it all began. Iona over the centuries has been a place of new beginnings. It was here in the sixth century that Saint Columba began his mission to Scotland. Having sailed from Ireland in penitent exile from his native land because of a battle he had incited, Columba experienced on this little island a grace of new birth that was to become also a birthing of Christianity for the whole nation. And since then countless pilgrims have come, also carrying within them the failures and hopes of their lives and nations, seeking here new beginnings for themselves and peace for the world.

It was on Iona in the late 1980s that I became deeply aware of the lost treasure of Celtic Christianity. In the ancient prayers of the Hebrides, especially in the collection known as the *Carmina Gadelica* ('Songs of the Gaels'), I found prayers that had been chanted for centuries at the rising of the sun and the setting of the sun, invocations for blessing at the birth of a child or the death of a loved one, rhythms of praise for the tides and the turning of seasons, and songs of thanks for planting and harvesting earth's fruits. These were different from the prayers I had grown up with in my Western Christian inheritance. The context was creation rather than church. Love of Christ and love of the earth were woven inseparably together. And I saw in them hidden gems for the journey of the human soul today.

Here on Iona I find myself wanting more often to pray in the ruins of the nunnery than in the rebuilt abbey church. And I am not alone in this desire. Although all of the attention historically has been focussed on the reconstructed thirteenth-century Benedictine abbey, a place of masculine spirituality, rather than on the ruins of the neglected Augustinian nunnery of the same period, a place of feminine spirituality, we are in the midst of a shift. When I first arrived on Iona in the late 1980s, the nunnery was not even included in the weekly pilgrimage around the island. Now it is not only a prominent stopping place on the Iona pilgrimage route but also a place where countless individuals pray in solitude and where groups of pilgrims can be found offering impromptu rituals and songs for the healing of the earth. What does this say? What is it about the nunnery that is speaking into the heart of the human journey now?

The nunnery sits open to creation. Whether in sun or in storm, whether in the open skies of a clear morning or the infinite stretches of space at night, in the nunnery one is aware of the elements, of birdsong, of ivy-leafed toadflax growing amid the red granite stones of the ruined structure, of unbridled wind. It is this that so many of us are looking for in our spiritual journey today, a connection between spirit and matter, the ancient bond between the wild and the sacred, an openness in relationship between prayer and the cosmos.

But the nunnery is not simply creation. It is not like praying in an open field of heather or on a rocky mountaintop. The nunnery has been a place of relationship, of intentional community, and of devotion to Christ and the cross. It has been a place where people have scrubbed potatoes together, shed tears at the news of births and deaths, and sung communal songs of the soul to the One who is beyond names but who is known as Love. It is this that many of us are seeking in the spiritual journey of humanity today, a vision of relationship, a sense of community at joyful and pain-filled transition points in life, and through it all a conscious yearning for the Living Presence.

But the nunnery is also a ruin. It is a place that reflects the brokenness of our lives and our world, as well as the failure of our religious institutions. It is a place that states clearly that we have not got it right and that we do not yet know exactly what shape the emerging spirituality of today will take. It is also a place that resounds with the neglect of the feminine that has so crippled our Western cultures and spirituality. It is this that many of us are longing for in the spiritual journey of the world today, a recognition that our imperial religious inheritance is collapsing, and that we desperately need to reintegrate the mystical, intuitive and earth-related fragrances of the feminine if we are to be alive to the deepest yearnings of the human soul.

George MacLeod, the founder of the modern-day Iona Community, is more associated with the rebuilt abbey than with the ruined nunnery. But he would not have claimed that the rebuilding of the Abbey was the definitive answer for today. At best it was a sign of the need to rebuild the spirituality that Iona historically represents. But new birthings need to happen in our lives and relationships and communities again and again and again. Long after Iona Abbey was rebuilt in the twentieth century MacLeod uttered a prayer that has been with me almost daily over the last number of years. In it he imagines Christ faithfully going to the Temple in Jerusalem, which represented both a place of ancient faith and at the same time a place that needed new vision.

MacLeod concludes the prayer by saying:

Give us grace in our changing day
to stand by the temple that is the present church,
the noisome temple

the sometime scandalised temple that is the present church,
listening sometime to what again seems mumbo jumbo.
Make it our custom to go
till the new outline of your Body for our day
becomes visible in our midst.

What is the 'new outline' of Christ's body for today?

What is the new birthing of spirituality that is trying to become visible within us and among us in our world now?

Philip Newell

Month 3 Day 14

Racial justice

Talking to strangers

Jesus' first experience of foreigners

At the beginning and close of Jesus' life are foreign bookends. Matthew, in the story we read at Epiphany, tells of wise men or Magi who come from the East in order to find the one whom they believe to be 'the new-born king of the Jews' (Mt 2:2). Where exactly they came from we do not know, but a frequent conjecture is Mesopotamia, later known as Persia and presently known as Iraq. If that were the case, it would be magnificent poetry, because on the way to Calvary Jesus is aided in carrying the cross by an African press-ganged into his service. His name is Simon and he comes from the region then called Cyrene, now referred to as Libya. So, appositely for a time when much of the world is engaged in an alleged War on Terror, we find that Jesus was positively associated with people who came from countries included in President George W. Bush's 'Axis of Evil'.

But, of course, that was not the only occasion on which Jesus had been helped by people from the continent of Africa. Matthew, who tells us about the Magi, also informs us that Jesus had to flee the country soon after their visit. Herod, who feared a rival monarch, decided to cull all boys aged two and under (Mt 2:16). We have no idea how long this episode lasted. What we do know is that by the age of eleven at the latest Jesus was living in the town of Nazareth with his parents (Lk 2:39).

It would be wrong to speculate as to what the experience of living in exile may have meant for someone so young. Its significance would probably be related through the years by his parents. But it might be sufficient for our purposes to recognise that here we have the Son of God experiencing a state similar to that known by refugees and asylum seekers – aliens in a land not their own, among people of a different language, with no security of tenure. Perhaps it was the hospitality shown to Jesus and his family in the alien land which made him keen to be accommodating to people of different ethnic and religious backgrounds throughout his ministry …

Three favoured foreigners

… We might note three of varied Gentile stock whom Jesus particularly appreciates.

The first is the grateful leper. One of ten, the rest presumably being Jewish, he alone returns to thank Jesus for effecting his cure. Does he do this because, as a non-Jew, he has no need to show himself to the priest like the others, or is it that he recognises in Jesus the fount of real rather than routine religion? We don't know, but we do know that on seeing him come back, Jesus expresses both admiration and amazement:

'Were not all ten made clean? The other nine, where are they? Was no one found returning to give praise to God except this foreigner?'(Lk 17:18).

The second non-Jew whom Jesus especially values is the woman referred to as

Syro-Phoenician (Mk 7:26) or Canaanite (Mt 15:22). Most people would today refer to her as being Syrian (another constituent member of the Axis of Evil). She has a daughter who is ill and wants Jesus to heal the child. The ensuing conversation has been interpreted in a number of ways, particularly the phrase Jesus uses when he says that it is wrong to take the children's bread and throw it to the dogs (Mt 15:26). Here he uses a crude vernacular term such as many nations have to refer to those they regard as inferior neighbours.

But the woman takes Jesus on and says that even the dogs (Gentiles) eat the scraps that fall from the children (of Israel)'s table. And in this, which some would see as a churlish riposte, he sees a statement of faith to which he can only respond by healing her child.

Thirdly we have the story of a healing which is requested by a man who is not a Jew. The story of the centurion is found in Matthew (8:5–13) and Luke (7:1–10) and each account has some original features.

The common ground is that the centurion comes to ask Jesus to heal his servant. Recently some scholars have indicated that the word used could refer equally to a domestic aide or to a younger man who was the centurion's partner. If, indeed, the latter were the case, that might help explain his reticence to have Jesus visit the household in case it in any way compromised Jesus. But irrespective of the status of the sufferer, Jesus is taken aback at the faith of the man who, using a military analogy, believes that as he commands men, so Jesus can command illness.

Jesus, astonished at his declaration of belief, says, 'Truly I tell you, I have never found such faith in all of Israel.' This expression is sufficient to indicate that the centurion was not a Jew and in all probability would be a Roman. Luke endorses this with the information that the Jewish elders made an urgent appeal to Jesus to respond positively to the man's request, '... for he is a friend of our nation and it is he who built our synagogue.' Matthew, in his account, records words of Jesus which slightly foreshadow the parable of the Sheep and the Goats, in which nations are judged not according to their religious affiliation but according to how they practise social justice and show generosity to the disadvantaged.

'Many will come from the east and the west to sit with Abraham and Isaac and Jacob in the kingdom of Heaven. But those who were born into the kingdom will be thrown into the dark …' (Mt 8:12)

Here again is evidence of Jesus' conviction, which is an offence to his listeners, that their espoused religion and treasured nation are no guarantee of salvation.

The icon of hospitality

Finally we should remember that fictional character whom Jesus chose to represent the model of care and hospitality.

In all Jesus' parables there is an element of surprise and occasionally offence. Many of the stories have an illogicality within them. For example, few fathers whose sons have squandered half their savings welcome such aberrant offspring back with a party. Again, irrespective of the century, it does not bode well for industrial relations if a man hiring labourers pays the same wage to those who have worked for a few hours as to those who have been on the job all day.

To the first hearers of the parable of the Good Samaritan (Lk 10:30–37), the title itself would seem something of an oxymoron. Just as there are Jewish lepers who don't return to thank God when they have been cured, so there are Jewish religious dignitaries who prefer to avoid the victim of a mugging than to help the injured person. And just as a Samaritan leper expresses exceptional gratitude, so it is a Samaritan traveller who cares for the injured man, transports him on his own donkey, and pays for his board and lodging with his own money.

This is the hero whose ethnicity alone suggested to the Jews that he was not one they would want to emulate. Malina and Rohrbaugh* suggest three reasons as to why the hero in the parable would be less than attractive:

a. the Samaritan was probably a trader, therefore of a dishonourable fraternity

b. the victim was ritually unclean and would contaminate whomever touched him

c. inns were establishments notorious for being run by and hosting people of bad reputation.

But there is perhaps also a sting in the tail of this parable.

The prelude to it was a lawyer asking Jesus, 'Who is my neighbour?' After telling the parable, Jesus asks the lawyer who was neighbour to the man who was mugged. The lawyer replies, 'The one who showed him kindness.' Jesus then enjoins him to 'go and do as he did'. But does that imply simply that the lawyer should help people in distress? Or – much more controversial – does it mean that in addition to being extravagantly kind, he also has to love Samaritans and whomever else helps the distressed. For indeed, the initial question was 'Who is the neighbour I have to love?' And the answer is not 'Go and do likewise.' The answer, on the basis of the parable, has to be: 'The person, irrespective of their race, who does good to others.'

In societies which are increasingly multicultural, where practitioners of world religions – Islam, Judaism, Buddhism, Christianity, Hinduism – can be found in all major world cities, one of the great strengths of the Christian faith is that its founder recognised that faith was not the property of one sect, but was a potential in all people. When a Muslim's faith leads him or her to so something sacrificial, it is not an inferior act because it is done by a non-Christian. It is something for which Christians should be grateful. For Jesus did not come to say that either the ancient Hebrews or the fledgling Christians were morally and spiritually superior because they were devoted to the true God. He came to recognise and to indicate that God was the ground of all goodness, the quality of which manifests in people of all religions and of none.

This does not undermine Christ's claim of uniqueness. Rather it endorses it, for he is uniquely able to recognise and to love the good in those who are 'not of this fold' (Jn 10:16).

John L. Bell

* *Social Science Commentary on the Synoptic Gospels, by Malina & Rohrbaugh (Fortress Press)*

Community

Creating local community

Coming away from the Iona Community plenary at Coatbridge, I found myself pondering the questions those present seemed to be asking themselves: 'What makes the Iona Community a community?' And 'What kind of community does the Iona Community want to be?' …

I've been a member since 1960, and the vision of community I caught on Iona has inspired everything I have tried to do since – working for community in society and being part of it in the Church.

I believe that the need to learn how to create community is perhaps the greatest challenge we face as post-modern human beings.

Pompous words? Not at all. For me this sentence is shorthand for a life's work. The basic line of approach was set for me by the SCM and by Iona, and the Rule of the Iona Community has kept me thinking about community and acting in accordance with it. But all sorts of other experiences have contributed to firm up the conviction expressed in the sentence. Now, all I can do is offer some stories from my past. They are just stories, not prescriptions for action, because each generation will tackle the challenge in its own way.

Some philosopher in the latter part of the nineteenth century commented that 'Abraham could travel as fast as my grandfather.' It is only in the last 150 years or so that the dramatic changes have occurred. Community used to be taken for granted. Until not so long ago those neighbours who had been given me by who I was and where I lived would have been my community.

I first began to reflect on this seriously when Irene (my wife) and I worked among village people in remote rural Zambia. At one time the people lived for security from wild animals and hostile enemies in fairly large fortified villages. If the chief needed to gather the people together all he had to do was beat a drum. The elders sat round in a communal area in the evenings. The men talked. The women sat around beyond the inner circle once their work was done, sometimes putting a word in, and children listened. During the day the women did most things together in a group, and the children were cared for mutually. Then came the Pax Britannica. Tribal warfare ceased, and the wild beasts were mostly hunted down and killed. It was now safe to live near the field where the crops were planted, so that you could scare the monkeys off the maize. People moved out of the villages into little individual nuclear family homesteads. In these places a wife and the children could work all day around the home without ever seeing another soul, except for any passer-by. What a difference in lifestyle! What about community now?

Just after Zambia received its independence in the 1960s, we were living in the small country town and administrative centre called Isoka, in the north of Zambia. Over two years, with very little money, entirely with their own labour, and help from others in the town, the local congregation of which I was pastor put up its first church building in permanent materials. No other white person was directly involved locally except myself. The previous building had been pole and mud with a thatched roof. This one had a cement floor, burnt bricks, glass in the windows and a corrugated-iron roof. Everybody in the town took an interest in it, many worked on it, and it was completed in 1969. There were a good few disputes among us in the course of getting it all done, but in the end it was the only community effort in the town that was finished on time and in budget. Many of the government schemes fell apart for various reasons, but the Church had offered a visible practical demonstration of what a local community could do if it set its mind to it and people worked together.

Later we lived in the capital city of Lusaka. We noticed that the people who gravitated to town looking for work tended to live together in one particular area, often where folk spoke their own tribal language. They created new communities in the new environment where they were now living; and so, begun by the local church and reflecting this in its own way, a Bible study group flourished in our home for expatriates a long way from their homes.

As the Protestant chaplain on the residential campus of the University of Zambia I was responsible for coordinating a weekly ecumenical service. We set up a student pastoral committee of twelve which met weekly at 9pm in one of the study-bedrooms. It planned the services and managed the offerings. But it also learned from its members who the students were who were having problems, and we considered how together we might help them. The group continued as the heart of the Protestant Christian community long after I left, and there are some remarkable stories of pastoral care.

Nowadays people are very mobile. I have a son and two daughters all married with families living around Guildford. As we visited them when they were younger, by our way of it they seemed to sit quite loose to any kind of local community. If a job necessitated a move to another part of the country, or to another country, they felt they could just get up and go, if the children's schooling could be worked out. It is true that telephones mean that they keep in touch with one another, and with us, so that there is a kind of electronic community, and they visit each other in their cars, but there are advantages and disadvantages in this. And have these been thought through? Ought there always to be a local dimension to one's community? And how do you define 'local' these days?

Our nearest local community here in Edinburgh is the group of eleven flat-owners who live with us in our tenement building. Irene and I worked with our neighbours at looking after the back garden, and arranging for the cleaning and painting of the common stair. When our roof started to leak, however, we knew that we had to get organised to

carry out expensive 'common repairs' together. With difficulty the work was done, but as soon as the crisis was over some of the owners refused to pay anything towards ongoing maintenance. And now there is no shared management of the building.

The church as community: when my sister and I were very small our parents moved away from the area where their families lived, the Lothians and Fife, to a totally new area for them – the city of Aberdeen. They became members of a local church, and as children we were completely integrated into it. Our mother died when I was five and our father when I was 13 years old. At that point our uncles, who were our guardians, had to decide what to do with us. The options were to split us up, each going to a different uncle or aunt, or to keep the home going in Aberdeen with the housekeeper, who had looked after us since our mother died. They decided on the latter policy. We were established in the neighbourhood and had other children as friends round the doors. And the local congregation was our other focus where there were folk who had known our parents and who cared for us. This was our community.

Everywhere we have moved since we were married, we have sought out a local church and tried to become part of it. In Africa these churches worshipped in local languages and we had to learn how to do that, but it paid tremendous dividends in fellowship with the local people. In the London suburb of Surbiton where we lived for eight years while our children were teenagers, our membership of the local Methodist church paid off in a quite incalculable way. There is a period with teenagers when they won't listen to their parents but they may listen to other adults they have come to know and trust. We were immensely grateful that other adults in that congregation, through the youth group, were able to pastor our children in ways that we just could not do at that time.

Robin Watt was a member of the Iona Community. He had been disabled from birth and the disabilities gradually progressed, though when I first knew him he was still practising law. He had qualified both in law and theology. For years he shared a house with Don Stubbings, another Community member, but then Don moved to his own place and Robin lived on his own. He became less able to do this, and the problem for his family was that Robin was a bachelor, and that one brother lived in London, and the other in the United States. They both came to Edinburgh from time to time, but were too far away, and Robin could neither see to type e-mails, nor talk easily on the phone because of his deafness.

A group formed round about him. Don, Iain Whyte and other Iona Community members visited him regularly. Iain, who had trained with Robin in Glasgow, organised other old friends to call from time to time. Irene (with CAB connections and medical experience) saw to his benefits and allowances, and kept an eye on the professionals who cared for his health. Another family friend, Susan, had him to lunch most Sundays and looked after his clothing and other needs. A lawyer friend kept his finances. I drove him to church every week. And through Susan we all reported to the brothers by e-mail. This was a great example of what 'care in the community', the current buzz phrase, could be all about. All the various professionals who dealt with Robin and encountered us were amazed – and no wonder. But for every person in need who enjoys this sort of care, there are so many who get little or none.

As for ourselves, the local congregation where my wife and I continue to worship each week is our key local community, and the various Iona Family Groups in which we have shared over the years since we returned to Britain have always enabled us to probe much more deeply our personal commitment to being and building community.

So I have come to believe that to think about community, and to try to create it locally, is perhaps the greatest form of evangelical service that a Christian can offer.

Jim Wilkie

Pilgrimage

Walking together

I remember that first pilgrimage we shared:
Iona
in a generous October sunshine;
and the two precious gifts which
all unknowingly
you put into my startled hands.

That was a pilgrimage rich with words…

I remember our last one together:
Lleyn
on a bright late-December day;
the slow walk up to the Holy Well,
and sitting companionably
on the wall where once the coffins were rested.

That was a pilgrimage gentle with quietness …

And in between?
Those times when,
coinciding,
we shared food and shelter;
explored the pleasures of poetry and place together;
and told and heard life's stories –
ones of both daylight and the darkness …

… Yes, I think they were often pilgrimages too.

Pat Bennett

Sexuality

God is intersex: from a conversation with Iona Community member Chris Gidden

'Courage, faith and cheerfulness' are words which spring to mind when I think of Chris Gidden, who has lived a life of great change – from working as an aircraft electrician in the RAF to becoming co-chair of CCND, from life as a man to becoming a woman. I spoke with Chris back in September 2011 when she was in Glasgow for an Iona Community Programme Committee meeting. Following is a short extract from that interview. (Ed.)

NEIL: You once said to me, and I've thought about it, something like: 'There is an in-betweenness of God. God is intersex.'

CHRIS: One of the things, particularly in the last fifteen years, that has really bugged me is the ownership of God that we as human beings try and make. And being in the Iona Community, and being exposed to women's liberation theology, made me start thinking about the women's Bible, women's prayers to God, with God as a woman; and trying to claim God for *a* particular gender. And I thought: why aren't trannies gaining this? And I thought about something which I think John Bell said some time ago in one of his books about: of course Jesus was a man. And I thought about that, because he was circumcised. But then I know with some intersex people you wouldn't know they were intersex because they have male genitalia, but they also have female genitalia as well, both complete, and that's not unknown. And for those, you could still be circumcised.

And then I thought: I've met a lot of very interesting people who are intersex – and they really need to claim their *identity* as intersex, and be *identified* as intersex, and be *accepted* as intersex. But there's so much bigotry, so much rant and rage over this, because whenever you start talking about gender, and if you're not normally one or the other, people get challenged within themselves – especially if they like you – about who or what you really are, and should I or should I not be liking this person, so much that I almost *love* them, but they're not of the right gender to be loved, as it were. Because of the norms of relationship, of our deep feelings, it's not right sometimes to express this. And I think that's where a lot of where the anger, the rage within oneself is, that we shouldn't be doing this love business.

And I thought, do you know, when you look at the anatomy of the human being at birth, at conception you actually *are* intersex: you have both. It's not until a little way along the conception line that the distinguishing paths are then branched: one is chopped off, the other one goes on – but for some people it isn't and it goes on to be both. And then you've got all these 'awkward' bloody people who are XXY, XYY … And the doctors, for a long time at Great Ormond Street, and it still sometimes happens, they've got to put down on the birth certificate are you a man or a woman: *there's no third option*. And that really has made me very angry. And I think this is an area that we've really got to fight. And I think this year of the census now, is a time that I can start something maybe.

My other thing is to step back and understand how the Bible was written up – *by* whom it was written, *for* whom it was written. Because at that time the people who wrote the Gospels, or who did writing of scripture, were scribes: It was men writing for men.

NEIL: So your being, your identity, your experience, and the people that you've met, have totally opened up that idea of God being both male and female.

CHRIS: Absolutely.

NEIL: And people like yourself can give us that vision, that wisdom, if we listen.

CHRIS: We need to completely rebalance everything here.

Month 3 Day 17

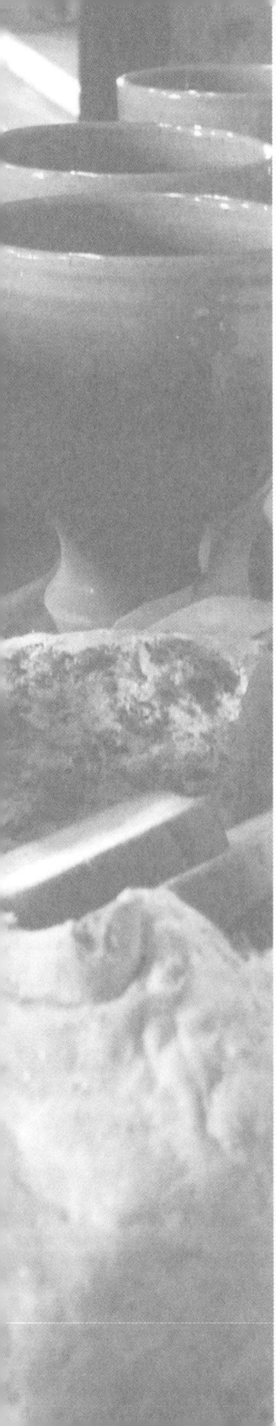

Healing

A touching place

She has travelled all her life,
dragging leg irons of disease,
to reach here.

This very spot.

In her aching belly
need has grown to desperation.
It drives her through her terror
and the gawking crowd.

He has travelled all his life
to reach here.

This very spot.

His shoulders ache with the weariness of others,
his brow lacerated by their twisted expectations.

Now her fingers tremble as they stretch
and brush the mud-spattered hem of his robe.

She finds a touching place.

You and I
have travelled our separate ways to here.

This very spot.

We stumble and trip over
our failure and success.

Driven by our need and compassion
we stretch out tentative fingers
and find in each other

a touching place.

Jim Hughes

Month 3 Day 19

Social Action

Night sight (on working as a street pastor)

I went into the city that is my home,
to be amongst those whom I usually wouldn't see.
The revellers and partygoers,
those forging new relationships, or escaping old ones;
those who sleep behind derelict churches,
and those who relieve themselves in alleyways.
Burly ones at doorways, and uniformed ones patrolling in twos,
we walked amongst them all.

Our clothing marked us out.
Others too were in costume, identifying their role, their purpose.

We were all there for our own reasons,
looking for something.
I, to deliberately place myself outside:
outside my comfort zone, my familiar experiences,
outside the people I choose to surround myself with,
alongside others.

I found open doorways I had never before noticed
leading to bright, loud places;
and the locked doorways I more commonly frequent
I found I share with others, who shelter there by night.
I found revelations of authenticity
normally repressed by light and sobriety,
and openness of hearts
touched by simple kindness.

To some we gave spikeys*, to others blankets,
for some we bought coffee, to others we gave water.
We listened to a story of an abusive marriage,
and many stories of 'boyfriend's gone off with best friend'.
We handed out flip-flops and plasters,
and collected discarded bottles and glasses.
And I found I belong there too,
and you will find me there again.

Elaine Gisbourne

** A plastic stopper that prevents drinks from being 'spiked'*

Month 3 Day 20

CHURCH RENEWAL

Bambalela: Never give up

In summer 2006 I was in South Africa, visiting a church in the township of Guguletu outside Cape Town with which the Iona Community has a partnership. Above the door of the sanctuary, so that people see it as they leave worship, are the words, 'Never give up'. And the congregation have a song, '*Bambalela:* never give up', which is regularly sung there in worship.

They need to sing it a lot, because this is a church with a huge mission and a huge heart, facing huge challenges. In a population of 300,000 in Guguletu around 30 per cent are infected with HIV. In the desperate poverty in which so many black South Africans live, treatment and good nutrition are often not available. There are many orphans and vulnerable children. In the midst of poverty, unemployment and illness, the people in Guguletu are living every day on the threshold between life and death.

But these are not people who give up easily, and in J.L. Zwane Presbyterian Church, they live hopefully. Every day, hundreds receive a cooked meal, others receive monthly food parcels. There are numerous support and counselling groups for people living with HIV, and for their families and children, and a team of homecarers. Others receive palliative care through a day hospice.

An after-school study programme is attended each day by 130 children, where they have a chance to have a meal, do homework, and receive additional study support, essential for children living in overcrowded homes with no electricity.

The centre has trained over three thousand people as HIV/AIDS educators. It runs a clinic in an informal settlement. It's involved in a rural outreach programme in the Eastern Cape, where a bakery, chicken farming, gardening, pig farming, forestry and an HIV/AIDS awareness programme have been established.

It has a sports development programme for under-13s, helping them to develop positive life skills. It started Siyaya, a performing group which does HIV/AIDS education through music and reaches hundreds in Guguletu each week. During worship each Sunday a person who is HIV-positive shares their story. (Can you imagine that happening week by week in your local congregation?) Yet to mention some of the many activities associated with this prophetic ministry is not really to describe what goes on there day by day. It is the work of the gospel, mediated through women and men who have been touched by the Spirit, and who, wounded and weary themselves, humbly companion the wounded and weary. Almost every person who works there is a volunteer. You would think that this kind of ministry would find universal affirmation and encouragement. Is it not putting the gospel into practice? I thought so. But, in fact, the church has attracted controversy and even disapproval for its work, because it welcomes everyone affected by HIV/AIDS. The minister of the church explained it this way:

'It is about people meeting people, listening to what they are going through and attempting to figure out where God is in all this. We have to try to walk with them. As a congregation we consciously decided to invite, embrace, include and engage people living with and affected by HIV/AIDS.'[1]

Like this man, who said, 'I think I've at least six things going against me these days. I'm poor; I'm unemployed; I'm HIV-positive; I've had my legs amputated; I'm black and I'm gay.'[2]

He found a welcome at the J. L. Zwane Church, but one woman in a different church was not so fortunate:

'I used to attend the local church but I don't any more. The pastor there believes that you can't be a Christian and have HIV. Two of my friends from the church used to keep telling me not to take any medicines, just to trust in Jesus to heal me. I couldn't accept that. I want to have Jesus and keep taking medicines. So I don't go to church any more, but I pray every morning for my family, for my son, for the doctors and everyone living with HIV/AIDS.'[3]

Within South Africa, and beyond, there is still a huge stigma attached to being HIV-positive. Many pastors in the churches continue to regard HIV/AIDS, which is so much linked to poverty and marginalisation, as a fierce judgement from God on human sin and they reject people who are HIV-positive, an understanding which has caused endless suffering to thousands.

Well, we are in no position to stand in judgement on these churches; how many of our churches offer a real, dignified, *unconditional* welcome to people who are poor, unemployed, HIV-positive, disabled, black, gay, a welcome that is not shot through with judgement, the belief that 'we know what's best for them'? When I was in Guguletu, a student from one of America's most famous theological seminaries, working in an affluent white Cape Town church, came to visit for a day. At the end of the day, having seen all that was being done, he said to one of the volunteers, 'This is all very well, but you are not preaching the gospel here. You are not telling the people about Jesus.'

I cannot tell you how angry and sad this comment made me. Aside altogether from the extreme Western arrogance of spending a few hours somewhere and presuming you know enough about it to pass judgement, it made me wonder deeply about the kind of Christianity he believed in.

Kathy Galloway

www.jlzwane.sun.ac.za/index.html

Notes:

1. Guguletu Journal, Peter Millar

2. Guguletu Journal, Peter Millar

3. Guguletu Journal, Peter Millar

Month 3 Day 21

Worship

New Orleans jazz and New Testament worship

There is an instructive affinity between New Orleans jazz and worship in the house churches which developed in the early centuries.

In New Orleans jazz the players bring to the music both a communal sensitiveness designed to produce the band sound and an appreciation of the gifts provided by particular instruments. A musical theme is taken up, in which all can share; then, by instinctive common consent, one of the instrumentalists is encouraged to pick up the tune and produce a spontaneous elaboration, before returning to the main theme with the rest of the players.

The basic requirement is to create a community-produced sound to which all contribute. When, by instinctive common consent, the rest of the players withdraw to allow a particular instrument to take the centre stage, this is to enhance the total musical offering, to refresh the main sound by producing a particular emphasis which enters the total fabric of sound to give colour and vitality to it. In the weaving of Harris tweed a particular pattern may prevail, but it can be made more attractive by colours which give it distinctive qualities – to produce in a fresh way contrast to or affirmation of some feature of the main pattern.

That is how Sir Alex Ferguson picks and trains football players. He has an eye for those who can play as members of a team – discounting players who cannot fit in, however crowd-pleasing may be their individual skills. He also assesses players so that particular skills can be used to full advantage through their placing in the field.

That is how the ordained should fulfil their assignments, seeking to

build up a community whose members are unselfishly concerned for one another, fitting their gifts together, as in a dry stane dyke where individual awkward shapes, deftly placed, can give strength and stability to one another.

The picture that St Paul gives of the Body of Christ affirms a prior concern above others – to form community, recognising the particularity of organs and limbs as resources to build it up, where all the parts, including the humblest, are given due value. As in New Orleans jazz, there needs to develop an awareness of the different gifts of the Spirit variously bestowed, a discernment about how these can fit together to express the mind of Christ in and for the world, and a readiness to bring particular gifts into play where appropriate. Distinctiveness, sensitively used, can provide a strengthening of praise and service.

Non-participant worship cannot match the vitality when manifold gifts of the Spirit are given space.

The relation of the small group to the larger assembly was to me best illustrated by the practice in Iglesia la Merced in Nicaragua. There the congregation on a Sunday comprised seven basic Christian communities. They had met during the week, shared knowledge of who and what should be prayed for, and worked on the biblical theme which would occupy the sermon period. The priest had a hand-held microphone which he passed around to build up the worship. Each member had already been engaged in identifying the main concerns the worship should cover. Each small community had its contribution enlarged and enhanced by the contribution of the other six. How rich is participant worship compared with that led solely from the front, which will have only one awareness and life experience to draw on for its content.

In house church worship, the spirit who guides and controls is the Holy Spirit. Those who open themselves to Her become one. When Paul urges Christians to be 'of the same mind' he is not looking for conformity to some set pattern of life but to the weaving of different gifts together in harmony. Within this harmony and building it up, particular gifts are given space: this member contributes a hymn (composed or sung), that member a word of guidance, the one who follows, a revelation (e.g. 'it came home to me in a flash that …'), the next an utterance in a strange language (speaking in tongues: an ecstatic experience). Two or three of those who have prophetic insight should be heard – provided they are ready to give way to others and not monopolise. All this (1 Corinthians 14:26–32) is under the guidance of the Holy Spirit who furnishes people with different gifts which are to be deployed to build up the church and refresh its worship.

What kind of spirit inspires New Orleans jazz?

It is a spirit who weaves into a harmony the offerings of different players, both by their participation in producing the band sound and in solos for which the band instinctively makes space. While solos in ballet contribute to the total performance, there is an element of the display of virtuosity as well – in New Orleans jazz particular instruments contribute a freshness to enhance the theme without drawing undue attention to themselves.

The Holy Spirit works creatively in the world – She is in no way confined to church. She bestows different gifts, welds into community those who make an offering of these, enriches the whole of life accordingly. To my mind the spirit at work in New Orleans jazz is the Holy Spirit.

It has been said that the description in Corinthians is an eccentric ecstatic form, not characteristic of the early church. The text says otherwise. It starts with the Greek word *hotan*: '*Every time* you gather, this is the way it goes in your worship.'

The Iona Community points a way forward. There is worship in Family Groups where the most recent and shyest member can get confidence to take part; in Iona Abbey, worship might be led by domestic or maintenance staff. It is a sign for the church and the world. Worship must be manifold. Worship must be participant.

Ian M. Fraser

Called to be One

Written on the wall

Elisabeth Miescher, an Iona Community member in Switzerland, reflects on her time working as an Accompanier with the Ecumenical Accompanier Programme in Palestine/Israel (www.eappi.org).

TO EXIST IS TO RESIST is spray-painted on the Wall in Bethlehem, next to the car gate.

Every Friday a small group of religious and lay people from the Bethlehem Children's Hospital, 6 to 10 men and women of different ages, pray at the wall. They resist at the actual separation wall. The group refuses to give up hope that walls can fall. Clémence, our Arabic language teacher, who owned land on the other side of the wall, is among them. Sometimes the EA Group of Bethlehem joins them. We resist resignation and despair …

At the entrance to the steel-caged gateway leading up to the huge checkpoint Gilo 300 in Bethlehem, there is another landmark:

GOD IS TOO BIG
FOR JUST ONE
RELIGION

He/She watches over the crowds of several thousand people who wait there every morning to cross over to Jerusalem to go to work – if they have obtained a permit. It is a humiliating passage. It takes easily up to three hours – and sometimes at 5:30 in the morning the entrance turnpike is still closed – when it should have opened at 5:00 sharp. I spent many mornings with the men there. And I asked God if She was just watching like a mother, or if She could convince the soldiers to do their work quickly. I was sure God was suffering with her children and crying at the huge separation barrier, listening to the harsh commands of the border police and to the sighing and anger within the silently waiting crowd …

Hearing VOICES FROM THE GHETTO our team went into the villages of the Bethlehem area to share in the work of a women's group preparing small lunches for the girls in the primary school. Due to the wall and fewer jobs, poverty has increased, and female students often get less food than their male siblings. Many of them come to school hungry in the morning.

Behind the wall, around Rachel's Tomb, is the Israeli military base for Bethlehem. Soldiers control the area of Aida Refugee Camp from their watchtower. Bethlehem is officially under Palestinian authority, with their own police, but the Israeli army is present everywhere.

The wall does not follow a straight line; it separates neighbours and forces them to take longer ways. One large house is now surrounded by the wall on three sides. The soldiers on the watchtower look directly into the rooms. Claire and her family, who live there, are in shock: they were landowners and had a tourist shop – now they have no income and no view.

Very near to their house I found these texts on Easter morning:

FROM THE ASHES OF OUR HOPELESSNESS
SPRING THE FLAMES OF HOPE …

A quotation by Gandhi, written in black, reads:

FIRST THEY IGNORE YOU,
THEN THEY RIDICULE YOU,
THEN THEY FIGHT YOU,
THEN YOU WIN

In red letters, a message by the Indian activist Arundhati Roy:

ANOTHER WORLD IS NOT ONLY POSSIBLE, SHE IS ON THE WAY.
MANY OF US WON'T BE HERE TO GREET HER,
BUT ON A QUIET DAY, IF YOU LISTEN CAREFULLY,
YOU CAN ALMOST HEAR HER BREATHING.

And a message by Nelson Mandela:

INJUSTICE MUST HAVE AN END, AS DAY MUST FOLLOW NIGHT.
WE WILL SEE THE DEATH OF TYRANNY
AND THE DAWN OF LIGHT AND MIRACLES.

This graffiti was like a sermon of Christ's resurrection – it moved me deeply.

Near Jerusalem, I came across:

I HATE ISRAEL – THIS WALL WILL FALL!

THIS WALL IS A SHAME
ON THE JEWISH PEOPLE,
ON MY PEOPLE!

On many shutters and doors of Arab residents in Hebron's Old City I saw the message:

GAS THE ARABS

This shows the hatred and despair of the 400 Jewish settlers in the inner, Old City of Hebron – 1600 soldiers are stationed there for their protection. They do not stop the many aggressive acts against the Arab population of Hebron. Jews and Muslims are both sons and daughters of Abraham – will there ever be peace between them? …

In 2007, on Israel Land Day, the 23rd of April, there was an alternative celebration, a beacon-lighting right near the Knesset. Many of those gathered together, including EAs, knew each other, having met at peaceful demonstrations around Bethlehem. Representatives of many peace groups made speeches, which ended with the lighting of a beacon. There was a strong wind blowing; the flames of the beacons flickered but withstood the force of the wind. By nightfall twelve beacons gave light to the crowd below.

Elisabeth C. Miescher

Month 3 Day 23

Mission

Retreat on the streets

Religious retreats conjure up images of country houses and pastoral calm, but a very different retreat took place a few years ago – on the streets of the East End of Glasgow.

The 'Retreat on the Streets' was offered by the city's Lodging House Mission, which supports people who are without permanent accommodation. The city's then-chaplain to homeless people, Ann Lyall, organised the event after hearing of similar retreats run by the ecumenical One City Project in Leeds.

More than a dozen people gathered at the Mission on a drizzly morning ready to spend seven hours on their own on the streets of Glasgow with just £1.50p to last them the day.

Ann said: 'The idea was to leave behind our money and possessions and simply spend an extended period of time reflecting on God's love for the city – and in particular His concern for the vulnerable and marginalised.

'Like many homeless people in the city, we had no agenda to keep us busy through the day and, having virtually no money, we learned a little of what it might be like to have few choices – and very little power.

'We were not pretending to be poor but we were trying, as best we could, to walk in the shoes of those who are. And after seven hours on the streets, we began to understand a little of what other people have to endure every day of their lives. For one thing, we were footsore and weary!'

Another of the participants was Anne Craig from UNLOCK in Glasgow, which encourages people in challenging urban situations to discover how their own stories relate to stories from the Bible.

Anne, who helped to organise the retreat, said: 'We knew that we would be going back to the Mission for a period of prayer and reflection when our time on the streets came to an end – and after that we would go back to our warm and welcoming homes. So, in that sense, we were not experiencing what it is to be poor or homeless ourselves.

'But it's interesting how, towards the end of the retreat, the imagination begins to kick in and you start thinking: *But what if I was not part of a supportive faith group? What if I didn't have a warm home to go to? What if I had to spend all night out on the streets? What if I had to spend every night on the streets?* And suddenly the words of Jesus about having been sent to bring good news for the poor acquire a new power and significance.'

The day, which was the third to have been run in the city, began with a simple briefing. This included the story of a woman who had taken part in an earlier retreat. Feeling tired after several hours walking the streets, she sat down on a wall in the city centre. By chance she fell into conversation with a homeless man who seemed to be interested in what she was doing.

She felt rather embarrassed to tell him that she was taking part in a 'retreat' on the city streets, but the man did not laugh at her as she expected. Instead he sat in silence for a few moments and then said: 'A lot of us on the streets believe in God, you know. We have no one else to cry to in the night.'

For some people the 'retreat on the streets' experience has an immediate and powerful effect. Participants say things like: 'This has really opened up the Gospel for me.' Or: 'I have lived here all my life, but never seen the city as I have today.'

Month 3 Day 23

Often they will say they felt surprisingly close to God on the streets, even though they never went near a church. Or that, like the woman in the story, people they met by chance seemed to speak something of God to them.

For others it may be months or even years before the experience begins to bear fruit. But it is interesting that many people ask to repeat the inner-city retreat experience. And for almost all of them, the retreat remains an important reminder of what the Gospel is about.

Now other groups, like the Church Urban Fund, are exploring this way of using the urban setting for prayer and reflection – and to be reminded that every part of our world, the beautiful and the not so beautiful, is loved by God. And every inch of our city streets is precious to Him.

David Rhodes

Month 3 Day 24

WORK

Western knitter

(Recollecting people who use their skills to serve those caught up in disasters)

Lifting her eyes to the hills of a lifetime
clouded by age, she sits in the sunset
hands knotted to aching, back bent from the burden
as a sheaf in the wind,

knitting in time to the throb of her thoughts
patterns of the past in colours of her kingdoms
with a stitch in the wrist and a turn in the yarn
and memories of those who once laughed.

Each winter, though harder, she works by the window
till word of the South feeds the world in her heart
and neighbours, now few, speak of sowing and growth,
and friends the winds scattered.

Her own grain now garnered, her face to her future,
she waits in the west for the word in the news,
linking the strands, and the shades, and the needs
of the children not hers she would serve.

As prices keep rising she saves on the heating,
sweeps the house slowly in search of the last coin;
lets pension and post send her parcel a pilgrim
to neighbours divided by ocean and favour

as she flings on the winds like a prodigal sower
her hopes and her warmth so that others find comfort,
sends bread on the waters, her gifts on the world
that knows nothing of her, for the word that knows all

of the pain of creation cast on from silence,
that the cold may be clothed in the love of a stranger,
that grain may fall open, that bread may be broken,
that the harvest abound.

Rosemary Power

Month 3 Day 25

POVERTY

A brand-new day

Fucking hell
stop ringing the bell
you're no getting in,
you're oot yir face,
get awa from my place,
I'm phoning the polis,
they're on their way,
now, do you want to stay?
Na, I didnae think so,
on yir toes, running like hell,
jist stop ringing my fucking bell …

The daddy-long-legs
outside the window,
it's raining,
it's struggling,
it wants in,
up and down it crawls,
still trying to get in,
I keep watchin',
will I, won't I
let it in?
Na, I just keep watching,

it flies away,
looking for sanctuary,
somewhere else I suppose …

I love the moon,
the stars, the sky
I go to bed
and wonder why

I wake up
look out the window,
the sun is shining
a brand-new day,
now I know why …

Bubbles, they're nothing but
trouble
so many young lives lost
at what cost?
They get so high, then so low
they're so young,
they don't know
hanging from the trees
is there gonna be
autumn leaves

No
their relatives are grieving
the only thing they'll be
receiving
is the thoughts of their small child
growing up

now every tree will hold a
memory
and that is so sad
not to look at a tree
cos you don't want that
memory.
Their son
whose life had just begun
now at an end
because of the latest trend …

I brought him in,
the poor soul,
he's good at that,
'poor poor me'
I wash his clothes
give him a bath
even trim his beard
how does he repay you?
He kicks you in the teeth
I fone the police
he scampers before they arrive
calling me a rat and a grass
bloody cheek! …

Heroin,
they say it's better than sex,
the needle
pumping it through your veins,
ahh bliss,
that's their kiss.

What about making love then,
but without the needle
you don't need heroin for that –
total ecstasy,
the human kind
smell, touch, feel, see, taste,
if you don't want that instead
then what a waste …

I stand next to him
I want to touch his skin
next to mine
we dance all night
Oh! What a night!
he pulls me close
his lips to mine
my eyes are closed
I open them
yes, he's still there
for I can't get free
his arms are still holding me …

He screams and shouts,
my ears are ringing
I can't stand the noise
he's out of his fucking face,
again,
I walk away,
pretend I'm singing ...

Looking up,
teardrops,

running down my face
no more pain,
I am numb,
I just stare ahead,
get up, walk away,
and close the door,
he won't see me no more …

Life
it cuts you like a knife
right through my heart
like a speeding dart
I feel the pain
if it wasn't for the kids
I'd go insane
fight your corner
stand upright
cos if you didn't
life would be shite …

Karen Buchanan

Karen Buchanan is a single mother of four children, ages ranging from 13 to 22. She lives in the centre of a Dundee housing scheme with a widespread culture of drugs and violence. She came to CraigOwl Communities to do a cooking class, then to a literacy class at which her writing talent was immediately obvious. She joined the CraigOwl Writers Group in the early spring of 2011 – these poems are just a fraction of her incessant output reflecting the harsh realities of her life. CraigOwl Communities is a voluntary organisation that seeks, through a range of provisions, to tap into the potential of those furthest from the job market. It has a strong record of both bringing people to 'job readiness' and finding actual employment.

Basic Christian Communities

Visiting Dungavel IRC

Monday evening and I'm coming up from the subway in Gorbals, Bridge Street. It's a dark, wet evening, one of those where the rain bounces off the pavement and you get wet just by looking at the rain. Across the car park I spot a familiar car and run through the puddles and jump in the back. 'Hi Alison.' 'Hi, hi, is that us?' 'Have you got the visit report from Thursday?' 'Yes, and I managed to get phone cards too – I think they are good ones. Talk Home and One Tel was what M. said would be good.' 'When were you last up there?' 'Two weeks ago.' 'Did you see F. then?' 'Yeah, she was doing well, making lots of jewellery. She gave me a gorgeous beaded bracelet she'd made.' And off we go. We chat away in the car about this and that, work and hillwalking, gardens and ceilidhs, recent weddings and plans for others. As we pass through Strathaven and wind up the wild hills beyond, we become more subdued.

Dungavel IRC is signposted (Immigration Removal Centre), and we swing into the drive and up to the car park. Around us are 30-foot-high fences topped with razor wire. Out come our passports and notebooks and paper and we go towards the first gate and ring the bell. We are let into a wire tunnel cage and asked to wait. We watch out for the drugs dogs that GEO have announced will be present for searches once a month as part of the security process. Beside us another, larger wire tunnel cage opens, and we see a blacked-out van drive in, the gates close behind it and then gates open in front as it drives into the compound. We stand and wait. Wet. A voice comes out of nowhere over the intercom. 'Hello.' 'Hi, we are befrienders.'

A long, laborious security process – one which I'd no doubt be in trouble for describing in any detail – follows. Bunches of keys, security wands, wrist bands, fluorescent paint, fingerprints, photographs, more bunches of keys, body searches and then suddenly we are inside the waiting room and hoping that soon those who have asked us for a visit will be down to the visits room to see us.

One by one they come down; 3 is our quota for the night, based on the IRC rules. Some are familiar faces, friends now, happy to see us. Some are keen to chat – football and the gym the main topics. One is drawn, thin, pale. 'He's not good,' says one of his fellow detainees. We talk, nothing heavy, just a few gentle words, conversation. I discover he speaks Arabic and ask for a short lesson. It works, and there is suddenly a laugh, a smile, and for a short time the roles are reversed and another language than bureaucratic-security-English is in play, and my attempts to speak it are a source of great hilarity. A woman comes down halfway through the hour we are allotted. We've not met her before, but she has just come from chapel. The prayer meetings are well-attended, we have come to understand, and important times of gathering.

Towards the end of the visit I go to the security guard on duty and ask permission to leave the phone cards, then fill in the names of those to receive them, and register a small sum of money that will be given to the one who is about to be deported the next day, passing the time of day with the guard as I do so. And then time is called and one by one we shake hands or hug our friends and say goodbye. There is always an awkward moment as we wait in the room, after they have gone, to be let out ourselves, but through a different door. We don't speak to each other, and the silence continues through the visits room as we are checked out of the Removal Centre. The same procedure as before: wands, fingerprints, photographs, keys, more keys. We walk between lines, scissors and stickers, warily watching for dogs, and then are back in the car park and the last door is locked behind us. And then we speak, anger and sadness woven through our conversation all the way back to Glasgow, and until we have gone our separate ways, until the next time.

Alison Swinfen

Non-Violence and Peacekeeping

Community Week Communion Address, Iona, 2008

Take my blood.
Take my death shroud and
The remnants of my body
Take photographs of my corpse at the grave, lonely.

Send them to the world
To the judges and
To the people of conscience
Send them to the principled men and the fair-minded.

And let them bear the guilty burden, before the world,
Of this innocent soul.
Let them bear the burden, before their children and before history,
Of this wasted, sinless soul,
Of this soul which has suffered at the hands of the 'protectors of peace'.[1]

The author of this poem, Jumah al Dossari, a thirty-three-year-old Bahraini national, is the father of a young daughter. He has been held at Guantánamo Bay for more than five years. In addition to being detained without charge or trial, Dossari has been subjected to a range of physical and psychological abuses. He has been held in solitary confinement since the end of 2003 and, according to the US military, has tried to kill himself twelve times while in the prison.

The poem comes from a book called *Poems from Guantánamo: The Detainees Speak*. The first time I read it, I could not help but hear in it the echoes of the words of Institution we say in the communion service. I read further in the book, and I found psalms, like this one:

I shall not complain to anyone or expect grace from anyone
other than God, so help me God.

O Lord, my heart is plagued with troubles.

I shall not complain to anyone other than You,
even if the seas complain of dryness.

My spirit is free in the heavens,
while my body is overpowered by chains.

Praise God, who has granted me patience in times of adversity
and gratitude in times of gladness.

Praise God, who placed a garden and an orchard in my bosom,
so they will be with me always.

Praise God, who has granted me faith and made me a Muslim.
Praise God, Lord of the world.[2]

And I found epistles:

I salute the brothers,
And pray peace to those who remain faithful.
I say hello to Shwayman,
And to everyone whom I love,
And to everyone who misses me.

Remember, pray to God for those whom I love.
Maybe God, with His kindness, will have mercy on me.[3]

And I realised that this too is a testament. It was a salutary reminder that testaments and psalms do not only belong to Christians. They speak because they are universal; they hold the fear and anger, but also the hope and the longing for

God of human beings of every description. That is what gives them their power to transcend time and place.

As a Christian community with an explicit commitment to peacemaking, we are well aware of the ambiguous nature of our scriptures, our liturgies, our histories, our religious language, our theologies, our practices. Violence and exclusion are woven through them like scarlet threads, as they are through all of life. These threads, as much as the faith in which they are embedded, continue to shape our modern world and the dominant ideological maps in both church and state.

Jesus asked his disciples, 'Who do you say that I am?' But even the act of interpreting and answering that question, of seeking to unpick the threads of violence in Christianity, has its own implicit violence; it uproots and disturbs, makes people homeless, carries bereavement within it, and we don't always account for the tears of relocation. As we attempt to live by the map of non-violence, we are aware of our complicity in violence at every level, from our own small deceits and betrayals to our involuntary collusions. Britain has this year become the world's biggest arms dealer. There are times when I feel so enmeshed in the web of violence, so aware of its implications, so despairing of the Christian community as a model of non-violence and reconciliation that it seems impossible to break free. And I hear once again, the question of Jesus to me, 'Who do you say that I am?' What am I holding on to in my commitment to non-violence?

In his Community Week sermon, David Lunan, our preacher, reminded us that it is when we are most aware of our brokenness, of the violence done by us and the violence done to us, at our most despairing, that God comes to us with a great unconditional 'yes'. And indeed, that is my experience and my testimony. But I want to say a little about how God comes to us. Speaking personally, God has never come to me through a proposition, a theology, a doctrine or a dogma. Hope and resurrection have quickened in me in the body and in the world. Deliverance, healing from violence, reconciliation have been always and only through the Word made flesh. Through my senses, in the infinite beauty of created things, in silence and songs and psalms and poems and the testimony of others, in touch and tenderness, in companionship and food and rain and sun; God comes to me when I am swimming in the sea; perhaps this is simply a preconscious memory of the womb, but I think God is a more stylish way of putting it! So I'm holding on to the Word made flesh, and the resurrection of the body.

And I'm holding on to the life and teachings of Jesus, because without them, the Word made flesh and the resurrection of the body make no sense; they disappear under obscure, forensic and violent theories of death. In the world of bodies and money and poverty and shame and hunger, Jesus affirmed the limitations and constraints of being human, did not separate himself from the condition of the hungry poor and identified himself with the excluded and the impure. He was unequivocal in teaching that his followers should love their enemies, do good to those who hate them, bless those who curse them and pray for those who ill-treat them, and he died doing exactly that. He made relationship, based on justice, kindness and humility, the central fact of his life; not belief, not piety, not conformity, and not power.

And because it's also through relationship that God has come to me as the Life of life, sometimes gently, sometimes humorously, sometimes with great rigour and challenge and struggle, I'm holding on to the Trinity, the community of God, that wonderful image of accountability and interdependence, a community of love in which each person is different yet equal, bound together through the power of mutual love. The members of the Iona Community are not always nice to me! I am not always nice to them! We often disagree! But I can live with that, because I love them and desire their well-being, and I believe that they love me, and I step out trusting in that love and unity, which is not of doctrine but of relationship.

My Christian formation as an adolescent was during the time of the American civil rights movement, and was hugely shaped by it. I am not black. I am not an

American. I did not suffer racism or segregation. But at the age of 15, I knew that this vision of Christianity, and this Jesus, articulated and embodied in the moral passion and costly commitment of Martin Luther King and his colleagues, and in people I knew personally as well, was something worth giving my life to. I have never changed my mind about that.

Martin Luther King is one of my saints, and I guess that most of us have them. But collectively the Iona Community has its own communion of saints. We name them every 31st day, and at our Hallowing Service. Every single one of these lives, flawed, wonderful human beings as they were, is a great testimony to the struggle for justice and the longing for peace. When I am weary, I hear one or another of them whispering in my ear, 'never give up'. Never give up the demanding common task of holding the space in which people who are different, who are in conflict, who are in pain, who are oppressed and divided, can meet. Hold the space, on Iona, at Camas, in Glasgow, in the Family Groups and in your neighbourhoods and churches and workplaces. Hold the space, that fertile and creative space, because within it, healing can happen, reconciliation is possible, justice becomes essential and grace abounds. I hear them whispering, 'You're all on a frontline somewhere. Hold the space. Never give up.' So I'm holding on to the communion of saints.

And I remember once being at the nuclear base at Faslane with some of the saints for a peace demonstration, and something extraordinary happened, which member Jan Sutch Pickard wrote a great poem about:

We shared Communion at the gates of Faslane:
one of the places in a broken world
where breaking bread and drinking bitter wine is most relevant.
We shared it to remember security –
not of barbed wire and missiles –
but of God's love that risks all and gives life.
We shared, in a warm circle of believers.
But later, when we sat down on the cold road,
we found that the bread and the cup had escaped,

and were still out there in the crowd,
being shared, carefully, among people of all kinds:
this paradox of pain and promise being passed from
hand to hand in a broken world.[4]

Somehow, in a place of great violence, a different kind of space came into being. The Holy Spirit, the spirit of Jesus, unexpected, unpredictable, uncontrollable, came among us in the power of non-violence, as the Spirit does when we hold the space for her. So I'm holding on to the promise and the power and the peace of the Spirit. I began with words from the Guantánamo Testament. Celebrating as we are on the night after the Feast of the Transfiguration, and between the anniversaries of the dropping of the atomic bombs on Hiroshima and Nagasaki, these words were a reminder to me that whatever belief, expectation or explanation I may bring to the table tonight, Jumah al Dossari in his Guantánamo cell is closer to the lived experience of Jesus. In his broken body, and in the broken bodies of everyone across the world who is dying violently, suffering violation and humiliation, suffering intolerable cruelty or hunger, I see again the total identification of Jesus with all flesh. And our prayer must be for the grace of God and action for justice to be in all the Guantánamos tonight. The memory of that which is intolerable to us is remembered in Christ's body, in which is named all the violence of the world. But our communion is not in the memory of suffering. Our communion is in the empty cross, in the hope of transformation, of new life, of blessing and sharing and laughter and delight. So tonight, I'm holding on to the feast. And I'm inviting you to share in it now.

Kathy Galloway

Notes

1. 'Take my blood …', by Jumah al Dossari, from *Poems from Guantánamo: The Detainees Speak*, University of Iowa Press, 2007. Used by permission of University of Iowa Press.

2. 'I shall not complain to anyone …' by Abdul Aziz, from *Poems from Guantánamo: The Detainees Speak*, University of Iowa Press, 2007. Used by permission of University of Iowa Press.

3. 'I salute the brothers …', by Abdulla Majid al Noaimi, from 'I write my hidden longing', from *Poems from Guantánamo: The Detainees Speak*, University of Iowa Press, 2007. Used by permission.

4. 'We shared Communion at the gates of Faslane …', by Jan Sutch Pickard, from *Out of Iona: Words from a Crossroads of the World*, Wild Goose Publications, 2003

Month 3 Day 28

INTERFAITH

Creative, Loving Spirit

In June 2010, the Iona Community Council set up an Inter-religious Relations Working Group. This paper is an edited version of one produced for the group.

Keep a world focus

Population migration, electronic communications and international travel have made us all much more aware of the diversity of religious belief and practice worldwide and in our own local communities. Scientific advances in understanding the natural world and ourselves as human beings have made it necessary for thoughtful believers to revise and reinterpret traditional statements of Christian faith. Historical and biblical scholarship has led us to new understandings of the authority of the Bible and the creeds of the church. Although in many places different faith communities live together happily and peacefully, in some places there is serious conflict between religious groups and brutal persecution of religious minorities. These are attributable to a variety of causes, some religious, some political, some both. Daily the media portray the heartbreaking consequences of such inter-religious strife – suffering, death, destruction and a pernicious climate of suspicion and distrust. These are aspects of the context in which our working group must prepare its report and the Community discern its response.

The Christian basis for our engagement

In discussing inter-religious relations, our focus as a Christian community should be on the gospel as it relates to today's world and the faith communities in it. It is the world in its variety and entirety that God loves; it is the world's salvation that God wills. God pours out his Spirit on all flesh, the many not just the few. Think what that means – no person, no religious community falls outside the sacred, loving purposes of God whose life-giving energy, encompassing goodwill and generous compassion infuse the whole of creation. Christians cannot claim a monopoly of the fruits of the Holy Spirit. Are not the gifts of the Spirit – love, joy, peace, patience, kindness, goodness, faithfulness, gentleness, self-control – as evident in Jews, Muslims, Sikhs, Hindus, Buddhists and indeed atheists, agnostics and humanists as they are in Christians? In the words of the prologue to the fourth gospel: Jesus is the light that lightens every person who comes into the world. As the writer to the Colossians affirms: in Jesus, God has united the things of heaven with the things of earth; in him the whole creation holds together.

Inter-religious relations today are not an optional but an essential Christian duty and privilege. Though Jesus was brought up in the Jewish tradition, learning the law and the prophets, attending synagogue and temple, he engaged with people of different faiths and cultures: for example, the Samaritan woman at the well, the Syro-Phoenician mother whose child was sick, the Roman centurion whom Jesus commended, saying he had 'never seen such faith as his before, not even in Israel'. Jesus firmly refused his follower's request to call down fire on a Samaritan village; the way of violent retribution was not for him. Pilate demanded that the inscription on Jesus' cross be written in three languages; it was a truth for the whole world as well as the Jewish and Roman leaders to read. At Pentecost people of different races, cultures and beliefs experienced the unifying presence of God through the Spirit. Paul's unwavering conviction that the gospel was for Gentiles as well as Jews ensured that Christianity became a world movement rather than remain a Jewish sect. Only with difficulty can we imagine the transformation in belief and lifestyle that his conversion from leading Jew to Christian apostle must have involved.

Do we now require a similar transformation of our accepted views? Do we need to make a step change in our thinking about those groups whose faith differs from ours? Are we able to recognise that the same Spirit is at work in different faith communities as well as our own? Or do we persist in focussing on our differences, too readily claiming a uniqueness and superiority for ourselves? Are we prepared to undergo a similar radical Paul-like transformation in order to embrace those whom we have been in the habit of regarding as outwith our circle? What crippling dogmas, what outworn practices do we need to discard, and what new passions do we need to kindle to respond to the Spirit today as it prompts us to value and engage with people of different faiths and seek with them the unity and peace of humankind? Is it possible for us to do so without feeling that we are abandoning our core beliefs or betraying our cherished religious and cultural traditions but rather that we are fulfilling our commitment to Jesus and maintaining our strong conviction that God's love is universal and unconditional? Christians have a responsibility to respect difference; to celebrate difference as a sign of the richness and diversity of God's world; to challenge difference where it hurts; and to reconcile difference when it is necessary to do so for the sake of health, justice and peace.

Month 3 Day 28

Sometimes religion is the problem rather than the solution

Religion is essentially a human activity and as such can be a force for both good and ill; a fount of grace, truth and loving-kindness on one hand and a rancid spring of violence, casuistry and selfishness on the other. The same spring seems able to bring forth sweet and bitter water. Perhaps you share some of my ambivalence about religion. I am amazed by the fatwas of the ayatollahs and shocked by the cruelty of Al Qaeda but excited by the Arab Spring and charmed by the kindness and friendliness of Muslim members of my local community. I am dismayed by the heavy-handed imperialism of the Vatican but frequently blessed by the love and prayers of my Roman Catholic relatives and friends. I am angered and saddened by the hostile statements from the Knesset but at the same time humbled by the admirable courage of 'Jews for Justice' dissenters in Israel and the scholarly wisdom of Jewish neighbours in my city. I am sometimes perplexed by the dreary formality, introspection and irrelevance of Scottish church synods and assemblies but continually inspired by the worship and vitality of some congregations and the devoted service of local Christian people. There is good and evil in every human endeavour, in each one of us and in our religions.

By definition, religions are exclusive and divisive. Although they have much in common (for example, belief in a divine being or beings, holy books and buildings, a moral code, forms of individual and shared worship, a recommended lifestyle, teaching about the origin and purpose of life, death and life beyond death) the differences between them have often been built up into unassailable dividing walls. I hope and believe that Christian churches and most world religions at their best have been an influence for good; but it is greatly to the shame of many faith

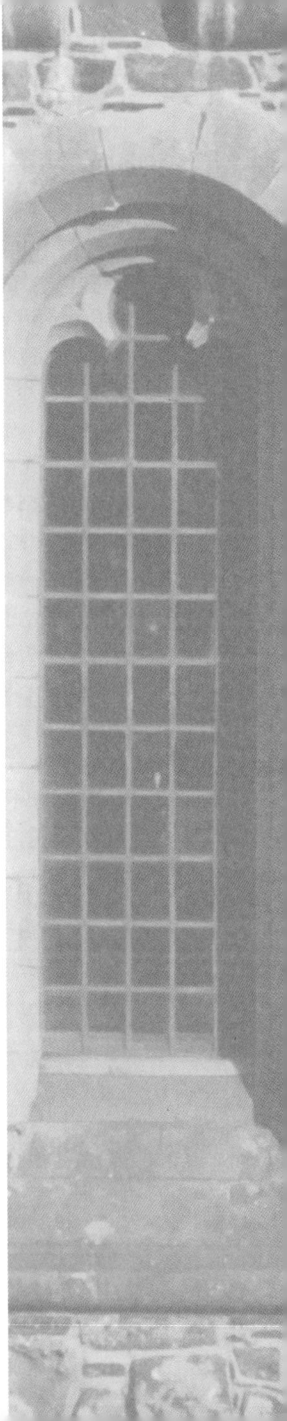

communities, including our own, that too often at their worst, they have not behaved responsibly – contributing to division, emphasising exclusiveness; seeking to achieve their goals sometimes by violent means, inflicting pain on others, generating animosity and distrust; resisting scientific progress. Religious systems, those in authority in them and their members, can be backward-looking, authoritarian, arrogant, spikily defensive, actively aggressive, self-serving and power-seeking. Religion can be destructive of freedom, love, joy, the human spirit and even life itself. Is it any wonder people in the West, spiritually hungry, searching for truth and meaning in life, are turning away from organised religion because they see it as self-serving and an obstacle to making a better world? Or give up on the church because they do not see the life of Christ in us?

Why did Jesus reserve his strongest criticism for the religious leaders of his day? I recall George MacLeod saying that the greatest contribution that Jesus made to religion was that he did away with it – or words to that effect. I also heard Hans Kung, speaking in Edinburgh in May 2000, say, 'There can be no peace without religious peace and no religious peace without dialogue between religions. If the churches in the former Yugoslavia had used the past 50 years for real dialogue, it would have been a different story today.'

I like this visionary verse by David Stevenson, an English Methodist. It is part of a poem entitled 'Dreams of a Kingdom':

Religion is no more – fragmenting humankind
with doctrine, creed and narrowness of heart.
Not darkly through a glass, truth stands at length
in beauty unaffected, a prospect indivisible.
Love is her only name.

So must we abandon organised religion altogether? Many in the UK have done so already. (Adult communicant membership of the Church of Scotland has fallen from 1,315,466 in 1958 to 474,937 in 2009, and other churches have experienced comparable decline.) Or should we commit ourselves to a new religious reformation? One that has already begun and will require of most of us and our churches not only personal rebirth and organisational regeneration but also a readiness to meet and learn alongside people of different faiths.

What has the Iona Community to offer?

There is little point in us duplicating work already being undertaken by other groups. All credit to those within religious organisations who have worked tirelessly to promote the sharing of knowledge, understanding and cooperation amongst faith communities. But if I am correct, much interfaith and inter-church debate is largely conducted defensively by those in official religious positions whose first loyalty must be to their own faith community.

The Iona Community stands within the Christian tradition but we are not a denomination with something to lose by deviating from the party line. The Community has always tried to put commitment to Jesus and the values of the Kingdom above loyalty to the accepted norms and doctrines of the denominations of its members. (That is one reason why, with all our denominational differences, we are still able to celebrate communion together in the Abbey and at Community gatherings.) For freedom Christ has set us free! So we can embark on inter-religious discussion and activity without some of the constraints which impede official church leaders with their orthodoxies. Indeed we can go further. In the past the Community at its best has been willing to encourage its members to go to Christ 'outside the camp' in their efforts to be faithful to their Christian calling; in the Spirit of Jesus to take risks by engaging with society in all its grubbiness and glory; even to break the rules where 'the letter killeth but the Spirit giveth life'. Religion can bind, divide and constrain: Jesus liberates, unites and empowers. Outside the camp one can find the fresh air of the real world with its necessary

compromises, its loving-kindness, friendship and generosity of spirit, its capacity to hurt and to heal, its freedoms, its conventions, the immediacy of life's pain and life's possibilities. One becomes aware of the Spirit moving, reconciling, healing, teaching, empowering. I write as one who was privileged to work as a hospital chaplain in the NHS, serving, alongside the clinical team, all who came through the hospital doors whatever their beliefs, meeting them as persons whose humanity I shared and whose beliefs I learned to respect. Living, working and serving together for the common good opens all kinds of doors.

In the NHS I also discovered that not everyone who claims membership of a faith community will accept the values, doctrines, lifestyle and moral precepts of that community or will find its liturgies helpful. So it is important to distinguish between faith communities with their creeds and the individuals who belong to them but have grown to find a living personal faith of their own. I also found many who had abandoned organised religion altogether because they could not with integrity believe the unbelievable or identify with any religious group. We must not lose sight of those who seek a credible faith but find it difficult to feel at home in today's religious communities. It is important to build relationships of respect, understanding and trust with them as well as with active members of faith communities; to meet in friendship as neighbours, exchanging information, sharing concerns and wherever possible acting together.

Religious belief and practice do not stand still: they evolve; and evolution is led mostly by those on the fringe. The Iona Community has demonstrated its capacity to evolve, to change itself and to generate change in the churches. It continues to be an inspiration to those on the fringes of organised religion. It is experienced in welcoming individuals as they are, orthodox, heretic and everyone in between. It prays for 'new ways to touch the lives of all'.

So we might ask, 'Should membership of the Community be open to those who belong to different religious groups, if they wish to join? We are already ecumenical: why not interfaith? Should worship in the Abbey be exclusively Christian? Should the Community stay close to its Christian roots?' These, I hope, are relevant questions for the Community to address. For the present, I cannot see any reason why we should not invite to Iona people from different faith communities, and especially those on the edges of these communities, to discuss the topics which lie at the heart of both the Jesus story and many other religious stories, topics which are of vital concern to many people both inside and outside religious communities: money and wealth, justice, peace, health, human relationships, personal growth in holiness, freedom, authority, life in community, revealed truth and learned truth, the trouble with religion; and in and through all these, the nature of God and the will of God for our time. Indeed there are compelling reasons why we should do so, humbly and hopefully, and I believe that the Community has the resources with which to embark on such a massive task.

Worship together might prove difficult to arrange but with humility, imagination, determination and goodwill it should not be impossible. Should we not try to find shared understandings, common words and lively actions to glorify in worship on Iona the Creative, Loving Spirit from which all life and many religions originate, the Spirit Christian people meet convincingly in Jesus? How good it would be to share the many things we have in common; to reform and strengthen our faith and ourselves and to do it better because we are doing it together; and to plan and work for a better future for all peoples and for all religions.

Stewart McGregor

COMMITMENT

No place like home

A letter from Warren Bardsley, volunteering as an EA with the Ecumenical Accompaniment Programme in Palestine and Israel (www.eappi.org):

Fawzieh Al Kurd is a remarkable woman. As you approach the house where she lives with her family – one of a row of dwellings on a hillside in the East Jerusalem neighbourhood of Sheikh Jarrah – your first impressions are of Israeli flags on adjacent houses and the presence of an armed security guard. In the foreground of the house is a spacious patio, and above the downstairs windows a large banner proclaims: THIS IS APARTHEID. At the back of the patio a group of young internationals are sitting or lying on mattresses. Fawzieh is a tall woman in her 50s; on meeting her, your first awareness is her smile and warm greeting; you know that she is genuinely glad to see you. In her eyes you also see pain and a steely determination. There is a transparent goodness about her, but she is no revolutionary activist. She simply wants to stay in the house in which she has lived for 52 years, where she was married, and where she has brought up her five children.

The story begins in 1956, when, following the birth of the state of Israel, the government of Jordan, which all that time had jurisdiction over East Jerusalem, gave land in Sheikh Jarrah for the building of homes for 28 refugee families with the help of UNWRA. Fawzieh came from a well-off family in West Jerusalem; her husband, Mohammed, is from the Jaffa area. It was agreed that ownership of the houses would be transferred to the families within three years. Following the Six Day War in 1967, two groups of Jewish settlers claimed ownership of the land, and over the next 25 years a series of legal battles ensued, during which it became clear that the settlers had no legitimate claim on the property. The Israeli Supreme Court did not, however, agree to rezone the land, and in the meantime, settler families began to infiltrate the neighbourhood.

Now, imagine this: You have recently built an extension to your home in order to accommodate your growing family, and in the hope that someday your sons, their wives and children will live there. An adjacent front door means that the apartment is separate but part of the main house. Imagine that after completion of this extension, a group of people claim that the property is theirs, have the locks on the extension door changed and move in. Such was the shocking experience of the Al Kurds, when in 2001, during their absence from Jerusalem on a hospital visit to Jordan, a settler family took over the extension to their home. Now try to imagine what life has been like for Fawzieh and her family for the past seven years, as they have tried to live a normal life in the face of constant provocation by settler families, who change frequently and for whom, it should be said, life must be extremely circumscribed. They make no attempt to communicate with the Al Kurds, who more than once have been offered large sums of money to move out, and it is little wonder that Mr Al Kurd's health has broken down. He is partially paralysed, has a heart condition and suffers from diabetes.

As Fawzieh sits with us on the patio outside her front door, she reflects on the latest developments. Two weeks ago, the settler family now occupying the extension fixed a large plywood structure to the wall, to celebrate Succoth, without saying anything to the Al Kurds. A new settler investment company has been recently formed, and in February of this year submitted a project to the municipality of Jerusalem, proposing the demolition of the 28 homes and the building of 200 settlement units to house Jewish immigrants. This is the real agenda. In July, the Israeli Supreme Court issued an order to evict the Al Kurd

family, a ruling that is being strongly contested by the Neighbourhood Committee's lawyer. Around mid-September the Court ordered the settler family to leave the house, but as a previous order was not enforced, Fawzieh is not over-optimistic. At best, it feels like a temporary reprieve. Recently, the nearby Hanoun family received an eviction order; the head of the household has just completed a three-month prison sentence for refusing to hand over the keys to their home. Fawzieh is grateful for the media attention that the campaign is receiving through the International Solidarity Movement, and for the support of EAs who regularly visit the family.

Fawzieh speaks with passion about her family, her faith in God, and the rightness of the cause. We are moved by her strength and resilience. Of course she is fiercely protective of her own. That is natural. But her resilience has become part of something bigger than herself and her household – the struggle for justice. There is something of the Rosa Parks spirit about her. She smiles again as we stand to say goodbye: *Masalaame*. The armed guard employed by the settlers passes us on his half-hourly 'check'. On the way out we see a large poster on the back wall stating in bold letters WE WILL NEVER LEAVE OUR HOME – an unambiguous declaration of intent. Knowing the power of the opposition they face, we continue to pray and hope with them for a just outcome. But we sense that time may well be running out.

There is a tragic sequel to this narrative: On Sunday, 9th November 2008, three days after this letter was written, a detachment of Israeli border police and military arrived at 3am, sealed off the Sheikh Jarrah area and evicted the Al Kurds from their home of 52 years. They moved into a tent on land adjacent to their home. One week later Mr Al Kurd, who had been seriously ill for a number of years, died. The tent has been taken down by the Jerusalem municipal authorities several times and re-erected. Fawzieh is now living with one of her sons in another part of East Jerusalem. The family are appealing against the eviction.

There was a crucifixion in Jerusalem
today.
Under cover of darkness they came.
Long before dawn.
Armed to the teeth.
Unjust sentence already passed,
separating a family
from their home of fifty years.
The usual suspects gather:
soldiers lounge at barriers,
smoking, drinking coffee.
Friends, neighbours watching,
from a distance,
seethe with impotent rage.
Black-clad religious
pass to and fro.
Notable absentees.
Sometime after noon
a word from the cross.
The indomitable Fawzieh
wheelchair-bound husband
by her side.
Voices vehement protest,
passionate faith that
right must prevail.
Still soldiers watch
waiting for the end.
There was a crucifixion in Jerusalem
today.

Warren Bardsley

The Rediscovery of Spirituality

The God of Grace: a sermon in Iona Abbey, Easter Sunday 2011

'What is your favourite day during Holy Week and Easter?'

Guests staying in the Abbey this week were asked this question on arrival.

A question to prompt our sharing with one another but also to highlight the opportunity presented to those of us participating in the programme in the centres here this week to journey with Jesus every day, every step of the way through the events of Holy Week. And we have done so against the charged backdrop of modern-day Israel and Palestine.

Most of us, most Holy Weeks, I suspect jump from Palm Sunday to Easter Sunday, not only because we are busy Monday-to-Friday people, not only because we naturally back away from suffering and pain, but also because we struggle to make sense of the events of Holy Week; we struggle to understand the meaning of the Cross.

This winter I took an evening class at Edinburgh University: 'The Megalith Builders of Northern Europe' – well, you have got to do something on those long dark nights – and I have always been fascinated by standing stones and ancient burial chambers. Who built them and why? How were they built and what do they mean? After my ten-week course I have learned a little of Neolithic funeral practices but on those big questions I am none the wiser. We don't know and can never truly know. I find it frustrating yet I love the mystery and all the many theories.

There is mystery at the heart of the experience of Easter. The big questions disturb and elude us as they have eluded followers of the crucified Jesus from that first Good Friday through the centuries. There are many theories, understandings, doctrines. Over the centuries one of those theories has become dominant to the exclusion almost of all others. Accepting that one understanding has become a test of faith. It runs like this.

Good Friday happened because God wanted it to happen, and we are told this by some interpretations of scripture passages, such as those dealing with the figure of the suffering servant in Isaiah, and by much of the teaching of the Church.

Humanity was so enslaved to sin, a hostage to wickedness, that a ransom had to be paid. God was so scunnered with humanity that reconciliation was only possible through the sacrifice of God's chosen one, Jesus the Christ, the Son of God. And there was blood, and a ransom was paid, and God was … God was what? Appeased? Happy? Satisfied?

When Lorn, my younger son, was a toddler he did something he shouldn't have. I can't remember now what it was that he did but I can remember what I did. I slapped him on his leg and I did it too hard, so hard that the mark of my cruel hand could be seen on his soft, pale skin. I cried. I cried because of the pain I had caused to someone I love; I cried because of my sense of failure and shame.

Now if that is how I felt as a very human, imperfect father then what kind of God is it that demands blood and sacrifice and death? That God is no better than I am – in fact that God is worse.

I do not believe in such a God – the God of the Grudge. That is not the God of Jesus Christ. Yet this is the God portrayed in so many of our hymns. Take for example an Appalachian hymn we sang one morning this week:

What wondrous love is this that caused the Lord of bliss,
to bear the dreadful curse for my soul, for my soul …

When I was sinking down beneath God's righteous frown
Christ laid aside his crown for my soul, for my soul.

There is a tragic disconnect between this dominant understanding of Jesus' death on the one hand and the message that he proclaimed.

So what does Jesus himself teach about forgiveness and debt, sin and

reconciliation? Should we not look to Jesus for understanding of these things? Surely the whole thrust of Jesus' life and teaching was to change our minds about the nature of God, a God of Love and Mercy, rather than to change the mind of a frowning God about us.

Previous generations of the faithful, in their attempts to understand the person and significance of Jesus, looked to ancient scripture which spoke of the coming of the Messiah, the Christ. The God of the Grudge has such a hold on humanity that rather than re-interpret passages like those which tell of the suffering servant in the light of the God revealed by Jesus, the opposite happened, leaving us with bloodthirsty theologies which confront us once more with the God of the Grudge.

Something in us finds it easier to believe in the frowning God of the Grudge than a God of Grace so we are forced on to our knees to pay homage to a God who acts more like a Mafia boss who sends out his hit men – pain, suffering and death – to put us in our place. It is very hard to escape the clutches of this Divine Don, as can be seen only too clearly in the history of the Church from the present day right back to the disciples themselves. Look at the disciples. When Jesus received a less than friendly welcome from a Samaritan village the disciples went into full Terminator mode, 'Lord', they said, 'do you want us to call down fire from heaven to destroy them?'

Despite them, Jesus proclaimed the Gospel of the God of Grace. He taught resistance to evil not through violence, fighting fire with fire. Not through an eye for an eye, blood for blood, but through love and compassion, forgiveness and healing, through justice and reconciliation.

Jesus died resisting evil, like thousands of women and men, known and unknown, martyred over the centuries. Jesus went to the Cross because the powers of this world demanded it – not God. Jesus was executed a common criminal because human beings declared him guilty by the due legal process of his day – not God.

God, scripture tells us, declared Jesus innocent and on the third day raised him up.

Ah, but now I am doing it – jumping ahead too soon as if the Resurrection somehow undid the suffering and injustice of the Crucifixion – cancelled it out. It does not. The execution of Jesus of Nazareth, his Cross, still stands for what it was – the legalised murder by the state and the religious authorities of a man who challenged the very basis of their power and authority.

Jesus' cruel, unjust death exposes the lie and the absurdity of the very notion of sacrificial religion. His cross still stands to remind us that we can never again believe that other human beings should be victimised, made scapegoats, demonised, killed, for the sake of some 'greater good'.

The arrest and crucifixion of Jesus convinced his scattered, shattered followers that the God of the Grudge had won. They had stepped out of line, flown too high. They had followed that dreamer, that rebel, walking away from their responsibilities, bringing shame on their families. They said it would all end in tears, they said it wouldn't last, they said that sooner or later they would pay for it. And they were right. So they abandoned him, denied him, ran away and hid.

Hiding behind locked doors those one-time followers of Jesus were once again enslaved by the God of the Grudge. And that is where it should have ended – Jesus and his Gospel of the God of Grace – crucified, dead and buried.

We are here two thousand years later because it was not the end, because those who ran away and hid emerged as bold as brass to speak of Resurrection and a Risen Lord. We are here because those who had denied ever knowing him now found the courage to be ready to die for him, and they did. We are here because those who had witnessed his bloody, humiliating death stood on street corners claiming victory over the powers of this world and over even death itself.

I learned on my course that the very first human rituals were associated with birth and death and that humankind's first monument was a tomb. Many a creed and philosophy has been nurtured and fed by the grave of a fallen leader, the burial place of a vanquished hero, the tomb of the ancestor. The tomb is thus the first cultural symbol – a symbol of remembrance, of belonging, of loyalty, of duty, of obligation. Alas for humanity, the tomb is also the place of grief and raw emotion and anger, the place where an eye for an eye can seem to make sense, where revenge is whispered as the answer to past injury and injustice and where redemptive violence raises up new heroes and fashions new tombs.

The God of the Grudge loves a tomb. And the powers of this world are practised at donning mourners' garb to stir up ancient hatreds, wrapping themselves in the flag of patriotism and divesting themselves of responsibility for the bloodshed and misery caused by their faults and follies. Jesus knew this, rebuking his religious opponents as recorded in Matthew's Gospel:

'You hypocrites! You make fine tombs for the prophets and decorate the monuments of those who lived good lives and you claim that if you had lived during the time of your ancestors, you would not have done what they did and killed the prophets. So you actually admit that you are the descendants of those who killed the prophets! Go on then, finish what your ancestors started.'

But the tomb of our dead leader was empty. There is no holy ground to be defended, no mummified body to be paraded on holy days, no relics to carry into battle, no wrong to be righted, no death to be avenged, no defeat to be repaid, for He is Risen and victory is won.

We are here because those first Christians experienced the power of the love of the Risen Christ; the Cross became for them a tree of Life sprouting green leaves of Hope. Nothing else can explain the transformation in them. We are here because we too have experienced that power or long to believe in it – that one day every tear will be wiped away, that one day there will be an end to poverty and injustice, violence and oppression. We are here because we too find hope in the Gospel of the God of Grace, in gathering together in Christ's name, in sharing bread and wine, friendship and faith.

A Frowning God did not demand sacrifice, but our Lord Christ Jesus said, 'This is my body broken for you. Do this in remembrance of me.' Amen

Peter Macdonald

The Thirty-First Day

My father's grave

My father died in the south of England, in the small town where he and my mother had raised their four children; far from his birthplace in Scotland.

He had passed on a strong sense of his roots to his children, though this seemed to be a generally unexpressed understanding, rarely put into words.

Many years later, I still feel that there was something missing while growing up, and I think it was a sense of place; a sense of belonging. We lived far from the sea and the hills, and it never felt like 'home': the place to go back to in later years. Even my Londoner mother was – and still is – happiest north of the border, where she now lives. Perhaps it is simply because Scotland is a beautiful country, overflowing with memories of good places and good people. For me, that includes staying with an aunt and uncle in Greenock. Those holidays were happy times, and well over fifty years later there are warm memories of the friendly people, exploring the shipyards with my father, paddle-steamer trips on the Clyde – and the best ice cream in the world. I can't claim that more than half my blood is Scottish, but it may be that something was transfused into it to tip the balance.

The time came for my father's funeral arrangements, and it turned out that there were none, except that he had asked for cremation: the rest was up to us. There was no obvious final resting place, so I let a lifetime of emotion – perhaps it was instinct – take over, and I suggested to my mother that we might take the ashes back to where they came from, and scatter them somewhere near the headwaters of the River Clyde, the great river that runs close to my father's birthplace. There was no discussion, and we agreed right there that we'd do it.

The funeral was a cold, brief ceremony conducted by a dutiful, but detached, clergyman, and held at a ghastly production-line crematorium in a neighbouring town – one of the bleakest of the early 'new towns'. The clergyman had already set the scene by telling us that he didn't regard my father – a Christian Scientist – as a Christian, never mind how devout he had been. Concentrating my mind on the northward journey to come, away from that desolate town, away from the harsh crematorium, away from the empty, comfortless ritual, made the event bearable.

A few days later we piled into a hired car and set off. On the way, I collected the urn from the undertaker, and was solemnly advised that I'd get a five-pound refund if I returned the empty urn.

It was a strange journey. We didn't know the exact spot that we needed, because the area wasn't my old stamping ground at all. Linda, my wife, remarked that we were fluttering about the landscape like birds in search of a nesting place. We found it, though. It's a quiet place where the River Clyde still runs fast, frolicking under an old bridge, with a good place for us to get down by the water. It wasn't very solemn or ceremonious: I simply emptied the urn into the river, watching the dust spread over the water, making patterns, disappearing into it, disappearing from us. Dust that had been an old man's body, discarded when he no longer needed it, became for ever part of a great river, something that will endlessly renew itself for as long as there are rivers.

Perhaps the ashes of my childhood drifted away in that moment too.

We walked along the riverbank, not saying much, our two young daughters pleased to have been part of taking care of their grandfather. 'Did you say a prayer?' someone asked me much later. No, I didn't. My mind was completely empty for a while, just glad that we had done what we had done, and having no doubt at all, then or since, that it was the best thing we could have done.

Whenever I come back to Scotland, I fly into Glasgow, and the plane sweeps over the great Firth of Clyde just before landing. I look out at the great expanse of water and the old industrial towns clustered along its shores, surrounded by the gentle green hills. And I look fondly, and perhaps proudly too, on my father's grave.

Andrew Foster

Month 4

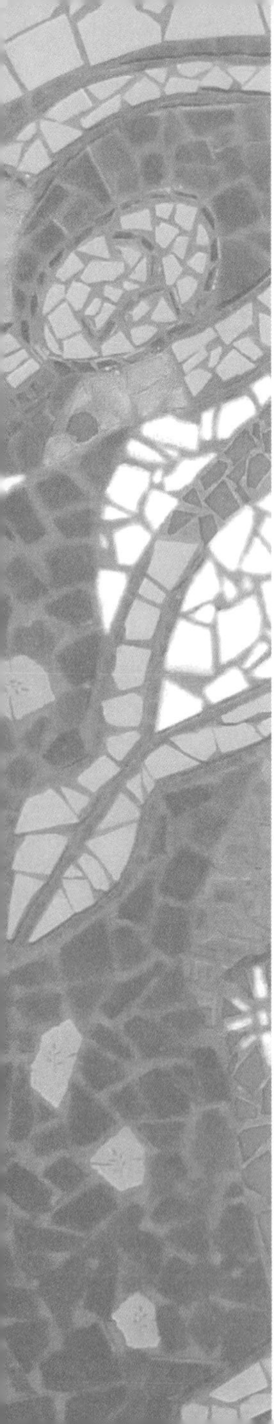

Month 4 Day 1

New Ways to Touch the Hearts of All

Lifted

Someone had fiddled with gravity
and this was no subtle tweak.
Earth's core was now repelling objects
and flinging them far into the sky,
where they gathered, uncertain,
like adolescents at a funeral.

Most were not impressed,
clutching vainly at treasures,
photos and phones, keys and cameras,
that spun off without farewell.
Emptying pockets was hazardous,
as the pilgrimage of possessions gathered pace.

The people remained,
tethered to the vacant earth.
Physicists sat, baffled and glum
at the selective sifting.
Losing their grip
to an alchemist of mass disorder.

Someone had fiddled with gravity,
I hadn't meant to – it was a careless prayer.
And yet, as I walked through the pert forest,
with its stargazing snowdrops,
whilst birds battled downwards
to the arcing telephone wires,
I couldn't help but feel this was manna in reverse,
and how my heart was lifted.

David McNeish

Month 4 Day 2

Economic Witness

Good money

I want to say a good word about money, because too many bad words are being said.

Money is just not good news at the moment for most people.

For some the budget has been a disappointment; for others the issue of MPs' expenses is a scandal; and for yet others the continuation of bumper rewards to bankers who have overseen financial failure is outrageous.

Money is not enjoying a positive profile.

Indeed it has accrued to itself a phalanx of adjectives which suggest that it is inherently corrupt:

Filthy lucre,
Black economy
Back-handers
Shady deals
Toxic loans.

What we fail to see is that the more we use such terms, the more we suggest that money is inherently contaminated. Therefore, when we are involved with it, we may subconsciously believe that we are dealing with something unhealthy. So we slip into being economical with the truth when we speak of financial matters. Married people refrain from telling their spouses how much they earn; close friends rarely discuss their personal wealth; and in the public realm deceit, silence or embarrassment surround the issues of expenses, taxation and the identity of those who are the gatekeepers of the black holes into which so much money seems recently to have disappeared.

Christians who refuse to be open about money, and who thereby encourage secrecy in high and low places, most need to be challenged. For the Christian tradition in its holy books never attributes a moral value to money, nor does it automatically dub wealthy people as duplicitous or malevolent.

Half of Jesus' parables mention money and never in condemnation. And when he upturns the tables of currency changers in the Temple, it is not coinage he is objecting to, but those who mishandle it.

It is ultimately our use of this commodity which has a beneficial or detrimental effect on other people. It is not pounds or dollars that are shady, it is how they are employed. It is not the economy that is deceitful, it is how banks, business, the government and taxpayers are transparent or furtive about their dealings.

The trickle-down effect was the process whereby the wealthy were encouraged to enhance their fortunes in the belief that financial amelioration would spread from the top down. The fact that it hasn't worked has nothing to do with a complex economic logjam. It has all to do with how benevolence, generosity and justice do not automatically flow from a huge income.

Money in itself is morally neutral. But its ability to benefit a society only becomes apparent when those who have it also have nothing to hide.

John L. Bell

Month 4 Day 3

Youth Concern

Letter to a grandchild on his blessing day

Dear Fergus,

It's a good day to be writing you a letter. The day of your blessing. Long ago when I was young (away back in the time of the Picts) lots of folk sent their grandchildren letters, but in this age of high technology it's much easier to send an e-mail or a text and to make it short. Perhaps you would rather have had an e-mail today: 'Hi Fergus, you sure sound like a cool dude. Love, Apse.'*

In a very short time your home will be in Toronto – quite a distance from the quiet lanes of East Bergholt. It won't take you long to discover a basic marker in our globalised world – that we are all interconnected as never before in human history. Given this reality, it is crucial that we never judge others by the colour of their skin, or their religious tradition, or their sexual orientation, or whether they are rich or poor, or old or young. If our planet is to survive we need one another, and when you are older I hope very much that you will do all in your power to

heal our wounded planet which today cries out in pain. It is a simple truth that all of life is sacred and precious, not just us human beings who, relatively speaking, have only been around for a short time.

Given the unpredictability both of human life and of our human future, I have been writing in my recent books about some of the qualities we all need. I need them. You need them. As you grow up, I would love you to slowly but surely realise that your life is held in God's hands. This means many things. It means we are made in God's image and empowered by the Spirit. It means we affirm God's goodness at the heart of humanity, planted more deeply than all that is wrong. It means that each day we can celebrate the miracle and wonder of life, and the unfolding purposes of God forever at work in ourselves and the world.

Walking in God's light means that people come before possessions – a hard truth in our culture where often what we have matters much more than who we are. It would be wonderful if you could carry in your heart and mind: integrity, compassion and the ability to take risks not just for yourself, but for others. Try not to forget that we live in a global village in which millions of our sisters and brothers are the victims of poverty, war and increasing injustice. And, in a world of many religions, if you do follow the Christian path, I hope you avoid a 'comfortable Christianity' and always believe in a God of surprises who can turn your life upside down.

Be able to laugh at yourself, and at silly jokes; and even if in a few years you strongly believe that your mum and dad know absolutely nothing about life, realise that if you do ever have children of your own, they will, before long, think the same about you! Sometimes that learning process may take sixty years, but hopefully you will get there in the end. This week, I loved reading about a guy who started to grow a ponytail at 85!

Earlier this year I had the privilege of helping with an interfaith book called *Reflections of Life: Words of Comfort and Encouragement*. It was published jointly by the National Health Service and the Scottish government, and copies have gone to all the hospitals in Scotland. Our hope is that the book will bring strength to many people in hospital, whether or not they have faith in God.

I would like to share with you one of my poems which is in this book. The poem is set in the Highlands of Scotland where your dad spent some of his teenage years, after returning from living in South India. The words reflect many of the things I believe about life. As you grow up I don't expect you to believe the same things as I do, but I do hope that you will be a person of love, of hope, of sensitivity and of awareness. And if you can, try growing a ponytail at 85!

Highland morning

On this quiet track
in early summer,
amid birch and larch and pine,
who could not sense the sacred
and feel creation's heart of love?

Fourteen centuries have passed
since Iona's monks –
at one with nature's pulse,
alive to crag and stream –
trod these Highland hills,
carrying Good News about the One
whose energies of light
pulsate through strath and glen.

This track is holy ground,
a sacred space,
where, walking lightly,
wonder becomes my companion.

Month 4 Day 3

I look through the trees
aware of the shy deer
who has grazed here longer than our centuries,
certain heir of mountain and forest.
And as I meet her gaze,
something in my spirit
leaps with joy,
for I feel at one with all that lives
on this glorious, Highland day.

Lots of love and go well on your travels.

Apse x

Peter Millar

** Apse – a family 'nickname'*

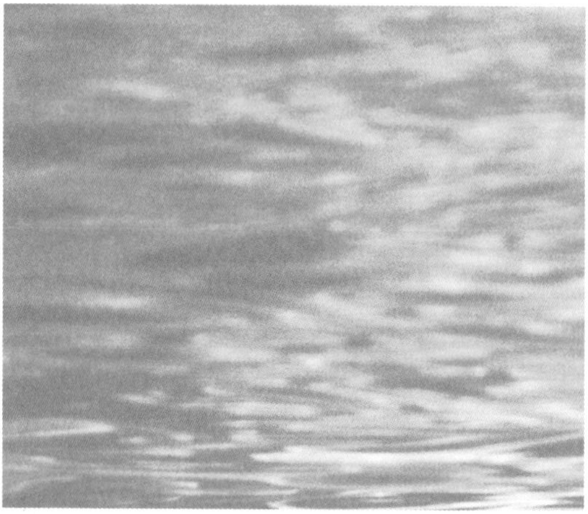

THE WORD

In 2007, a group of Iona Community members and associates travelled to Cuba to meet with fellow members and associates. During that time many connections were made and stories and feelings shared. Following are two poems by Neil Squires which came out of the visit.

Rene

During our time in Cuba, we were privileged to meet
Rene Castellana,
a 94-year-old lay Presbyterian.

Originally a psychologist,
he is a legend within the Presbyterian Church in Cuba
and is much loved and respected for the contribution
he has made over the years,
particularly in a pastoral role.
He is also an amazing dancer
and has a phenomenal knowledge of dances from
all around the world.

He took great delight in dancing for us and with us
and also told us a lovely story … He said:

'When I die, I'll teach the angels to dance.
And I'll know how to teach them to use their feet;
I'll know how to teach them to use their shoulders;
I'll know how to teach them to use their hips;
but I won't know how to teach them to use their wings.'

A grandmother's gift

Many families have become split up since the Cuban Revolution, as family members have gone to live overseas. The costs of travel and restrictions on leaving/entering Cuba have made it difficult for them to be reunited. Often mail does not reach its destination and Internet connections are unreliable, so written communication is also problematic.

A small, brown package …
Inside, a children's Bible.
And a letter, lovingly written
from a mother to her son she's not seen for fifteen years
and a grandmother to a grandson she's never met.

Pride and pain.
Yearning and resignation.
Hope, that someday soon she might travel the long journey
to be reunited …
To embrace her son, hold him
and talk into the night.
To experience the joy of her grandson.
Tell him stories, read to him,
until he falls asleep …
and maybe dreams of Cuba.
Until then, this gift
sent very special delivery
will do just fine …

Back in Scotland
I realise, this simple, uncomplicated act,
this kind of everyday, mundane thing,
is something I've taken for granted all my life.
The package slips effortlessly into the postbox.
And leaves Inverkeithing … bound for Spain.

Neil Squires

Month 4 Day 5

Hospitality and Welcome

Death row

It was his first day sentenced.
They put him in a cage:
no place unseen, to wash or weep,
no place to rest, no choice to sleep;
demanding lights, destroying noise,
the bruise of chains, the shouting guards
cut into all he'd been.

'Your name, son?' said the orderly
to the body by the wall.
He whispered it, the man yelled out:
'Neil Crossan, dead man come.'

The cages rattled, men roared out
his name along the cells.
The televisions blared their wares –
he'd heard the tales, he knew the code
and cowered there for violent death
from hands of men mad as their words
each in their private hell.

The plastic supper sent and done,
the anger loud, the sounds' rebound,
rocked round along the walls.
The orderly returned and swept

without a word or look or hope
a bag beneath the bars.

Neil Crossan sat and stared the hours,
in muteness though the noise,
imagining what horrors now
were presents to new boys.

With lights dimmed down for sleeping,
the pain exhausted sank.
He braced his soul to bear the worst
and opened up the bag.

For scorpions, faeces, filth and scorn
he was prepared that night,
and found there toothpaste, chocolate, soap,
a comb, and smokes and lights.

The morning orderly came by.
Neil asked: 'How can I pay?'
'You cannot pay except to give
when some damned soul comes through.

Now this is life and this your home
for twenty years, or worse.
We are the bad, the mad, the sad
the ignorant and base,

who walk like you through death's dark row,
where evil, hate, may breed,
but each may choose, down years, down life
to meet unspoken need.

We likely did some evil act
our souls may hate, forget;
still limitless and free is grace
for those the world rejects.'

Rosemary Power

The charity Life Lines, a secular organisation, looks for mature individuals to write to people on death row in the United States: www.lifelines-uk.org

Month 4 Day 6

This is the Day

Sauntering*

Now that I'm old I'll learn to saunter.
My hips will swing as I notice what
puts me in mind of forgotten roistering
and I'll wink at strangers.

I will encounter pleasures, some dark, dank –
as you find in vast canal warehouses,
with tapping sounds in the roof where
pigeons' wings whine.

Sauntering, I will find that time saunters too.
It will expand without effort while I listen

to the blather of children, strangers, lonelies
and mad old souls.

Sauntering, I will walk on holy ground.
My loose gait will disturb no small animals:
they will sense harmlessness
and carry on snuffling.

Sauntering will lead to baths at midday,
night swims, afternoon films and eating
nothing but smoked salmon all week,
and stew in bed.

Wouldn't put it past me to saunter
into verse, write tomes of rude red politics –
but so quietly that passing birds will flirt,
giving me the eye.

Sauntering, I will learn its manifold
advantages; so this poem will never end,
as sauntering throws up more tricks and
grand surprises.

But can you saunter through the world's woes?
Did Jesus and the Marys, did Gandhi and Mandela,
did they saunter while they fed and led
and told the truth?

Margaret Legum

** Saunter: from the old French 'sainte terre', meaning 'holy ground'*

The Iona Experience

The 'Just Across' group: from Wrexham to Iona

Four trains, one-night B&B in calm and sunny Oban, two ferries and one bus trip later – and Zimbabwe, the Ukraine, Eritrea, England and Wales were represented at the MacLeod Centre by 14 people, including two toddling Zimbabwean boys.

We shared worship twice a day in Iona Abbey, chores, meals, entertainment and company with the volunteer and resident staff and a few other guests from Norway. We explored the beautiful island together – walking along white beaches, and up Dun I, giving us a chance to see beyond the island to the Paps of Jura, Colonsay, the north of Mull and Staffa. Some of the party even went into the sea – and I mean *into*! Freezing to say the least.

There was a chance on Monday to sail to Staffa in a small boat, which six of the group did. Words were too hard to find to describe the trip. On our return journey we sailed by five or six dolphins, dancing about together in the sea. What more could we ask for?

As the group reflected on the week it became very clear that folk had truly appreciated the opportunity to see beyond the town of Wrexham and to be part of a community for a week. Someone reflected: *'I have had the chance to do three things I have never done before – travelling in a boat, climbing a "mountain", and going to a beach and in the sea. Thank you for giving me the opportunity.'* This 'Just Across' group became more than a group of people from the weekly drop-in – we became family. A very special family, which felt blessed in every way. Thanks be to God.

Biddy Crossfield

Month 4 Day 8

Life in Community

Change

'Be the change you want to see in the world.'*

I want to
clear the temple, loot the vaults,
lance every boil, fix all faults.
Heal the land, clean the air,
neuter pain, cure despair.
Restore every broken home.
Renew every broken vow …

So much change is needed.
And Gandhi – I feel a little overwhelmed.
Must do better, do more, do well.
Or can I just be?
Is faith the decision to plough just one furrow
and trust the rest of the field to others?
Here is hoping.

David McNeish

* *Gandhi*

Women

Women of dignity

I want to share some stories of women who exemplify for me the power of human dignity. In 1998, I attended the Women's Festival held at the General Assembly of the World Council of Churches in Harare, Zimbabwe. While I was there, I met a French-speaking Methodist deaconess, Marie-Thérèse. She came from the Democratic Republic of the Congo, a huge country in which all the problems that beset Africa are present to a desperate degree. It is the scene of a bloody and rumbling war, complicated not only by warring factions but by the undisciplined forces of half a dozen other African countries, which breaks into open conflict regularly, and where low-grade hostilities are a normal way of life. It has enormous numbers of refugees and displaced peoples. HIV/AIDS is a huge problem. And, though it is a beautiful country rich in natural resources, the combination of asset-stripping, war and chaos has left the people tremendously impoverished.

On the last day, I went to see Marie-Thérèse off on her journey home. She was there with a group of other women from the Congo, all of them involved in church and community projects in their towns and villages – caring for people with HIV/AIDS, for refugees and war victims, for some of the many orphans created by the tragedies of their country, for women struggling to support big families with few resources. They had travelled to Zimbabwe by a rickety bus that looked as if it wouldn't get to the end of the street, never mind back to the Congo. When it started up, it made terrible noises and belched fumes. These women were going to spend three days and nights on this bus, driving through some of the most dangerous parts of Africa, sleeping and eating on the bus. It was a profoundly humbling experience to meet these women; I could hardly imagine the struggles and difficulties they faced. And yet, the astonishing thing about them was how joyful, how full of laughter and hope they were.

I asked them why they had made this long, uncomfortable and dangerous journey to East Africa. 'It's so important for us to have this chance to meet Christian women from other parts of the world,' they replied. 'It's an encouragement for us; we feel we are not alone. We want to learn about the problems women face in other places, and to share faith with them.' I think they had found that encouragement; I certainly know I had found it in them.

Another friend of mine in Scotland recently took a very long walk. She walked the West Highland Way (a 95-mile rural trail) in the company of a number of young people from the poorest parts of Glasgow. They weren't young people who were used to outdoor pursuits, so they had to do a lot of training in the gym and on practice walks to get fit enough for their expedition, and my friend gave up her spare time to do it with them. They had to raise money for proper equipment. She's someone you couldn't blame for sitting back and enjoying what leisure time she has – she is a single parent who had experienced considerable personal tragedy in her life, and has survived what would stop most of us in our tracks. But she's chosen instead to try to give something positive and creative to young people who have very little positive and creative in their lives. She too dares to care.

Volunteering in an HIV programme in Kenya, my daughter met Jayne Mutahi, who runs Hands of Compassion, an outreach project. Jayne has, in the past four years, accumulated nine tents and a second-hand vehicle and made it her objective to take HIV-testing and medical treatment to the Masai tribe, who often live as far as ten hours from any health care. The Masai are a popular attraction with Western tourists visiting Kenya but their numbers are declining. They have continued to practise their ancient rituals and ceremonies, choosing a peaceful way of life that is centred on rearing their cattle, but their polygamous practices accelerate the spread of HIV throughout families.

Jayne relies on intermittent sponsorship and donations from friends and volunteers to carry out the mobile clinics. On a typical four-day clinic, over three hundred people are assessed and given treatment by the nurses and a hundred are tested for HIV. Everyone who comes for treatment or testing is given food and water and there is daily worship in English, Masai and Swahili, so that a strong sense of unity and friendship develops between the many different tribes and cultures involved with the project. The clinics are the only link the people have to information about health issues, family planning or HIV, and they mean a great deal to them.

Kosuke Koyama challenges us:

What is love if it remains invisible and intangible? Those who do not love a brother or sister whom they have seen cannot love God whom they have not seen. The devastating poverty in which millions of children live is visible. Racism is visible. Machine guns are visible. Slums are visible. The gap between rich and poor is glaringly visible. Our response to these realities must be visible … It is the 'see, hear, touch' gospel that can nurture the hope which is free from deception.[1]

There are three things I notice about people who get involved in these ways. The first is that they are always *practical;* they are about making changes through what people can do together. The second is that they are always *learning.* Through becoming involved, they also learn a considerable amount about the people and places they are seeking to support. Care is always most meaningful when it is informed – and this is a virtuous circle, because learning enriches both those who are being supported, and also those who are doing the supporting. And the third thing that I notice is that this kind of working and learning together builds *community.* It involves an investment of time and money; it also involves a lot of laughter and creativity. It gives value to the people who are being supported. But it also gives value to the people working together in this way. It is the 'see, hear, touch' gospel in action.

This involvement reflects a real solidarity with those who, as Koyama says, the powerful try to make invisible, those people who live on the margins.

Kathy Galloway

Note:

1. From an address given by Kosuke Koyama at the 8th WCC General Assembly, Harare, Zimbabwe, 1998

Prayer

Warm and alive

It was a fine night, no wind, and was mild as could be expected considering the ground was freezing. The views were simply superb in all directions. To my left was the gully curving upwards and out of sight. In the other direction I could see the Inaccessible Pinnacle, while straight ahead and below was the corrie, with its small snow-covered lochan, then the moors with the lochan Fhir Bhallaich and beyond that Glenbrittle Bay.

For the first hour or two I watched the sunset. It was a lovely sight as it sank behind a mass of coloured clouds. I dreaded its disappearance, but when it did at last vanish the temperature didn't seem to drop much. Soon the stars began to appear between the clouds, and the sea was bathed in moonlight. It was curious to notice how the further lochan altered with the change of light. As the sea and the distant moors grew darker and darker until I could not distinguish the one from the other, so the snow-covered lochan became brighter as the contrast between it and its surroundings increased. Most of the night I was gazing intently in its direction as it was there I expected first to see the light which would indicate the approach of the rescuers.

The advent of the night had however one slight advantage. Until the sun set there were frequent tiny ice falls above me. Apparently some ice fell off the vertical walls, and rolled down the bed of the gully with a placid tinkling sound. These tiny icefalls did no real harm, but before the cold of the night stopped them, they had covered my rucksack, my loose glove, and nearly all the rope and ice axe. There were two curious phenomena which might have seemed ghostly had I not found the explanation. Some time after my partner had left, but before there was any chance of a search party's arrival, I heard what sounded like a rhythmic beat of axe on ice, apparently coming from below. I looked down, but there was, of course, no one there. Several times this was repeated, with the same result. Eventually I noticed that it was always followed, at regular interval, by one of these icefalls, and the sound must have been that of ice pealing off the rocks above. It occurs to me that the footsteps sometimes heard on the hills at night might have had the same kind of explanation, for example, a delayed movement of the ground that had just been passed and compressed.

Then, after about two hours, I saw what seemed like a very faint light, appearing and disappearing, as would be the case if held by someone walking over rough ground, just where I supposed the path by the lochan to be. The light was so faint, as in the case of a star, it could be seen best by looking slightly away from it. But as it remained in exactly the same place I eventually had to give up hope, and realise that it was not a light but a patch of ice or water which varied in brightness inversely as the density of the clouds in front of the moon.

Later on, partly to keep up my spirits, and partly to help keep awake, I started to sing Gaelic songs and hymns. I was amazed to find how much better my voice sounded than usual, possibly owing to the great walls on either side. I do not normally approve of singing or shouting on mountains, believing silence to be one of their greatest attributes, but felt that the occasion was exceptional. In fact, I was so pleased with the feeling of warmth and comradeship it produced, especially the singing of the hymns, that I thought of greeting my rescuers with a song, but at once rejected the idea as they would be bound to think that I was light-headed or that there was nothing the matter with me, and neither theory would bear any relationship to the truth.

And then it happened – the moment for which I had waited and prayed for so long arrived, and I saw, on the far side of the lochan, a light. There was no mistaking this one: it was bright yellow and moving. It would be difficult to exaggerate the wonder, the thrill of seeing that light for which I had been looking so intently and for so many hours, and to know that my efforts had been rewarded, as I was wide awake, still free from pain and apparently unaffected by the exposure. The light seemed to advance quite quickly until the steeper part of the lower corrie was reached, when it disappeared from view for some time, and became visible again in the upper corrie.

Meanwhile, other lights had come into view, and it was thrilling and wonderful to watch their flickering progress and realise its significance. It was as though the cold dead mountainside had become warm and alive.

Roger Gray, an early member of the Iona Community and peace activist, after fracturing his thigh in a climbing accident

Justice and Peace

Curve of a human hand

Curve of a human hand
warding off danger:
symbol of shelter, more than a gesture –
stretched as far as a curve can,
fragile, resilient, and
a shape we know in our bones;

sixty years ago, jetsam of war
was put to good use from Tiraghoil to Kintra:
there's still an Anderson shelter on most crofts –
nothing is wasted here –
so these little sheds house chickens,
store onions, keep tools from rust;
thrawn, rusting themselves,
humble structures with bowed roofs, just
like the curve of a human hand …

thirteen centuries have passed
but on the Garvellachs
the beehive huts still stand, battered
by time and sea winds, but not demolished;
like chambered shells, broken open
showing the beauty of their convolutions;
places to read creation's great book,

space to turn the eye inward,
refuge from the wind's fury
and angry clamour of the news;
skilfully built, the subtle arch of the roof – look –
like the curve of a human hand …

minutes ago, more shellfire;
a bomb explodes over huddled houses
far from these peaceful islands;
in a war that threatens us all,
we glimpse people with no refuge –
in Gaza, right now,
the camera gazes into the terrified eyes
of a woman holding her child, while
the other hand's raised …

the curve of a human hand
warding off the raging world,
stretched as far as a curve can:
a little refuge of humanity,
resilient, fragile, and
more than a gesture, a symbol of shelter –
this shape we know in our bones.

Jan Sutch Pickard

The Integrity of Creation

The Listener

A child at the window.
His ears tuned
to the whisper of the sky.

'No more, I ask, please!
The poison hurts,
the smoke you feed me.'

A child at the farm.
His ears tuned
to the murmur of the crops.

'Stop, stop, please listen!
The toxin aches,
the chemicals you bathe me with.'

A child at the beach.
His ears tuned
to the mutter of the sea.

'Cease, please, I seek of you!
The venom burns,
the oil you coat me in.'

The world cries in pain,
the boy says.
But nobody bothers, nobody cares,
nobody listens.

Euan Stuart, at 13 years old

Columban Christianity & the Celtic Tradition

Associate members of the Iona Community are invited to renew their vows annually in June; many do so on St Columba's Day (June 9th).

Worship for St Columba's Day

Call to worship

Breath of God,
Breath of life,
Breath of deepest yearning,
COME, HOLY SPIRIT.

Comforter,
Disturber,
Interpreter,
Enthuser,
COME, HOLY SPIRIT.

Heavenly Friend,
Lamp-lighter,
Revealer of truth,
Midwife of change,
COME, HOLY SPIRIT.

The Lord is here
GOD'S SPIRIT IS WITH US.

Song: ('The God of heaven', John L. Bell and Graham Maule, *Iona Abbey Music Book,* Wild Goose Publications)

Prayers of approach

The ever-changing sea, the strong hills, the life-giving air,
the interplay of shadow and sunshine and stars,
all announce a Creator's goodness.
PRAISE TO YOU, O GOD

In the craftworker's skill, the designer's ideas,
the insight of artist and writer and musician,
the impatience of the prophet and the patience of the carer,
you have called human beings to partnership in creation.
PRAISE TO YOU, O GOD

Your living word, carried across the earth
by apostle, saint and martyr,
came to our shores with men and women
who, in their common life of work and prayer,
tested the gospel promise and found its truth.
Centuries on, we gather,
proof that their seed landed in fertile soil.
PRAISE TO YOU, O GOD

Creator God,
you turned Columba from the sound of conflict
to become a bearer of the gospel of peace,
putting in his mouth the song of the Trinity.
Grant us that same courage, faith and cheerfulness,
that we may recognise our place in the gospel story
and live it in our lives.
AMEN

Gospel and reflection

Chant: ('Iona Gloria', *Iona Abbey Music Book,* Wild Goose Publications)

Commitment

On this, St Columba's Day, we commit ourselves as Associate Members of the Iona Community

(Associate Members of the Community stand and say)

IN THE PRESENCE OF OUR SISTERS AND BROTHERS, NEAR AND FAR,
AND IN THE NAME OF GOD,
CREATOR, REDEEMER, SUSTAINER,
WE COMMIT OURSELVES TO THE PURPOSE AND
THE PRAYER LIFE OF THE IONA COMMUNITY.

WE, BEING MANY, ARE ONE IN CHRIST.
WE WILL CELEBRATE THE WHOLENESS OF OUR LIFE TOGETHER.
WHERE IT IS FRACTURED, WE WILL WORK FOR RECONCILIATION.
WHERE IT IS DIMINISHED, WE WILL STRIVE FOR ITS FULLNESS.
SO GOD HELP US NOW AND ALWAYS.
AMEN

May they not fail you
NOR WE FAIL THEM

Affirmation

WE BELIEVE THAT GOD IS PRESENT
IN THE DARKNESS BEFORE DAWN;
IN THE WAITING AND UNCERTAINTY
WHERE FEAR AND COURAGE JOIN HANDS,

CONFLICT AND CARING LINK ARMS,
AND THE SUN RISES OVER BARBED WIRE.

WE BELIEVE IN A WITH-US GOD
WHO SITS DOWN IN OUR MIDST
TO SHARE OUR HUMANITY.
WE AFFIRM A FAITH
THAT TAKES US BEYOND THE SAFE PLACE:
INTO ACTION, INTO VULNERABILITY
AND INTO THE STREETS.

WE COMMIT OURSELVES TO WORK FOR CHANGE
AND PUT OURSELVES ON THE LINE;
TO BEAR RESPONSIBILITY, TAKE RISKS,
LIVE POWERFULLY AND FACE HUMILIATION;
TO STAND WITH THOSE ON THE EDGE;
TO CHOOSE LIFE
AND BE USED BY THE SPIRIT
FOR GOD'S NEW COMMUNITY OF HOPE
AMEN

Song: ('I will always bless the Lord', John L. Bell, *One Is the Body,*
Wild Goose Publications)

Prayers of thanksgiving and intercession

Creator God, we give thanks
that those who brought the gospel to these lands,
and whose cells and abbeys were close to wind and sea and soil,
heard the Spirit of God in the freshening leaves and the rush of water.
So we pray for the creation which nourishes and sustains all that lives.
Renew in us the sense of its value

that we may not squander its riches,
or so bend it to our will that we find we have destroyed it.

Understanding God, we give thanks
for the place given to learning in the communities of work and prayer
from which the gospel spilled into our land –
the knowledge of scripture,
of medicine and healing,
and the schooling of the young.
So we pray for honesty and openness in learning,
clarity and truthfulness in communication
and a respectful and enquiring spirit
as we discover more about the world and its peoples.

Reconciling God, we give thanks
for the earliest disciples in these lands,
who sought in community the way of generosity,
who confronted warring powers, challenged injustice
and offered the peace of Jesus Christ to all they met.
So we pray for a society that deals justly with all its members,
especially the most vulnerable ones,
and for all who labour in councils and committees,
who ask questions and write letters
and work for communities in which all may live in peace
and a world in which all are valued.

Joyful God, we give thanks
for those whose days and nights were shaped by prayer,
and whose utterances were rich in the words of the Psalms.
So we pray for the stirrings of the Holy Spirit,
within us and amongst us,

that we may live our lives in intimacy and kindness
and know the companionship of Jesus beside us.

Nurturing God, we give thanks
for the love of beauty and gifted imagination
of those who brought us the gospel,
as they decorated the scriptures,
worked in metal and stone
and made melodies to delight the heart.
So we pray for the valuing of the imagination
and the encouragement of creative gifts,
even when we find them in unlikely places.

Spirit of the living God,
you breathe in us, on all that is inadequate and fragile.
You make living water spring even from our hurts themselves.
Through you, the valley of fears becomes a place of wellsprings.
So, in an inner life with neither beginning nor end,
your continual presence makes new freshness break through.
We pray in your name with confidence … *(Lord's Prayer)*

The bread we share is one
THOUGH WE ARE MANY, WE ARE ONE BODY.
LET THERE BE ENOUGH FOR EVERYONE, EVERYWHERE.

Sharing the Peace

Blessing

LIVING GOD, BLESS US
AS TOGETHER WE GO OUT
EMPOWERED BY OUR LONGING,
STRENGTHENED BY OUR SOLIDARITY

HUMBLED BY OUR NEED
TO LOVE AND SERVE THE WORLD.
AMEN

Sung blessing: ('The peace of the earth be with you', Guatamala, CH4)

Kathy Galloway

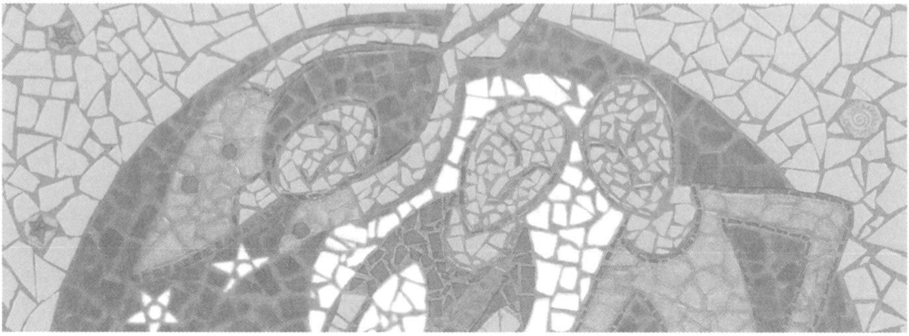

Month 4 Day 14

RACIAL JUSTICE

Principalities and powers

I was sitting in Hendon Methodist Church in London on a cold January Sunday morning listening to the sermon by the minister. The first real indications of the mess that unrestricted capitalism has caused were beginning to fill the newspapers as the full story of the incompetence and corruption of those charged with running financial institutions began to be apparent. From the pulpit came the challenge to look beyond the easy economic headlines and ask questions about what really was going on. In the middle of the sermon the minister asked for contributions from the congregation about the really important priorities for Christian folk at this time. From this multi-ethnic congregation came some trenchant comments and divergent views. Integrity has always been very important for Robert.

In December 1971, three young Zimbabweans arrived in Community House in Clyde Street, Glasgow in exile from white-ruled Rhodesia. They had come through Malawi, assisted by long-time member of the Iona Community Tom Colvin. One of them was Robert. Robert took an accountancy course at what is now Glasgow Caledonian University. Whilst in Scotland he went to Iona several times and ended up as a youth leader in the old Abbey camp. He also met Molly, a Zimbabwean nurse, whom he married six years later. Robert and Molly returned to Zimbabwe after Independence and settled in Argyle Avenue, Harare, an address which reflected the chequered Scottish heritage of the old Rhodesia.

Everything was going well in their lives – double income and the birth of their first of three boys, Farai. Robert was working for a tea company and Molly practising midwifery. After a few years the Zimbabwe government had an appointment for an accountant in a new palm oil venture close to the South African border and the family moved to Mwenzi in the south. Robert was well-respected and was asked to accompany a Zimbabwe government team to Bulgaria.

He went off to Sofia with senior civil servants and a trade minister. The visit was a diplomatic success and a lucrative deal was about to be signed. Robert was asked to look over the financial details. He became worried. There was obviously a great deal of financial benefit, but not necessarily for the government, still less for the people of Zimbabwe. So he asked questions and didn't get clear answers. He asked more questions.

Then he was taken aside by the Minister. In a scene reminiscent of *A Man for All Seasons* where Thomas More is under pressure to sign against his conscience and to go with his colleagues 'for fellowship', Robert was given a cosy chat. 'You're a young man,' said the Minister, 'with a great future in front of you.' The rest was unsaid. It didn't need to be.

Robert did not go along with the scam despite a great deal of attempted persuasion in the next few days. Sitting in his kitchen in north London many years later, he told me that he didn't think that it made much difference – the deal was signed. But it did keep his integrity intact. Some politicians in Zimbabwe, as in Britain, often can't understand what they see as 'gestures conscience'. One of the most corrosive attacks on principles is often justified by an appeal to 'live in the real world'. It's not a new temptation. A man in the Middle East two thousand years ago was told by well-meaning followers and co-religionists as well as his enemies to 'live in the real world' and bend his principles to save his life. Fortunately for us all he was willing to practise what he preached about those who seek to save their skins losing the essence of their lives.

For Robert it was not a smooth path to his ministry today. His job went, and things deteriorated so badly in Zimbabwe that he had to leave his native land and go into exile once more. He trained for the Methodist ministry just before the age limit debarred him.

His raw evangelical background was considerably changed by the experience of hospital chaplaincy, which enabled him to see spirituality in a very much wider context. He now ministers to one multi-racial congregation, and another in a different part of north London which is predominantly white. He has great pastoral skills. What you see with him is what you get. In being true to God whom he serves, he is also true to himself.

'What does anyone gain by winning the whole world at the cost of destroying himself?' (Luke 9:25, REB)

Prayer

We see compromise in politics, business, education and in the church and we don't like it and often despise it.

We compromise every day in our own lives and we persuade ourselves that it is necessary, even right.

We easily identify the lack of integrity in our society, our world, and we distance ourselves from it, failing to admit to its reflection in ourselves.

God, help us to be truer to ourselves and therefore truer to you.

Iain Whyte

Month 4 Day 15

Community

The family

He had no wife, no family,
he had no children of his own;
he once had been a refugee,
despised but never left alone.
To all the widowed and the fatherless
he showed the love that none had shown.

He liked to watch as children played
and knew the lyrics of their song;
he cared for those that lived at risk,
the ones whose rights had all gone wrong.
The plight of helpless and homeless folk
would always in his heart belong.

He had no job to pay the rent,
but women gave him house and food;
they saw in him no hidden threat,
his singleness was safe and good.
And those whom no one ever listened to
discovered that he understood.

He chose to eat in simple style
beside the wounded, hurt and poor;
he told them tales to make them laugh
and, for their stigma, was the cure.
In crowds and circles of rejected folk
his generosity was sure.

Those whom he calls his family
are this through love and not reward:
sisters and brothers we can be,
if we but take him at his word.
And so we join to celebrate the life
of Jesus Christ, our friend and Lord.

Wild Goose Resource Group

Pilgrimage

Explorers not mapmakers

(Meditation on the story of the Transfiguration, Luke 9:28–32)

How good it is that we are here.
This is It. We have arrived.
We will put up tents,
shelters, chapels, churches …
Others coming to this place
will see what we think we know.
Why move on?
We have found Identity and Meaning.
We will hold on to this experience
for dear life and human sanity.

But there is no holding on.
The cloud is upon us.
We are covered in shadow
and immobile in fear.
Risen and free, he dances ahead
and we must let go.
What we attempt to contain
within our poverty of understanding
is here no longer.
We leave behind one mystery

to follow another mystery –
a continual exploration
which allows no settlement
in the safety of the known.
No pitching of tents,
or making of shelters,
to protect our visions.

One who goes before
moves with all speed,
leaving as we arrive;
showing us that discipleship
is and always will be
the ever-new, ever-changing search
for what we have always known.

Joy Mead

Sexuality

Trapped inside my suitcase

From closing remarks at an Affirmation Scotland event, Saturday 30th April, 2011

When I embarked on a career in ministry nearly forty years ago, among all the things I might have fantasised about doing – and don't ask! – I never dreamed I would be standing before a gathering supported by Affirmation Scotland, as a heterosexual minister (I never thought there was any other kind) supporting gay clergy and others, at a meeting prior to a General Assembly, in a time of vital importance for the Church. I never dreamed … because I could never have conceptualised that this would be an issue which has come to the fore as it has done; I could not have believed it would be a matter which has exercised the collective mind of the Church as it has done in recent times; and I would never have thought it would come to matter so much to me.

But here I am … because … in forty years, society has changed beyond recognition. I had a father who was one of the nicest men you could ever meet, and a Kirk elder, but who referred to gay people as 'poofters' and 'shirt-lifters', and saw homosexuality as an evil aberration. He wouldn't now … And in forty years the Church has changed – but that would take too long to elaborate on … And in forty years I have changed. I am no longer the fresh-faced, clean-shaven, shinty-playing, teetotal, Christian-Endeavour-educated, prayer-meeting-attending, fervent-evangelical, everything-is-certain Christian I was when I was 20 – thank God!

But then, I didn't know my faith as I know it now … I hadn't sat by the bedsides of dying people who agonised about their relationship with the Church because of their sexuality; I hadn't embraced gay people in their bereavement because they couldn't grieve openly for their partner; I hadn't become best friends with a gay priest, and blessed his relationship, and known the pain he still carries about his relationship with his denomination and his calling because of his sexuality; I hadn't confirmed the relationship of a gay couple who had been rejected by the Church; I hadn't conducted the funeral of a gay 28-year-old woman; and I didn't have a gay daughter.

So much has changed … And now I find myself at the sharp end of an issue that I never expected to be passionate about. So why? Why does it matter so much?

Why did I cry in front of the Special Commission when I was there with Mary, my wife, when I didn't expect to? Why would I now go to the ends of the earth for inclusiveness in the Church – and, indeed, what lies beyond inclusiveness? Is affirmation not even more important?

Not because of a personal campaign, nor because I am a single-issue person; nor because I'm on a bandwagon or a soapbox or because I always espouse liberal causes … But because of theology …

And here's the erudition for this section … You'll know, because of your intimate knowledge of ecclesiastical history and classical languages, that Augustine of Hippo defined the Latin *theologia* as 'reasoning or discussion concerning the Deity'.

My trouble was … what did this Augustine of Hippo know about my modern Christian life? What reasoning or discussion was required, for goodness sake? I knew who God was, what God was like … my faith was certain; my theology was pure; my definitions were solid; I knew my product … I was God's salesman, with a case full of good things to sell, things I believed in, certainties I was sure of, faith that I was committed to. I had used the products myself. They were good things. I wasn't flogging them round unsuspecting customers because I had to or because I was paid to. I wanted them to have a better life, to believe as I believed, to know the God that I knew – the God that I carried around with me in my salesman's case.

And, somewhere along the line – probably because of my time in the hospice – God said, *'Listen, pal. We need to talk about this. My mate, Augustine of Hippo, was right, you know. There's some reasoning to be had, some discussion to be entered into.*

You think you've got me trapped? But you know little or nothing of me. I am not to be confined to your suitcase. I am not a series of products to be sold. Listen, pal, we need to talk about this …'

So I've been involved in theology, in *theologia*, 'reasoning or discussion concerning the Deity' … And the God I now know, I hardly know at all … for his grace is too big for me to conceptualise; his embrace of humanity is more wonderful than I can ever understand; his creative presence is way beyond my imagining … so we desperately need an acceptance of theological diversity, which for me is an acceptance of the width and wonder of God.

And before I get accused – as I have been often enough through the years – of not being a proper Christian or not Christocentric enough – let me continue by mentioning Jesus. How do I now know what God is like? Because of the Incarnation … And what does the Incarnation mean? God becoming flesh so that the whole of creation might be redeemed … God becoming flesh – human flesh; sexual flesh; hurting flesh; craving flesh; cleaving flesh; loving flesh; in the person of Jesus … so that I might know what God is like – fully human: fully sexual; fully hurting; fully craving; fully cleaving; fully loving. And if it's any less than that, then God is diminished, and trapped in our suitcase again.

Does Jesus reveal a God who is any less than that? I hope not. Do I understand it all? No, I do not. Am I pleased I get a glimpse that matters, that I understand a wee bit, enough to give me hope? You bet I am. The key is helping people to understand the nature of that God and not becoming all wrapped up in a sterile debate about scripture.

And this incarnate God comes to redeem the whole of creation … everyone created in his own image – certain people, and not-so-sure people, and don't-know-people; gay people and straight people; right and left people (and all the middle-ground people); ordained people and lay people; Christian people and humanist people; me, my friend, my gay daughter, my heterosexual daughter and son, my grandson; you … and

all the people you know who rejoice and are hurt; who are broken and healed; who feel included and rejected; the whole of creation … and if it's any less than that, then God is diminished, and trapped in my suitcase again.

So, the God I now know is a God who makes sense of things that I can't make sense of … The God that I know is a God who laughs at our desire for 'purity' in the Church, and reminds us that when we are 'pure', there is no learning; where there is certainty, there is no growth; when there is only law and dogma, there is no grace.

As the late, lamented Roland Walls said to us in New College in the 1970s: 'Let's take all the books of dogma and put them in a bin … and let's put a lid firmly on the bin … and let's all together sit on the lid – just to make sure the dogma doesn't get out again!'

You don't 'dogmatise' people into the Kingdom: you love them, and let God do the rest … (and to do that, we need to be patient, and not strident).

So, no matter what the Church becomes, God calls you to believe in God as God is, as God is revealed to you.

No matter what happens at the General Assembly, God is still God, and God calls you to believe in a God who is beyond your imagining.

No matter what fractures appear in Church structures, God calls you to believe in a God who will not be broken or threatened by what the Church does or doesn't do, for this is a God who was never to be trapped in the Church in the first place!

No matter what pain you and I go through, God calls us to believe in a God who has much yet – so much more than we could ever imagine – much yet to reveal to us of his nature, his grace, his healing and his inclusiveness and affirmation. The stories of our lives that we have to tell – our testimonies – are powerful and effective: they speak volumes, beyond words and dogma – and they will create openness to the God we seek to reveal.

No matter what rejection you feel, or what pain you carry because of the rejection of people you love, believe in a God who has broken out of the suitcase and is waiting to welcome you as you are. We need to communicate that in an intelligent and honest fashion to those beyond our circle.

No matter how much you know God and are certain of your faith, believe in a

God who is bigger than you will ever know, and who, even now if we are open to it, taps you on the shoulder and says: *'Listen, pal, we've got some reasoning and discussing to do ...'*

No matter how fearful you feel about what might happen at the General Assembly, and as you hold to your passion for the peace and unity of the Church, believe in a God who still believes in *you,* and what *you* stand for, and what is communicated through your inclusive and affirmative compassion *you* show to a world which craves for that image of God.

No matter how outside you might feel or are made to feel, believe in a God – this loving, amazing, surprising, enlivening, incarnate God – who is outside the structures as well as inside, a God who will be where you are, where I am, where my friend and my daughter are ... over there, with arms wide open, calling out, *'You are mine.'*

Tom Gordon

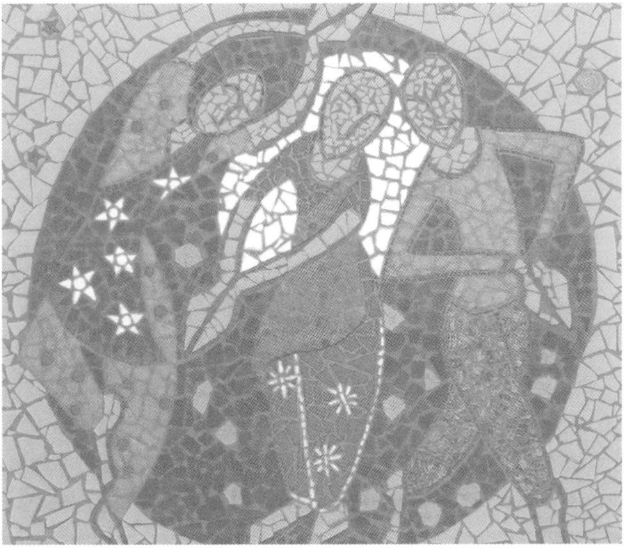

Month 4 Day 18

Healing

The prayer shawl ministry

Jane came to talk to me after the Christian Unity Week service at her church. 'I don't know if you heard,' she said, 'but my husband passed away in November.' I said I was sorry and that I wished I had heard earlier. 'He loved his shawl, right to the end,' Jane said. 'Every time he went for treatment he had it wrapped round his shoulders or his knees, and it was never far from him at home.' She went on to tell me how much she missed him, how she didn't know what to do without him. I looked at the dark-pink scarf Jane was wearing against her navy coat. I pulled out the pink-and-lilac shawl I had in my bag and wrapped it round Jane's shoulders. 'I think you need a shawl now.' She went back to her friends, pulling the shawl tightly round her.

A few weeks later, Olwen spoke to me at one of the churches I serve as a lay preacher. 'I wasn't here last time you came,' she said, 'but the shawl you sent me in hospital – well, it got me through, and it was a great talking point with the other patients as well.'

One of our 'Knit & Natter' members got a shawl from me when she was admitted to hospital with a very scary angina attack – before she left hospital she passed it on to a nurse whose daughter had breast cancer.

Every week we give shawls away to people in all sorts of difficulty, from diagnosis and treatment, to bereavement, shocks and traumas of every kind, as well as to people in joyful circumstances. It was a delight to send a shawl to someone to give to her daughter when her baby was born, and to hear she had it round her shoulders when feeding the baby.

Less than two years before we had sent a shawl to the same mother when her first baby was stillborn.

I first read about Prayer shawl ministry in one of the many knitting magazines which have sprung up in the revival of knitting and crochet in Britain. The founders, Janet Bristow and Victoria Cole-Galo, combined their ideas of ministry with their love of knitting and crochet while they were at Hartford Seminary in Connecticut. They and others have published several books including patterns, prayers and experiences of giving shawls. The shawls are always given away – I have accepted donations from people who want to give them, for our group's expenses and to buy more yarn, but never from the recipient.

In 1995 I started a 'Knit & Natter' Group at Emmanuel URC in Cambridge, just before we moved to Liverpool, and combined three elements in the development of the group, which is still going strong. Firstly, there are masses of unused knitting yarn lying around in people's cupboards and boxes, and if you ask in your local paper you will soon have more than you need! Secondly, there are people who like to knit and crochet, but have no one to knit and crochet for. Some of these people would welcome another social group to join: they're isolated by widowhood, their children have moved miles away, and they really enjoy the company of new friends. Thirdly, there are international charities who would like to take knitted and crocheted clothes and toys to people in need: Samaritan's Purse (Operation Christmas Child, the Shoe Box campaign), Hope and Aid Direct (who take van-loads of warm things to Kosovo every six months), as well as local centres for homeless people and asylum seekers. Local nursing homes also welcome knee-rugs for immobile residents. So it's not hard to find places to send the bags and bags of knitted things any group will produce.

When I came to Liverpool I soon got involved in starting three groups in the South Liverpool area, two of which meet at our churches. Women come from around the neighbourhood to these groups, along with a smaller number of church members. As well as meeting once a week we have Christmas parties and coach trips (with a nice lunch – very important). We enter a team in the church quizzes every six months (calling ourselves 'The Woolly Thinkers' was irresistible) and have stalls at the spring fair.

It's the Shawl ministry, though, which I find most rewarding. We have given shawls to families who have suffered a murder or road death, sending them through the Police Family Liaison team, who have been very appreciative of having something to bring when they visit a family. We have made tiny, fluffy shawls for children whose mothers died suddenly, and heard they were still wearing them or carrying them around weeks later. One of our knitters sent a shawl to her son's mother-in-law in Japan, who was widowed suddenly; and received a lovely card written in halting English, to join the dozens of cards and letters of appreciation from other recipients. A lady having chemo told us she put the crocheted shawl under her pillow and wrapped her fingers through and round it when she was feeling frightened at night.

The founders of Shawl ministry in the U.S. meet in church groups and consciously pray as they make and send the shawls. Sometimes shawls are blessed in church by the minister before they go. Ours are not specifically church groups but everyone knows that the shawls are prayers and good wishes which we send or give to people who very much need them. We have a simple card which we send with the shawls, naming the person who made the shawl, and conveying our prayers and love.

And all I can say is, it works. People 'get it'. You don't need words when there is a warm hug in a shawl. I carry a shawl in my bag whenever I can, and people ask me for them: ministers, church members, whoever. It should be surprising how many times people tell us we have given them a shawl in their favourite colour, but it's not, of course (shades of George MacLeod: 'If you think that's a coincidence…').

What moves me most of all is when one of the group says something like: 'My neighbour had a fall and broke her hip, so I sat up two nights and crocheted her a shawl. She was made up!' (Scouse for 'thrilled'). In the properly working church, deacons, church wardens, elders or stewards take care of the community, without waiting for ministers to tell them what to do. In good communities, neighbours do the same. My husband, Gordon, a minister, is always amazed how Shawl ministry keeps on working. I've lost count of the times he has come back from visiting a widow and has told me: 'She was wearing your shawl.'

A few extras: for boys and men, I often make a big warm scarf; only for older and immobile men do big crocheted rugs seem really appropriate. I decided to put a care label with the shawls as well after someone washed one in hot water and it stretched out of shape. We happily replaced it but the lady was distressed by what she'd done.

We had an article about our 'Knit & Natter' groups in *Simply Knitting magazine* (Issue 46, November 2008). After that I had calls from all over the country from people who'd read the article and then made a shawl for someone in need – one for a niece in New Zealand who had lost a baby: 'I was just wondering what on earth to do for her, then I read your article.'

You knit us together

Tune: Mayenziwe (South African trad.)

You knit us together though far apart,
a fabric of beauty, of warmth and art.
So bind us together, through time and through space,
to grow into your garment of grace,
to wrap the world in love's Embrace.

You knit us together, all shapes and size;
the fabric you make is your great surprise.
So bind us together, through time and through space,
to grow into your garment of grace,
to wrap the world in love's Embrace.

You knit us together, all shades and hue:
the gold of our joy and our sorrow's blue.
So bind us together, through time and through space,
to grow into your garment of grace,
to wrap the world in love's Embrace.

You knit us together, to serve and share.
The wounds that we bind show your healing care.
So bind us together, through time and through space,
to grow into your garment of grace,
to wrap the world in love's Embrace.

You knit us together, your seamless robe,
to care and to comfort around the globe.
So bind us together, through time and through space,
to grow into your garment of grace,
to wrap the world in love's Embrace.

You knit us together in so many ways,
to live with each other, and sing your praise.
So bind us together, through time and through space,
to grow into your garment of grace,
to wrap the world in love's Embrace.

Anna Briggs

www.shawlministry.com

Social Action

From Atlanta, Georgia to Glasgow's East End

As we flew down the St Lawrence River, with Quebec on one side and Maine on the other, with New York some miles ahead, the sky cleared, apart from a few clouds whose reflection on the water made them appear like floating islands on the sparkling sea. It felt like the final stretch down to Atlanta where the adventure and life-changing experience would start – a chance for me to become a volunteer for three months at the Open Door Community, helping each week with the Thursday evening foot clinic and the Tuesday morning breakfasts, and sharing in the Sunday afternoon Communion and the fine meal that followed.

Our first contact with the Open Door (or '910' as it's known locally: it's a big house at 910 Ponce de Leon Avenue near downtown Atlanta) was in 2000 when Norman, my husband, spent a month of his 'sabbatical' as a resident volunteer there. He'd been back for a couple of short visits since then and some of the Open Door people had visited Glasgow and Iona, including a week that Murphy Davis and Ed Loring, two of the Open Door's founders, had led at the Abbey in 2002. But now, during Norman's three months as a visiting scholar at Columbia Theological Seminary, Decatur, just half an hour's bus ride from 910, I was to have the chance myself to find out what he was so enthusiastic about!

At 910 (for over 30 years now) there is a community of committed people, some of them formerly homeless, who provide hospitality for homeless people (mostly male, African American or Hispanic), inviting them into their home for meals, 120 or so each day, and offering them support in the form of counselling, showers, clothing, toiletries, etc. All the Open Door's work is rooted in prayer and worship, and includes prison ministry and political activism – campaigning against poverty, racism and the death penalty.

It was a very powerful, heart-warming and memorable experience for me, out of which grew the idea of starting a foot clinic in Glasgow. I realised, after three months of working with destitute men and women in Atlanta, that this was something that I could do on returning home – using my skills as a physiotherapist in the sort of way I had been looking for since retiring. So I approached the Lodging House Mission, a church-related day-centre in Glasgow's East End mostly for folk who are homeless or in hostels and supported accommodation, about the possibility of starting a foot clinic there, and they readily agreed. The plan was to base the practicalities broadly on what happens each week at the Open Door, although I recognised that there would be significant differences due to context and culture (and I've certainly discovered that most of the people who come to the foot clinic are better off than those we dealt with in Atlanta, owing to the lack of welfare benefits in the US). Some of the local churches helped with donations of foot-baths, sprays, scrubs, cream, towels, scissors, clippers, etc, as well as giving money, and this generosity is ongoing.

What happens each fortnight on Tuesday mornings? We rely on people referring themselves; so introductions, initial conversations and explanations of what we do are important. People who come naturally can be apprehensive: taking off your socks and shoes for this purpose makes you vulnerable (and you can't escape in a hurry!), people can be embarrassed about dirty feet and so on. Clearly we are not trained podiatrists. What we offer is foot-washing, using foot-spas, basic chiropody (e.g. cutting nails, removing hard skin and corns), massage and general advice on footwear, foot care and other minor problems (e.g. muscle strains, infections). We have a supply of shoes and socks. As well as giving advice, if there are more serious problems, we encourage the men and women to attend a nearby medical clinic. The maximum number of people we have treated in the two-hour period is 12, and it tends to vary each time, depending on how long it takes to deal with each person who comes.

We deliberately sit at a lower level than the folk who come. Apart from being more comfortable and the practical reasons (relating to foot treatment) for this, it puts the relationship on a more level playing field, and we feel this is important.

After all, in what's happening the vulnerability is mutual – for the giver as well as the receiver, and this helps achieve a sense of sharing and equality in this basic and intimate task.

Why is this important to us and how does it relate to our faith? In general the folk who come initiate, and are keen to engage in, conversation about their story and circumstances; and we often have the sense of opportunities missed and young lives wasted. Occasionally they ask us why we are doing this. Sometimes they tell us about their family and how they became homeless – very often because of family break-up and addiction problems. They often speak of their dream to be in some sort of employment (even more difficult, of course, in the present economic situation).

As far as the faith dimension goes, I feel there is something sacramental in what we are doing. Jesus cared for the marginalised and needy, washed the feet of the disciples and told his followers to do likewise in loving and caring for one another. One example of that is Mary, who according to the Gospels washed the feet of Jesus, using expensive ointment, even before he washed the disciples' feet: so Mary can be seen as the model disciple. And I'm reminded too of the old saying, which happens to be prominently displayed just inside the entrance of the Open Door: 'Often we meet Christ in the stranger's guise.'

Ruth Douglas Shanks

www.lhm-glasgow.org.uk
www.opendoorcommunity.org

Church Renewal

Lippen on the Holy Spirit

The stories I tell here have already been shared as particular items at particular times. But they belong to one journey. Here I thread them into one necklace, each one in order of time. I do so because I have thought: *Should I be given the chance before I die to leave one word of advice, what would it be?* Without hesitation I knew. It would be 'Lippen on the Holy Spirit: lean on, trust in, keep turning to, develop a living relationship with the Holy Spirit'.

Faced with contemporary decisions and choices, some say, 'I must ask myself what Jesus Christ would have done in this situation.' For one thing, they don't seem to realise what a huge task they set themselves. They would need to divest these situations of contemporary factors, re-clothe them in a Palestinian first-century context and follow through with what would be prescribed as Christ-like in the present day – in my judgement an impossible task.

For another, Christ Jesus has different advice: 'When the Spirit of truth comes, he will guide you into all the truth; for he will not speak on his own authority, but will speak only what he hears and he will make known to you what is to come. He will glorify me, for he will take what is mine and make it known to you. All that the Father has is mine – and that is why I said: "He will take what is mine and make it known to you"' (John 16:13–15).

'Lippen on the Holy Spirit' is the advice of Jesus Christ Himself; for when we are faced with decisions and choices in our own time, and seek to deal with these according his mind, the Spirit will make his mind known.

How this works out is clearly illustrated in Acts 13 and 16.

At the start of Chapter 13 we are given a picture of prophets and teachers in Antioch who strenuously seek the will of the Spirit in prayer and fasting. The Holy

Spirit responds with 'Set Barnabas and Paul apart for me, to do the work to which I have called them.' The work is not specified. They will find, as they take the road, what is required of them at each stage.

Features of a journey are revealed in Acts 16. Paul and his companions are prevented from delivering the message of the Church Council to inhabitants of Asia (at that time a province not a continent). What stops them? The Holy Spirit! They go on and attempt to enter Bythnia, but the way is barred again by the Holy Spirit. Paul, an evangelist to his fingertips, is denied opportunity to preach to people who did not even know the name of Jesus – by the Holy Spirit! They either skirt or go straight through Mysia, and come to Troas. There a Macedonian appears in a night vision, appealing to them to 'cross over to Macedonia and help us'. Then they 'set about getting a passage to Macedonia, convinced that God has called us to take the good news there'.

Paul and his companions were able to begin the mission to Europe only because they disciplined themselves to be attentive to the Holy Spirit both when they were told 'Speak up' and 'Shut up'. (Oh, that some contemporary evangelists heard the second command as well as the first! The gift they might give at times would be to step aside and to sit at the feet of ordinary people and learn what the Spirit is saying to the churches.)

The journey which I undertook in 1980 was to Mexico, Guatemala, El Salvador, Nicaragua, Panama and Venezuela, visiting basic Christian communities and carrying news of the work of the Spirit manifest in their development in different parts of the world which I had visited.

To understand what follows, it is necessary to appreciate that my and Margaret's marriage was like a coin with two sides. On the one hand, we were given to one another to delight in one another. We had a special gift for that. We were utterly charmed, all our days, to share life. On the other hand, we were given this togetherness to fulfil Kingdom assignments. What these would be we could not anticipate. We had simply to be alert to read the signs given on the way.

Margaret was especially good at reading these signs and jaloosing what should come next. Whatever I had to do on my own (e.g. for the World Council of

Churches) would get her blessing. Except in this instance! She almost dug in her heels and tried to dissuade me from this journey. The problem was that, at that time, Guatemala and El Salvador were killing fields and she knew that I would not be with protected tourists but with those counted eliminable. First she tried the line that there was enough information about these two countries available in print and I could miss them out without loss. My reply was simply that, as she knew, reports of others were not good enough – I needed to find what I needed to find. She left it a few days. Then she said that not only reports but people were coming from these two countries – I could seek them out and get direct information of the kind I wanted. I replied that, as she knew, I needed to see people and sniff out the reality of situations in their natural context, not away from it. She gave up. I went with her reluctant blessing after all.

Was it that my conviction overcame her hesitations? That was not our way. We were together-people. I believe she came to see that she was looking on our marriage as if it had only one side, the delight in one another. She was scared for my well-being, even for my life. I believe she worked things out so that she came to the point where perfect love casts out fear. She consented to what she came to see as a Kingdom assignment, part of the package which was our marriage.

The visit to Mexico was straightforward. Bishop Mendez Arceo had developed his diocese on a basis of space given for small communities to flourish. I was able to get updated about their recent history and share with them insights from the life of communities in other parts of the world.

Four hours before my flight to Guatemala my Mexican host, Dr Gaxiola Gaxiola, got a phone call. It was to say that all my contacts in Guatemala and El Salvador had been killed, or had fled the country or gone underground – there would be no one to meet me to provide links with the small communities. Dr Gaxiola suggested I had better give up on the trip and fly back to Britain. But that would have meant that an interested party would not have been consulted – the Holy Spirit. I asked leave to go away by myself for 10-15 minutes to think things through. All I did was open myself to the Spirit.

In my experience the guidance the Spirit gives is not resoundingly clear. It may edge slightly to one way rather than another way and you simply have to make a judgement and plunge. You know, in any case, that if you have chosen rightly, your initiative will be gathered into a large divine initiative, and if wrongly, that it will be covered by an entirely sufficient forgiveness. I came back to my host and said I was going to continue with the journey.

What are you to do if you land in a strange country and all your contacts (except one priest, who I knew would not be at the airport) are eliminated? If I remember rightly, the person who was originally to meet me was called Sister Angela. I approached some of those who were meeting new arrivals and asked if they had seen Sister Angela. Some did not know her, others had not seen her recently. I knew this would be so. The whole idea was to make some sort of human contact in the hope that something might come of it.

Two nuns whom I approached were expecting two other nuns, who disembarked behind me. When these arrived, they all moved off in a great flurry of greetings and welcoming conversation. The word came to me 'Stand around and look forlorn'. In fact these exact words came to me. I remember the word 'forlorn' in particular. How on earth could such an irrelevant thought come from the action of the Holy Spirit? All I knew was that strange pointers like this had, in the past, proved to have substance in them which I could not see at first. At the entrance to the airport I stood around looking forlorn.

At that time the entry to parking areas and the exit from the airport were close to one another. After some time the car with the four nuns appeared, ready for departure. The driver saw forlorn me, changed direction, swung alongside and asked if Sister Angela had not turned up. When I said she had not, the nun said that there was still a spare seat in the car. They would want to help – but could only do so if the place I wanted to reach was in the direction they had to take. I mentioned

Iglesia la Merced. 'No problem. That's on our way. Hop in!'

If I had taken a taxi into the centre of the city, I would have been met by a closed and darkened church and would have been quite lost. As it was, the nuns knew the church house, which was in a warren of side streets. They took me there. A priest was putting away his car. He said that if I had arrived five minutes earlier, he would not have been there. If I had arrived five minutes later, no one would have answered the door. Too often a gun had been poked through a space in the metal grill and the person who answered had been shot at. The priest was the one person whose name I still had, not only in Guatemala City but in the whole country. I was provided with a base from which to operate.

On arrival in El Salvador, I adopted a different tactic. I made for Bishop Romero's headquarters and asked around, seeking some sort of lead. I got none. I went out the front door. To the left of it was an open space about the size of a school playground.

Two men were walking diagonally across it, talking. I took the chance to bring them into conversation and found that one of them was Romero's liaison link with basic Christian communities! Once again I had purchase on a situation which seemed to yield none. His companion was in charge of the Roman Catholic radio station which bravely provided knowledge of what was really happening in the country. Though it was towards shutdown time in the evening he invited me to look around before the station closed – I could leave my rucksack in one of the rooms. So we wandered across a few hundred yards and I was shown around. At shutdown I wandered back – to find that the room in which I had left my rucksack was locked for the night and no one who was still there knew how to gain entrance. I found that this was because of a device that had been adopted. The military, hostile to Romero and all that he stood for, were liable to raid the church headquarters without notice, looking for 'subversive material'. Evidently they were not allowed to make forced entry to particular rooms. So each room had a locking up arrangement which was not shared – so that others could genuinely tell the military that they did not know how to get access. My rucksack was out of reach.

As the headquarters closed down, I realised I had two options. One was to sleep rough, in the open air. I was accustomed to rough sleeping. That was not the problem. The problem was death squads, wandering about at night, indiscriminately killing, leaving corpses to be picked up in the morning. The alternative was to try to get a bed in a modest residence. But I had no baggage, no airline tickets, no passport or other identification, no money – the police would be called, and El Salvadoran jails were not known for their gentleness and comfort. At that point I put my hand in my pocket – and found that Romero's basic Christian communities linkman, who lived outside the city, had given me his card, which I had pocketed without thinking. I also found some El Salvadoran coins. For the life of me I cannot say how they got there – I had not bought anything which would have produced change. They were exactly the amount needed for a phone call. (George MacLeod would have said 'If you think that is a coincidence, I wish you a very dull life!') I made contact and was told that, not far from where I was, I could find a house which a family had abandoned because of pressure from an anti-Romero military neighbour. There was still a caretaker there – he would provide a bed for the night. The next morning no one was earlier than me at the church headquarters, anxious to retrieve the signs of legitimacy and identity which the rucksack held!

In Nicaragua, I stayed first of all with Xavier Gorostiaga, the economic supremo of the new Nicaragua – produced by a brilliant people's revolution (eventually undermined and befouled by Reagan's illegal Contras and all manner of interference and dirty tricks by the USA). I had found Xavier in Ruskin College. (Developments in Nicaragua meant that he had a year to spare after Ruskin. I got him to come to Selly Oak Colleges as Third World lecturer, or something like that. We had flexibility in Selly Oak and could make appointments according to need as long as resources could be found.)

After some days in the Jesuit Centre which Xavier had as his

base, I moved to Ciudad Sandino, a barrio which had four Jesuit priests at its heart, with whom I teamed up for some more days, experiencing the outburst of gratitude and hope which marked the first anniversary of the success of the revolution. From the barrio, members of basic Christian communities had gone out to join the guerrillas when they came down from the hills to capture Managua, in one instance with sticks and stones assaulting the armoured cars (48 if I remember rightly) supplied by Britain to the dictator Somoza. There could not have been, at any other point of history, such a commitment of Christian believers in a revolutionary struggle.

I then moved on to Panama. I understand how difficult it might be for some readers to credit the story which follows. All I can do is supply a record.

Sometimes I had minimal information for getting in touch with small Christian communities. They did not advertise themselves. They might be beavering away, living the faith imaginatively under the noses of the official church without that church realising that they existed.

When I had to journey (as Abraham and Paul did) on a basis 'go and I'll show you on the road what to do', I had a prayer which went something like this: *'Look, God, I may have misread signs – or maybe you want me out of the road to act through other people. If this journey appears to me to be fruitless, fair enough – you know the total scene. But if you want it to bear fruit, please put the people I need to work with in touch with me.'*

In the case of Panama, I flew in with nothing to go on except the name of the person who linked the basic Christian communities. I had no address. I might well have spent the three days I had allowed for the visit searching without being able to find him.

This is what happened: When I was flying to Panama he was driving on some assignment well away from the airport. He experienced a very strong sensation that he was required to turn back on his tracks. He realised that such an irrational feeling must not be given weight and tried to drive on. The pressure to turn round became so strong that he yielded. He drove up to the airport just as I was coming out. We did not know one another but recognised one another at once. I found I had arrived at a rare time when the Panamanian communities had three days of interchange – not meeting in a block but visiting one another in a process of mutual learning and mutual sustaining.

Thereafter I moved on to Venezuela, to a Pentecostal centre in Barquimento which I used for a base and for occasional consultations. On one occasion, my awareness that something new was stirring (though words such as basic Christian communities or basic ecclesial communities were still not current) led me to set up a five-day gathering of those involved, from Puerto Rico right round to Venezuela. The provision at the centre was absolutely basic – had we met in a hotel, participants would have been tongue-tied with culture shock. In the Pentecostal centre they met at a level which did not disturb or confuse them. While I was at Barquimento, I heard of shanty towns growing up around Caracas, as poor people in the countryside moved into the city to try to make a living. The concern of the Participation in Change programme, coordinated for the World Council of Churches, remained with me with its focus on how the poor were coping with change. So I got my ticket altered to spend a day or two in Caracas on the way back. But, try as I would, I could get no means of contact with people in Caracas, to give me entry to the shanty towns.

On the way to the plane I took God to task, 'Look Lord, a covenant is two-sided. You have your bit to do as well as I have. So please get off your butt and do something – unless a fruitless journey is what you actually want.'

The pilot was a show-off. Never in my life have I been in a plane which took off at such a steep angle. When he straightened it out, a lass came forward from further down the plane with my plastic file in her hand. With the angle taken by the plane on take-off, it had slipped through the back of the seat beside me, and slid down to land at her feet. I thanked her. Then she said, 'I wanted an excuse to see you in any case: I think you work for the World Council of Churches in Switzerland.'

I wondered furiously what committee or commission we might have worked on together. It was not that. 'It's just that, some time ago, I went on the tour of the World Council headquarters and I think I saw you there. When you came on board I recognised you. The landing of your file at my feet gave me an excuse to come and talk.'

So she sat beside me and we chatted. *Did she stay in Switzerland and have business in Caracas?* No, Caracas was her home city. She had been on a course in Switzerland which was not obtainable outside Europe, and now she was on her way back. *What type of course was it?* It was designed to equip her better for some work in the social services, her job in Caracas. *What kind of organisation did she work for? Religious, medical, political?* She was on the social services staff of Caracas City Council. *Was there any line of work for which she had particular responsibility?* Her main job was to be a liaison between the Council and the slum dwellers in the hills around the city.

There is a mystery in all this. Did I prove to be inadequate martyr material? I was not killed even once, by death squads or by other means! I was not even jailed. I came within a whisker of that in the Philippines. The dictator Marcos had gone to spend time with his pal Ronald Reagan. Specially close watch was kept on exits for the dissemination of undesirable information! I had volunteered to carry records of assassinations, tortures, etc to London to post to different justice and peace committees in different parts of the world. They were almost found on me.

That would have been rough.

Margaret never complained that I returned safely from each visit! Sure, the Holy Spirit was guide, comforter and friend. But that does not guarantee survival in this life. However, I shared Margaret's relief.

Ian M. Fraser

WORSHIP

The promised presence

(An Iona Community Associates' meeting at Acton Scott Village Hall)

Quartz-ray heaters and a smell of damp
and woodlice where the skirting is decayed.
We gather where the shuttlecocks have flown
looked down on by the village cricket team,
The Queen and unnamed chairs of WI:
a circle in the lines that say you're 'out'.

I turn and see myself in all at prayer:
the greying heads, the well-lined, well-veined cheeks,
and feel with them the westward call that tugs
with ever-crossing Celtic interlace
binding each mind it laced so long ago,
so far away from this quiet, country scene.

Before us, in the centre, bread and wine –
His promised presence where the village class
of country dancers make their steps entwine
with slap of shoe and happy breathlessness.
And yet it feels more holy than a church:
the mouldy air makes village bread seem fresher,
the stale sweat gives the wine a sweeter taste –
and round all, through all, of all in that room
the Spirit weaves the threads of human grace.

Rob Walker

Called to be One

A Palestinian cookbook, a leg without an ID, and two washing machines

A letter from Warren Bardsley, volunteering as an EA with the Ecumenical Accompaniment Programme in Palestine and Israel (www.eappi.org):

In the theme of this letter there is a strong hint of the bizarre! It highlights the absurdity of some of the things that happen at checkpoints and customs barriers here and which reflect the day-to-day experience of Palestinian people. Let me say straight away that I hope I never lose my capacity to be shocked by what I see and hear at these soul-destroying places. According to the latest figures from the United Nations Office for the Coordination of Humanitarian Affairs (UNOCHA), there are now over 600 checkpoints of various shapes and sizes around Jerusalem and the West Bank, in an area about the size of Wales. It is almost impossible for a Palestinian to travel anywhere without going through one or more of these barriers, which means quite simply that you can never plan to make and keep an appointment. A journey which would normally take half an hour can last three or four hours depending on the whim of IDF soldiers manning the checkpoint or the amount of traffic going through. Many precious hours of many lives are lost, simply in waiting.

Some months ago a member of an NGO was returning to Norway and was carrying in her luggage a Palestinian cookbook. Going through customs, her bags and cases were thoroughly searched (a common experience here). In the course of this investigation the officials came across the object in question, scrutinised it, consulted, then said to her, 'We will have to confiscate this item. We can't give you an explanation but you will understand that it is for security reasons.' Anything, apparently, can be justified in the name of security!

Even more bizarre, was the experience of the Palestinian family who were returning from Jerusalem to a West Bank village, carrying with them an item in a long wooden box. When they were questioned by the soldiers at the checkpoint, they explained that they had been with their father who had just undergone major surgery in a Jerusalem hospital involving the amputation of a leg. They had left him in hospital, where he was making a good recovery, but they wanted to return home to bury the leg in the family grave. The soldiers demanded that the box be opened; they examined the leg, then asked the family if the limb had an ID. They said, naturally enough, that as the leg belonged to their father, the ID was with him in Jerusalem. The post commander had in the back of his mind some recollection of a soldier who had recently sustained an accident involving a leg and his suspicions were aroused. After some discussion the soldiers decided that they couldn't allow the leg through without an ID. So the family had to return to Jerusalem, recover their father's papers, make their way back to the checkpoint and then travel home. By this time, as you can imagine, the leg was smelling offensively. It was almost dark when they arrived at their village and the journey had taken eight hours – four times its normal length. I relate these stories not to ridicule Israel nor to deny the state's proper security concerns, but to point out the nonsense of this extreme, inhuman inflexibility and to illustrate the daily humiliations to which Palestinian people are subjected under this Occupation.

And what about the two washing machines? Ghassan Burquan, a Palestinian stonecutter living in the Israeli-controlled side of Hebron, saved up for months and bought a washing machine. Since he is not allowed to drive a car to his home – Palestinian vehicles being banned on that stretch of the street –

he parked nearby and carried the machine on his head, accompanied by his wife, five children and his brother. Border police stopped him and asked to see what was inside the boxed appliance. His brother got upset and before long the checkpoint was surrounded by armed men; Ghassan ended up in jail badly bloodied and accused of trying to steal a gun from the Border Police. Unusually, he was later released on bail by the Appeals Court.

But the washing machine had disappeared.

The incident, reported by Haaretz journalist Gideon Levy, was read by two Israeli friends, Gershom and Elliott, who live in Jerusalem. They decided that, in memory of a friend who had just died, they would buy a washing machine and deliver it to Ghassan, someone completely unknown to them. Accordingly, they made arrangements, and Yehiel, an acquaintance who works with Rabbis for Human Rights, offered to drive the washing machine to Hebron. At the various checkpoints, soldiers concluded that the three men were Jewish settlers and waved them through. Ghassan and his brother met them in Hebron and they crowded into the backseat of the car. They arrived at the small apartment where Ghassan and his family live, and as they shared food and drink together the three Israelis explained that they had brought the machine, not only in memory of their friend but because it was what their faith required of them.

Gershom concluded: 'We are not suggesting that bringing a washing machine to the West Bank will lead to peace, just as I wouldn't claim that one donation will end poverty. But as Rabbi Tarfon said: *"You are not expected to finish the task and you are not free to refrain from it".*'

It may be that when the madness of the Occupation ends, and the final chapters are written, acts of human compassion and solidarity like these will be seen to have played a not insignificant part in ending it.

Warren Bardsley

Mission

The girl who had barely blinked

A reflection on working on a Communications Workers Union Humanitarian Aid convoy, bringing donations to hospitals, orphanages and Roma schools in Bulgaria …

It was simply the biggest CWUHA convoy ever to take to the road – eleven vehicles, twenty-two drivers. With broad accents from Dublin, Liverpool, Edinburgh and Newcastle, to name but a few, we couldn't begin to worry about understanding any Bulgarian! The upside of having many hands on deck for unloading hardly needs stating; and after each long and emotion-charged day, there was the solidarity of shared experience, talked through at length and sometimes with unembarrassed tears.

The hospital at Vidin, our first destination, was a 'gentle' opener. We saw the good news first. Funds raised by team members had been sent ahead of our trip and spent well at local suppliers. Several of the children's wards were already boasting their brand-new blue and orange beds, cots and bedside lockers. With incredible timing, while we were there, a further delivery arrived and brand-new incubators came onto the premises, also the result of convoy fundraising. There was no taking away from the celebration of such tangible achievements. And there was equally no denying the shock of seeing those wards where old furnishings had not yet been replaced with new. In the midst of the gratitude expressed, we learned that this was the most generous charitable giving the hospital had ever received, and it was also the first time that aid had been targeted at helping the children's wards.

There was similar joy to be had at Montana. It was not a place to retreat in horror at the prospect of being a patient there yourself, but compared with what we know at home, it was a huge step back, in time, in technology, in facilities.

Montana was a tale of two hospitals – the rather dilapidated one in use, and the potentially upgraded version, in its towering naked-brick, semi-constructed state. The new-build had been halted indefinitely. There was no more money.

Sofia's hospital was the one place we did not all venture, city-centre trucking being, to borrow from another of the team's many tongues, 'pure mental'. Thankfully there were enough of us to handle the most challenging unloadings of a number of operating tables. How they made it to the theatres, we can only guess – just getting them off a truck nearly cost a finger.

And so to our other destinations – a different kind of place. For some of us, it was the first experience of being in an orphanage. But whether first or umpteenth, these are hard places to be. Kula is a community of cared-for young people with many kinds of disability, physical and psycho-neurological. The Day Centre building was a promising facility, its airy activity rooms decorated with the children's artwork. The neighbouring residential building looked even brighter and more modern, until we stepped inside.

Even looking later at a photograph of the abysmal toilets, my lip still curls involuntarily, recalling the near nausea felt at the time of taking the shot. The downstairs kitchen and laundry were pitiful sights. Appliances belonged to some bygone age and the long, cold basement corridor was reminiscent of some derelict warehouse. Back upstairs, one of the bedrooms seemed at first to be empty too, but peeking round the door, it transpired one bed was occupied. A little girl of unidentifiable age was lying awkwardly, fully clothed and half-covered with a patterned sheet.

Her high, wide forehead and the strange angles of her limbs disclosed perhaps spina bifida. She was wide awake and taking in this stranger. I wished I knew her name. I wished I knew her language. I wondered what chances she had to be out of that bed and playing. I wished I had a cuddly toy to leave in her arms. But with what we had – time and touch and murmurings, smiles and coos and gazes – we communicated. First came clasping hands, then a huge smile, a beautiful giggle, and a lively bouncing of those crooked legs. What was her story and how will life be for her in five, ten years?

We met others who had, strictly speaking, outgrown the age and stage of residential care. The staff at Kula had set up a 'Protected House' – a garden cottage for four older boys, who proudly showed us round their home, despite its walls surely bulging at finding capacity for 22 sudden guests! In such tiny corners, there was real hope, but precarious hope. Can these young men stay in this protected, marginally independent base indefinitely? Who will decide and what alternatives could they possibly thrive on?

Kyustendil too was filled with unanswered questions, though it's impossible to say which is worse – to be left wondering or to find out the facts. Bulgaria has 160 orphanages and, cultural norms as they are, it is rare for disability to be accepted and embraced within the family. But that was not the relevant issue at Kyustendil. Our first deliveries and visit were to the misnamed 'Mother and Baby Centre'. The stark, spartan rooms of cots set side by side are an affront to our every idea of what childhood should be. Yet some were there because their families believed they would be better off in the care of the state than remaining with economically impoverished parents of the Roma underclass.

There were two children who stood out to me in the toddlers' dorms. The first, because of his natural inquisitiveness and trust. With curly hair, an angelic face and a bright-red jumper, he stood alert and curious in his cot, as though not wanting to miss a move of this invasion of big people. He loved being tickled and squirmed happily in my arms, looking round in every direction from the higher than usual vantage point, then homing in with fascination on my camera case, fingering the straps and discovering the funny sound Velcro makes and how the zip zipped. It wasn't really me he didn't want to let go

of – only the camera case!

A few cots away, a second curly-haired, wide-awake child occupied her cot. She was lying on her back with motionless arms spread-eagled beside her head, palms up. Crouching down to appear less fearsome, I offered a hand through the wooden cot bars. No reaction. With one finger, I played 'round and round the garden' in one of her tiny palms. No reaction. Only a hollow unblinking stare: the saddest and most perturbing non-encounter with a child that I have ever had.

It was hard to be there. And harder still to walk away. The staff we met were no doubt doing their under-resourced and unapplauded best. Only later did we learn of the genuine incredulity at our presence and aid being a promise carried through. It seemed that grand intentions declared from other well-meaning quarters had led only to disappointment. The difference we had made was now stacked high in the corridors and ready for unpacking after our departure – new cots, mattresses, clothes, toys, all kinds of play equipment and much more.

Wonderfully, within a fortnight of returning home, an e-mail arrived with a batch of photographs showing off the newly kitted-out playroom at the Centre. Children we had met only in their cots were on bikes, trikes and seesaws, exploring playhouses and clutching balls and dolls. I clicked onto the next photo and suddenly there was the girl who had barely blinked.

She still looked aloof and unsmiling, but she was there, active and playing.

Ironically, the children growing up in the ghetto-like shanty town of the Roma village we visited were absolute live wires. But here we witnessed a moment that summed up all too well the dire circumstances of the families living there.

It all started in the dusty field between school and village that passed as their playground. The sight of ten lorries rolling in had brought all ages teeming from nearby houses and streets. Among the multitude were as many adults as children – young mothers and wizened grandmothers, all vying for a share of our gifts, and smiling as they received toys and other goodies, to be given to the infant in their arms or a toddling latecomer. Included in the offerings were knitted teddies by the boxful (no convoy is complete without them). One particular boxful was rapidly emptying into the eager hands of children and adults alike, creating a buzz of movement and voices.

One woman arrived late on the scene and approached the hub of activity, only to see that the last teddy had just gone. She pointed at the box, which was upturned and shaken as a gesture of explanation and apology. The woman pointed at the box again, speaking her own language. 'Does she want the box? Do you think she's asking for the box?' Hesitantly, for fear of having picked her up wrongly, the box was gingerly offered. Big smiles, more chatter, and it was taken and paraded away. Did we really witness this? A woman made happy by the acquisition of a large cardboard box? But the story had not ended.

A few minutes later she returned, this time carrying a plastic bag half-filled with fruit and vegetables. These were handed to her astounded benefactor, to express profuse gratitude.

Jo Love, 2010

www.cwuha.org

Work

The bondage of busyness ... a plea for taking and making time

There's a marvellous book by the German author Michael Ende. It's called *Momo*; it was written in 1973 and it's about time thieves.

It observes, through the eyes of an outsider, how people are seduced into overwork. And in the process busyness displaces friendship, schedules displace compassion, and the time for others which makes life rich is stolen.

Not long before Ende's novel was published, we had a series of prime ministers who would take afternoon naps, write books, go to the theatre and delight in being bon viveurs; and nobody thought it was wrong.

Now, if the present incumbent in Downing Street were known to be playing bridge of an afternoon or went to a West End cinema every Thursday night as a matter of course, there would be an outcry. We expect public servants, especially those who are our political masters, to be dedicated to duty 24 hours a day. And if their health should suffer, then those who yesterday were demanding a pound of flesh will today say take it easy, so that tomorrow the same degree of busyness might be exacted.

Perhaps we expect this of figures in political life because so many of us have bought into or become victims of a stress-obsessed society, and we wouldn't want those at the top to have more time on their hands than we have on ours.

Or perhaps we fear time in the same way as some people fear silence. Not sure of what to do with it, we retreat into busyness and defend ourselves by saying that we are the victims of a demanding job and a full diary.

And in the process time becomes the enemy, and we speak of it in hostile terms: we talk about time beating us, or about having to kill time.

Maybe, for our own good, we should befriend time rather than demonise it. Maybe, just as in our most prudent moments we budget our money and take stock of the consequences of over-spending, so we should budget, discuss, decide on and befriend our time.

And maybe part of that process is blowing the whistle on always saying 'yes' and finding the courage sometimes to say 'no'.

Being known as a busy but obliging person and being regarded as indispensable may massage our ego; but such things may also destroy the very ego they flatter.

And if not saying 'yes' every time seems rather 'un-Christian', then maybe we should look again at Christ. Jesus didn't heal everybody who was ill, he never entered every debate that was on offer. But he did know some facts of life which we may have forgotten … namely that God is not a time-thief. God is a holiday maker; and time is not a threat, it's a gift.

John L. Bell

Month 4 Day 25

POVERTY

Inspired by love and anger

Inspired by love and anger, disturbed by need and pain,
informed of God's own bias, we ask him once again:
'How long must some folk suffer? How long can few folk mind?
How long dare vain self-interest turn prayer and pity blind?'

From those forever victims of heartless human greed,
their cruel plight composes a litany of need:
'Where are the fruits of justice? Where are the signs of peace?
*When is the day when prisoners and dreams find their release?'**

In 1947, in the middle of the worst winter of the century, a young Church of Scotland military chaplain with British forces in Germany was approached by a former Luftwaffe bomber pilot, who told him about the plight of 80,000 nearby German refugees, who were nearly frozen to death. Could the minister help? Douglas Lister went with him to see the refugees. He was horrified by what he saw. He found babies wrapped in newspapers. The refugees had very little to eat. He knew he had to help these starving people.

High Command refused permission on the grounds that it would be fraternisation with the enemy. Douglas approached his friend, Captain John Althorp, for his advice. 'Good God,' said Althorp, 'these poor people are no enemies! Fight the High Command!'

He did. 'As my order as chaplain is to serve people regardless of race, colour or religion, I wish to appeal against the rule in question,' he said in his letter to the High Command. 'I consider it my duty to help those people in their need if I possibly can. I would be grateful if you could give me permission to do so.'

He won the appeal. Letters were sent to Scotland asking for support, to help the German refugees survive the winter hardship – all this only two years after a war in which many Scots had lost loved ones. As a result of the campaigning efforts of Mr Lister and Captain Althorp, and chaplains across Europe, many churches rallied to the cause. The lives of hundreds of so-called 'enemies' were saved. As a result of this cooperation, the Inter-Church Refugee Service was born. It developed in time into Christian Aid.

I am grateful to Ron Ferguson for sharing this story. It is a vivid reminder that from the beginning, three things were true of the movement that eventually became Christian Aid. The first is that people inspired by love and anger, disturbed by need and pain, decided something needed to be done, not just felt. The second thing is that they turned to the churches to do it. And the third thing is that theirs was a challenging cause. It called on a war-weary people to do what Jesus asked them to do, to love their enemies, do good to those who had hated them and pray for those who had persecuted them. The task was complex, disturbing, fraught with practical and political and pastoral difficulties. But from its inception, Christian Aid was rooted in the conviction that the gospel commands us to seek peace founded on justice, and that costly reconciliation is at the heart of the gospel.

Today, Christian Aid works in over 40 countries, with and through hundreds of partners. The majority of these are Christian: national denominations, Councils of Churches and ecumenical Christian NGOs. We are part of the ACT (Action of Churches Together) Alliance, a global partnership of churches and related agencies working to save lives and support communities in emergencies worldwide. Sometimes we work with partners who are of other faiths or no faith to make the greatest impact on overcoming poverty.

I want to share three contemporary stories with you.

Joseph lives in the Mbeere region of Kenya. As in many parts of sub-Saharan Africa, Mbeere has been significantly and negatively affected by unpredictable climate change. This is one of the main reasons why so many rural people have moved to Nairobi, millions of them, unable any longer to make a living and putting enormous pressure on the city's infrastructure, living in vast slums like Kibera. It's one of the reasons there are so many street children in Nairobi. In the Mbeere region, crop yields have been diminishing, and as they have no access to the kind of technological advances in agricultural production that farmers in the West take for granted, they have an over-reliance on ancient farming methods. Never mind tractors, many food producers in Africa don't even have oxen and plough. They farm with hoes and machetes. Nor do they have access to something we take for granted, a simple thing like the weather forecast. This mattered less when weather patterns were predictable; now they are anything but. So the first obstacle that Joseph faces as a farmer is climate change, the second is lack of access to scientific and technological advances. And his third problem is having to rely on middlemen to sell his goods. They are often unscrupulous, which means that he is less likely to get a fair price or make any profit for his very hard work.

Maria lives in the Beni region in Northern Bolivia. Bolivia is the poorest country in South America and Beni is part of the Amazon basin. Maria is another farmer with big problems. Poor and excluded indigenous communities in this region have suffered very badly through logging and deforestation of the rainforest destroying their traditional livelihoods. Though they have lived there since time immemorial, indigenous communities cannot produce the kind of land titles we in the West are used to – in the past, they never needed them anyway. Nor do they have the access to lawyers which could help them claim their land rights. So big logging companies can destroy the rainforest with impunity. The World Bank estimates that 80% of all logging in Bolivia is illegal. The deforestation has also increased flooding, as it has in many parts of the world. So Maria and her people needed to find new crops to farm that are more resilient to flooding.

Lawrence is a farmer in Ghana. He's had a very hard time in the last fifteen years or so. Since the trade liberalisation of the 1990s (that's when poor countries were forced to open up their home markets to Western goods by international institutions like the IMF, the World Trade Organisation and the World Bank, usually because of the global debt crisis), Ghana's agricultural economy has been drastically affected by subsidised foreign imports. You know that idea that kind-hearted people in the West had about European butter mountains and food surpluses, that the thing to do with them was to send them to Africa – it was a very bad idea indeed! So in Ghana, rice and tomatoes were among the main products, but now, two-thirds of rice growers are operating at a loss, and 90% of the tomato paste is imported. The offloading of European and American surpluses on to African and South American markets simply put local producers like Lawrence out of business. Heavily subsidised Western goods lower prices to such an extent that local traders cannot compete. Stringent regulations placed by Western-controlled bodies like the World Trade Organisation, the International Monetary Fund and the World Bank on trade and markets in developing countries forbid subsidies, but these regulations are not observed by the very countries which impose them. It's a question of 'do what we say, not what we do'.

These stories are a direct link with the origins of Christian Aid. Still today, we are promoting contentious causes like climate justice, land rights, tax and trade justice, which are complex, disturbing, fraught with practical and political and pastoral difficulties. But the cruel plight of Joseph and Maria and Lawrence composes a litany of need, and so we go on in the conviction that profound poverty and injustice is not God's will and that we are called to respond across all worldly barriers.

This is a difficult time financially for many in rich countries. But for those in the poorest countries already living on the margins of destitution, the financial crisis can make the difference between life and death – their export orders are tumbling, investment finance is drying up, money sent by relatives working in the West is falling, unemployment is increasing and aid is already being cut by rich countries. Commodities speculation, now that property is a busted flush, is causing food prices to soar. The money to realise the Millennium Development Goals is disappearing into a global taxation system that allows the world's richest to evade their responsibilities as corporations, as citizens, as human beings, and I commend to you Christian Aid's Trace the Tax campaign.

This is especially a challenging time for fundraising in South and Central America. Earlier this year, the UK Department for International Development cut its funding to Latin America, on the basis that these are middle-income countries and don't need it! But three-quarters of the world's poorest people live in middle-income countries – the truth is that these are the world's most unequal countries, where hugely wealthy elites live alongside people in the most appalling poverty. So Christian Aid continues to support its partners there.

At Community Week this summer, I invited the Community to support

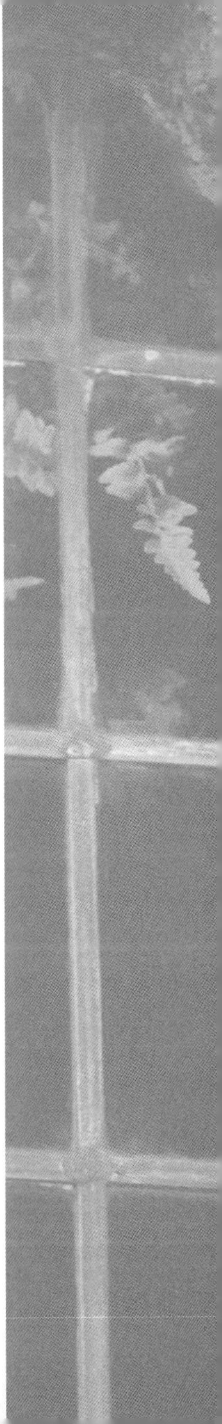

Christian Aid's work in the conflict-ridden country of Colombia, where key food security resources, such as water and fertile soil, are seriously compromised by the dominance of extractive industries, mainly oil and coal, who occupy and contaminate significant tracts of land. The situation is made worse because poor rural people, subject to constant human rights violation, lack effective and peaceful channels for political participation, especially at the local level. This perpetuates a culture of violence, where violence and violence alone is the preferred method to manage differences, advance vested interests or exert public authority. Christian Aid supports grassroots partners aiming to reduce poverty and human rights abuses, particularly empowering women and young adults in local communities. Overcoming violence, increasing human rights, challenging vested interests, supporting women and young people, are not the easiest causes to raise money for. But Christian Aid is rooted in taking up difficult tasks, and these ones are at the heart of the Iona Community's Peace and Justice Commitment. So I invite members, Family Groups, associates and friends to consider supporting this work in your fundraising and disbursement, and to now help to grow hope in a troubled and beautiful country.

God asks, 'Who will go for me?
Who will extend my reach?
And who, when few will listen,
will prophesy and preach?
And who, when few bid welcome, will offer all they know?
And who, when few dare follow,
will walk the road I show?' *

Kathy Galloway (Head of Christian Aid Scotland), 2011

* *From 'Inspired by Love and Anger', by John L. Bell and Graham Maule, from* Love and Anger: Lively Songs of Social Justice, *Wild Goose Publications*

www.christianaid.org.uk

Basic Christian Communities

Angel in Camden Town Market

I used to hear him busking in Camden Town Market. He was a dwarf, or little person; his features sharp, and twisted from a difficult birth; beaten and scarred from a hard life. His arms were like broken wings that had healed, and set crookedly. He played an autoharp, and sort of strummed it with one hand and his long yellow nails. It sat in his lap. He was perched on a high stool. There was cap lying on the ground for passers-by to throw change in.

The first time I heard him he was singing 'Summertime'. I was lost in the maze of market stalls and myself, and was feeling cold and numb. His voice made me stop … and shiver … as it opened me up.

His voice was a cry … In moments, soothing … victorious:

But one of these mornings …
you're gonna rise up singing.
You're gonna spread your wings
and take to the skies …

But until that morning …
nothing's gonna harm you.

So hush, little baby,
don't you cry …

It was a grey London day – cloudy, heavy, pressing, depressing. He looked like an angel, perched on that stool: the autoharp was all silvery-sounding. He sang 'Summertime' over and over. Like he was reciting a psalm. Like he was praying for

his broken self; and for every broken soul pushing and dragging themselves through Camden Town.

One time I stood and listened to him singing 'Summertime', and saw a flock of skylarks fly from out of his twisted mouth – bursting from the cage of his body, and trailing in a graceful arc up over scaffolding and steel and glass and rain-streaked concrete tombs …

I was working for a homeless shelter in King's Cross at the time. I went round London talking to people sleeping rough (my patch was Camden Town, the Strand, Kingsway, Temple, Piccadilly Circus …). I walked and rode around London so much that by the end of the day my snot was black with car exhaust and soot from the Underground.

But the real smell of London for me is the sweet fragrance of 'Old Holborne' rolling tobacco: its incense filled just about every conversation I had. I had a pouch of Old Holborne, and a packet of Rizla rolling papers, the shelter supplied me with. I'd offer folk I met a roll-up: 'Need a roll-up, mate?' It was a good 'opener' and a way in; we'd sit and talk. Later I'd ask them if they needed a kip for the night, and would invite them back to the shelter for a meal, a break from the wind and cold, some hours of unguarded sleep …

I had the angel's voice singing in my head all through one day doing street work …

… Talking to a young guy on the Strand, who'd just got out of prison. In prison he'd spent all his free time using the weights and exercise equipment in the yard, he tells me. At first, it was a way to stay sane and out of trouble, but then he got into it – and now his idea is to do a moduled course at college he heard about, and then get a job in a health club: showing other people how to use the machines, and helping them to get healthy and fit.

He can do it, he tells me, with sinew in his voice – and I believe him … He can do anything, survive anything, he says. One time he almost died from drugs and drink. He OD'd and passed out: he remembers the blackness. 'Like a pit.' … They rushed him to hospital and gave him a shot of adrenaline in his heart … He feels himself when he's working out, he says to me.

I offer him a roll-up but he says he doesn't smoke. 'Oh, of course,' I say … I offer him a kip back at the shelter but he tells me he's moving on tonight. Whenever he feels like he's getting sucked into a pit now, he moves on. He rolls up his jacket, and shows me his arm, tattooed with a bald eagle – it's like solid rock.

> *… you're gonna spread your wings,*
> *and take to the skies …*

Talking to another young guy, skippering outside Burger King; who, after his silent, hard friends all leave, admits to me that he's scared … Scared of going to court and being sent back to jail. 'Scared of going down the cages and getting slashed' …

He wants his mum, he says, sucking on a bottle of beer. And I want to hug him.

> *… So hush, little baby,*
> *don't you cry …*

Talking to old Harry. Sitting cross-legged on the cold stone floor of King's Cross station, sharing a big bottle of cider as he recites to me his poem about the American West. About Geronimo and Sitting Bull, and how the U.S. government betrayed the Native American people and stole their land.

Harry was a miner; his family had worked the land for generations: 'Until Thatcher came ridin' into town and gave the country to the corporations and bankers.'

After that – after the marches and the battles with police on horseback, and then the years of never being able to find any real work – he 'lost heart' and 'something deep down inside of him died'. He calls himself a drunk, a failure: he ran out on his family.

But his heart's alive when he recites his beautiful, human poetry. He waves his arms like a prophet, like a shaman. And everyone just walks past the dirty old drunk – radiating light; intoxicated with the Spirit … And as the Transport Police cowboys come to arrest him to dump him in a cell overnight, he is as stoic as Sitting Bull; his face deeply life-lined as Geronimo's in the American neon light.

> *... But until that morning*
> *nothing's gonna harm you ...*

Talking to young Robbie on the steps of St Pancras Church. About the Beatles, and their song from *Revolver* 'Tomorrow Never Knows': 'Play the game ex-is-tence to the end ... of the beginning,' he intones, and laughs hollowly, and stares at me with his wide, dead eyes. Like black holes. He drones that he's looking forward to dying and becoming atoms ... to being infinite and for ever. And I'm not sure what to answer. I get sucked up into his eyes for a moment. I see oblivion, I see Hell ... There are no stars in young Robert's eyes any more; and I turn away as he finishes shooting up.

> *... One of these mornings ...*
> *you're gonna spread your wings*
> *and take to the skies ...*

Talking to Chas up near Westminster Station – who runs up and tells me that he made the Homelessness World Cup football team! He went for a try-out – and made the team! And now he's going on an aeroplane to Brazil to play for his country!

> *... you're gonna spread your wings*
> *and take to the skies ...*

Talking to a guy whose girlfriend and best friend were killed together in a car crash, and who's got a lot of pills on him, and keeps popping them while we're talking, washing them down with a bottle of vodka he keeps slugging back. He hands over the bottle of pills at one point, but then takes them back again when I fumble around nervously and say something stupid, when I lose hold on the conversation and it seems like I'm not *really* listening and don't *really* care. I think of snatching the bottle back, but everything's happening so fast; and as I'm just about to, he lurches off into the Underground. I push my way through a crowd, but by the time I get inside the station he's far away. And as I watch him riding deep down on the conveyor belt of death, and disappear, I say a short prayer:

But until that morning …
nothing's gonna harm you …

Talking to a tired, faded-looking woman who tells me her name is Rose; who escaped her husband: who was over 300 pounds, and made her cook and clean up after him. Who made her wipe his arse while he called her mother.

She's got nowhere to go now – nowhere to go but she's free, she says, and tilts her face up to the pale London sun; and there's a trail of perfume of something like roses from a smartly-dressed woman who passes, on her way to the theatre.

… Nothing's gonna harm you …

Talking to an old guy kipping in a little park, who's dying for a smoke; who plays the harmonica, and tells me that it's nice to play in the early morning with the birds singing … I sit with him on the bench, and he talks to me about dancing with his wife. 40 years ago at a dancehall in London. He wore a zoot suit; she wore a long flowing ballgown that shimmered with light when she moved … He tells me that he'll see her again in heaven, and that they'll dance again together there; and sits and smokes, and quietly plays his harp.

But one of these mornings
you're gonna rise up singing …

So hush, little baby,
don't you cry …

Talking to the Rastafarian who feeds the birds, who has feathers and twigs matted in his long, cabled hair; who tells me that the

songbirds can communicate with the angels. And also with the free and funky-great spirit of William Blake, who lives in Soho Square.

Talking to Marcus, who's waiting to get the keys for his new place: He started a new job as a bricklayer, and took his first pay and put it down on a room. Before, he was a miner, a labourer … He won't get in until the first of the month, but that's OK, he says – he's got a job. Meanwhile, he keeps to himself; keeps himself tidy, keeps away from the drink. 'Sometimes you just gotta wait,' he says, and sits and waits. Listens to football on his transistor radio …

He says that when he moves into his flat, the first thing he'll do is to make himself a nice big meal – a nice fry-up: eggs, sausages, beans, tomatoes, mushrooms – he's got a television a friend's keeping for him – and sit and watch football and eat his fry-up. He's really looking forward to that, he tells me.

… But until that morning …
nothing's gonna harm you …

Talking to Kostas from Greece, who carries a terrible weight of papers around with him everywhere in an old backpack. Papers that prove who is: where he was born; where he's lived – in a hostel in Germany, in a refugee camp in France; where he's worked – picking fruit in Spain, hops in Kent, cleaning toilets in an old-age home …

'My dream is that – one day – I will carry on me only a phone, a wallet, and keys,' he says, and sets his burden down a minute to rest and have a roll-up. I give him a light and he sighs out smoke; closes his baggy eyes a moment … Then takes a deep breath, and picks up his heavy backpack again. I watch him walk off down Euston Road, bowed like Atlas.

… one day …
You're gonna spread your wings and
take to the skies …

Talking to Mary, who was knackered; and who winced and cried and went through bloody hell with her swollen legs and infected foot to make it to the night shelter with me – on the bus, on the tube, on the tube, on the bus – getting dragged up and down the fucking stairs and escalators … And who, by the end of the night, was somehow singing and dancing to country-and-western music in the shelter common room.

But one of these mornings …
you're gonna rise up singing.
You're gonna spread your wings and
take to the skies …

But until that morning …
nothing's gonna harm you.
So hush, little baby,
don't you cry …

Neil Paynter

'Summertime', by George and Ira Gershwin, from the opera Porgy and Bess.

www.simoncommunity.org.uk

Month 4 Day 26

NON-VIOLENCE AND PEACEKEEPING

Try-out

He grew up in a town where red and blue mattered
more than rain and power cuts. Had a try-out,
once, for his best mate's Sunday juniors team.
Laughed off the pitch five minutes later,
dragged bootlaces through puddles, launched his ball
into the duck pond. Moorhens
scattered, bits of duckweed fountained, wet air.

Saturdays were shiftless, snicket gates
and washing lines flapping like flags. Smoking
by dockyard walls, sneering at the here-we-goes.
Lock-outs, dole queue, Jobcentre; then the army.
Blue in a garish glare of sky;
red in fountaining sand, stink of scorched metal.
But they were kindly hands that wrenched him
out of wreckage, blotted the blood and grit
of his coughing on a chequered *keffiyeh*.

Medals, discharge, amputations later
and he's back in that desert, painting
18-yard boxes on bomb-parched ground.
Hot brown children try and catch him out,

dribble footballs
between the real leg and the plastic one.
Indoors, their fathers draw from hookahs
and talk of re-planting the fields.

Andy Humphrey

Month 4 Day 28

INTERFAITH

The Peace Initiative

Is there something more important to do than pray for peace, and in particular to pray for peace within the family of Abraham and Sarah and Hagar? The shadow side of Christianity, Judaism and Islam is at the heart of some of the most conflicted places of hatred and violence in our world today. We know the frightened and angry countenance of religion. We need to look it in the face and denounce it as a false expression of religion. But do we also know that deep within our religious inheritance are visions and practices of peacemaking that hold the key to transformation in our lives and world? We desperately need to access these now. Without peace in the family of Abraham there will not be peace among us as nations.

Praying with the Earth (SCM/Canterbury), along with its companion CD of meditative chants, *Chanting for Peace*, is a peace-offering from within the Christian household. Every morning and evening in the new prayer book, sentences from the Quran, the Hebrew Scriptures, and the teachings of Jesus are used in order to pray for peace. And the same is true in the new collection of chants, allowing words from other parts of the family to draw us back to the true roots of our inheritance, the oneness of the human soul and the essential unity of the earth.

The inspiration for this project grew out of my teaching relationship in the high desert of New Mexico with Nahum Ward-Lev and Rahmah Lutz, a Rabbi from Santa Fe and a Sufi Muslim teacher from Abiquiu. Every summer Ali and I co-teach with Nahum and Rahmah on themes of peace within the Abrahamic community. Our daily pattern is to take it in turn. Whichever one of us is teaching offers words of scripture from our respective tradition for the group to take into silence before shared reflection and conversation.

The first summer together I offered our class words from St Matthew's Gospel. As people meditatively walked in the desert landscape or sat prayerfully in the coolness of the adobe chapel, I noticed that Rahmah's face was radiant. Her countenance always shines but on this occasion she looked like Moses coming down from Mount Sinai. I wondered what was happening in her heart. When we gathered, she was the first to speak. She said, 'I so love Jesus, peace be upon him. He is so compassionate. He is so truthful. He is so merciful. I so love Jesus, peace be upon him.' Most of us in the circle were from the Christian household. And many of us sat with tears in our eyes. As I looked at Rahmah I thought, 'You are teaching us how to speak about Jesus.'

If Jesus' wisdom is again to be recovered within the Christian household, in ways that will enable us to lead the world in peace rather than divide the world in hatred, I believe its rebirth will come largely from outside Christianity. Other parts of the Abrahamic family have not forgotten the essence of Jesus – his compassion, his truthfulness, his mercy. It is from them that we will be helped to remember the true heart of Jesus. And it is from them that we will be helped to remember how to truly follow Jesus.

We need one another. Our traditions are given not to compete with each other. They are given to complete each other. This is my hope in *Praying with the Earth*. This is my intention in *Chanting for Peace*. In listening to the true heart of Islam and Judaism, we will be led not away from the true heart of Christianity. We will be led to a recovery of our distinct treasure, the wisdom of Jesus, who taught us to pray for peace, and who showed us how to live love.

These new resources are only two particular expressions of the way forward. It is of course not just a prayer book and a collection of meditative chants that we need. Our deep need and our truest desire is for greater relationship within the Abrahamic family. Relationship, relationship, relationship is what will change us as individuals and as traditions. And it is the re-establishing of relationship that will heal us. The 'Praying for Peace Initiative' (see www.salvaterravision.org) which I and others launched at the beginning of 2011 is committed to praying and chanting for peace by using the words and wisdom of other parts of the family. It is a way of becoming more deeply aware of one another's treasure. Many members of the Christian household have never read the Quran, let alone used its words to pray. Shall we choose in new ways to live in relationship?

People often think that peace is a pipe dream. In part this is because the word 'peace' has been limitedly associated with a future kingdom or a perfect realm of God on earth. And so the impression has been created that if true peace were to come it would be forever, as if eternally established. But is this the nature of relationship? Who are the people who are most important to us in our lives? They are the people who have chosen again and again and again to look to our heart and to remain in relationship with us even when we have been false. And the reverse is also true about the most important relationships of life. In every moment of our lives and world we have the capacity to choose to be untrue, whether as individuals, as nations, or as a species. This is the challenge, as well as the beauty, of life in its interwovenness. True relationship must always be chosen. This is its greatest blessing. I can look to your heart and honour you now or I can look away from your heart and dishonour you now. And so the way of peace is not about thinking that we need to create a perfect realm of relationship that will hold forever. It is about choosing to be true to one another in every moment, again and again and again. The time of peace is now. Now is the time to make our offering.

To the home of peace
to the field of love
to the land where forgiveness and right relationship meet
we look, O God,
with longing for earth's children
with compassion for the creatures
with hearts breaking for the people and nations we love.
Open us to visions we have never known
strengthen us for self-givings we have never made
delight us with a oneness we could never have imagined
that we may truly be born of You
makers of peace. [1]

Philip Newell

Note:

1. Philip Newell, from Praying with the Earth, SCM/Canterbury, 2011

Commitment

Are you coming?

Come!

I can't do it.

You can do it.

I'm too heavy. I'll sink.

Lay down your burdens and you'll be light enough.

I'm not strong enough.

You don't have to be strong. The water will hold you up.

I might get wet.

Yes, you will.

I might sink.

Only if you panic.

I might drown.

You won't drown. Just let yourself float, and the water will carry you.

People will see me.

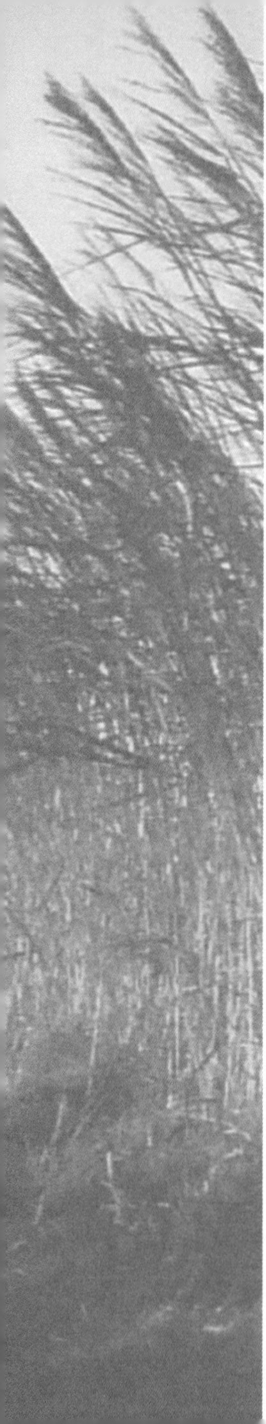

Yes, they'll definitely see you. You might encourage some of them to try it too.

But some of them might try to stop me, for my own good.

Yes. But you can't live out of other people's fears.

Some of them might throw stones at me.

That's a risk you'll just have to take.

Some of them might laugh at me.

Yes. But you'll be the one walking on the water.

The water's very dark.

That's just because you're standing in the shadow. From here, it's a beautiful green.

There might be monsters.

Yes. But there are monsters where you are now.

How will I know which direction to walk in?

Just keep your eyes on me.

What if I can't see you for the waves?

I'll still be here.

I'm very scared.

We're all scared. But don't trust your fears. They're not reliable.

What will I trust?

Trust your love.

But what if I get that wrong?

Then trust my love. They come from the same place.

But what if … ?

This conversation's becoming very circular. I'm not going to stand here all day while you theorise. Now you have to move your body. Action will remove the doubt. Are you coming?

Kathy Galloway

Don't tell me of a faith that fears

Don't tell me of a faith that fears
to face the world around;
don't dull my mind with fickle thoughts
of grace without a ground.

Chorus: I need to know that God is real,
I need to know that Christ can feel
the need to touch and love and heal
the world, including me.

Don't speak of piety and prayers
divorced from human need;
don't talk of spirit without flesh
like harvest without seed.

Chorus

Don't sate my soul with common sense
distilled from ages past,
inept for those who fear the world's
about to breathe its last.

Chorus

Don't set the cross before my eyes
unless you tell the truth
of how the Lord who finds the lost
was often found uncouth.

Chorus

So let the Gospel come alive
in actions plain to see,
in imitation of the one
whose love extends to me.

Wild Goose Resource Group

The Rediscovery of Spirituality

Towards a spirituality for today (from a talk)

Perhaps a good place to start, as we come to reflect on the theme of a spirituality for today, is to remind ourselves that the word 'spirituality' is not a biblical term. 'Spirit', especially the Holy Spirit, and the gifts and fruits of the Spirit, are what the Bible is interested in. And it was an English Quaker of the late nineteenth and early twentieth century who, for me at least, summed up very neatly the biblical approach to spirituality. 'To be a Christian', wrote William Littleboy, 'consists not in feeling but in following; not in ecstasy, but in obedience.'

That said, there is clearly a huge interest today in spirituality; and on Iona we have experienced this very intensely, particularly in relation to the phrase 'Celtic spirituality'.

This has had at least two significant effects on us in the Iona Community.

On the one hand, it has made us examine quite carefully the Celtic heritage that we have inherited, in order to avoid the danger of romanticism, of reading back into the 6th and 7th centuries inappropriate echoes of the 20th and 21st.

On the other hand, it has challenged us to try to think through what we mean by our own 'spirituality'.

In a moment, I want to share with you some reflections on what I think we can take from these early centuries, in order to help us on our faith journey today. But first, a word about the spirituality of the Iona Community.

I was once asked, when I was Leader of the Iona Community, to give a talk to a group in Aberdeen on the spirituality of the Iona Community. On my way up, I stopped off in Edinburgh to visit George MacLeod, then in his 90s. Looking for a good opening quotation for my talk, I asked him: 'What would you say if someone asked you what was the spirituality of the Iona Community?' Without a moment's hesitation, the old rascal replied, 'I'd say I had another appointment and leave the room!'

George MacLeod, however, has in fact said much more than that about spirituality. In one place, he has written, 'The true mark of Christian spirituality is to get one's teeth into things. Painstaking service to humankind's most material needs is the essence of spirituality.' Another well-known Community member, John Bell, has said, 'Spirituality is the oil which fuels that machinery by which we relate to God, to God's world and to God's people.' And Kathy Galloway has written, 'Spirituality is that which ultimately moves you – the fundamental motivation of your life.'

I think these attempts at defining spirituality give a pretty clear indication of how the Iona Community understands the meaning of the word. We see it to do with relationships – getting the right balance, if you like – between God, ourselves and the whole of God's creation. We reject entirely any suggestion that spirituality is about escape from the world, or that it is to do primarily with the state of one's individual soul. And we are not interested in trying to get back to an earlier stage in history, searching for some purer, cleaner, more natural past – which of course never existed. God calls us forward, not back – and is always ahead of us anyway – and the Church is called to be a movement, not a monument. As one Church member once memorably said at one of our General Assemblies, when people had been referring to Elders as 'pillars of the Kirk': 'What the Kirk needs today are not pillars, but propellers.' Amen to that.

Nevertheless, what we have gradually come to appreciate is the heritage that we do receive from our Celtic past. As we have already seen, it's very difficult to get as close to this as we might wish; and it is equally difficult to avoid the danger of reading back into it echoes of our own concerns. And as I now attempt to offer some reflections on what we can take, in this matter of spirituality, from our Celtic heritage, I am under no illusion that I will be any more successful than others in avoiding those dangers.

Central to the faith of the Celtic Christians, it seems to me, were three fundamental convictions:

They believed in the Church, the Body of Christ in Heaven and on Earth, with themselves totally incorporated in it.

They believed in God's revelation of himself, in Christ, in scripture, in the ongoing life and teaching of the Church, in the whole of his creation, and in the human heart.

And they believed in the absolute necessity of our response to that revelation – in confession, in praise, and in practical love and care for our fellow creatures in the spirit of Jesus, available to us through grace alone.

It is clear to me that these basic beliefs are to be found in all that we know of them, both from their own writings, and from the material written about them from later times. That they believed in the Church can be seen not only from what they themselves wrote – there is a lovely poem, for instance, attributed to Columba, in praise of the Pope – but also in the way they built their lives around the Sacraments and practices of the Church, and in their love and promotion of the Communion of Saints. Their commitment to the Bible is evidenced, for instance, in their painstaking copying of scripture, so often beautifully illustrated and illuminated, of which we still have examples in the Book of Kells and the Lindisfarne Gospels. It is well-known how they saw God's revelation all around them in the natural world, and even in some of the pagan practices which they came to replace. And everything we know about them confirms their belief in what we would simply call 'practical Christianity' – or as George MacLeod would say, 'getting one's teeth into things'.

Behind and within these three basic beliefs, we can, I think, detect a distinctive spirituality which has much to offer us as we go forward today.

There is, for instance, a joyful acknowledgement of the connectedness of all things. The artwork of these early centuries, found on their stone crosses, their jewellery and their illuminated manuscripts, has made us familiar with what is called the Celtic knot – the interweaving lines which have no beginning and no end. Many have come to see this as an expression of their sense of connectedness – the connectedness of heaven and earth, of the spiritual and the material, of here and eternity.

This sense of connectedness, it seems to me, is something we deeply need to recover, we who have lived through the growing individualisation and disconnectedness of the past 20 to 30 years. Indeed, the roots of the disintegration that afflicts the life of Western society go much deeper, back to the rationalism and the so-called Enlightenment of the 17th and 18th centuries.

For the Celtic Christians, the sacred and the secular were not opposites: life was a whole, and God was involved in all of it. So it was natural for Columba to have as much care about the bardic, and often pagan, poets of Ireland, and about the welfare of a wounded crane, as it was for him to care deeply about carrying the good news of the Gospel to the surrounding pagan Picts. In George MacLeod's well-known phrase, for the Celtic Christians God was either 'Lord of everything or Lord of nothing' – and what God offered, in Christ, was not soul salvation but whole salvation. There was a connectedness there – and it grew, of course, as much from their reading of the Bible as it did from their culture of their times – and it draws us still, it speaks to us still. One member of the Iona Community, Kate McIlhagga, put it very succinctly when she wrote: 'Spirituality is where prayer and politics meet.'

Another feature detected in Celtic Christianity – a feature which, like most of them, is by no means unique to the Celts – is what one of the early writers in praise of Columba called 'a sense of balance'.

Their spirituality was one which recognised the need, for instance, for a balance between the corporate and the personal in life. The Celtic Christians, especially the missionaries among them, lived in the constant tension between the need to work and pray in community with their fellows, and the burning desire to withdraw to a place of utter isolation, for prayer on their own before God.

This sense of balance – the balance between activity and retreat, between speech and silence, between work and worship, to name but three areas – is found, of course, in almost every religious tradition, and in all generations. For Christians, it takes its origin from the Bible, from the balance in God's work of creation in the Genesis poem, from the balance in Christ's life and ministry in Galilee, in the Gospel accounts. On Iona, we have a symbol of it, built into the walls of the medieval Benedictine abbey. If you stand by the Communion table, and look up at the window on the south wall, you can spot, about halfway up, on the stonework on either side, two little carvings. On the one side, a cat – symbol of reflection, retreat. On the other side, a monkey – symbol of activity, advance. A balanced life, and an integrated one, was a goal of the Celtic Christians, as it still is for millions today.

Another aspect of their spirituality, and one which is largely ignored, is the place in their lives of discipline. We have examples from these centuries, for instance, of what are called the 'penitentials', codes of discipline, often quite harsh, at least to our ears, relative to various levels of misdemeanours in the monastic life. One such, for instance, taken it seems from a similar code drawn up for monks in Egypt, calls for the penitent to stand up to the waist in water, reciting the Psalms. That sounds like something that could even be enjoyable in the heat of the desert – less so, perhaps, in the cold of an Iona winter! But they did it, all the same.

Columba's life, we are told, was a disciplined one – and he demanded discipline from his monks. There may have been – there probably was – an element in this of the mortifying of the flesh. The Christian Church has always had to struggle with its attitude to the body – a struggle very much before us today – trying, again, to get the balance right, between too much love of the flesh and too little. It doesn't seem, though, as if the Celtic Christians sought to abuse the body – rather, they seem to have

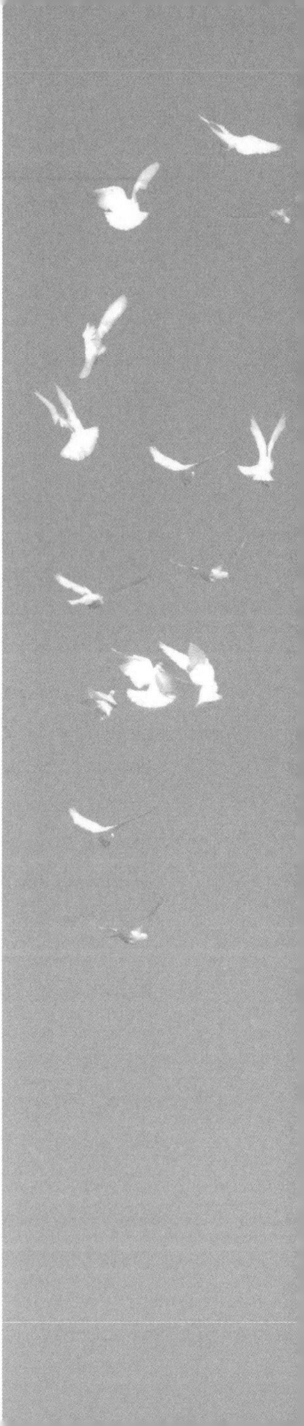

taken their cue from St Paul, seeking always to keep the body, and its appetites, under control. And the discipline they exercised was a mutual discipline – accountability to each other, in charity, lay at the heart of it, with accountability to the Superior, representing Christ, as the final part of the process.

The disciplined Christian life, in a spirit of mutual accountability, and in love, rather than any sort of fierce individualistic fanaticism, is surely something we can take from our Celtic forbears. Church life in our society has often, has it not, seemed to swing between two extremes – a rather liberal, formal observance on the one hand, and a more rigid and personal commitment on the other. Again, we come back to balance and connectedness. Discipline, even hard discipline, has its place, if it is balanced – and accountable – and appropriate. The Celtic Christians understood this well, it would seem.

Much is made, by most modern writers on this theme, of the Celtic Christians' ability to delight in the natural world, and to find evidence of God's self-revelation in nature. We certainly have plenty of evidence to support this – remembering, of course, that the world of nature was really the only world they knew – and this encourages us, in our day, to rediscover the place of the natural world as a focus for ongoing revelation, and the importance of our stewardship of the created order.

What has not perhaps received so much attention – and what may in fact have something quite important for us in our post-modern, eclectic culture – is the way in which the Celtic Christians related to the pre-Christian culture of their pagan neighbours.

It can perhaps best be summed up in the phrase 'critical involvement'. Living as they did in a culture which was just emerging from centuries of paganism, they sought to tread a careful path between total rejection and dangerous assimilation. Thus, St Patrick would take the pagan symbol of the Irish shamrock – a guard, so it is said, in paganism against the evil eye – and turn it into a Christian symbol of the Holy Trinity. St Patrick, again, was the one who confronted the pagan Druids, and called on all the great forces of nature – the heavens, the sun, the moon, the lightning, the sea, the rocks, many of which were regarded as deities in the pagan pantheon of the time – to come to his aid as the creatures of the one Creator God. St Columba, as we have seen, took pagan wells, and turned them from dwelling places of pagan spirits into places for baptism, sacramental sites for the revelation, not of evil spirits, but of the good God known in Jesus Christ.

There is a challenge to us today, is there not, which is not too dissimilar to this challenge to the Celtic Christians? We live in a world of many faiths and of none. The temptation is often to say either, 'a plague on all your houses', as many do, or else to suggest, again as many do, that all are really the same.

With the Celtic Christians, however, might we not be better trying to see how God seeks to reveal himself in and through these many faiths.

Who are we, after all, to deny that, even as God sought to reveal himself to the pre-Christian Celts in the forces of nature all around them, so he is still today seeking to reveal himself to our post-Christian neighbours, in many ways which, at first sight, seem strange, and even dangerous, to us? The Celtic Christians had the faith and the courage to enter into this challenge – we could do worse than attempt the same.

There is, to be sure, much more to be said – much more that has been said, and well said – about the spirituality of the Celtic Christians, and how it might help us today. We could speak, for instance, of their love of pilgrimage – of going on pilgrimage for Christ, leaving all that they held dear in this world for the sake of the Gospel. We could speak of the importance that they placed on hospitality – reflected in the Celtic rune, 'Often, often, often, goes the Christ in the stranger's guise.'

For myself, I think the thing I take most from these Celtic ancestors of ours is the sense that God is NOW. God is in the here and in the now – and in whatever I am doing; if I seek to do it in the spirit and by the power of the risen Christ, then God will bless me, for he is not 'I was', or 'I will be', but 'I AM'. That, and the sense I have so very strongly that for Columba and all the others, what really mattered was that God was bringing them, despite all their faults and failings, to the full stature of

Jesus Christ, that is, to the fullness of the humanity that God intended us to have from the beginning.

So I end with the words, not of a Celt at all, but of the martyred German theologian of the Nazi era, Dietrich Bonhoeffer, which I used to end my preface on Worship in the last two editions of the Iona Community's worship book. We believe, I wrote there, in what Bonhoeffer believed – and it is, I think, what the Celtic Christians believed too: that *'the Christian person is not a religious person, but simply a human being, as Jesus was a human being, profoundly this-worldly, characterised by discipline, and the constant knowledge of death and resurrection'*.

John Harvey

Month 4 Day 31

THE THIRTY-FIRST DAY

In death there is life: Zena's story

'Can I come to your church?' said a small Asian-Scottish lady as we shook hands at the close of a service in the winter of 1977.

Zena Bell, born of a Scottish mother and Indian medical student father in the same year that saw the births of Queen Elizabeth and Lady Thatcher, was taken shortly after her birth to Quarriers Homes.

In the pre-Second World War years life was tough for a four-foot-ten young girl of different ethnic origins. Zena used to speak much later of the harsh discipline and bullying. She was an able and determined youngster, and in time she secured a place to train as a nurse. This she did for some years. Then another blow struck.

Nervous breakdowns, which even today still carry stigma, are no longer 'acceptable' reasons for terminating employment, let alone dumping you in a psychiatric hospital and throwing away the key. But in the early 1950s, with no family and no one to speak for her, that is exactly what happened to Zena Bell. She had a great spirit and she was a rebel. She was tranquilised by drugs and electric shock treatment. Yet that spirit could not easily be broken.

Over a quarter of a century later the Labour Government instituted a programme of 'care in the community' to help long-term psychiatric patients leave institutions. It was well-resourced in medical and social work terms and so Zena, in 1977, found herself in a 'halfway house' in Paisley, close to the flat in which she was to live for the next twenty years.

Zena was so institutionalised that all her conversation at first was about 'Doctor X' or 'Nurse Y'. We had to show her how to boil a kettle or cook an egg and ask for things in the shops. She started coming to Merksworth Church, and joined the tea and coffee team, who enveloped her despite her habitual downing of dishtowels and running out when she thought someone was 'looking at her'. She babysat for our family, found a wee cleaning job, and gradually had members of the congregation round for a cuppa. Zena was a lifelong Rangers fan and lived within spitting distance of Love Street. I always teased her, when I looked in after the St Mirren games, that the P.A. had announced Rangers were 3-0 down. She shook her fist at me.

When in hospital, Zena had been befriended by a certain Iona Community family in Linwood. When Colin and Carol Morton moved to Prestonpans, Zena visited them, but when they went to Jerusalem she was devastated. 'What am I going to do?' she asked me. 'Visit them,' I replied with little belief that she could. One Saturday I drove her to the airport and watched her board a plane to Tel Aviv.

Colin later told me stories about her wandering round the Old City and accosting an Israeli soldier nearly twice her size and demanding to get on the bus to Tiberias. She went to Disneyland in California the next year, taking her boyfriend, Jimmy, with her. Life had opened up for Zena like a sunflower.

And then, around her seventieth birthday, Zena developed inoperable cancer. It shook her friends more than her. Her determination to live her last days as fully as possible was as inspiring as her calm faith and life-affirming stubbornness.

One of the great privileges of my life was to conduct a communion service round her bed in the Accord Hospice in Paisley, surrounded by those she now regarded as her friends. Poor Jimmy was told in no uncertain terms to remove his bunnet: 'Ye'r ignorant, Jimmy, so ye are' came the comment from the bed. He loved her to the last, as we all did. And that service for me was an overcoming of death in all its fears and captivity. Zena made it so.

Zena died shortly after, in the middle of a World Cup. 'When Scotland play next I'll be in heaven,' she said to me. 'You'll get a better view Zena,' I said, 'but you might want to change the channel.'

My last memory of her was of a cheeky laugh from this sister who once said to us 'I'm a besom, so I am.' She was indeed, we loved her for it. And after such a rocky start, in her last days she brought resurrection to us all.

Prayer

God who brings light out of darkness and who at Easter brought signs of victory over death and destruction, we, who seem to have so much, rejoice in those unlikely folk whose thrawn determination and courageous persistence have brought resurrection to our lives in the most unlikely ways. We delight in their memory, we take strength from their legacy, and we pray that we be in some way worthy of them.

Iain Whyte

End Piece

Blessing

May God write a message upon your heart,
bless and direct you,
then send you out –
a living letter of the Word.

Iona Abbey Worship Book

Prayers for the Days

Day 1 – 'New ways to touch the hearts of all'

Pray for 'new ways to touch the hearts of all'.

For writers, musicians, artists, dancers, liturgists …
For all those working creatively in the fields of politics,
community development, human relations …

For risk takers,
for enablers …

God, you are always calling your people
to follow you into the future,
inviting them to new ventures, new challenges,
new ways to care,
new ways to touch the hearts of all.

When they become fearful of the unknown, give them courage.
When they worry that they are not up to the task,
remind them that you would not call them
if you did not believe in them.

When they get tired,
or feel disappointed with the way things are going,
remind them that you can bring change and hope
out of the most difficult situations.

Day 2 – Economic witness

Pray for organisations working to bring about a more just economic order; people and countries held captive in the chains of debt.

Jesus Christ, Lord of all,
help me to live more simply
and with greater faith in you.

Day 3 – Youth concern

Pray for children
and for youth.

May children be protected, nurtured and encouraged.
May they have the chance to learn,
the space to dance,
the room to grow.

May youth be valued and heard,
supported and challenged,
and be given real opportunities
to help in the reshaping of the Church and the world.

Day 4 – The Word

For the word of God in scripture,
for the word of God among us,
for the word of God within us,
thanks be to God.

Day 5 – Hospitality and welcome

Pray for houses and centres of hospitality and welcome.

For those who are not welcomed:
refugees and asylum seekers;
all who are homeless.

As the poor widow welcomed Elijah,
let me be open
to the richness and miracle in meeting.

As Abraham and Sarah welcomed passing strangers,
let me entertain the possibility of
angels in disguise.

Let my eyes be opened
that I may recognise in my neighbour
the divine presence of Christ.

Day 6 – This is the day

God, your kindness has brought the gift of a new day.
Help me to leave yesterday,
and not to covet tomorrow,
but to accept the uniqueness of today.
Amen

Day 7 – The Iona experience

You are an island in the sea, O God,
you are a hill on the shore,
you are a star in the darkness,
you are a staff to the weak.
O, my soul's healer,
when I am lost and tired and stumbling
you shield and support me.
God, help me to give light, love and support to others.

Day 8 – Life in community

Pray for all those living and working in intentional communities,
giving thanks for their counter-cultural witness.

For volunteers everywhere.

May people find meaningful ways to contribute to their communities.
May their gifts and talents be recognised and encouraged.

Day 9 – Women

Pray for women who are discriminated against,
who are marginalised,
who suffer violence and abuse.
For women bearing heavy responsibilities and pressures:

women on the way to the well
women supporting whole families by themselves …

For equal opportunities
and women's issues.

Jesus, women were always close to you,
did not run away –

from pain
from commitment
from grief and emptiness.

May the contributions, wisdom and strength of women
be recognised in wider society.

Day 10 – Prayer

Lord, give me a moment to be still:
to listen for your voice within my heart.

Day 11 - Justice and peace

The Spirit of the Lord is upon me.
He has chosen me to bring good news to the poor.
He has sent me to proclaim liberty to the captives
and recovery of sight to the blind;
to free the oppressed
and announce that the time has come
when the Lord will save his people.

Luke 4:18–19

DAY 12 – The integrity of creation

Pray that nations may have the political will
to protect this fragile planet,
and that people everywhere
may think globally and act locally.

Pray for fair trading organisations
as they seek to guard the rights and incomes
of work forces in developing countries.

Pray for the indigenous peoples of the world.

O Christ, there is no plant in the ground
but it is full of your virtue.
There is no form in the strand
but it is full of your blessing.
There is no life in the sea,
there is no creature in the ocean,
there is nothing in the heavens
but proclaims your goodness.
There is no bird on the wing,
there is no star in the sky,
there is nothing beneath the sun
but proclaims your goodness.

Christ, help me to consider the effects of my lifestyle;
to make daily choices prayerfully.

George MacLeod

Day 13 – Columban Christianity & the Celtic tradition

O God, be a bright flame before me,
a guiding star above me,
a smooth path beneath me,
a kindly shepherd behind me.

Attributed to St Columba

Day 14 – Racial justice

Pray for racial justice,
for those working to overcome racism in our society,
and pressing for changes in nationality law and immigration policy.

Peace between nations,
peace between neighbours,
peace between lovers,
in love of the God of life.

Day 15 – Community

Pray for the local community, community development and community relations;
for the community of the world.

May diversity be valued, barriers crossed,
and ordinary people empowered.
May neighbourhoods be places
where all have a part to play.

Day 16

Pilgrimage

Pray for all pilgrims and seekers
and companions on the way;
for all travellers.

Christ, may I walk with you,
in solidarity with the poor
and with all of God's creation.

Day 17 – Sexuality

Pray for lesbian, gay and transgender rights.

May the One
who has lovingly created human life with such diversity and potential,
be with all who challenge prejudice and abuse of power
and all who work for a fairer, more inclusive society.

Day 18 – Healing

Pray for health, wholeness and the ministry of healing.
For victims of violence and injustice.

Compassionate God, use ordinary people,
people with their own needs,
to bring life and hope to others.

Day 19 – Social action

Pray for prisoners of conscience;
for political prisoners;
for those who are tortured
and detained without trial.

Living God,
you have taught that faith without works is dead,
so temper our faith with love and hope
that we follow Christ and give ourselves freely to people in their need:
then the lives we live may honour you for ever.
Amen

Day 20 – Church renewal

Pray for local church renewal;
local church community.

May your churches be centres of justice and joy, O Christ
where your love is shared,
and your life made real in the world.

Day 21 – Worship

Pray that the worship of the Church may be renewed
through scripture, song and honest prayer.

May worship serve to strengthen and inspire your people
to do what you require, O Lord.

Day 22 – Called to be One

Pray for relations between denominations in Britain
and the world.

May differences be celebrated.
May Christians be made one in Jesus,
who died to bring peace and reconciliation.

Day 23 – Mission

Pray for church centres
and church organisations.

For an approach which is open, inclusive and sensitive;
imaginative and risk-taking.

O God, who gave to your servant Columba
the gifts of courage, faith and cheerfulness,
to carry the word of your gospel to every creature,
grant your church a like spirit and energy.

Day 24 – Work

Pray for the unemployed,
for industrial mission,
for those whose work is exploited.

For those who have no work, and those who have too much;
for work that is meaningful and shared;
for a society where people are valued for themselves.

In the name of the God of work and rest.

Day 25 – Poverty

Pray for the poor and disadvantaged.

For those who choose to live and work
in areas of multiple deprivation;
for all involved in homeless projects and credit unions.

May the poor become empowered
and the world be turned upside down.

Day 26 – Basic Christian communities

Pray for basic Christian communities throughout the world,
giving thanks that, amid poverty and oppression,
people are finding a biblical faith that empowers and liberates,
as they work together for grassroots change.

Day 27 – Non-violence and peacekeeping

Pray for organisations involved in international aid and peacekeeping;
for individuals working in the peace movement
and engaged in non-violent resistance.

For victims of war and violence;
for the abolition of nuclear weapons.

Lord, make me an instrument of your peace.
Where there is hatred, let me sow love,
where there is injury, pardon
where there is doubt, faith
where there is despair, hope
where there is sadness, joy.

O Divine Master,
grant that I may not so much seek
to be consoled as to console,
to be understood as to understand,
to be loved as to love.
For it is in giving that we receive,
it is in pardoning that we are pardoned,
it is in dying that we are born again
to everlasting life.
Amen

St Francis

Day 28 – Interfaith

Pray for interfaith dialogue;
for people of other faiths and ideologies;
for situations and places in the world
where there is war and conflict.

May people of different faiths and beliefs find understanding
in their common search for meaning.

Day 29 – Commitment

O most merciful Redeemer, friend and brother,
may I know thee more clearly,
love thee more dearly,
follow thee more nearly:
for ever and ever.

St Richard of Chichester

Day 30 – The rediscovery of spirituality

Pray for the growth and deepening of the spiritual life.

God help me to maintain a spirituality that is both tough and tender,
and to seek you not only in the sacred places
but in the midst and the margins of daily life.

Day 31 – The thirty-first day

Pray for those who have died
and for those who grieve.

As you were before us at our life's beginning
be you so again at our journey's end.
As you were beside us at our soul's shaping,
God be also at our journey's close.

Prayer sources

Prayer for Day 1, Kathy Galloway, adapted from *The Pattern of Our Days*, Wild Goose Publications
Prayer for Day 3, Brian Woodcock (youth prayer)
Prayer for Day 4, *Iona Abbey Worship Book*, Wild Goose Publications
Prayer for Day 5, Neil Paynter, *Iona Abbey Worship Book*, Wild Goose Publications
Prayer for Day 6, *Iona Abbey Worship Book*, traditional (adapted), Wild Goose Publications
Prayer for Day 7, Gaelic traditional, adapted from *Each Day & Each Night*, J. Philip Newell, Wild Goose Publications
Prayer for Day 9, Neil Paynter
Prayer for Day 10, Peter Millar
Prayer for Day 12, Brian Woodcock/Celtic traditional/Neil Paynter
Prayer for Day 14, Traditional (adapted), *Iona Abbey Worship Book*, Wild Goose Publications
Prayer for Day 15, Brian Woodcock
Prayer for Day 17, Brian Woodcock
Prayer for Day 18, Brian Woodcock
Prayer for Day 19, Iona Community, *Iona Community Worship Book*, 1988 edition, Wild Goose Publications
Prayer for Day 20, Brian Woodcock
Prayer for Day 23, *Iona Abbey Worship Book* (adapted), Wild Goose Publications
Prayer for Day 24, Brian Woodcock
Prayer for Day 26, Brian Woodcock
Prayer for Day 30, Brian Woodcock
Prayer for Day 31, Traditional, *Iona Community Worship Book*, 1988 edition, Wild Goose Publications
Prayer concerns for the days, Brian Woodcock or Neil Paynter;
other prayers for the days, Neil Paynter

Bible Readings

New ways to touch the hearts of all

Psalm 33:3; Psalm 40:3; Psalm 98:1; Isaiah 43:19; Ezekiel 11:19; Matthew 9:17; Luke 5:36; Luke 24:28–35; John 13:34; Romans 6:4; Romans 7:6; 1 Corinthians 11:25; 2 Corinthians 5:17; Colossians 3:10

Economic witness

Leviticus 25:10–14; Jeremiah 6:13–16; Matthew 6:19–24; Luke 12:13–27; Luke 12:32–34; Luke 21:1–4

Youth

Ruth 1:16–17; I Sa 17:33; Matthew 9:18–26; Matthew 11:25–26; Matthew 18:1–6; Matthew 19:13–14; Luke 2:41–52; Luke 7:11–15; Luke 10:21–24; Luke 18:15–17; 1 Timothy 4:11–16

The Word

Psalm 56:10–11; Psalm 119:105; Isaiah 40:8; Amos 8:11; Matthew 4:4; Luke 8:11; Luke 11:1–4; John 1:1–14; Acts 4: 31; Hebrews 4:12

Hospitality and welcome

Genesis 18:1–15; Exodus 22:21; Leviticus 19:33–34; Deuteronomy 24:17; 1 Kings 17:8–24; Matthew 2:13–15; Matthew 10:40–42; Matthew 26:6–13; Luke 10:38–42; Luke 15:11–32; Luke 19:1–10; John 2:1–11; Acts 28:1–10; Hebrews 13:1–2

This is the day

Genesis 1:5; Psalm 118; Matthew 5:14; Matthew 26:6–13; Mark 1:16–17; Mark 4:21; Mark 9:2–8; Mark10:13; Luke 2:1–7; Luke 16:19–31; John 1:14–18; John 14:27; John 20:1–18; Romans 13:11–14; 2 Corinthians 6:1–3; Ephesians 3:18–19; I Thessalonians 5:15–22

Women

Genesis 18:11–15; Exodus 2:1–10; Joshua 2:1–7; 1 Samuel 2:1–11; Matthew 26:1–13; Matthew 27:55–56; Matthew 28:1–20; Luke 1:26–45; Luke 1:46–55; Luke 8:1–3; Luke 24:1–12; John 4:27–30; John 19:25–27; Acts 9:36–43; Acts 16:13–15; Acts 18:24–28; Romans 16:1–2; Philippians 4:1–3

Prayer

1 Chronicles 29:10–20; Psalms 4:1–3; 19:14; 39:12; 46:10; 55:1–2; 61; 62:1–2; 66:20; 69:13–18; 86:1–7; 88; Isaiah 37:14–20; Matthew 6:5–24; Matthew 7:7–13; Matthew 26:38–46; Luke 18:1–14; John 17:1–26; Acts 1:12–14; Acts 4:23–31; Acts 16:25–26; Romans 8:26–27; Ephesians 3:14–21; Philippians 4:4–7; James 5:13–20

Justice and peace

Old Testament: Genesis 9:8–17; Deuteronomy 30:9–14; 1 Samuel 2:1–10; Psalms 9; 10; 22; 51; 72; 85:10; 96; 97; 98; 113; 140; Proverbs 8:20; Isaiah 2:1–5; 42:1–4; 58:1–12; 61:1–4; Jeremiah 31:31–34; Amos 5:10–24; Micah 4:1–4; 6:1–8; Malachi 3:1–5

New Testament: Matthew 5:1–20; 16:24–26; 23:1–4, 23–24, 37; 28:1–10; Luke 1:46–55; 4:16–30; 6:20–38; 12:13–21, 32–34; 18:18–30; John 20:19–29; Acts 4:32–36; 2 Corinthians 8:1–9; Ephesians 2:13–22; James 2:1–5; 5:1–6; 1 Peter 3:8–17

The integrity of creation

Genesis 1:26–31; Genesis 6–9; Exodus 17:1–6; Job 12:7–10; Job:38; 39; Isaiah 24:4–6; Psalms 8; 29; 46; 65:5–13; 67; 72; 80; 84; 96; 104; 147; 148; Isaiah 24:4–6; Ezekiel 34:18–19; Matthew 6:25–31; John 4:7–14; Romans 8:18–25; Colossians 1:15–20

Racial justice

Genesis 11:1–9; Luke 10:29–37; Acts 2:1–13; Acts 10:34; Acts 17:22–34; Romans 2:11; Colossians 3:9–15

Community

Exodus 16:1; Psalm 133; Matthew 5:43–48; Matthew 7:1–5; Luke 19:35–40; Luke 22:7–38; John 13:6–20; Acts 2:1–21; Romans 12:9–21; 1 Corinthians 11:17–34; 1 Corinthians 12:1–31; 1 Corinthians 13:1–13; Galatians 5:22–26; Ephesians 4:1–16; Ephesians 4:25–32; Colossians 3:12–17; 1 Thessalonians 5:11–28; 1 Timothy 6:11–16; James 4:11–12; 1 Peter 3:8–12; 1 John:3:18; 1 John 4:7–12

Pilgrimage

Genesis 12:1; Exodus 15:22–27; Exodus 16:1–36; Numbers 20:2–13; Numbers 21:4–5; 1 Chronicles 29:15; Psalm 23; Jeremiah 31:21; Luke 24:13–29; Ephesians 5:8–10; Hebrews 12:1–2

Relationships

Genesis 2: 15–25; Ruth 1–4; 1 Samuel 18:1–5; Song of Solomon 1–8; John 15:1–17

Healing

Psalms 6; 13; 16; 27:13–14; 28:6–9; 30; 34; 36:7–9; 40:1–3; 42; 51:15–17; 139:1–18; Isaiah 43:1–4; Matthew 5:1–12; Matthew 8:1–17; Matthew 8:28–34; Mark 1:29–45; Mark 5:1–20; Mark 8:22–26; Luke 5:12–26; Luke 13:10–17; John 5:1–18; John 10:10; John 11:1–44; Acts 3:1–10; Acts 8:14–25

Action

Exodus 4:10–16; Matthew 7:21–23; Matthew 11:2–6; Matthew 21:28–32; Matthew 25:34–36, 40; Luke 4:16–21; Luke 11:37–54; Luke 12:32–35; Luke 19:1–10; John 4:1–15; Ephesians 6:13–16; James 1:22–25; James 2:14–26

The Church

Acts 9:31; Acts 11:19–26; 1 Corinthians 1:10–31; Revelation 2:1–22

Worship

Exodus 32:1–6; Psalms 95:1–7; 98:1–6; 100; 134; 149; 150; Amos 5:21–24; Acts 13:13–52; Acts 14:1–7; Acts 18:12–14; 1 Corinthians 14:26

Called to be One

John 17:18–23; Acts 2:1–21; Acts 17:22–34; 1 Corinthians 12:12–16, 26–27; Galatians 3:28–29; Ephesians 4:1–16; Colossians 3:1–17

Mission

Psalm 37:31; Matthew 5:13–16; Matthew 10:5–42; Luke 5:1–11; Luke 10:1–20; Luke 21:5–19; Luke 24:44–49; Acts 27:13–26; 2 Corinthians 3:1–3; 2 Corinthians 5:20–21; 2 Corinthians 6:1–13; 2 Corinthians 11:16–33; 2 Timothy 2:1–7

Work

Psalms 118:22; 127:1; 135:15–18; Amos 8:4–6; Matthew 4:18–22; Matthew 11:28–30; Matthew 20:1–16; Matthew 25:37–40; Luke 16:1–18; John 2:13–16; John 6:27–34; Ephesians 2:19–22; 1 Thessalonians 5:12–22; 2 Timothy 2:15; Philemon 23–25; James 5:1–6

Poverty

Job 24:1–8; Psalms 9:18; 113:2–8; Isaiah 58:6–9; Jeremiah 22:13–16; Matthew 19:16–30; Matthew 25:37–40; Luke 2:1–7; Luke 14:15–24; Luke 16:19–31; Luke 21:1–4; James 2:1–7

Basic Christian communities

Jeremiah 18:4–5; Mark 1:16–20; Luke 1:46–53; John 3:8; Acts 1:12–14; 1 Corinthians 14:20; 1 Corinthians 14:26–33; Galatians 5:1; Ephesians 4:1–16

Non-violence and peacekeeping

Isaiah 2:1–4; Isaiah 53:4–7; Matthew 5:9; Matthew 5:38–45; John 18:3–12; Romans 12:14–21; Philippians 4:4–7; Revelation 22:1–2

Interfaith

Read from a book from another faith or belief – The Upanishads, The Bhagavad Gita, The Dhammapada, The Koran, the Tao Te Ching …

Commitment

Matthew 3:13–17; Matthew 4:18–22; Matthew 10:5–42; Matthew 14:28–30; Matthew 16:21–28; Matthew 19:16–30; Mark 2:13–17; Mark 10:46–52; Luke 9:57–62; John 15:1–27; Hebrews 13:12–16

The thirty-first day

Psalm 23; Matthew 5:4; Matthew 28:5–6; John 14; 2 Corinthians 4:16–18; Hebrews 12:1–2; Revelation 21:1–4

Sources and Acknowledgements

'On Money' – by Alison Swinfen. A version of this talk formed part of a discussion organised by Kathy Galloway of Christian Aid Scotland. An extract was published in *The Expository Times*: 'And Finally ... On Money' (122:12) 624, 2011, and in *Coracle: the magazine of the Iona Community*, autumn 2011. Used by permission of Alison Swinfen

'Jesus was young' – by Kathy Galloway, from *Getting Personal: Sermons and Meditations*, Kathy Galloway, SPCK, 1995, © Kathy Galloway. Used by permission of Kathy Galloway

'Steve the Satanist: unless a seed dies' – by Nancy Cocks, from *Invisible We See You: Tracing Celtic Threads through Christian Community*, Nancy Cocks, Novalis, 2003, and Wild Goose Publications, 2006, www.ionabooks.com

'Reflections on working with an asylum seeker: Michael's story' – by John Prysor-Jones, from the *Iona Community e-bulletin*

'A threshold experience' – by Peter Macdonald, excerpt from the 'Iona Community's Annual Report', 2010, from *Coracle: the magazine of the Iona Community*, spring, 2010

'Among unchosen neighbours: a reflection from Iona' – by Rowena Aberdeen, from the *Iona Community e-bulletin*

'Angel in disguise' – by Rowena Aberdeen, from *Acorns and Archangels: Resources for Ordinary Time – The Feast of the Transfiguration to All Hallows'*, Ruth Burgess (ed.), Wild Goose Publications, 2009, www.ionabooks.com

'Aliah bakes bread' – by Jan Sutch Pickard, from *Between High and Low Water: Sojourner Songs*, Jan Sutch Pickard, Wild Goose Publications, 2008, www.ionabooks.com

'Qualandia Terminal: First Friday of Ramadan' – by Warren Bardsley, from *Letters from Jerusalem: Reflections of an Ecumenical Accompanier*, Warren R. Bardsley, Church in the Marketplace Publications, 2010. Used by permission of Warren Bardsley

'First on the list' – by Annika Spalde, from *Heart on Fire: Living as a Mystic in Today's World*, Annika Spalde, Wild Goose Publications, 2010, www.ionabooks.com

'Heartbeat of creation' – by Chris Polhill, from *A Heart for Creation: Worship Resources and Reflections on the Environment*, Chris Polhill (ed.), Wild Goose Publications, 2010, www.ionabooks.com

'Reconnecting with the roots – a future for Celtic spirituality?' – by Rosemary Power, from *Coracle: the magazine of the Iona Community*, autumn 2009

'Unite against fascism' – by Philip Jakob, from the *Iona Community e-bulletin*

'On the Victoria Line' – by Bryan Owen © Bryan Owen

'So many kinds of awesome love' – by Nicola Slee, from *Praying Like a Woman*, Nicola Slee, SPCK, 2004. Used by permission of Nicola Slee and SPCK.

'Starfish' – John L. Bell, based on a story by Loren Eiseley from *The Promise of Paradox* (Servant Leadership Press, Washington DC. 1993 by Parker J. Palmer), from *He Was in the World: Meditations for Public Worship*, Wild Goose Publications, 1995. Used by permission of the Wild Goose Resource Group © Wild Goose Resource Group, 1995, www.ionabooks.com

'Born into complicity' – by Kathy Galloway, from *Sharing the Blessing: Overcoming Poverty and Working for Social Justice*, Kathy Galloway, SPCK, 2008. Used by permission of Kathy Galloway and SPCK

'Secularism' – by Ian M. Fraser, from *Coracle: the magazine of the Iona Community*, autumn 2010

'The saints of God' – by Ian M. Fraser, from *Candles & Conifers: Resources for All Saints' and Advent*, Ruth Burgess (ed.), Wild Goose Publications, 2005, www.ionabooks.com

'Lighting up the ordinary' – by the Wild Goose Resource Group, from *Present on Earth: Worship Resources on the Life of Jesus*, WIld Goose Resource Group, Wild Goose Publications, 2004, www.ionabooks.com, © 2002 Wild Goose Resource Group

'Work is a curse – until you don't have any' – by John Davies, from www.johndavies.org

'Metanoia' – by Martin Scott, from *A Heart for Creation: Worship Resources and Reflections on the Environment*, Chris Polhill (ed.), Wild Goose Publications, 2010, www.ionabooks.com

'Christ in the face of the stranger and prisoner: the Open Door Community, Atlanta, Georgia' – by Peter R. Gathje, from *Sharing the Bread of Life: Hospitality and Resistance at the Open Door Community*, the Open Door Community, 2006 © Peter R. Gathje. Used by permission of Peter R. Gathje

'Boundaries' – by Jan Sutch Pickard, from *Coracle: the magazine of the Iona Community*

'A heart broken open' – by Ray Gaston, from *A Heart Broken Open: Radical Faith in an Age of*

Fear, Ray Gaston, Wild Goose Publications, 2009, www.ionabooks.com

'The return of Godflesh: barking bark' – by Donald Eadie, from *Coracle: the magazine of the Iona Community*, winter 2010/11

'Surprising gifts' – by Warren Bardsley, from *Touched by Grace: Walking the Path of Grief,* Warren R. Bardsley, Church in the Marketplace Publications, 2005. Used by permission of Warren Bardsley

'Surrounded by a cloud of witnesses' – by Kate McIlhagga, from *The Green Heart of the Snowdrop*, Kate McIlhagga, Wild Goose Publications, 2004, www.ionabooks.com

'Suffer the little children: A reflection from Uganda' – by Willie Salmond, from *Coracle: the magazine of the Iona Community*, autumn 2010

'I don't like the dark' – by Brian Woodcock, from *Coracle: the magazine of the Iona Community*, winter 2011/12

'Lessons in love and anger: Rima and two weeks in May' – by Alison Swinfen, from *Coracle: the magazine of the Iona Community*, winter 2009/10

'An open letter to the UK Border Police' – by Alison Swinfen, from the *Iona Community e-bulletin*

'I would have almost certainly guaranteed come out of jail in a box' – from *Coracle: the magazine of the Iona Community*, winter 2009/10

'Not counting' – by Ruth Burgess, from *Bare Feet and Buttercups: Resources for Ordinary Time – Trinity Sunday to the Feast of the Transfiguration*, Ruth Burgess (ed.), Wild Goose Publications, 2008, www.ionabooks.com

'Looking at the environment through the lens of prophecy' – by Eurig Scandrett, from *Coracle: the magazine of the Iona Community*, summer 2011

'Iona: Icon of marginality and engagement' – by Bonnie Thurston, from *Coracle: the magazine of the Iona Community*, summer 2011

'I will leap into love' – by Lesley Orr, from *Wrestling and Resting: Exploring Stories of Spirituality from Britain and Ireland*, Ruth Harvey (ed.), CTBI, 1999. Used by permission of Lesley Orr and Ruth Harvey

'God's wide embrace: what is "natural" and what is "in Christ"' – by Ian M. Fraser, from *Coracle: the magazine of the Iona Community*, winter 2011/12

'Cracking up' – by Margaret Silf, from *Coracle: the magazine of the Iona Community*, autumn 2010. Used by permission of Margaret Silf.

'Planting potatoes' – by Helen Steven, from *Now More Than Ever, Here More Than Anywhere: 50 Years of Scottish Songs for Nuclear Disarmament*, Penny Stone (ed.), 2008. Used by permission of Helen Steven and Penny Stone. *Now More Than Ever …* available from the Edinburgh Peace and Justice Centre, or Scottish CND.

'The candle we light …' – by Joy Mead, from *Where Are the Altars?*, Joy Mead, Wild Goose Publications, 2007, www.ionabooks.com

'How to strip an olive tree' – by Jan Sutch Pickard, from *Between High and Low Water: Sojourner Songs*, Jan Sutch Pickard, Wild Goose Publications, 2008, www.ionabooks.com

'The Poverty Truth Commission' – by John and Molly Harvey, from *Coracle: the magazine of the Iona Community*, summer 2011

'A simple prayer' – by Martin Johnstone, from *Coracle: the magazine of the Iona Community*, summer 2011

'Affirmation – from *A Storehouse of Kingdom Things*, Ian M. Fraser, Wild Goose Publications, 2010, www.ionabooks.com

'A small part of the picture' – by Iain Whyte, from *Coracle: the magazine of the Iona Community*, spring 2010

'Meeting the Black Panther of the Blue Mountains: A letter from Australia' – by Peter Millar, from *Coracle: the magazine of the Iona Community*, spring 2008

'Step by step' – by Ruth Burgess, from *Coracle: the magazine of the Iona Community*, winter 2011/12

'A time of great taking: a global *saquao*' – by Peter Millar, from *Coracle: the magazine of the Iona Community*, autumn 2011

'Rekindling community: on the 2011 UK uprisings' – by Dan Glass, from *Coracle: the magazine of the Iona Community*, autumn 2011

'He was a storyteller' – by Ruth Burgess, from *Acorns and Archangels: Resources for Ordinary Time – The Feast of the Transfiguration to All Hallows'*, Ruth Burgess (ed.), Wild Goose Publications, 2009, www.ionabooks.com

'Transfiguration – a moment in Iona Abbey' – by Nancy Cocks, from *Invisible We See You: Tracing Celtic Threads through Christian Community*, Nancy Cocks, Novalis, 2003, and Wild Goose Publications, 2006, www.ionabooks.com

'Life in all its fullness: from the Camas Diary' – from *Coracle: the magazine of the Iona Community*, autumn 2011

'Millennium Development Goals: Gender equality and empowerment of women' – by Lesley Orr, from *Coracle: the magazine of the Iona Community*, winter 2011/12

'How am I supposed to pray' – by David McNeish, from *Coracle: the magazine of the Iona Community*, autumn 2011

'We all bleed red' – by Alison Swinfen, from *Coracle: the magazine of the Iona Community*, winter 2011/12

'Walking the track' – by Joan Jones, from the *Iona Community e-bulletin*

'The "new outline" of Christ's body for today' – by Philip Newell, from *Christ of the Celts: the Healing of Creation*, Philip Newell, Wild Goose Publications, 2008, www.ionabooks.com

'Talking to strangers' – by John L. Bell, from *10 Things They Never Told Me about Jesus: A beginner's guide to a larger Christ*, John L. Bell, Wild Goose Publications, 2009, www.ionabooks.com, © 2009 WGRG, Iona Community, Glasgow G2 3DH

'Creating local community' – by Jim Wilkie, from *Coracle: the magazine of the Iona Community*, summer 2011

'God is intersex: from a conversation with Iona Community member Chris Gidden' – from *Coracle: the magazine of the Iona Community*, winter 2011/12

'A touching place' – by Jim Hughes, from *Praying for the Dawn: A Resource Book for the Ministry of Healing*, Kathy Galloway and Ruth Burgess (eds), Wild Goose Publications, 2000, www.ionabooks.com

'*Bambalela:* Never give up' – from *Sharing the Blessing: Overcoming Poverty and Working for*

Social Justice, Kathy Galloway, SPCK, 2008. Used by permission of Kathy Galloway and SPCK

'Written on the wall' – by Elisabeth Miescher, from *Coracle: the magazine of the Iona Community*, summer 2008

'Retreat on the streets' – by David Rhodes, from *Coracle: the magazine of the Iona Community*, spring 2010

'Western knitter' – by Rosemary Power, from *Coracle: the magazine of the Iona Community*, spring 2011

'A brand-new day' – by Karen Buchanan, from *Coracle: the magazine of the Iona Community*, summer 2011

'Visiting Dungavel IRC' – by Alison Swinfen, from *Coracle: the magazine of the Iona Community*, winter 2011/12

'Community Week Communion Address, Iona 2008' – by Kathy Galloway, from the *Iona Community e-bulletin*

'No place like home' – by Warren Bardsley, from *Letters from Jerusalem: Reflections of an Ecumenical Accompanier,* Warren R. Bardsley, Church in the Marketplace Publications, 2010. Used by permission of Warren Bardsley

'The God of Grace: a sermon in Iona Abbey, Easter Sunday, 2011' – by Peter Macdonald, from the *Iona Community e-bulletin*

'Lifted' – by David McNeish, from *Coracle: the magazine of the Iona Community*, autumn 2011

'Good money' – by John L. Bell, from *All that Matters: Scripts from BBC 4's "Thought for the Day" and other Musings*, John L. Bell, Wild Goose Publications, 2010, www.ionabooks.com, ©2010 WGRG, Iona Community, Glasgow G2 3DH

'Rene', and 'A grandmother's gift' – by Neil Squires, from *Coracle: the magazine of the Iona Community,* autumn 2008

'Sauntering' – by Margaret Legum, from *Learning to Saunter*, Margaret Legum, Kalk 'n Cheese Press, 2007 © Margaret Legum

'The "Just Across" group: From Wrexham to Iona' – by Biddy Crossfield, from *Coracle: the magazine of the Iona Community*, spring 2011

'Change' – by David McNeish, from *Coracle: the magazine of the Iona Community*, autumn 2011

'Women of dignity' – from *Sharing the Blessing: Overcoming Poverty and Working for Social Justice*, Kathy Galloway, SPCK, 2008. Used by permission of Kathy Galloway and SPCK

'Warm and alive' – by Roger Gray, from *Roger: An Extraordinary Peace Campaigner*, Helen Steven, Wild Goose Publications, 1990, www.ionabooks.com. (Originally from *Cuillin Adventure)*

'Curve of a human hand' – by Jan Sutch Pickard, from *Horizontal: Gatherings 9*, Jan Sutch Pickard © Jan Sutch Pickard

'The Listener' – by Euan Stuart, from *Coracle: the magazine of the Iona Community*, autumn 2010

'Worship for St Columba's Day' – by Kathy Galloway, from *Coracle: the magazine of the Iona Community.* (Affirmation, *Iona Abbey Worship Book*)

'The family' – by John L. Bell and Graham Maule, from *Love and Anger: Songs of Lively Faith and Social Justice*, John L. Bell and Graham Maule, Wild Goose Publications, 1997, www.ionabooks.com, © 1997 Wild Goose Resource Group

'Explorers not mapmakers' – by Joy Mead, from *Where Are the Altars?*, Joy Mead, Wild Goose Publications, 2007, www.ionabooks.com

'The prayer shawl ministry' – by Anna Briggs, from *Coracle: the magazine of the Iona Community*, summer 2010

'You knit us together' – by Anna Briggs, from *Coracle: the magazine of the Iona Community,* summer 2010

'From Atlanta, Georgia to Glasgow's East End' – by Ruth Douglas Shanks, from *Coracle: the magazine of the Iona Community*, summer 2011

'Lippen on the Holy Spirit' – by Ian M. Fraser, from *A Storehouse of Kingdom Things: Resources for the Faith Journey*, Ian M. Fraser, Wild Goose Publications, 2010, www.ionabooks.com

'A Palestinian cookbook, a leg without an ID, and two washing machines' – by Warren Bardsley, from *Letters from Jerusalem: Reflections of an Ecumenical Accompanier,* Warren R. Bardsley, Church in the Marketplace Publications, 2010. Used by permission of Warren Bardsley

'The girl who had barely blinked' – by Jo Love, from *Coracle: the magazine of the Iona Community*, spring 2010

'The bondage of busyness ... a plea for taking and making time', by John L. Bell, from *Thinking Out Loud: Collected scripts from Radio 4's "Thought For The Day"*, John L. Bell, Wild Goose Publications, 2008, www.ionabooks.com, © 2008 WGRG, Iona Community, Glasgow G2 3DH

'Inspired by love and anger' – by Kathy Galloway, from *Coracle: the magazine of the Iona Community*, autumn 2011

'Angel in Camden Town Market' – by Neil Paynter, from *We Journey in Hope: Reflections on the Words from the Cross*, Neil Paynter & Peter Millar, Wild Goose Publications, 2011, www.ionabooks.com

'Try-out' – by Andy Humphrey, from *Coracle: the magazine of the Iona Community*, spring 2009

'The Peace Initiative' – by Philip Newell, from *Coracle: the magazine of the Iona Community*, summer 2011

'Are you coming?' – by Kathy Galloway, from *Getting Personal: Sermons and Meditations*, Kathy Galloway, SPCK, 1995, © Kathy Galloway. Used by permission of Kathy Galloway

'Don't tell me of a faith that fears' – by John L. Bell and Graham Maule, from *Love and Anger: Songs of Lively Faith and Social Justice*, John L. Bell and Graham Maule, Wild Goose Publications, 1997, www.ionabooks.com, © 1997 Wild Goose Resource Group

'Blessing' – by Neil Paynter, from *Iona Abbey Worship Book,* Wild Goose Publications www.ionabooks.com

Some Books by Authors in *Living Letters of the Word*

Warren Bardsley:
Against the Tide: The Story of Adomnán of Iona, Wild Goose Publications
Letters from Jerusalem: Reflections of an Ecumenical Accompanier, Church in the Marketplace Publications
Passion and Power: Conflict and Change in Seventh-century Britain, Church in the Marketplace Publications
Touched by Grace: Walking the Path of Grief, Church in the Marketplace Publications

John L. Bell and Graham Maule, the Wild Goose Resource Group, the Wild Goose Worship Group:
All that Matters: Collected Scripts from Radio 4's Thought For The Day, Volume 2, Wild Goose Publications
Cloth for the Cradle: Worship Resources and Readings for Advent, Christmas and Epiphany, Wild Goose Publications
Come All You People: Shorter Songs for Worship, Wild Goose Publications
Courage to Say No: Songs for Lent and Easter, Wild Goose Publications
Enemy of Apathy: Songs and Chants for Lent, Eastertide and Pentecost, Wild Goose Publications
God Comes Tomorrow: Music for Advent and Christmas, GIA Publications
God Never Sleeps: Songs from the Iona Community, Wild Goose Publications
Hard Words for Interesting Times: Biblical Texts in Contemporary Contexts, Wild Goose Publications
He Was in the World: Meditations for Public Worship, Wild Goose Publications
Heaven Shall Not Wait: Songs of Creation, the Incarnation and the Life of Jesus, Wild Goose Publications
I Will Not Sing Alone: Songs for the Season of Love, Wild Goose Publications
Innkeepers and Lightsleepers: Seventeen Songs for Christmas
Jesus & Peter: Off-the-record Conversations, Wild Goose Publications
Last Journey: Seventeen Songs for Times of Grieving, Wild Goose Publications
Love and Anger: Songs of Lively Faith and Social Justice, Wild Goose Publications
Love From Below: Sixty-two Songs of Discipleship and the Church's Sacraments and

Seasons, Wild Goose Publications
Many and Great: Songs from the World Church, Wild Goose Publications
One Is the Body: Songs of Unity & Diversity, Wild Goose Publications
Present on Earth: Worship Resources on the Life of Jesus, Wild Goose Publications
Psalms of Patience, Protest and Praise, Wild Goose Publications
Sent by the Lord: World Church Songs, Wild Goose Publications
Stages on the Way: Worship Resources for Lent, Holy Week and Easter, Wild Goose Publications
States of Bliss and Yearning: The Marks and Means of Authentic Christian Spirituality, Wild Goose Publications
Take This Moment, Wild Goose Publications
Ten Things They Never Told Me about Jesus: A Beginner's Guide to a Larger Christ, Wild Goose Publications
There is One Among Us: Shorter Songs for Worship, Wild Goose Publications
The Singing Thing: A Case for Congregational Song, Wild Goose Publications
The Singing Thing Too: Enabling Congregations to Sing, Wild Goose Publications
Thinking Out Loud: Collected Scripts from Radio 4's Thought For The Day, Wild Goose Publications
We Walk His Way: Shorter Songs for Worship, Wild Goose Publications
When Grief is Raw, Wild Goose Publications
Wrestle and Fight and Pray: Christianity and Conflict, St Andrew Press

Ruth Burgess:
A Book of Blessings, Wild Goose Publications
Acorns and Archangels: Resources for Ordinary Time – The Feast of the Transfiguration to All Hallows', Wild Goose Publications
Bare Feet and Buttercups: Resources for All Saints' and Advent – Trinity Sunday to the Feast of the Transfiguration, Wild Goose Publications
Candles and Conifers: Resources for All Saints' and Advent, Wild Goose Publications
Eggs & Ashes: Liturgical & Practical Resources for Lent and Holy Week (with Chris Polhill), Wild Goose Publications
Fire & Bread: Resources for Easter Day to Trinity Sunday, Wild Goose Publications
Friends and Enemies: A Book of Short Prayers and Some Ways to Write Your Own, Wild Goose Publications
Hay and Stardust: Resources for Christmas to Candlemas, Wild Goose Publications

Hear My Cry: A Daily Prayer Book for Advent, Wild Goose Publications
Praying for the Dawn: A Resource Book for the Ministry of Healing (with Kathy Galloway), Wild Goose Publications

Nancy Cocks:
Growing Up with God: Using Stories to Explore a Child's Faith and Life, Wild Goose Publications
Invisible We See You: Tracing Celtic Threads through Christian Community, Wild Goose Publications, Novalis

John Davies:
Walking the M62, John Davies, Lulu

Donald Eadie:
Grain in Winter: Reflections for Saturday People, Epworth Press

Ian M. Fraser:
A Storehouse of Kingdom Things: Resources for the Faith Journey, Wild Goose Publications
Many Cells – One Body: Stories from Small Christian Communities, World Council of Churches
Salted with Fire, St Andrew Press
The Way Ahead: Grown-up Christians, Wild Goose Publications

Kathy Galloway:
Dreaming of Eden: Reflections on Christianity and Sexuality, Wild Goose Publications
Getting Personal: Sermons and Meditations, SPCK
Living by the Rule: the Rule of the Iona Community, Wild Goose Publications
Praying for the Dawn: A Resource Book for the Ministry of Healing (with Ruth Burgess), Wild Goose Publications
Sharing the Blessing: Overcoming Poverty and Working for Justice, SPCK
Story to Live By, SPCK
Struggles to Love: The Spirituality of the Beatitudes, SPCK
Talking to the Bones: Poems, Prayers and Meditations, SPCK
The Dream of Learning Our True Name, Wild Goose Publications
Walking in Darkness and Light: Sermons and Reflections, St Andrew Press

Ray Gaston:
A Heart Broken Open: Radical Faith in an Age of Fear, Wild Goose Publications

Tom Gordon:
A Blessing to Follow: Contemporary Parables for Living, Wild Goose Publications
A Need for Living: Signposts on the Journey of Life and Beyond, Wild Goose Publications
New Journeys Now Begin: Learning on the Path of Grief and Loss, Wild Goose Publications
Welcoming Each Wonder: More Contemporary Stories for Reflection, Wild Goose Publications
With an Open Eye: Parables with Meaning for Today, Wild Goose Publications

John Harvey:
Bridging the Gap: Has the Church Failed the Poor?, Wild Goose Publications

Margaret Legum:
It Doesn't Have To Be Like This: Global Economics: A New Way Forward, Wild Goose Publications

Kate McIlhagga:
The Green Heart of the Snowdrop, Wild Goose Publications

Joy Mead:
A Telling Place: Reflections on Stories of Women in the Bible, Wild Goose Publications
Making Peace in Practice and Poetry, Wild Goose Publications
The One Loaf, Wild Goose Publications
Where Are the Altars?, Wild Goose Publications
Words and Wonderings, Wild Goose Publications

Peter Millar:
An Iona Prayer Book, SCM-Canterbury Press
Finding Hope Again: Journeying Beyond Sorrow, SCM-Canterbury Press
Iona: Pilgrim Guide, SCM-Canterbury Press
Our Hearts Still Sing: Daily Readings, Wild Goose Publications
Surprise of the Sacred: Finding God in Unexpected Places, SCM-Canterbury Press
Waymarks: Signposts to Discovering God's Presence in the World, SCM-Canterbury Press

J. Philip Newell:

A New Harmony: The Spirit, the Earth and the Human Soul, John Wiley & Sons
Book of Creation: An Introduction to Celtic Spirituality, SCM-Canterbury Press
Christ of the Celts: the Healing of Creation, Wild Goose Publications
Each Day & Each Night: Celtic Prayers from Iona, Wild Goose Publications
Listening to the Heartbeat of God: A Celtic Spirituality, SPCK
Praying with the Earth: A Prayerbook for Peace, SCM-Canterbury Press

Lesley Orr:

A Unique and Glorious Mission: Women and Presbyterianism in Scotland, 1830–1930, John Donald
In Good Company: Women in the Ministry, Wild Goose Publications

Bryan Owen:

Blue Daffodils and Other Poems, Matador
Praying on the Edge: Human Rights for Concerned Christians, Covenanters Press

Neil Paynter:

Around a Thin Place: An Iona Pilgrimage Guide (with Jane Bentley), Wild Goose Publications
Blessed Be Our Table: Graces for Mealtimes and Reflections on Food, Wild Goose Publications
Down to Earth: Stories and Sketches, Wild Goose Publications
50 Great Prayers from the Iona Community, Wild Goose Publications
Gathered and Scattered: Readings and Meditations from the Iona Community, Wild Goose Publications
Growing Hope: Daily Readings, Wild Goose Publications
Holy Ground: Liturgies and Worship Resources for an Engaged Spirituality (with Helen Boothroyd), Wild Goose Publications
This Is The Day: Readings and Meditations from the Iona Community, Wild Goose Publications

Jan Sutch Pickard:

Between High and Low Water: Sojourner Songs, Wild Goose Publications
Dandelions and Thistles: Biblical Meditations from the Iona Community, Wild Goose Publications
Out of Iona: Words from a Crossroads of the World, Wild Goose Publications

Chris Polhill:
A Heart for Creation: Worship Resources and Reflections on the Environment, Wild Goose Publications
Eggs & Ashes: Liturgical & Practical Resources for Lent and Holy Week (with Ruth Burgess), Wild Goose Publications
Pilgrim's Guide to Iona Abbey, Wild Goose Publications

Rosemary Power:
The Celtic Quest: A Contemporary Spirituality, Columba Press

David Rhodes:
Faith in Dark Places, SPCK
Sparrow Story: The Gospel for Today, SPCK
See: www.turbulentbooks.co.uk

Eurig Scandrett:
Scotlands of the Future: Towards a Sustainable Economy, Luath Press Limited

Margaret Silf:
Daily Readings with Margaret Silf, Darton, Longmann & Todd
One Hundred Wisdom Stories from Around the World, Lion Hudson
Taste and See: Adventuring into Prayer, Darton, Longmann & Todd

Nicola Slee:
Doing December Differently: An Alternative Christmas Handbook (with Rosie Miles), Wild Goose Publications
Praying Like a Woman, SPCK
The Book of Mary, SPCK

Annika Spalde:
A Heart on Fire: Living as a Mystic in Today's World, Wild Goose Publications
Every Creature a Word of God: Compassion for Animals as Christian Spirituality (downloadable book), Wild Goose Publications

Helen Steven:
No Extraordinary Power: Prayer, Stillness and Activism, Quaker Books
Roger: An Extraordinary Peace Campaigner, Wild Goose Publications

Alison Swinfen:

Through Wood: Prayers and Poems Reconnecting with the Forest, Wild Goose Publications

The Open Door Community:

A Work of Hospitality: The Open Door Reader, 1982–2002, Peter R. Gathje, Editor, Open Door Community, Atlanta, Georgia

I Hear Hope Banging at my Back Door: Writings from Hospitality, Ed Loring, Open Door Community, Atlanta, Georgia

The Cry of the Poor: Cracking White Male Supremacy – An Incendiary and Militant Proposal, Ed Loring, Open Door Community, Atlanta, Georgia

Bonnie Thurston:

Belonging to the Borders: A Sojourn in the Celtic Tradition, Liturgical Press

For God Alone: A Primer on Prayer, University of Notre Dame Press

Simon Varwell:

Up the Creek without a Mullet: A Hair-brained Journey across the Globe, Sandstone Press

Iain Whyte:

Scotland and the Abolition of Black Slavery, 1756–1838, Iain Whyte, Edinburgh University Press

Brian Woodcock:

Advent Readings from Iona (with Jan Sutch Pickard), Wild Goose Publications

Some Iona Community classics:

A Wee Worship Book, Wild Goose Worship Group, Wild Goose Publications

Chasing the Wild Goose: The Story of the Iona Community, Ron Ferguson, Wild Goose Publications

Daily Readings with George MacLeod, Ron Ferguson, editor, Wild Goose Publications

Every Blessed Thing: An Evening with George MacLeod (double CD based on the one-man play about the life of George MacLeod), Ron Ferguson and Tom Fleming, Wild Goose Publications

George MacLeod: A Biography, Ron Ferguson, Wild Goose Publications

Iona Abbey Music Book, Wild Goose Publications

Iona Abbey Worship Book, Wild Goose Publications
Iona Community: Today's Challenge, Tomorrow's Hope/Sermon in Stone (DVD), Wild Goose Publications
Iona God's Energy: The Vision and Spirituality of the Iona Community, Norman Shanks, Wild Goose Publications
Meditations from the Iona Community, Ian Reid, Wild Goose Publications
Only One Way Left, George MacLeod, Wild Goose Publications
Reinventing Theology, Ian M. Fraser, Wild Goose Publications
The Pattern of Our Days, Kathy Galloway, Wild Goose Publications
The Twelve Together, T. Ralph Morton, Wild Goose Publications
The Whole Earth Shall Cry Glory: Iona Prayers, George MacLeod, Wild Goose Publications

Iona can be the home of the New Reformation. But it must recover its genius: keep acting its insights at whatever risk if its insights are to be clarified and the next obedience seen. If, as a community, we write at all it can be no more than passing calculations in the sand, to point to the next Obedience.

George MacLeod

Wild Goose Publications, the publishing house of the Iona Community established in the Celtic Christian tradition of Saint Columba, produces books, e-books, CDs and digital downloads on:

- holistic spirituality
- social justice
- political and peace issues
- healing
- innovative approaches to worship
- song in worship, including the work of the Wild Goose Resource Group
- material for meditation and reflection

For more information:

Wild Goose Publications
Fourth Floor, Savoy House
140 Sauchiehall Street,
Glasgow G2 3DH, UK

Tel. +44 (0)141 332 6292
Fax +44 (0)141 332 1090
e-mail: admin@ionabooks.com

or visit our website at
www.ionabooks.com
for details of all our products and online sales